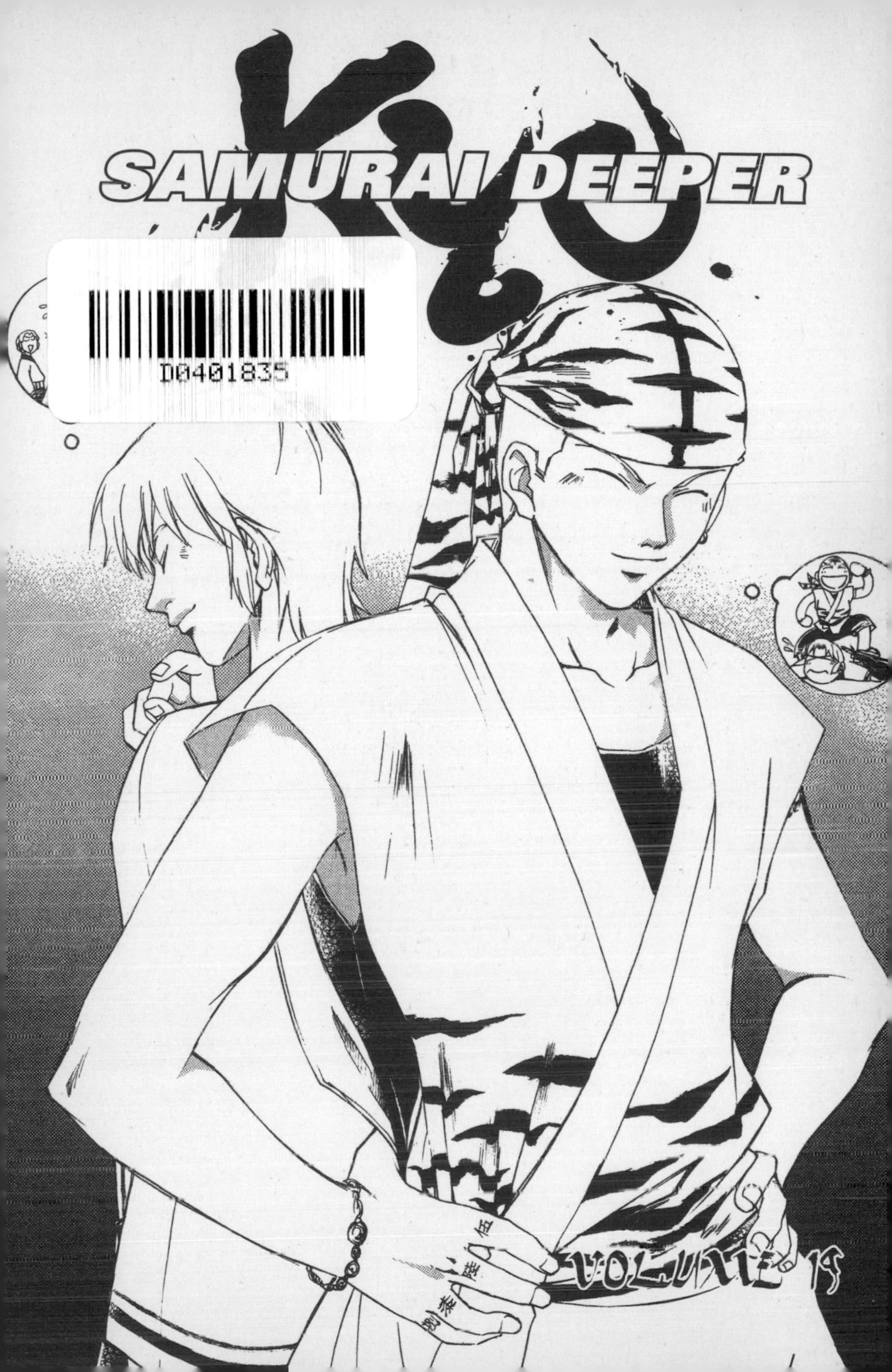
KYO
SAMURAI DEEPER
VOLUME 19

Samurai Deeper Kyo Vol. 19
Created by Akimine Kamijyo

Translation - Alexander O. Smith
English Adaptation - Rich Amtower
Retouch and Lettering - Jennifer Carbajal
Cover Design - Louis Csontos

Editor - Carol Fox
Digital Imaging Manager - Chris Buford
Production Manager - Elisabeth Brizzi
Managing Editor - Sheldon Drzka
Editor-in-Chief - Rob Tokar
VP of Production - Ron Klamert
Publisher - Mike Kiley
President and C.O.O. - John Parker
C.E.O. and Chief Creative Officer - Stuart Levy

A  Manga

TOKYOPOP Inc.
5900 Wilshire Blvd. Suite 2000
Los Angeles, CA 90036

E-mail: info@TOKYOPOP.com
Come visit us online at www.TOKYOPOP.com

ISBN: 1-59532-459-3

First TOKYOPOP printing: August 2006
10 9 8 7 6 5 4 3 2 1
Printed in the USA

SAMURAI DEEPER Kyo

Vol. 19
by Akimine Kamijyo

HAMBURG // LONDON // LOS ANGELES // TOKYO

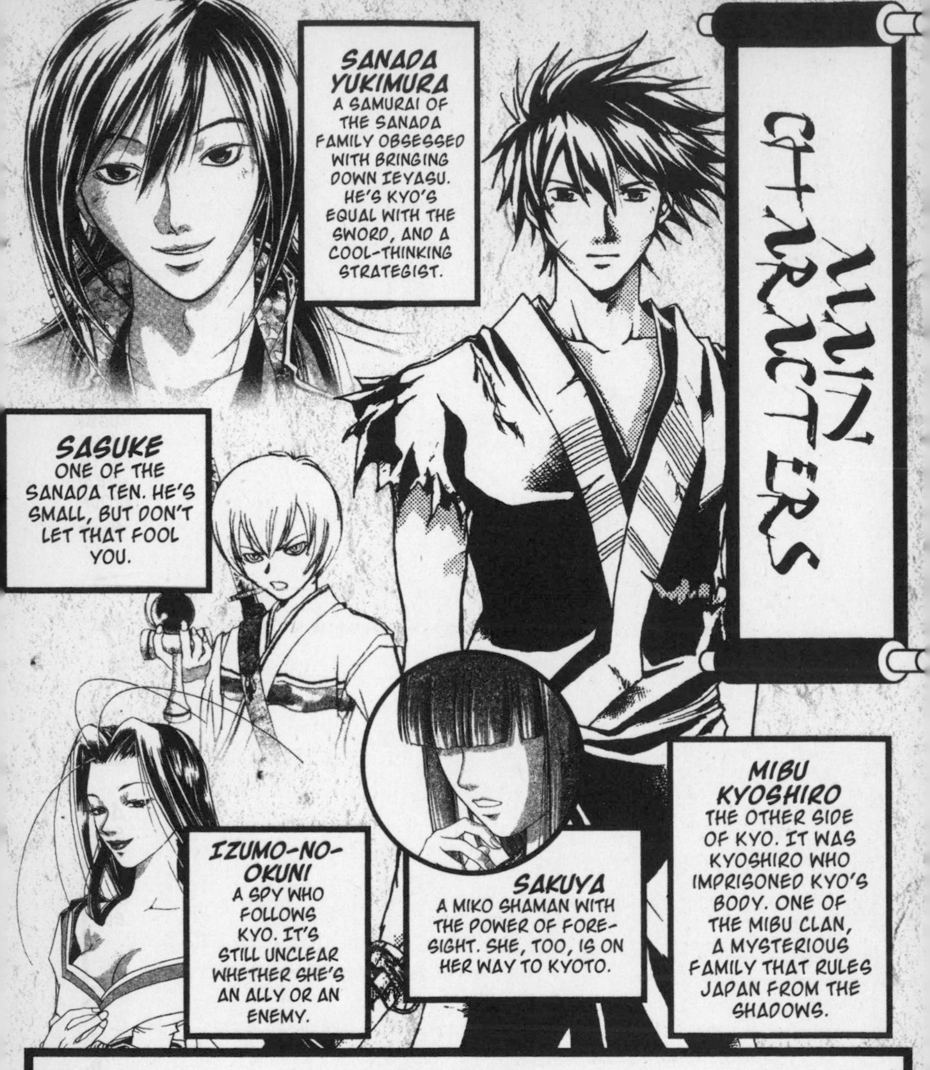
MAIN CHARACTERS
SANADA YUKIMURA
A SAMURAI OF THE SANADA FAMILY OBSESSED WITH BRINGING DOWN IEYASU. HE'S KYO'S EQUAL WITH THE SWORD, AND A COOL-THINKING STRATEGIST.
SASUKE
ONE OF THE SANADA TEN. HE'S SMALL, BUT DON'T LET THAT FOOL YOU.
MIBU KYOSHIRO
THE OTHER SIDE OF KYO. IT WAS KYOSHIRO WHO IMPRISONED KYO'S BODY. ONE OF THE MIBU CLAN, A MYSTERIOUS FAMILY THAT RULES JAPAN FROM THE SHADOWS.
SAKUYA
A MIKO SHAMAN WITH THE POWER OF FORE-SIGHT. SHE, TOO, IS ON HER WAY TO KYOTO.
IZUMO-NO-OKUNI
A SPY WHO FOLLOWS KYO. IT'S STILL UNCLEAR WHETHER SHE'S AN ALLY OR AN ENEMY.

THE STORY

THANKS TO SHINREI OF THE FIVE'S WATERWYRMS, YUYA HAS ONLY EIGHT HOURS LEFT TO LIVE. KYO AND THE REST CONTINUE TOWARD THE FORMER CRIMSON KING, BOTH TO SAVE YUYA AND TO UNCOVER THE SECRET OF KYO'S BIRTH.

AFTER FIGHTING THROUGH THE FIRST GATE OF THE MIBU LAND, PROTECTED BY HOTARU, THEY REACH SAISHI AND SAISEI'S SECOND GATE ONLY TO FIND THE TRAITOR YUKIMURA WAITING FOR THEM.

MORTAL COMBAT ENSUES AT THE SECOND GATE. STEPPING IN FOR THE WOUNDED KYO, AKIRA FACES OFF AGAINST SAISEI, THE FIGHT IS BITTER, AND SAISHI LAUGHS AT HER SISTER'S RESOLVE... ANGERING AKIRA WHO TAKES HER DOWN NEXT.

AT THE THIRD GATE STANDS CHIMEI, THE MAN RESPONSIBLE FOR THE TRAGIC DEATH OF MAHIRO'S SISTER AT MURAMASA'S HOME FOUR YEARS BEFORE. MAHIRO ATTACKS TO AVENGE HER SISTER, BUT CHIMEI WIELDS THE POWER OF EARTH, MANIPULATING GRAVITY TO HOLD MAHIRO AT BAY. CHIMEI LAUNCHES HIS COUNTERATTACK, BUT NOW HE FACES A FAR MORE FEARSOME FOE: KYO!

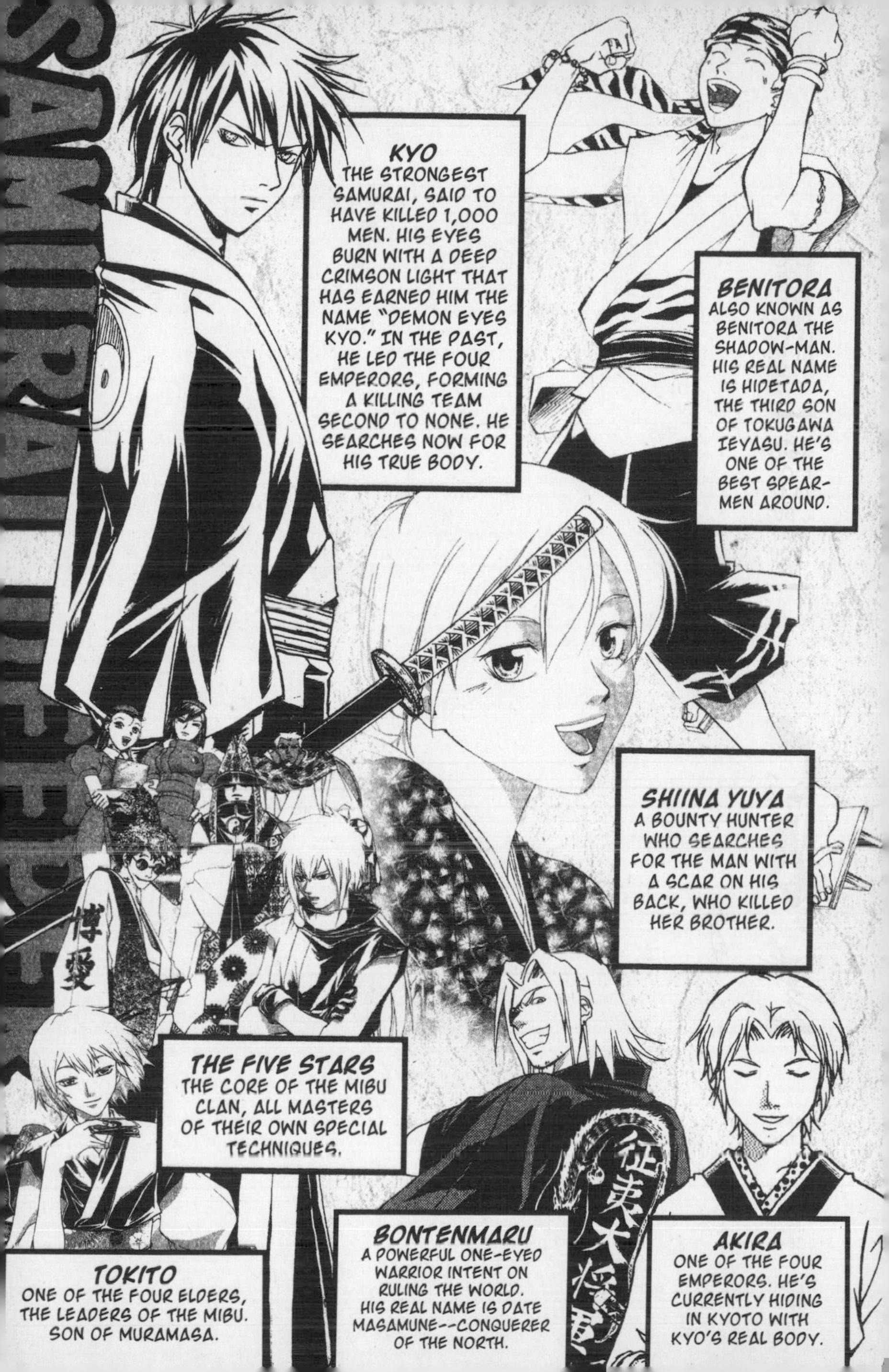
SAMURAI DEEPER
KYO
THE STRONGEST SAMURAI, SAID TO HAVE KILLED 1,000 MEN. HIS EYES BURN WITH A DEEP CRIMSON LIGHT THAT HAS EARNED HIM THE NAME "DEMON EYES KYO." IN THE PAST, HE LED THE FOUR EMPERORS, FORMING A KILLING TEAM SECOND TO NONE. HE SEARCHES NOW FOR HIS TRUE BODY.
BENITORA
ALSO KNOWN AS BENITORA THE SHADOW-MAN. HIS REAL NAME IS HIDETADA, THE THIRD SON OF TOKUGAWA IEYASU. HE'S ONE OF THE BEST SPEARMEN AROUND.
SHIINA YUYA
A BOUNTY HUNTER WHO SEARCHES FOR THE MAN WITH A SCAR ON HIS BACK, WHO KILLED HER BROTHER.
THE FIVE STARS
THE CORE OF THE MIBU CLAN, ALL MASTERS OF THEIR OWN SPECIAL TECHNIQUES.
AKIRA
ONE OF THE FOUR EMPERORS. HE'S CURRENTLY HIDING IN KYOTO WITH KYO'S REAL BODY.
BONTENMARU
A POWERFUL ONE-EYED WARRIOR INTENT ON RULING THE WORLD. HIS REAL NAME IS DATE MASAMUNE--CONQUERER OF THE NORTH.
TOKITO
ONE OF THE FOUR ELDERS, THE LEADERS OF THE MIBU. SON OF MURAMASA.

OF KYO!

WHERE DID KYO MEET ALL HIS FRIENDS? WHO DID THEY FIGHT? SWIFTER THAN KYO CAN SWING HIS SWORD, HERE'S A RECAP OF ALL THAT'S HAPPENED IN SDK SO FAR!

一 (1) THE JOURNEY OF KYOSHIRO AND YUYA BEGINS! (SDK VOL. 1)

▲ MIBU KYOSHIRO

▲ SHIINA YUYA

THE BEAUTIFUL BOUNTY HUNTER YUYA MEETS MIBU KYOSHIRO BY CHANCE (OR WAS IT FATE?!). WHEN THEY FOUGHT THE BANTOUJI BROTHERS, KYOSHIRO'S OTHER SIDE WAS REVEALED: THAT OF DEMON EYES KYO!

COME ON!
YOU'RE NEXT!

WANTED: DEMON EYES KYO

二 (2) THE WOMAN IZUMO-NO-OKUNI (SDK VOL. 1-2)

THEY MEET THE WOMAN IZUMO-NO-OKUNI AT AN INN TOWN--AND SHE SEEMS TO KNOW A LOT ABOUT KYO AND KYOSHIRO'S PAST. THEN, IN THE VILLAGE OF DESERTERS, KYO AWAKENS AND SHOWS HIS FULL STRENGTH!

四 (4) KYO AND YUKIMURA MEET! (SDK VOL. 3)

A DRUNK CALLS OUT TO THEM AT A TEAHOUSE--AND TURNS OUT TO BE A SWORDSMAN OF SUCH SKILL THAT HE CAN SLIP PAST EVEN KYO'S DEFENSES!

▸ SANADA YUKIMURA

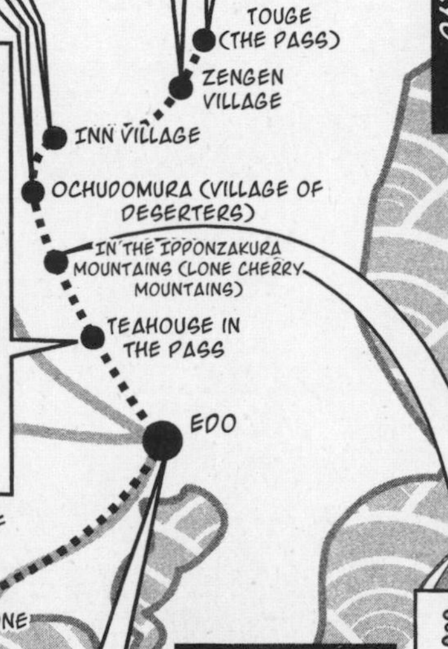

TOUGE (THE PASS)
ZENGEN VILLAGE
INN VILLAGE
OCHUDOMURA (VILLAGE OF DESERTERS)
IN THE IPPONZAKURA MOUNTAINS (LONE CHERRY MOUNTAINS)
TEAHOUSE IN THE PASS
EDO
THE FOREST OF AOKIGAHARA
HAKONE
MT. FUJI

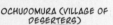

三 (3) BENITORA JOINS THE PARTY! (SDK VOL. 2-3)

THE PARTY GETS INTO A FIGHT WITH A TREASURE-SEEKING GROUP OF ASSASSINS KNOWN AS THE KITOU FAMILY SANSAISHU. ONE OF THEIR NUMBER, BENITORA, ENDS UP JOINING SIDES WITH KYO. KYO FIGHTS THE SHIROKARASU (WHITE CROW) AND AWAKENS FULLY! KYOSHIRO, HOWEVER, IS NOWHERE TO BE SEEN.

▲ BENITORA

▸ THE REAL TOKUGAWA IEYASU

五 (5) FIGHT BEFORE THE SHOGUN! (SDK VOL. 3-5)

KYO, YUKIMURA, AND BENITORA ENTER A TOURNEY HELD BY THE RULER OF THE LAND, TOKUGAWA IEYASU. BUT THE TOURNEY WAS A TRAP! SET UPON BY TOKUGAWA'S ELITES, THE THREE MANAGE TO DESTROY THEM ALL WITHOUT BREAKING A SWEAT! THEN YUKIMURA TELLS KYO A SECRET: THE LOCATION OF HIS BODY!

THEY'RE NOT HUMAN...
THEY'RE DEMONS.

IN JUST 3 MINUTES!

LEARN THE LEGEND

六 (6) MORTAL COMBAT VERSUS ODA NOBUNAGA AND THE TWELVE GOD SHOGUNS! (SDK VOL. 5-10)

KYO'S BODY LIES HIDDEN IN THE DEEPEST REACHES OF THE AOKIGAHARA FOREST AT THE FOOT OF MT. FUJI. BUT BETWEEN KYO AND HIS BODY STAND THE TWELVE--GUARDIANS OF THE MASTER, ODA NOBUNAGA. AFTER A STRING OF BLOODY BATTLES, KYO'S DEMONBLADE, MURAMASA, RELIEVES NOBUNAGA'S BODY OF ITS HEAD, BUT AKIRA MAKES HIS ESCAPE WITH KYO'S BODY!

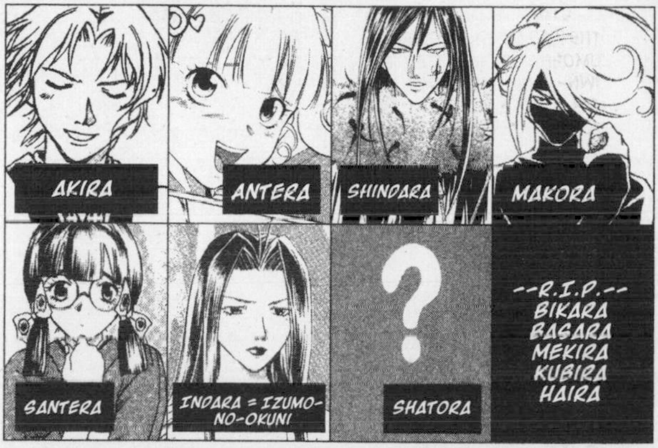

AKIRA
ANTERA
SHINDARA
MAKORA
SANTERA
INDARA = IZUMO-NO-OKUNI
?
SHATORA
--R.I.P.--
BIKARA
BASARA
MEKIRA
KUBIRA
HAIRA

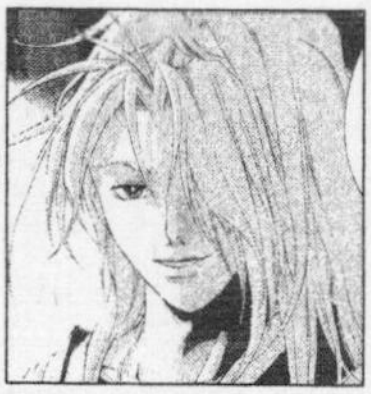

NOBUNAGA AWAITS THE TIME OF HIS RESURRECTION IN THE VILLAGE OF THE MIBU, DEEP WITHIN THE LAND OF THE FIRE LOTUS.

▲ ODA NOBUNAGA

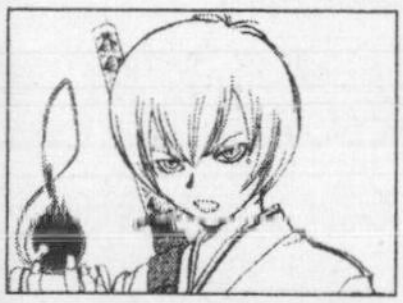

◀ SASUKE

ONE OF THE SANADA TEN. HE RETURNED TO THE FOREST WHERE HE WAS BORN ON YUKIMURA'S ORDERS.

八 (8) FIERCE FIGHTING AGAINST THE PRIDE OF THE MIBU CLAN! (SDK VOL. 11-)

THE ENIGMATIC MIBU FAMILY HOLDS THE KEY TO THE MYSTERY BEHIND KYO'S BIRTH. AFTER HOLDING THE POWER TO CONTROL JAPAN'S HISTORY FROM THE DARK SIDE, SUDDENLY THE FACE-TO-FACE SHOWDOWN HAS BEGUN! AT THE SAME TIME, THE POWER TO SAVE YUYA'S LIFE LIES WITH THE ENEMY. KYO HAS CONFRONTED THE FIVE STARS, THE FOUR EMPERORS AND, MOST RECENTLY, THE CRIMSON KING (AKA NO OU), HIS LATEST ULTIMATELY STRONG FOE. ON THE OTHER HAND, KYO IS MARCHING INTO ENEMY TERRITORY ARMED WITH THE MUMYO JINPU TECHNIQUE THAT MURAMASA TRADED HIS LIFE TO OBTAIN.

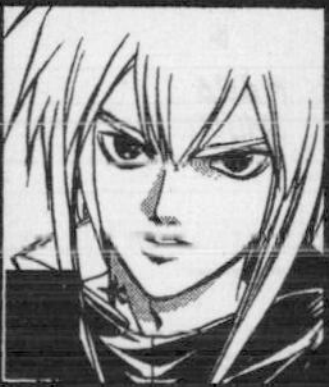

SHINREI

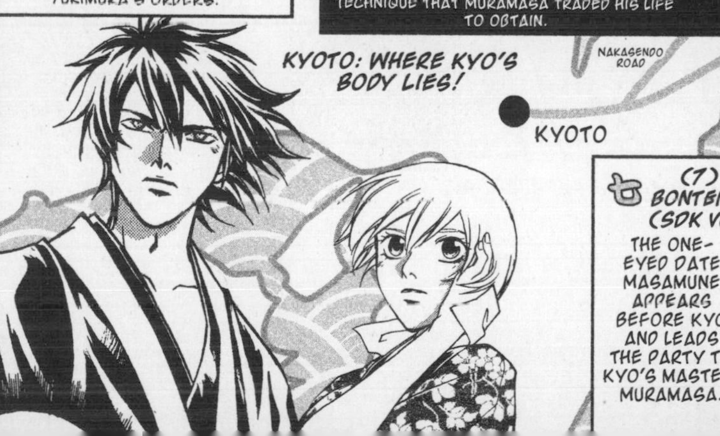

KYOTO: WHERE KYO'S BODY LIES!
NAKASENDO ROAD
TOKAIDO ROAD
OWARI
KYOTO

七 (7) ENTER BONTENMARU! (SDK VOL. 10)

THE ONE-EYED DATE MASAMUNE APPEARS BEFORE KYO AND LEADS THE PARTY TO KYO'S MASTER, MURAMASA.

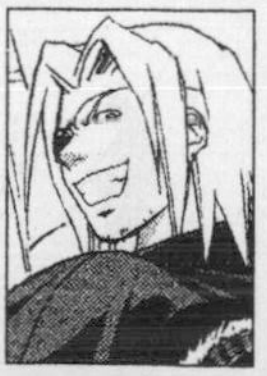

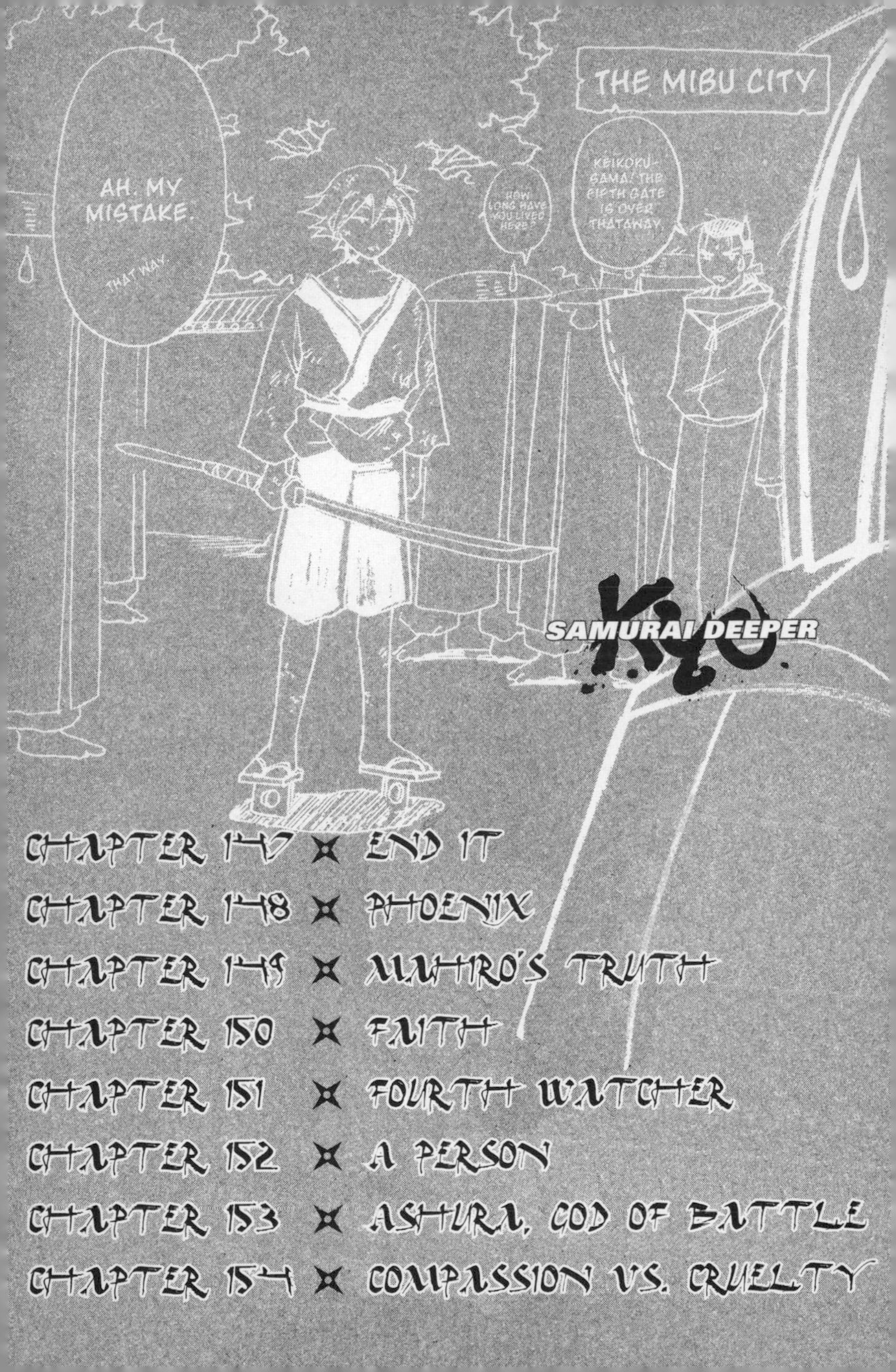
THE MIBU CITY
KEIKOKU-SAMA! THE FIFTH GATE IS OVER THATAWAY.
HOW LONG HAVE YOU LIVED HERE?
AH. MY MISTAKE.
THAT WAY.
SAMURAI DEEPER KYO

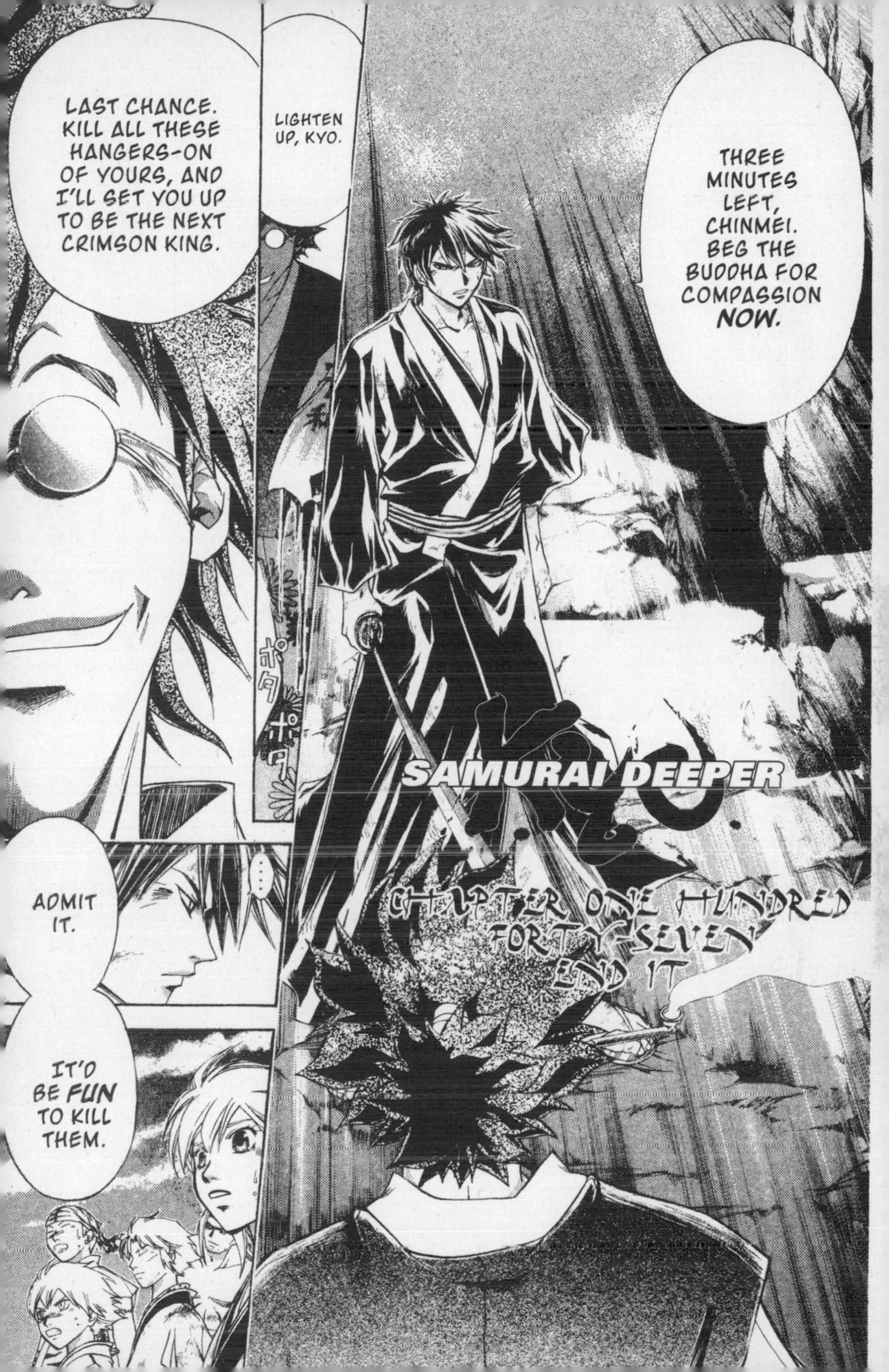
THREE MINUTES LEFT, CHINMEI. BEG THE BUDDHA FOR COMPASSION NOW.
ポタ ポタ
SAMURAI DEEPER
CHAPTER ONE HUNDRED FORTY-SEVEN
END IT
LIGHTEN UP, KYO.
LAST CHANCE. KILL ALL THESE HANGERS-ON OF YOURS, AND I'LL SET YOU UP TO BE THE NEXT CRIMSON KING.
...
ADMIT IT.
IT'D BE FUN TO KILL THEM.

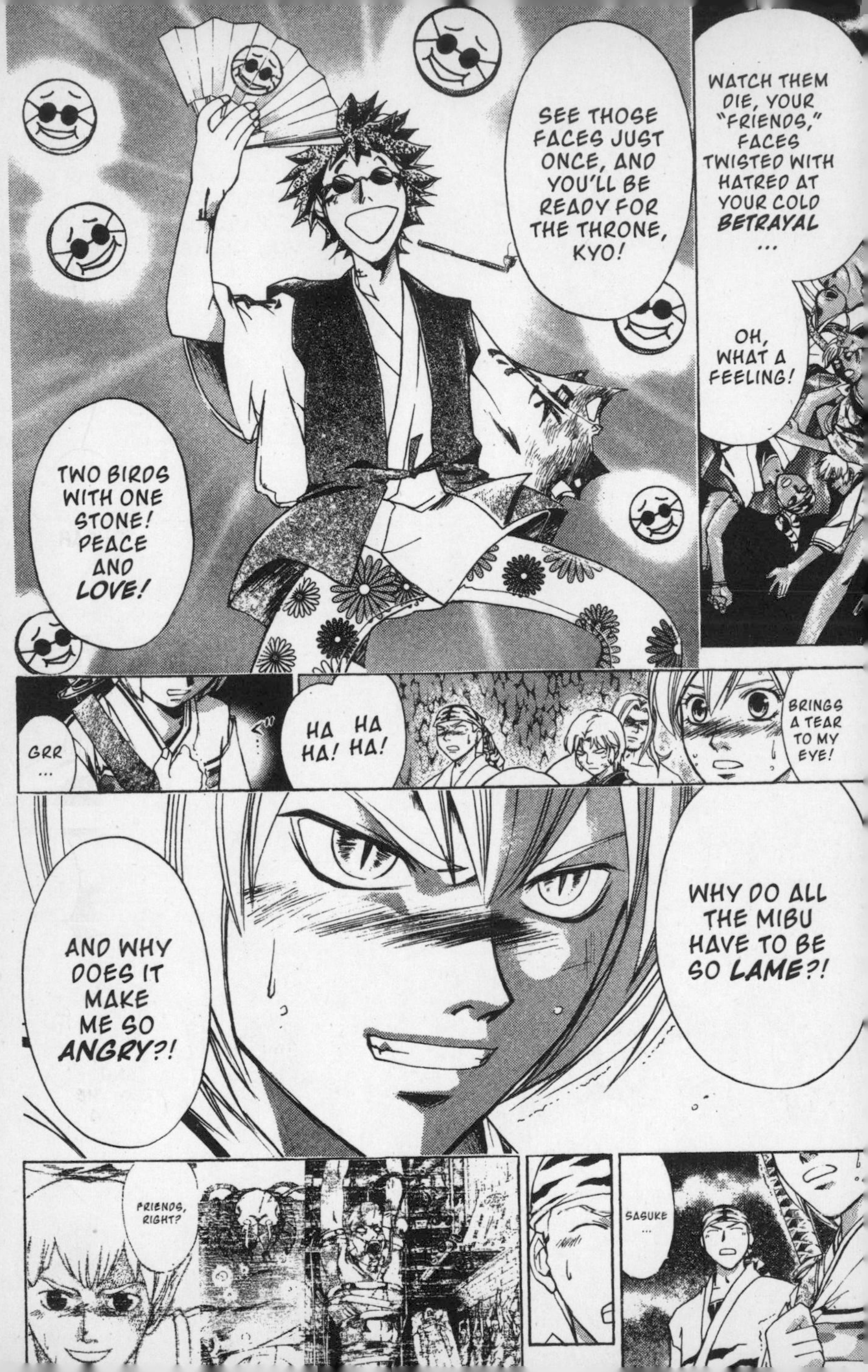
WATCH THEM DIE, YOUR "FRIENDS," FACES TWISTED WITH HATRED AT YOUR COLD BETRAYAL ...
OH, WHAT A FEELING!
SEE THOSE FACES JUST ONCE, AND YOU'LL BE READY FOR THE THRONE, KYO!
TWO BIRDS WITH ONE STONE! PEACE AND LOVE!
BRINGS A TEAR TO MY EYE!
HA HA HA! HA!
GRR ...
WHY DO ALL THE MIBU HAVE TO BE SO LAME?!
AND WHY DOES IT MAKE ME SO ANGRY?!
SASUKE ...
FRIENDS, RIGHT?

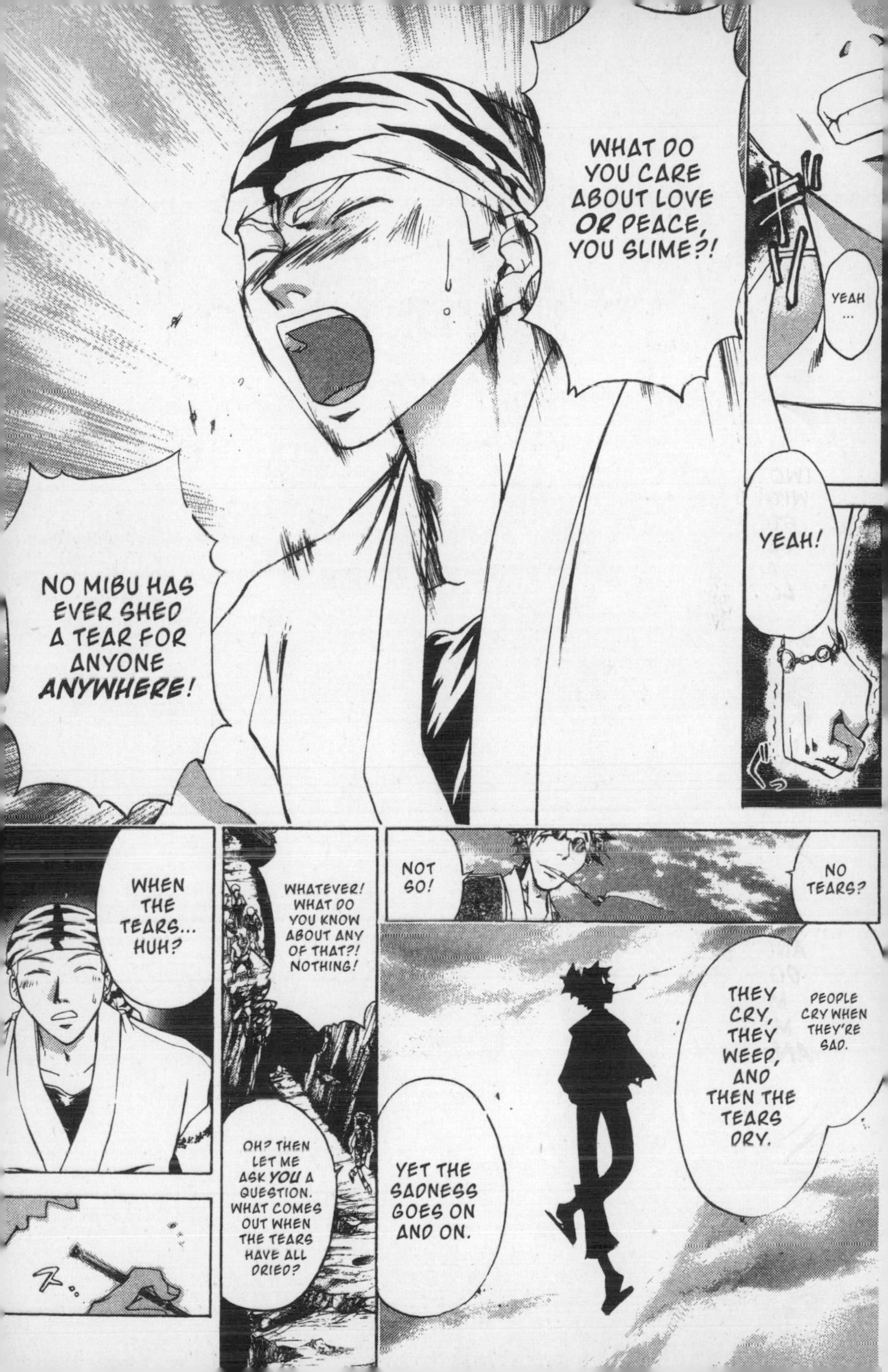
YEAH ...
YEAH!
WHAT DO YOU CARE ABOUT LOVE OR PEACE, YOU SLIME?!
NO MIBU HAS EVER SHED A TEAR FOR ANYONE ANYWHERE!
NO TEARS?
NOT SO!
PEOPLE CRY WHEN THEY'RE SAD.
THEY CRY, THEY WEEP, AND THEN THE TEARS DRY.
YET THE SADNESS GOES ON AND ON.
WHATEVER! WHAT DO YOU KNOW ABOUT ANY OF THAT?! NOTHING!
OH? THEN LET ME ASK YOU A QUESTION. WHAT COMES OUT WHEN THE TEARS HAVE ALL DRIED?
WHEN THE TEARS... HUH?

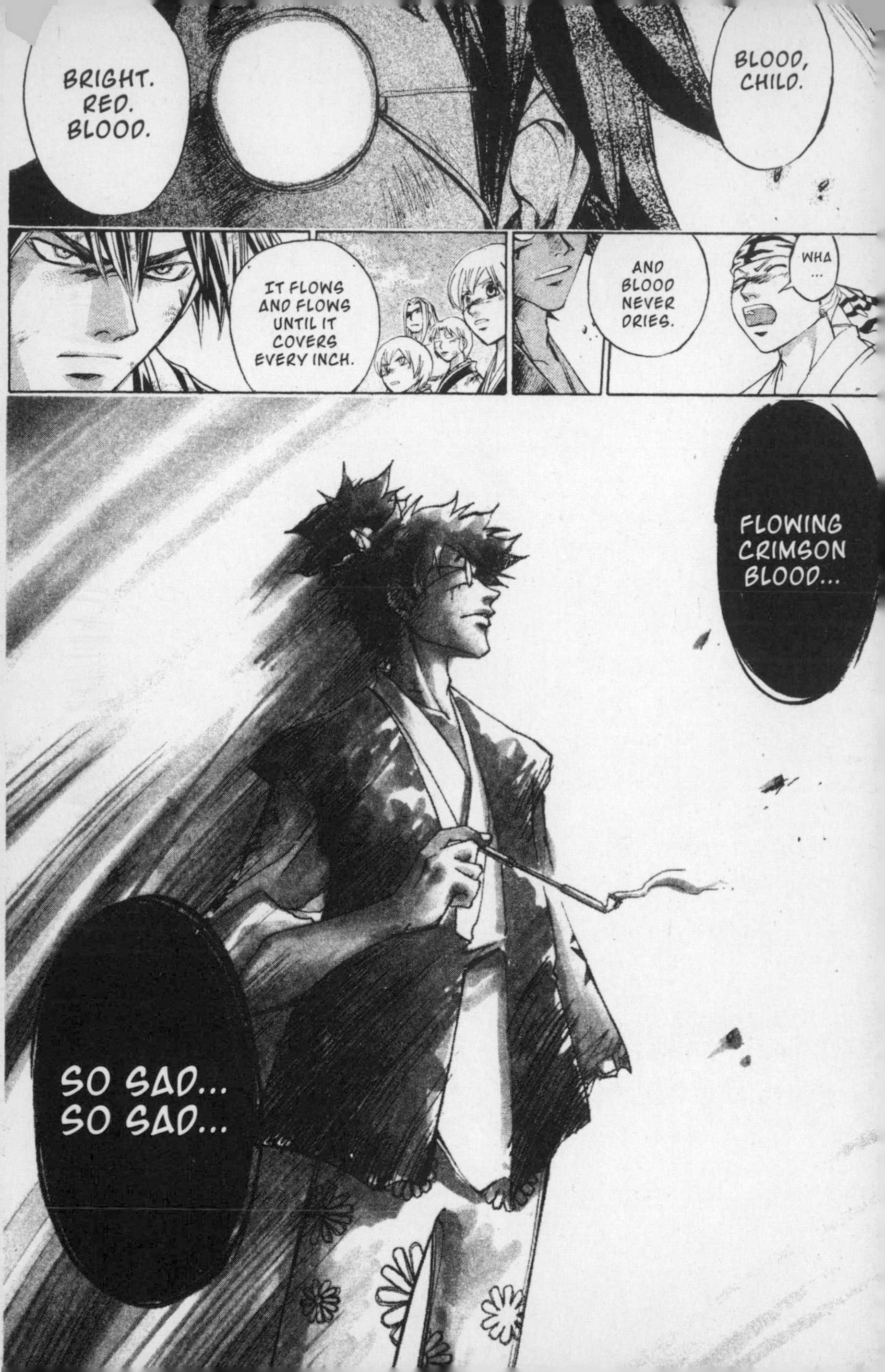
BLOOD, CHILD.
BRIGHT. RED. BLOOD.
WHA ...
AND BLOOD NEVER DRIES.
IT FLOWS AND FLOWS UNTIL IT COVERS EVERY INCH.
FLOWING CRIMSON BLOOD...
SO SAD... SO SAD...

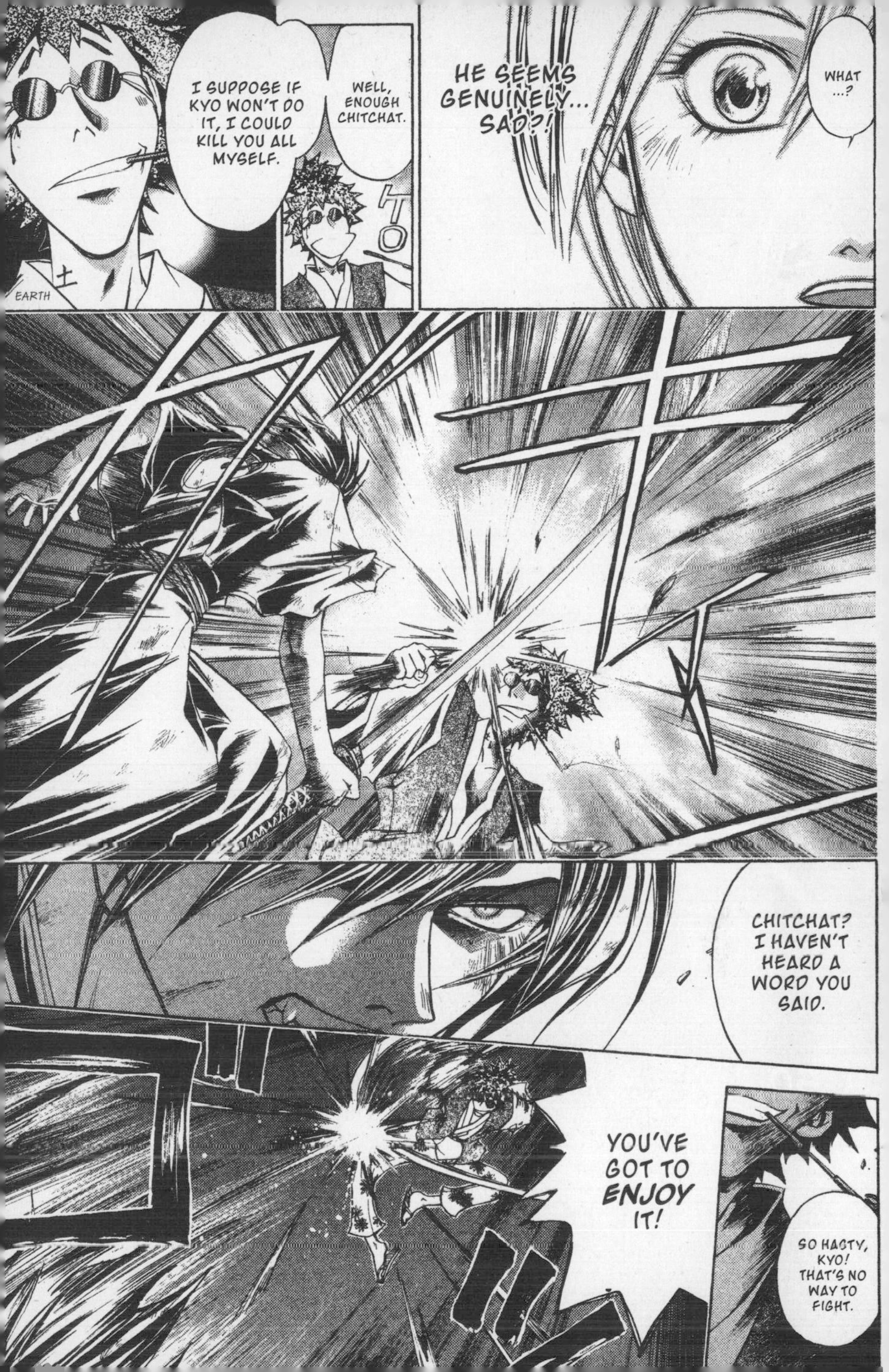
WHAT ...?
HE SEEMS GENUINELY... SAD?!
WELL, ENOUGH CHITCHAT.
I SUPPOSE IF KYO WON'T DO IT, I COULD KILL YOU ALL MYSELF.
EARTH
CHITCHAT? I HAVEN'T HEARD A WORD YOU SAID.
SO HASTY, KYO! THAT'S NO WAY TO FIGHT.
YOU'VE GOT TO ENJOY IT!

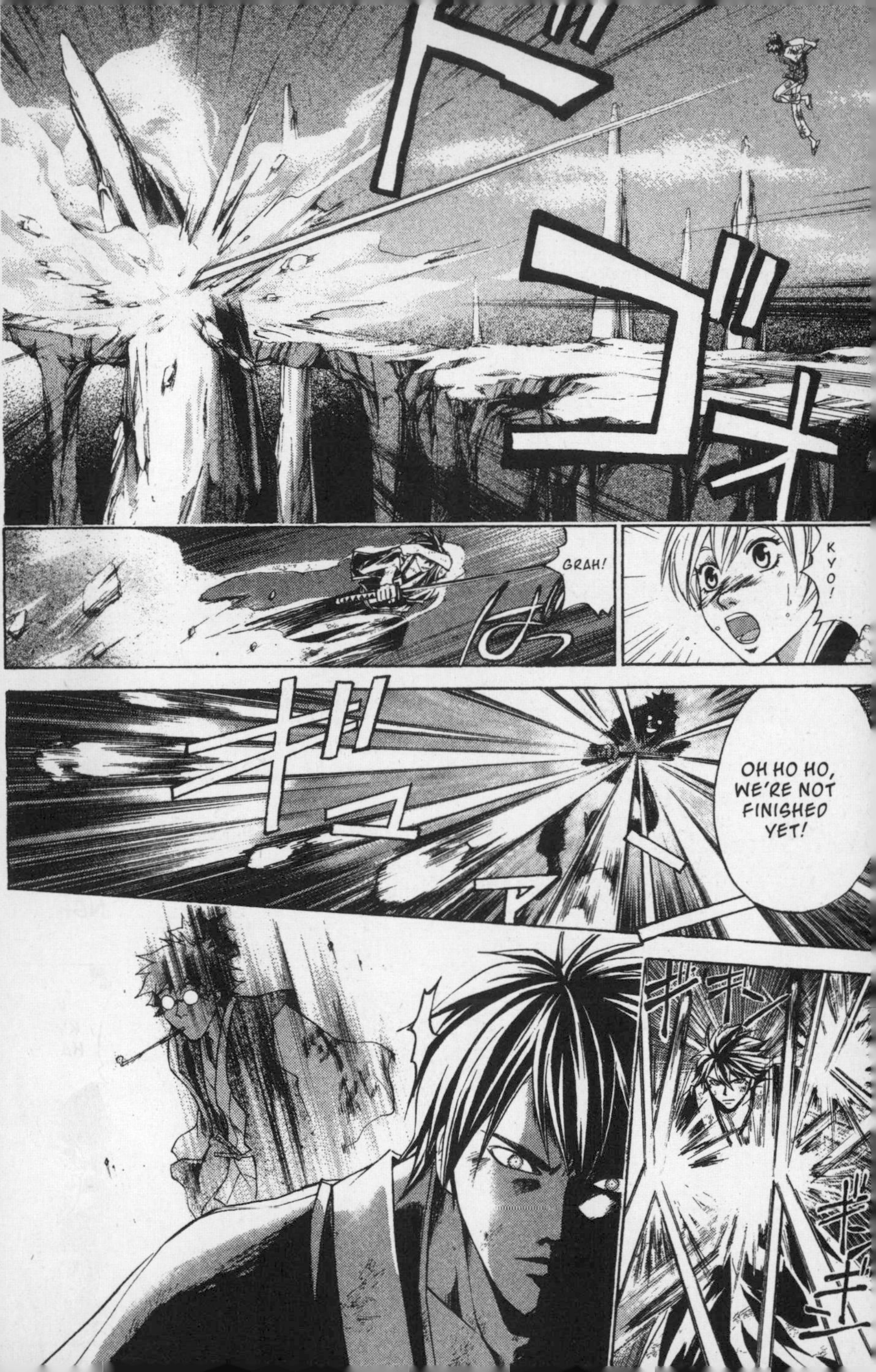
KYO!
GRAH!
OH HO HO, WE'RE NOT FINISHED YET!

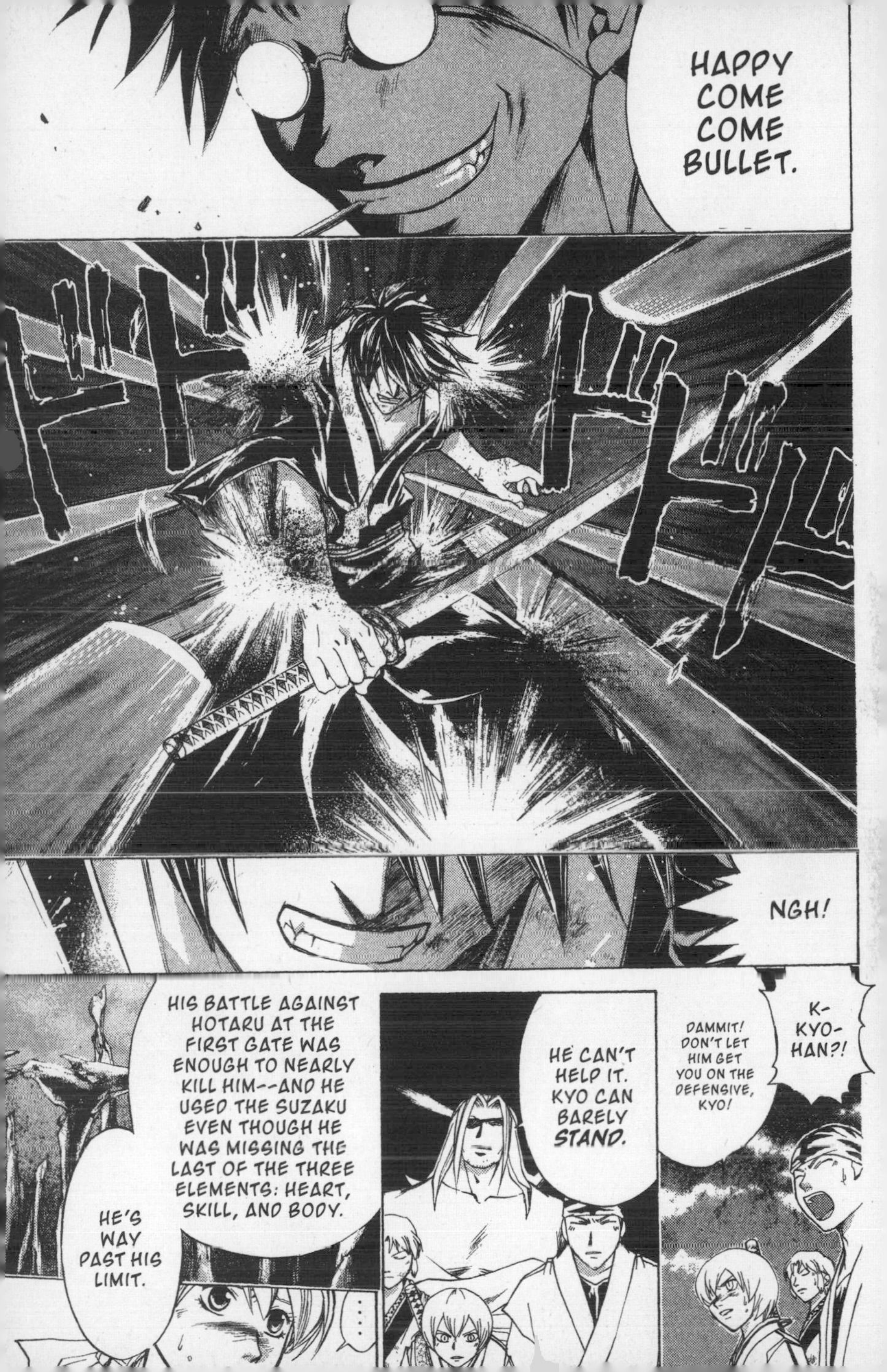
HAPPY COME COME BULLET.
NGH!
K-KYO-HAN?!
DAMMIT! DON'T LET HIM GET YOU ON THE DEFENSIVE, KYO!
HE CAN'T HELP IT. KYO CAN BARELY STAND.
HIS BATTLE AGAINST HOTARU AT THE FIRST GATE WAS ENOUGH TO NEARLY KILL HIM--AND HE USED THE SUZAKU EVEN THOUGH HE WAS MISSING THE LAST OF THE THREE ELEMENTS: HEART, SKILL, AND BODY.
HE'S WAY PAST HIS LIMIT.
....

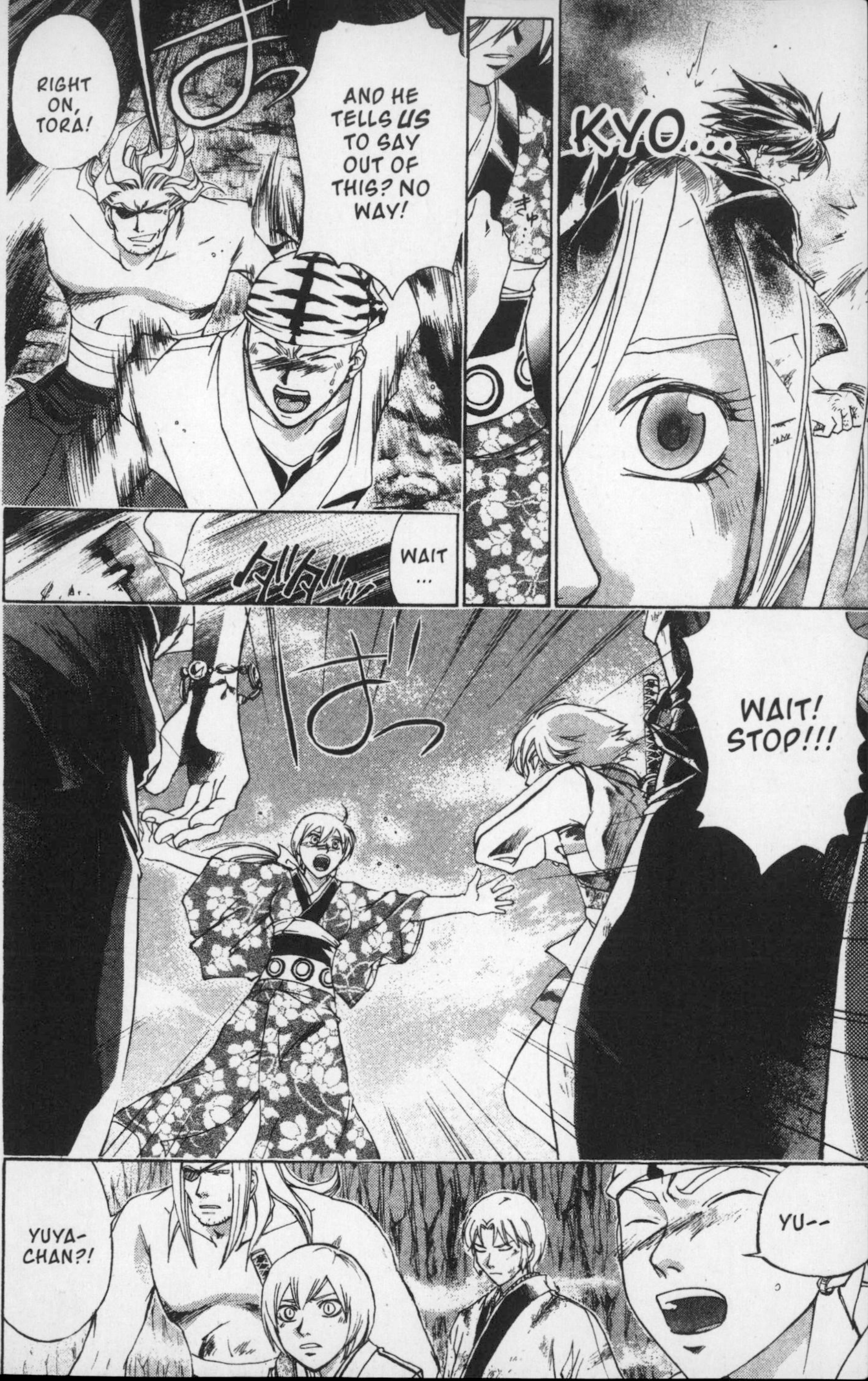
KYO...
AND HE TELLS US TO SAY OUT OF THIS? NO WAY!
RIGHT ON, TORA!
WAIT ...
WAIT! STOP!!!
YU--
YUYA-CHAN?!

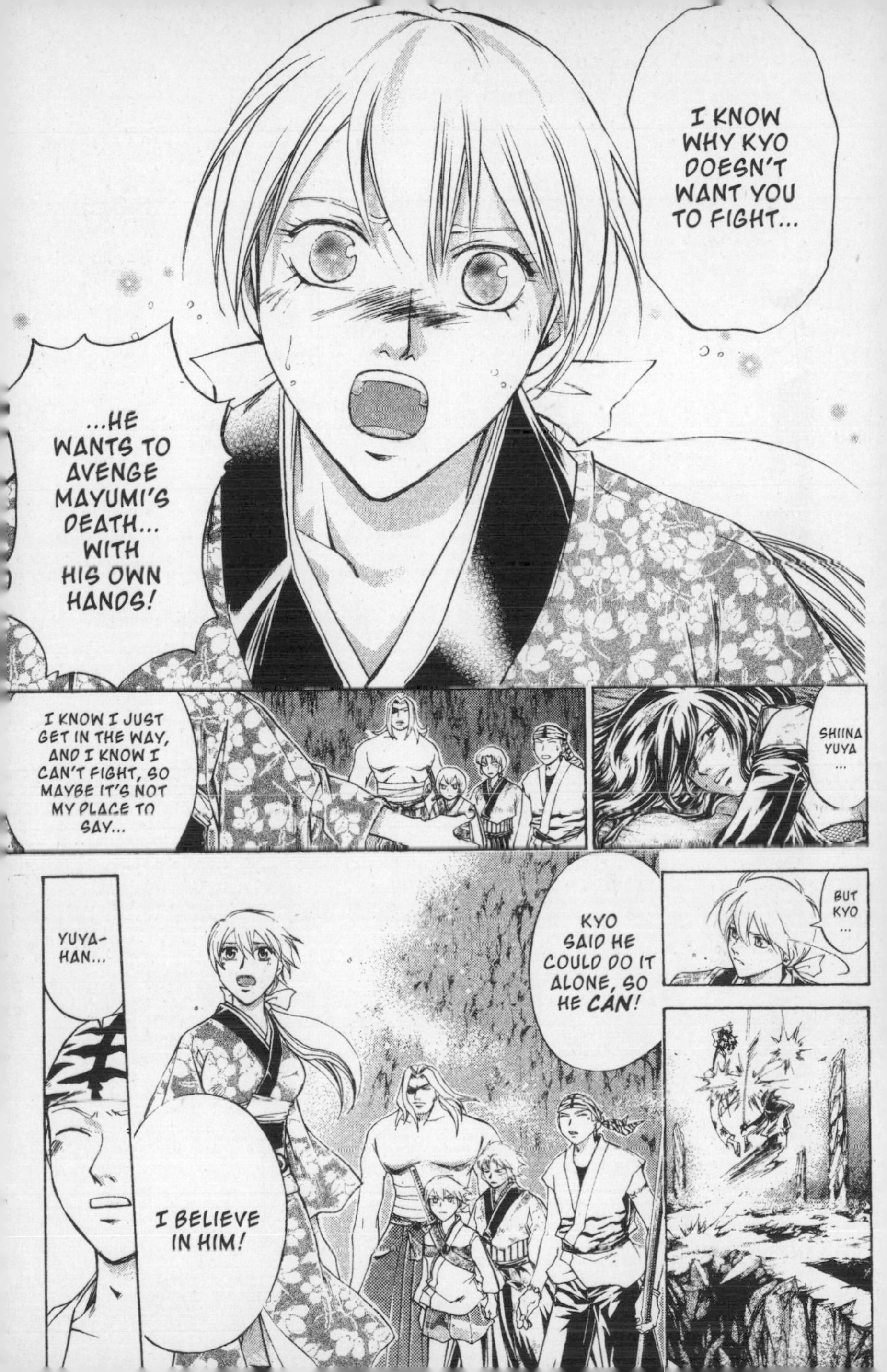
I KNOW WHY KYO DOESN'T WANT YOU TO FIGHT...
...HE WANTS TO AVENGE MAYUMI'S DEATH... WITH HIS OWN HANDS!
SHIINA YUYA ...
I KNOW I JUST GET IN THE WAY, AND I KNOW I CAN'T FIGHT, SO MAYBE IT'S NOT MY PLACE TO SAY...
BUT KYO ...
KYO SAID HE COULD DO IT ALONE, SO HE CAN!
YUYA-HAN...
I BELIEVE IN HIM!

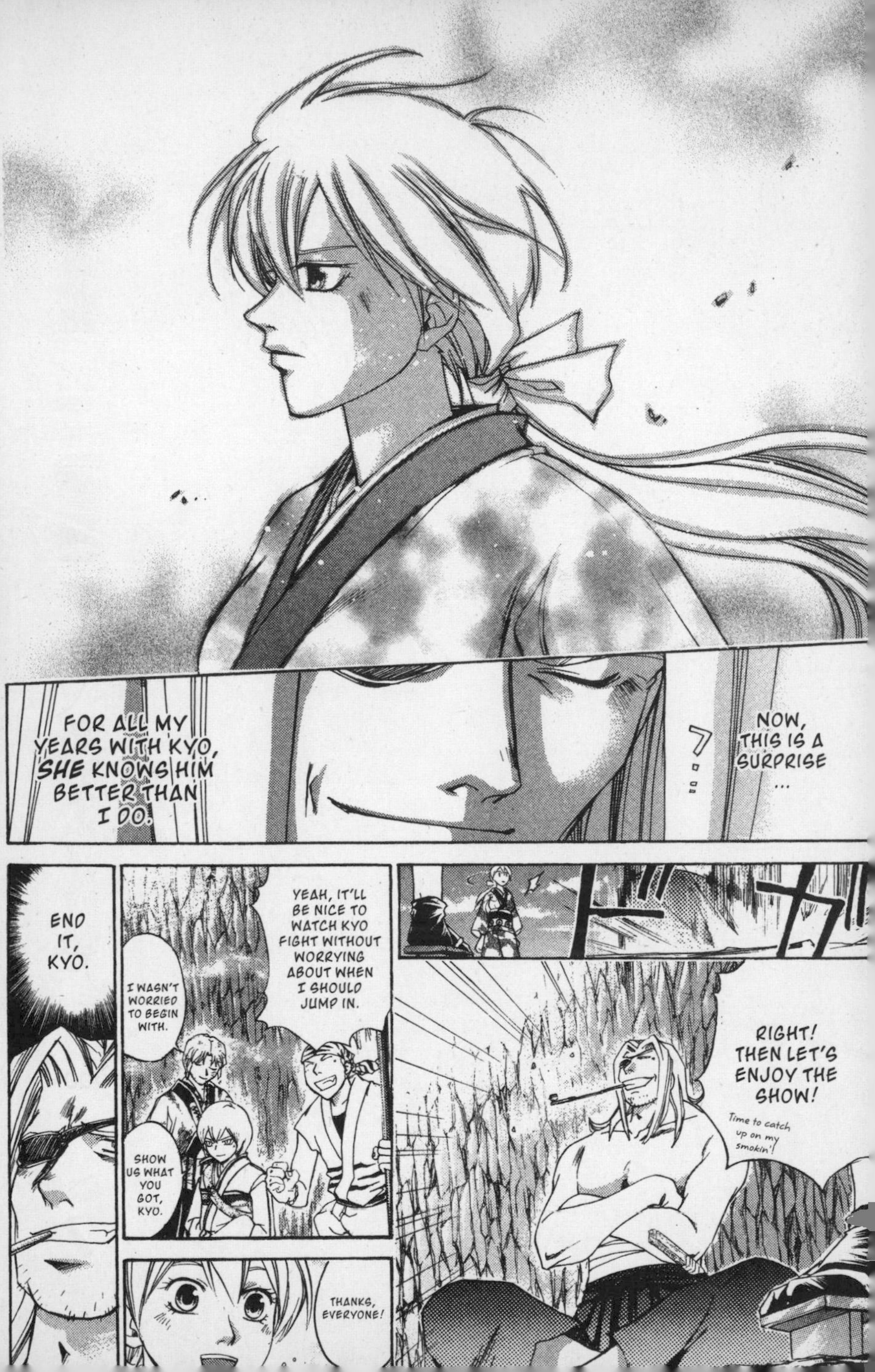

NOW, THIS IS A SURPRISE ...
FOR ALL MY YEARS WITH KYO, SHE KNOWS HIM BETTER THAN I DO.
RIGHT! THEN LET'S ENJOY THE SHOW!
Time to catch up on my smokin'!
YEAH, IT'LL BE NICE TO WATCH KYO FIGHT WITHOUT WORRYING ABOUT WHEN I SHOULD JUMP IN.
I WASN'T WORRIED TO BEGIN WITH.
SHOW US WHAT YOU GOT, KYO.
THANKS, EVERYONE!
END IT, KYO.

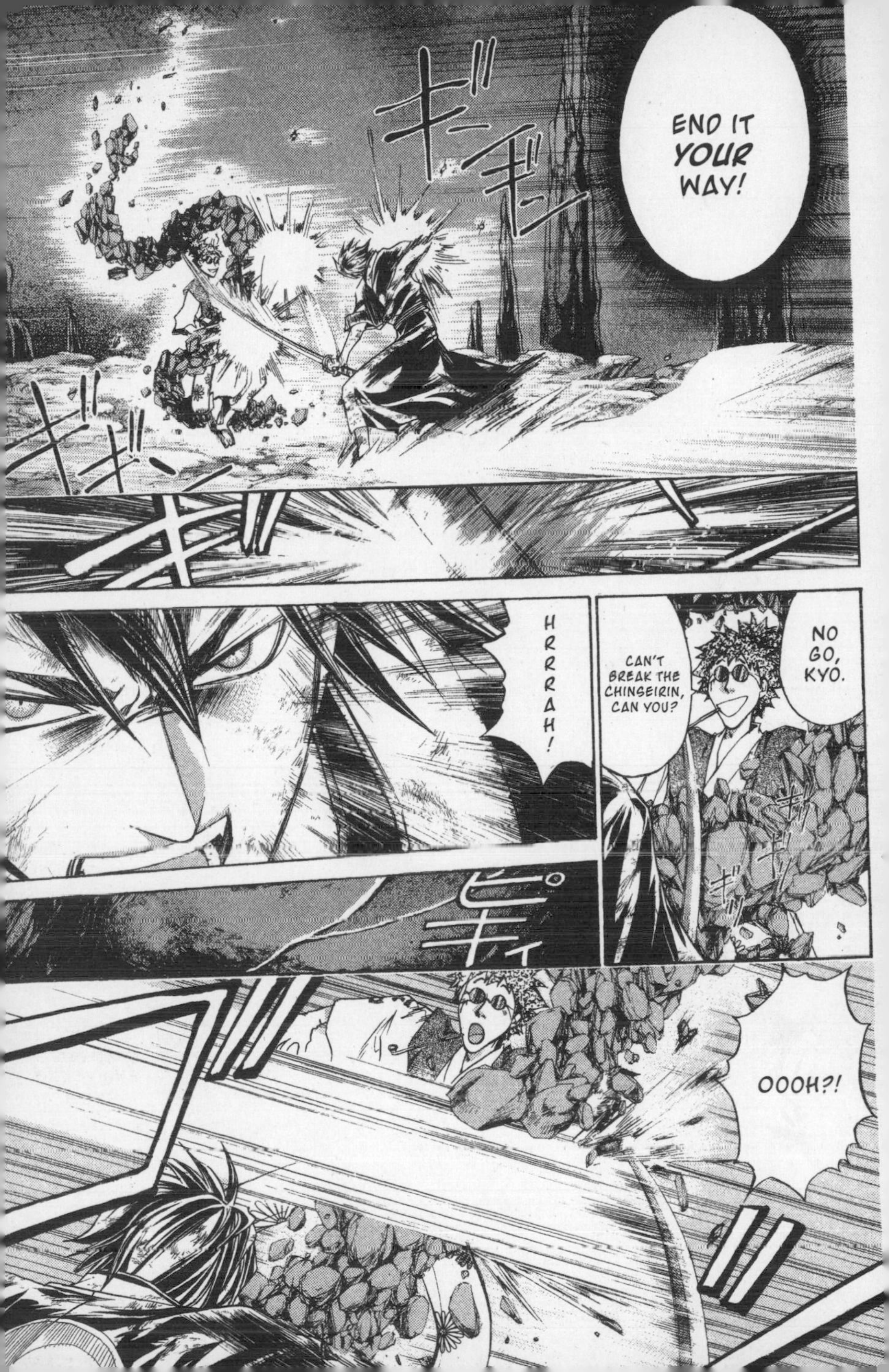
END IT YOUR WAY!
NO GO, KYO.
CAN'T BREAK THE CHINSEIRIN, CAN YOU?
HRRRAH!
OOOH?!

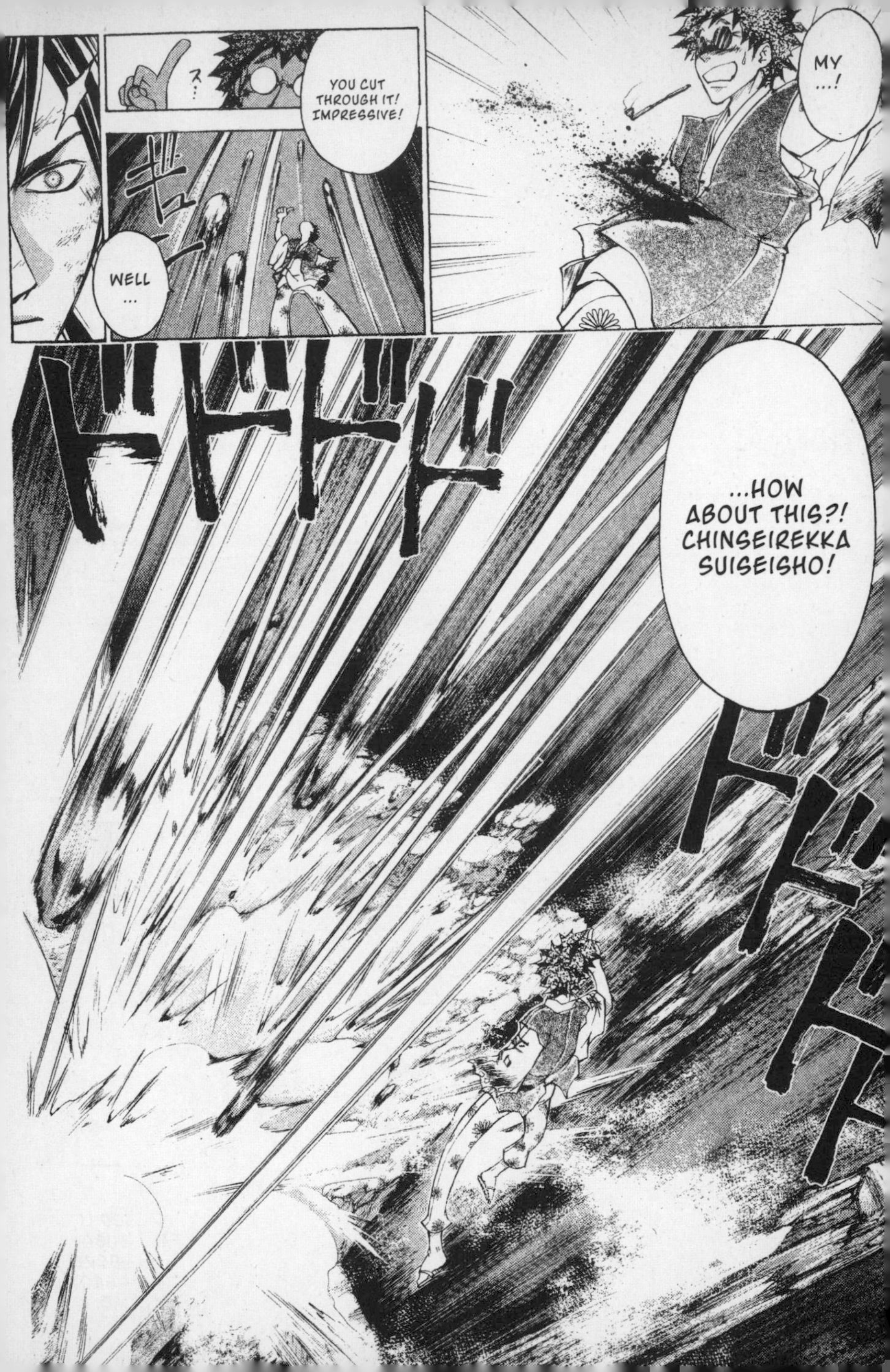
MY ...!
ス…
YOU CUT THROUGH IT! IMPRESSIVE!
WELL ...
...HOW ABOUT THIS?! CHINSEIREKKA SUISEISHO!
ドドドド

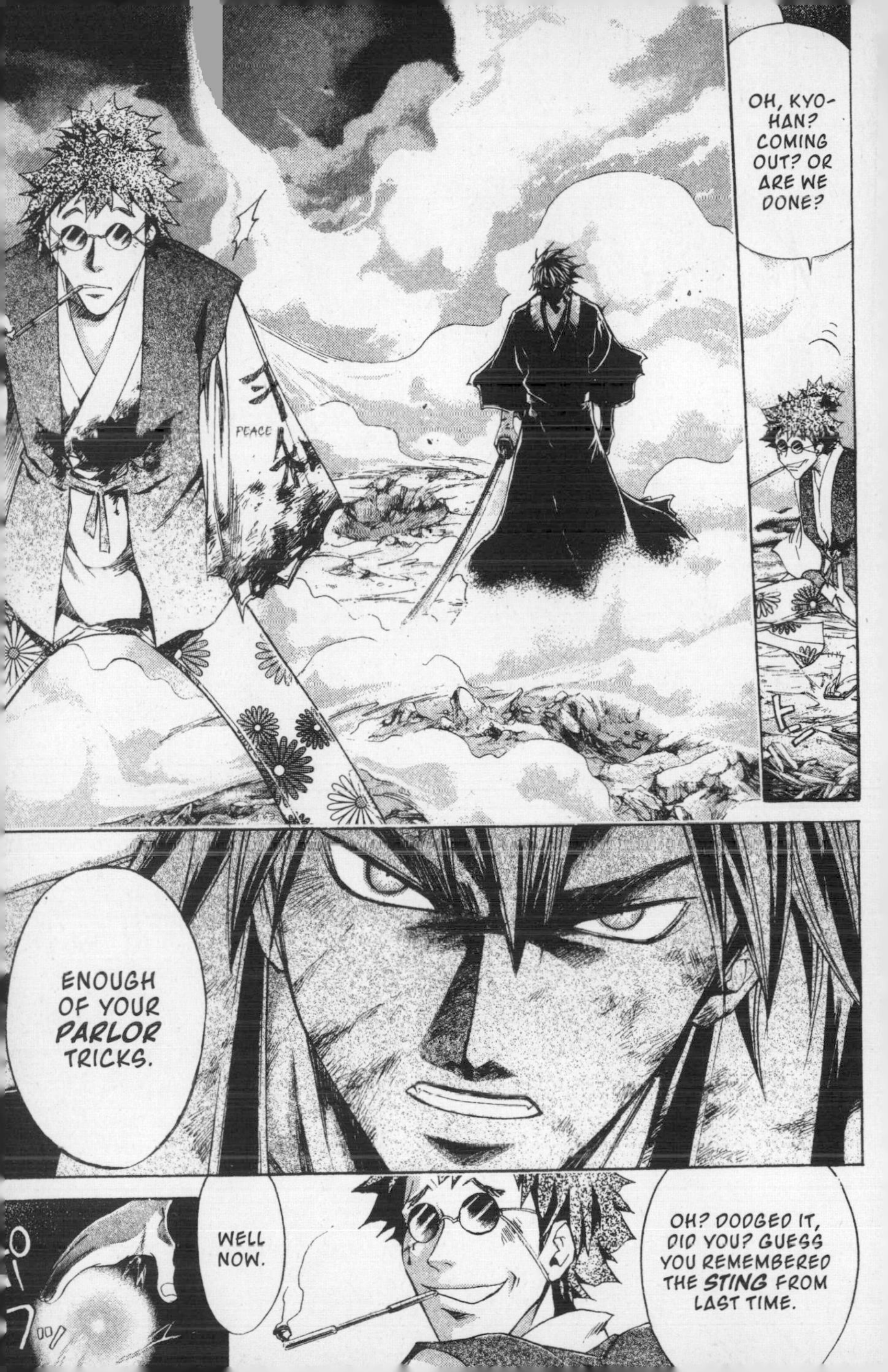
OH, KYO-HAN? COMING OUT? OR ARE WE DONE?
PEACE
ENOUGH OF YOUR PARLOR TRICKS.
OH? DODGED IT, DID YOU? GUESS YOU REMEMBERED THE STING FROM LAST TIME.
WELL NOW.

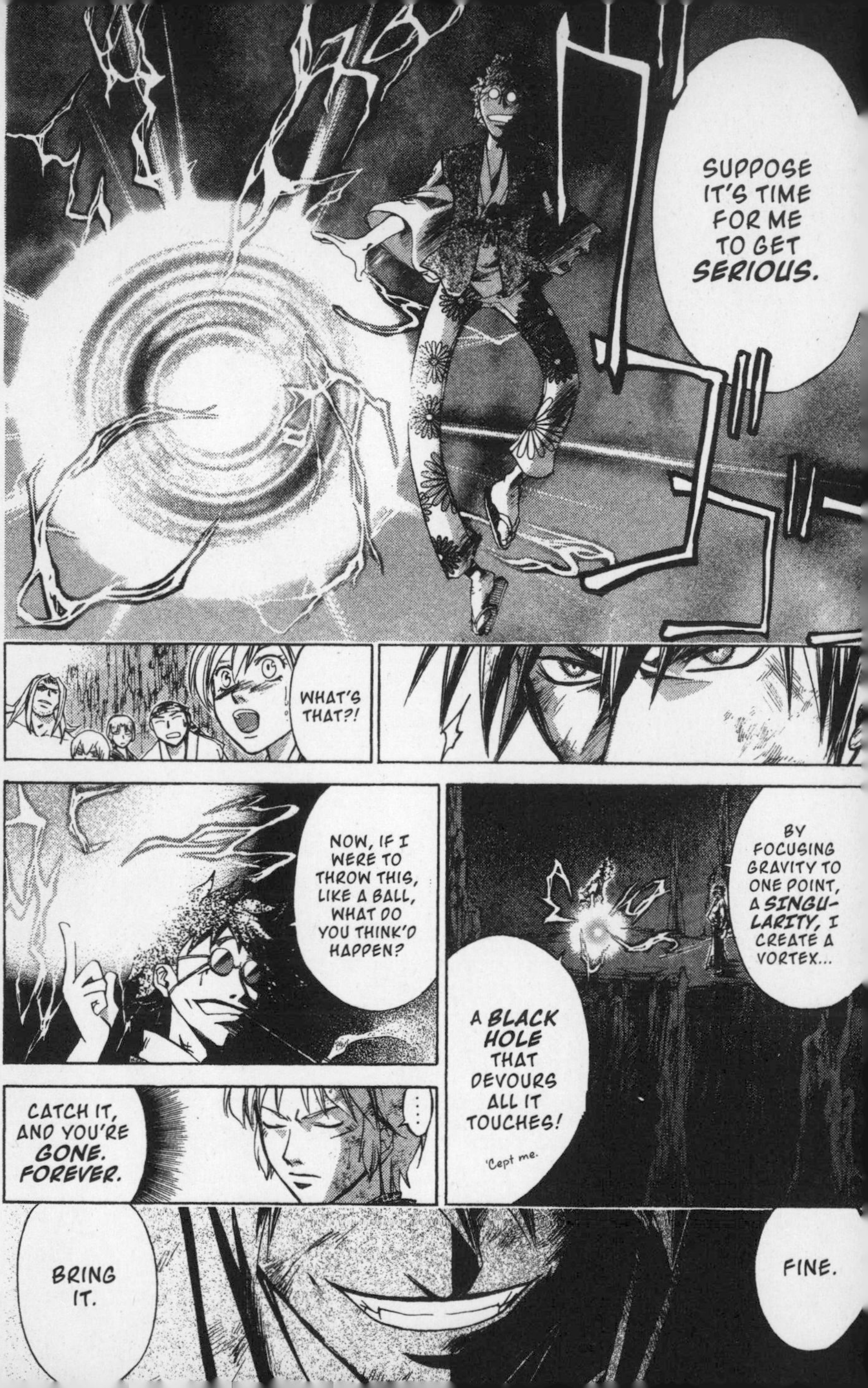
SUPPOSE IT'S TIME FOR ME TO GET SERIOUS.
WHAT'S THAT?!
BY FOCUSING GRAVITY TO ONE POINT, A SINGULARITY, I CREATE A VORTEX...
A BLACK HOLE THAT DEVOURS ALL IT TOUCHES!
'Cept me.
NOW, IF I WERE TO THROW THIS, LIKE A BALL, WHAT DO YOU THINK'D HAPPEN?
...
CATCH IT, AND YOU'RE GONE. FOREVER.
FINE.
BRING IT.

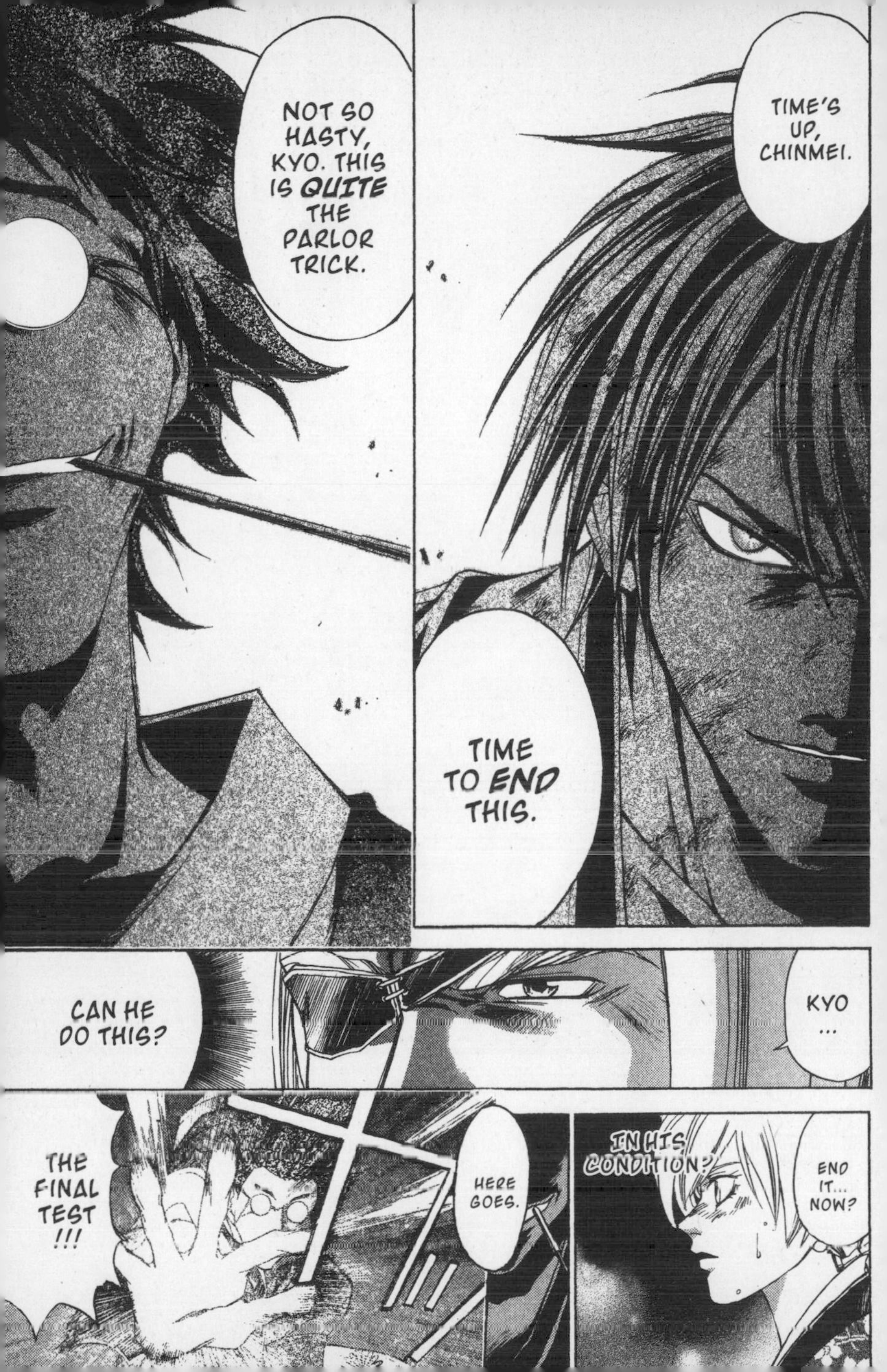
TIME'S UP, CHINMEI.
TIME TO END THIS.
NOT SO HASTY, KYO. THIS IS QUITE THE PARLOR TRICK.
KYO ...
CAN HE DO THIS?
END IT... NOW?
IN HIS CONDITION?
HERE GOES.
THE FINAL TEST !!!

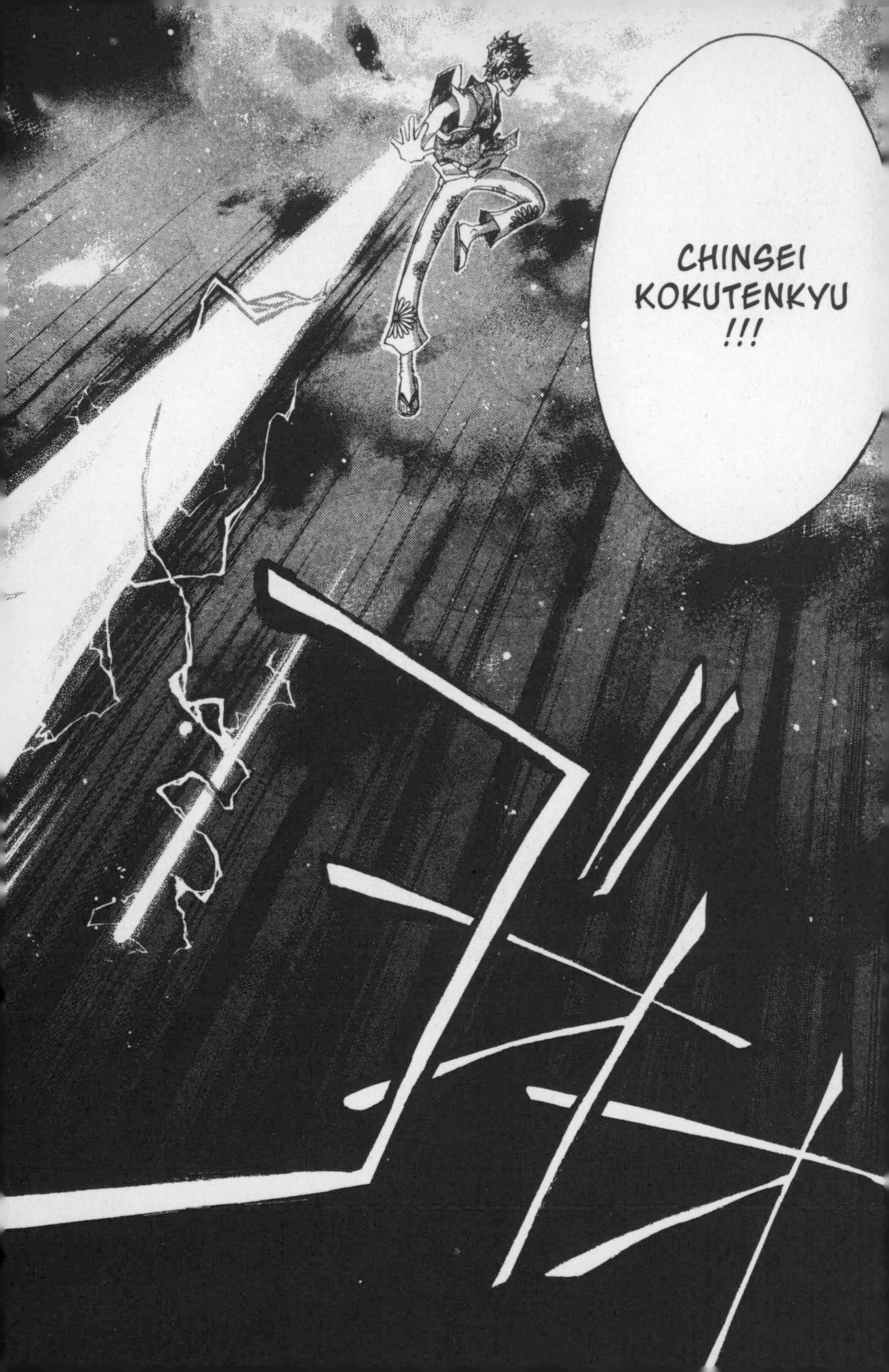
CHINSEI KOKUTENKYU !!!

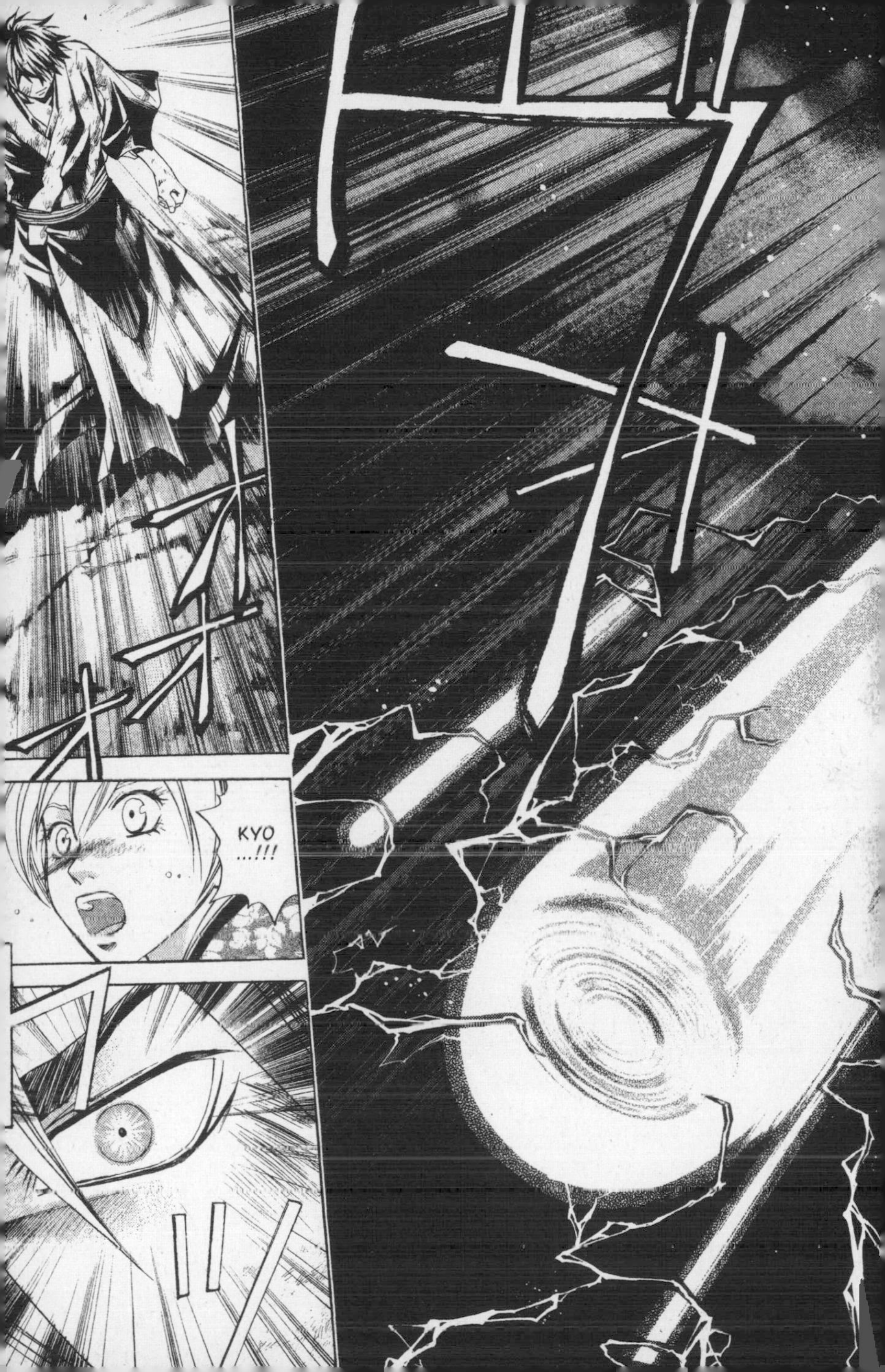
KYO
...!!!

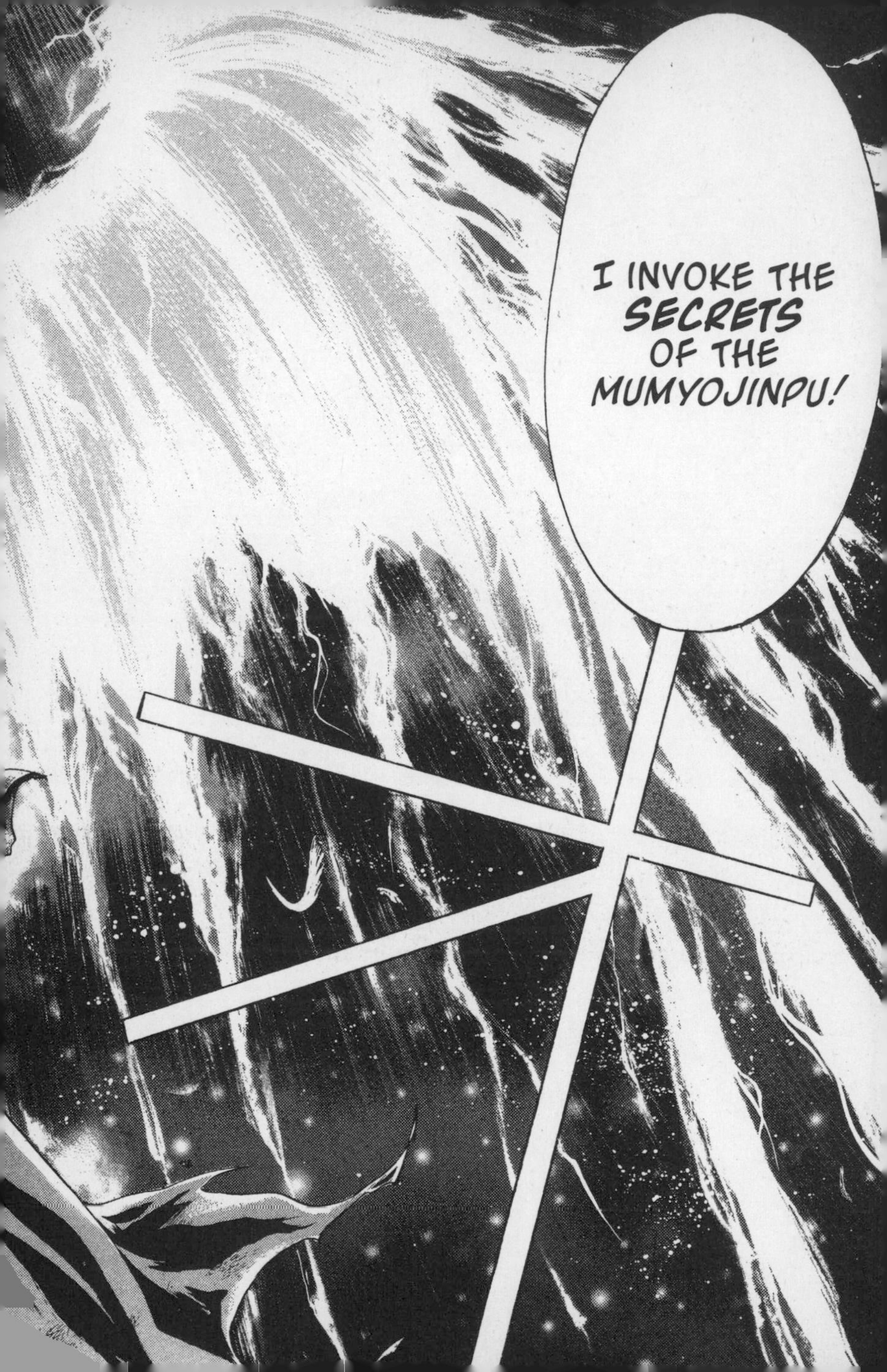
I INVOKE THE SECRETS OF THE MUMYOJINPU!

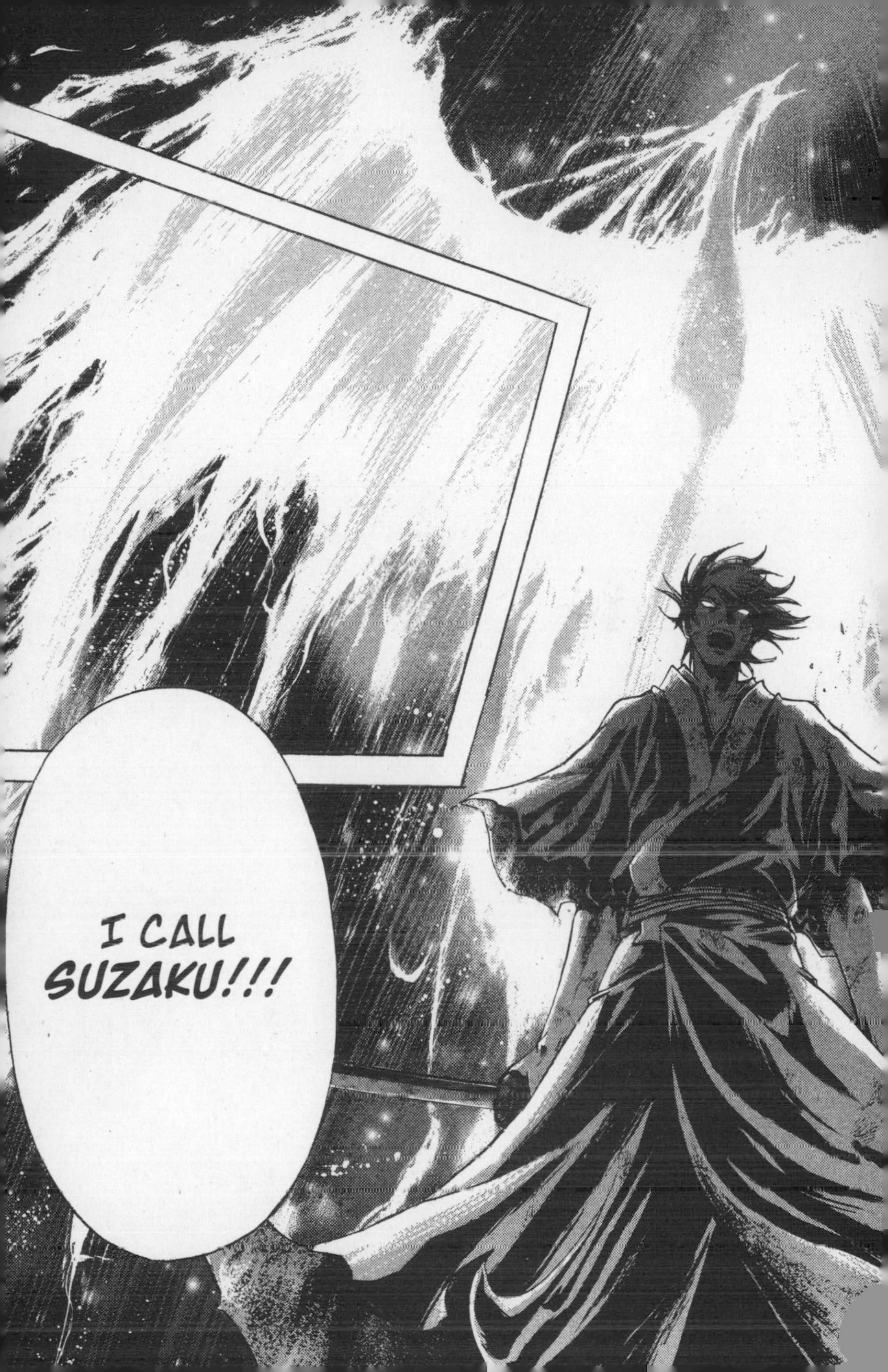
I CALL SUZAKU!!!

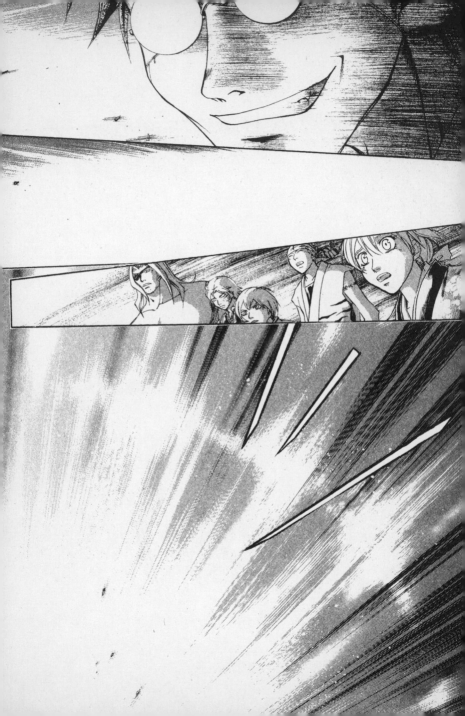

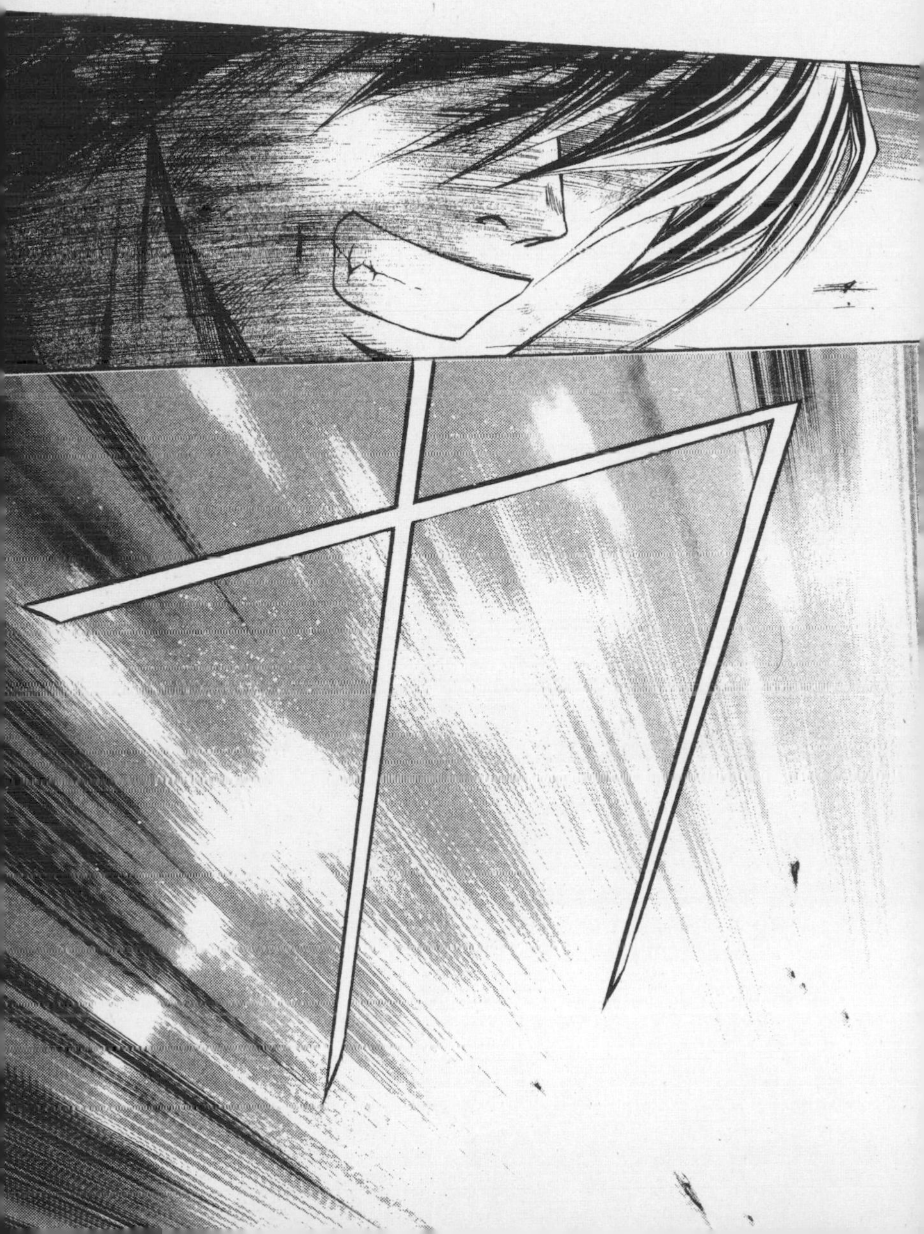

The Kamijyo Report

MY NIECE

I GAVE MY SISTER A FAN WE MADE FOR A GIVEAWAY.
COOL BABIES ARE HAPPY BABIES!
SEE? EVEN KYO CAN HELP RAISE A KID!
OOH! FEEL THE BREEZE!
I GOT A PICTURE LATER.
WOW, SHE'S GOTTEN SO BIG!
HUH?
SHE WAS EATING IT.
DON'T YOU HAVE ANY-THING TO SAY FOR YOURSELF, KYO?!
IT MADE ME HAPPY.
Really!
I'LL SHOW HER WHEN SHE'S OLDER.

Yo! Kamijyo, here, drinkin' a bit too much! (Jus' kiddin'! Only one a day!) Wow, Volume 19 already! Most manga would be thinking about wrapping up by now! But the readers (you!) demand more, so here it is, thanks to you! We've still got a way to go, and it'll just get better!
I thought I had lots of extra pages in this volume, but in the end...I had room for only ONE Kamijyo Report! But while I'm here, let me ask you...

[Draw Like Kamijyo Poll: Which is Better?]
1. A few big postcards (current format)
2. Lots of smaller postcards

Of course, I want to print all your postcards! But we only have so many pages, so I want to make those the best I can. Let me hear what you think!

So long for now, everyone. See you in Volume 20! 'Til then.

***Thanks for all the letters, folks! I read them all (really!)--I mean, how could I not?!**

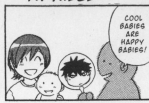

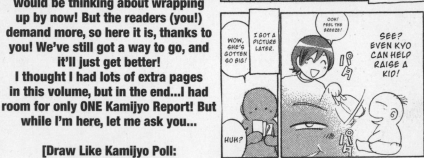

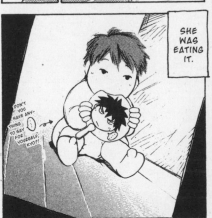

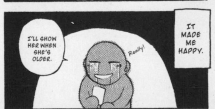

The Kamijyo Report

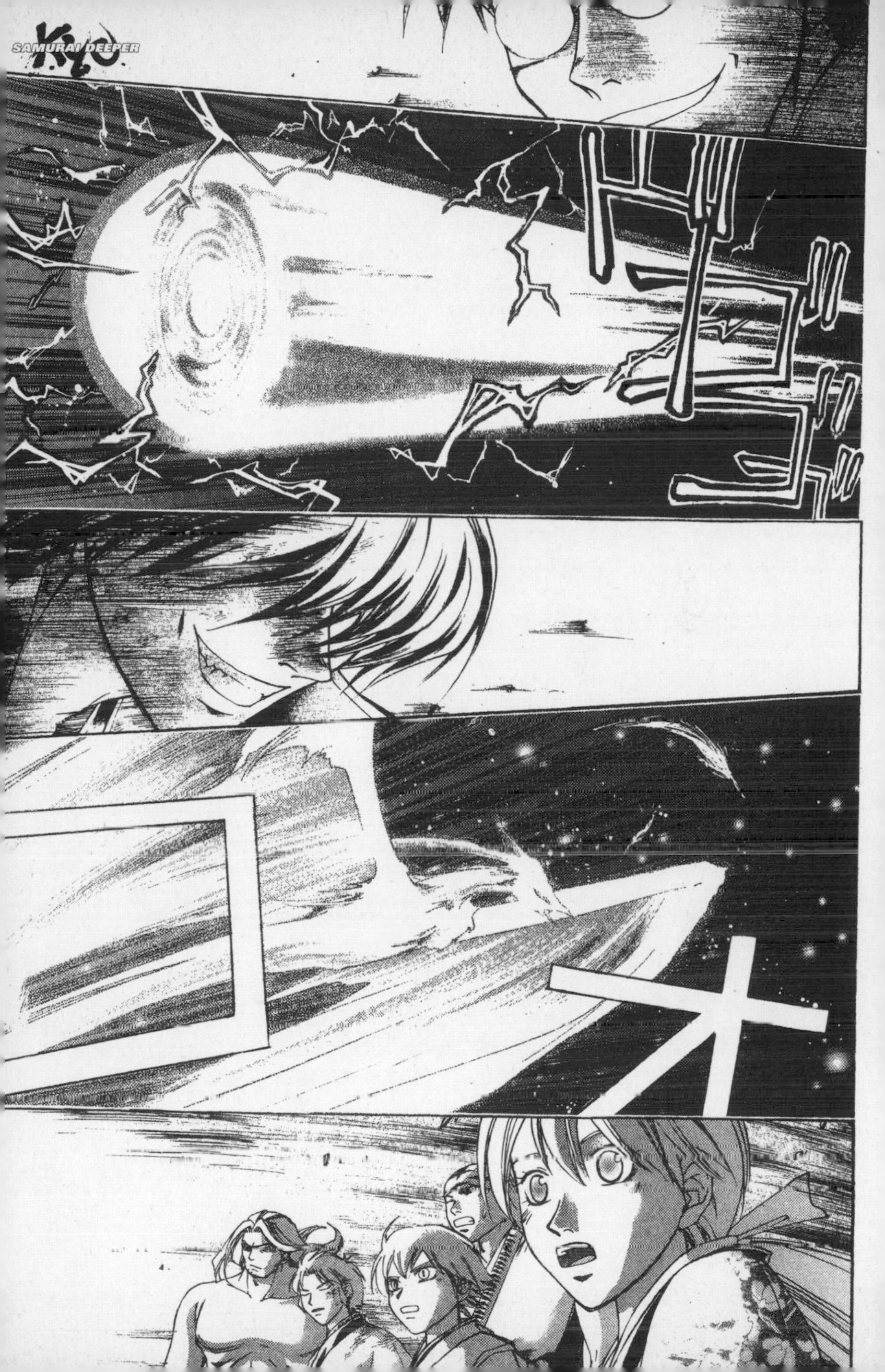

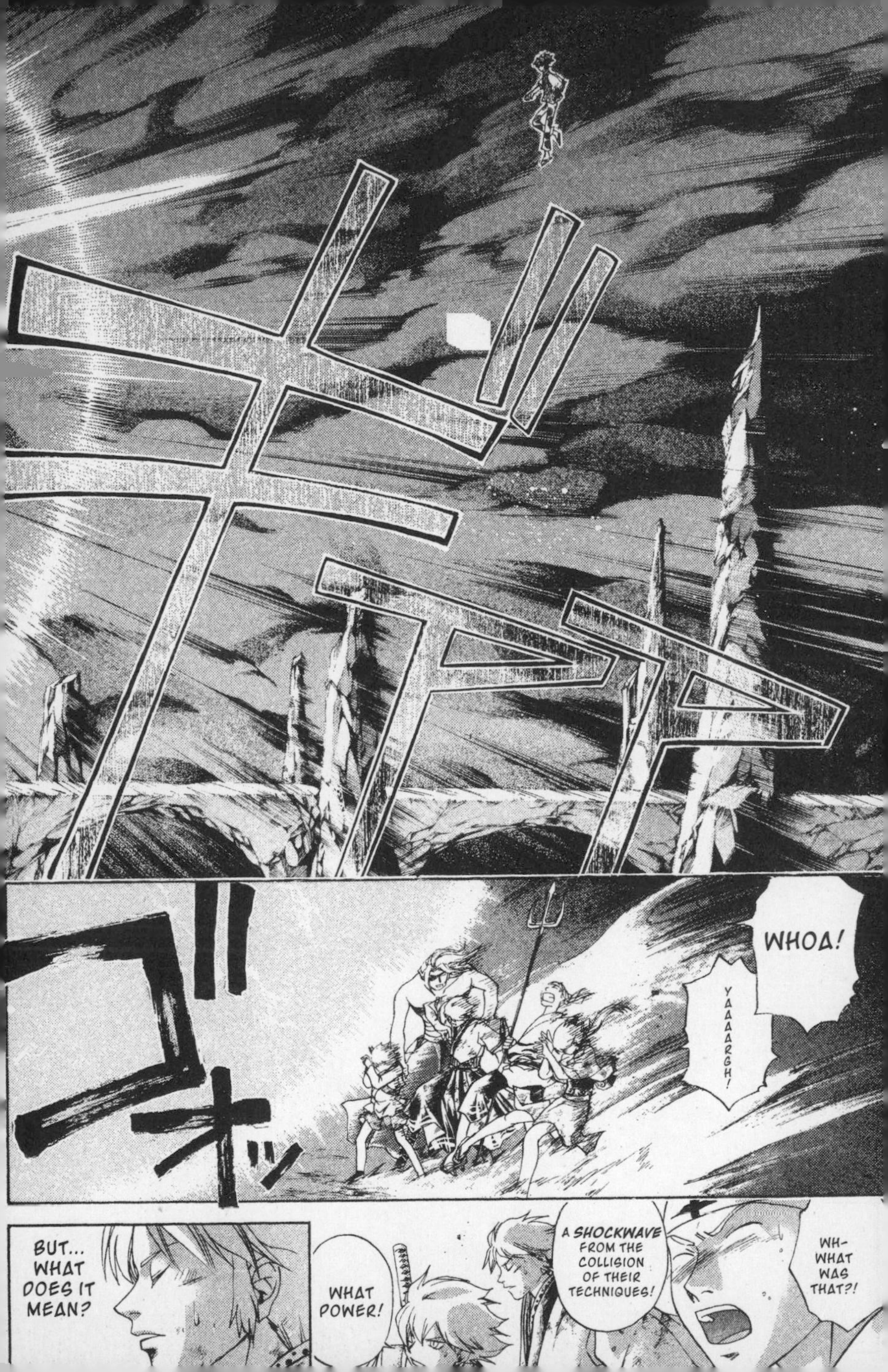
WHOA!
YAAAAARGH!
ゴオッ
WH-WHAT WAS THAT?!
A SHOCKWAVE FROM THE COLLISION OF THEIR TECHNIQUES!
WHAT POWER!
BUT... WHAT DOES IT MEAN?

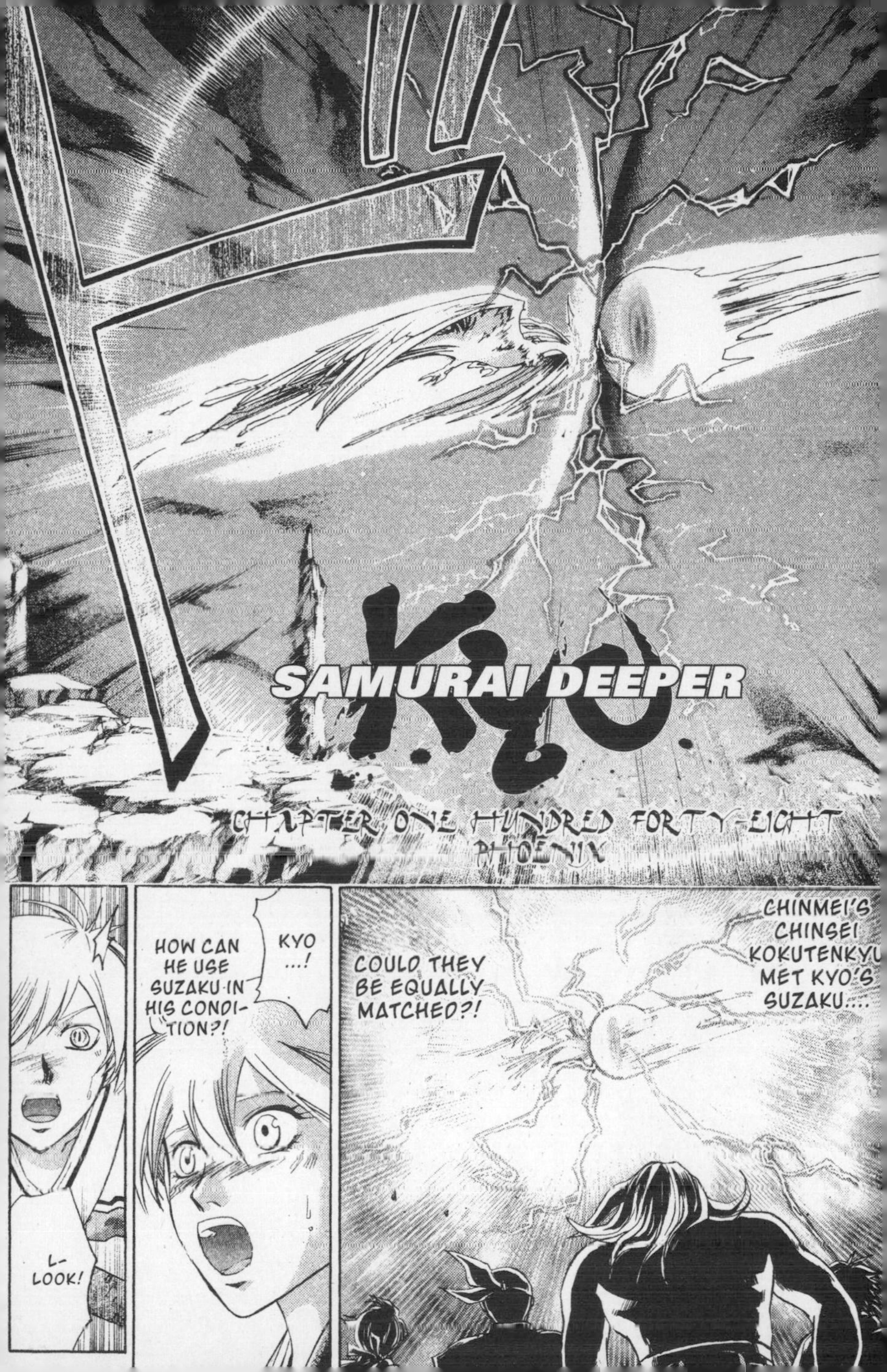
SAMURAI DEEPER KYO
CHAPTER ONE HUNDRED FORTY-EIGHT
PHOENIX
CHINMEI'S CHINSEI KOKUTENKYU MET KYO'S SUZAKU....
COULD THEY BE EQUALLY MATCHED?!
KYO ...!
HOW CAN HE USE SUZAKU IN HIS CONDITION?!
L- LOOK!

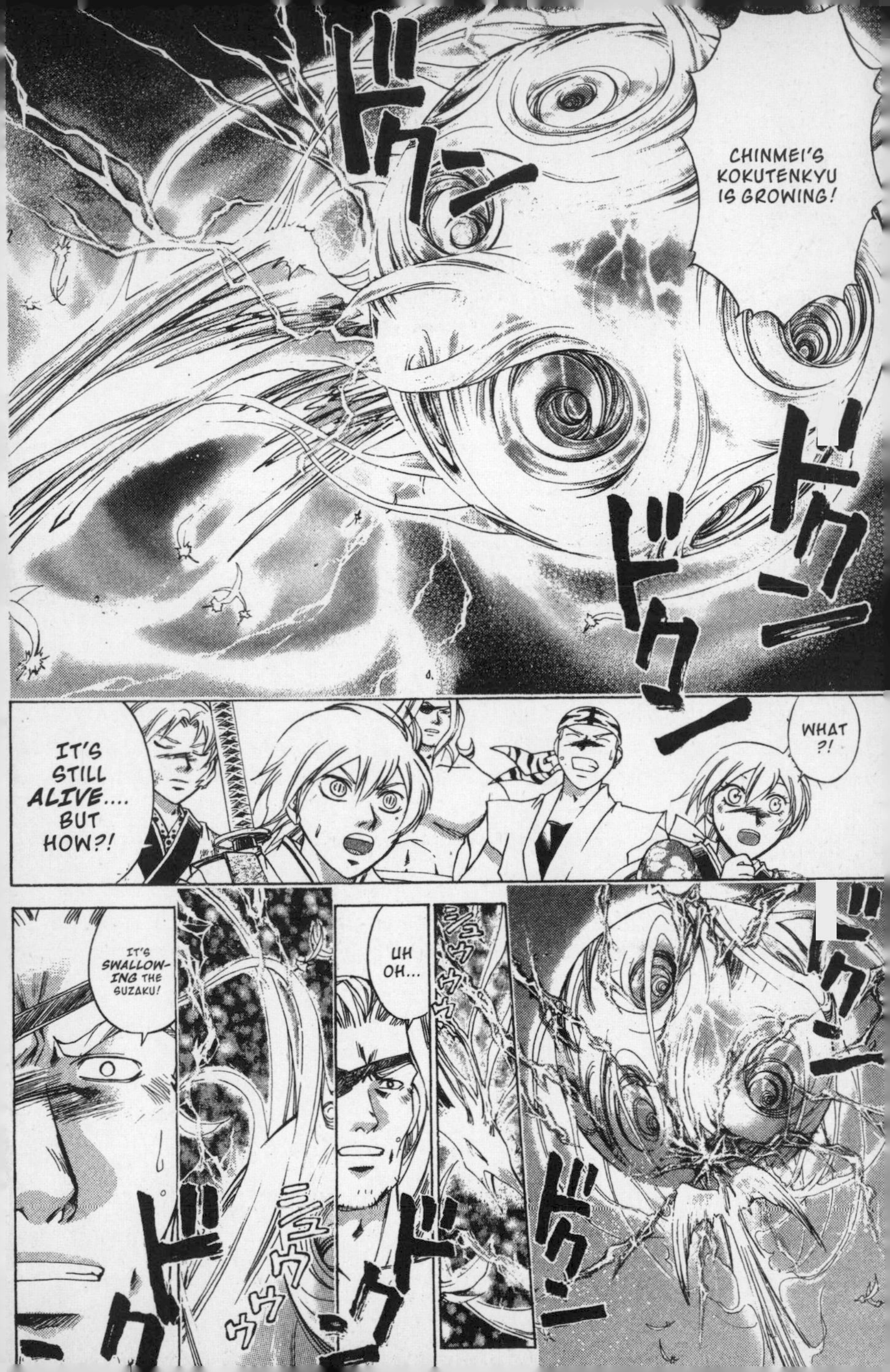
CHINMEI'S KOKUTENKYU IS GROWING!
WHAT ?!
IT'S STILL ALIVE.... BUT HOW?!
UH OH...
IT'S SWALLOWING THE SUZAKU!

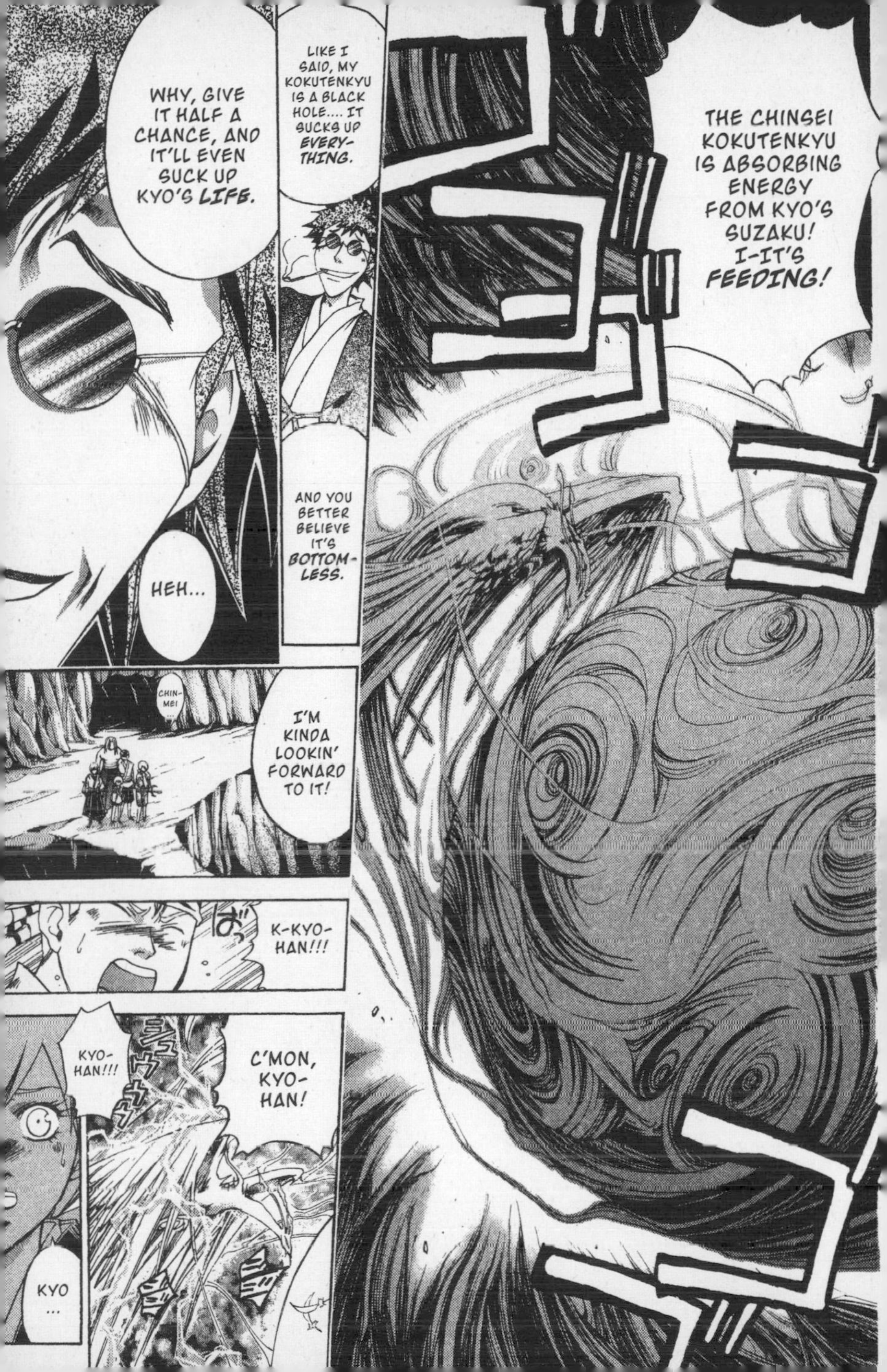
THE CHINSEI KOKUTENKYU IS ABSORBING ENERGY FROM KYO'S SUZAKU! I-IT'S FEEDING!
LIKE I SAID, MY KOKUTENKYU IS A BLACK HOLE.... IT SUCKS UP EVERY-THING.
AND YOU BETTER BELIEVE IT'S BOTTOM-LESS.
WHY, GIVE IT HALF A CHANCE, AND IT'LL EVEN SUCK UP KYO'S LIFE.
HEH...
I'M KINDA LOOKIN' FORWARD TO IT!
CHIN-MEI ...
K-KYO-HAN!!!
C'MON, KYO-HAN!
KYO-HAN!!!
KYO ...

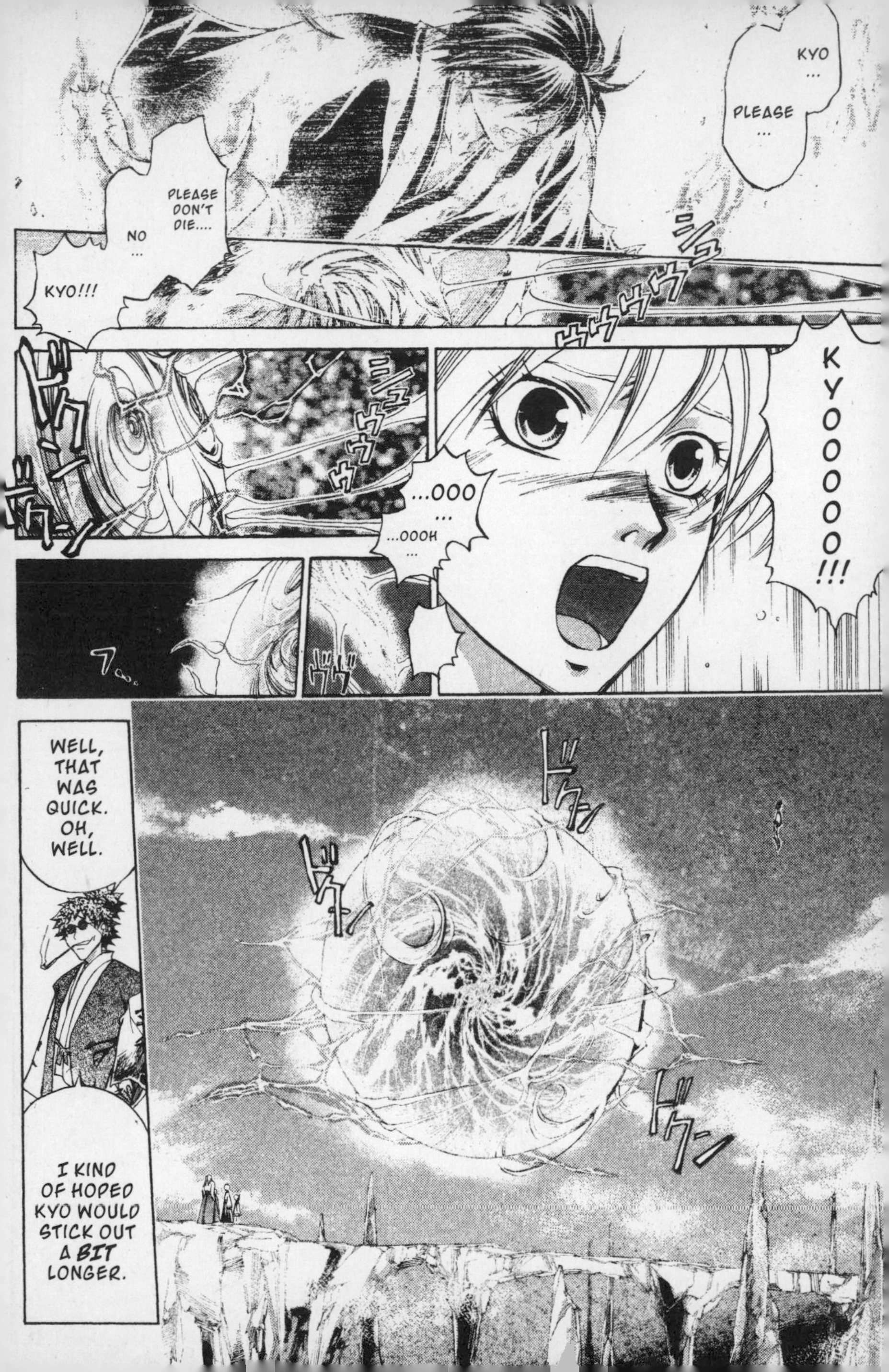
KYO ... PLEASE ...
PLEASE DON'T DIE....
NO ...
KYO!!!
KYOOOOOO!!!
...OOO ...
...OOOH ...
WELL, THAT WAS QUICK. OH, WELL.
I KIND OF HOPED KYO WOULD STICK OUT A *BIT* LONGER.

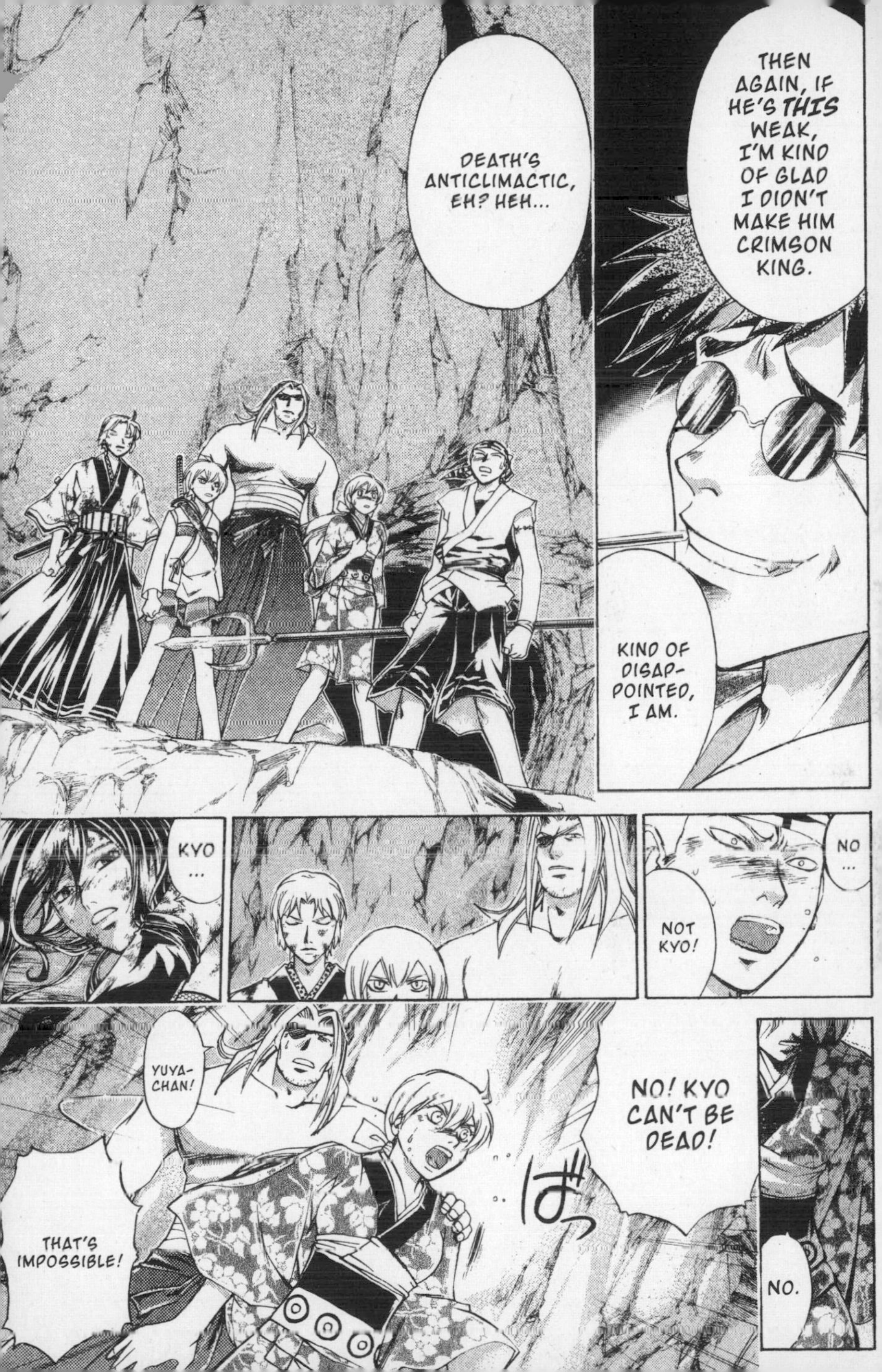
THEN AGAIN, IF HE'S *THIS* WEAK, I'M KIND OF GLAD I DIDN'T MAKE HIM CRIMSON KING.
KIND OF DISAPPOINTED, I AM.
DEATH'S ANTICLIMACTIC, EH? HEH...
NO ...
NOT KYO!
KYO ...
NO.
NO! KYO CAN'T BE DEAD!
ばっ
YUYA-CHAN!
THAT'S IMPOSSIBLE!

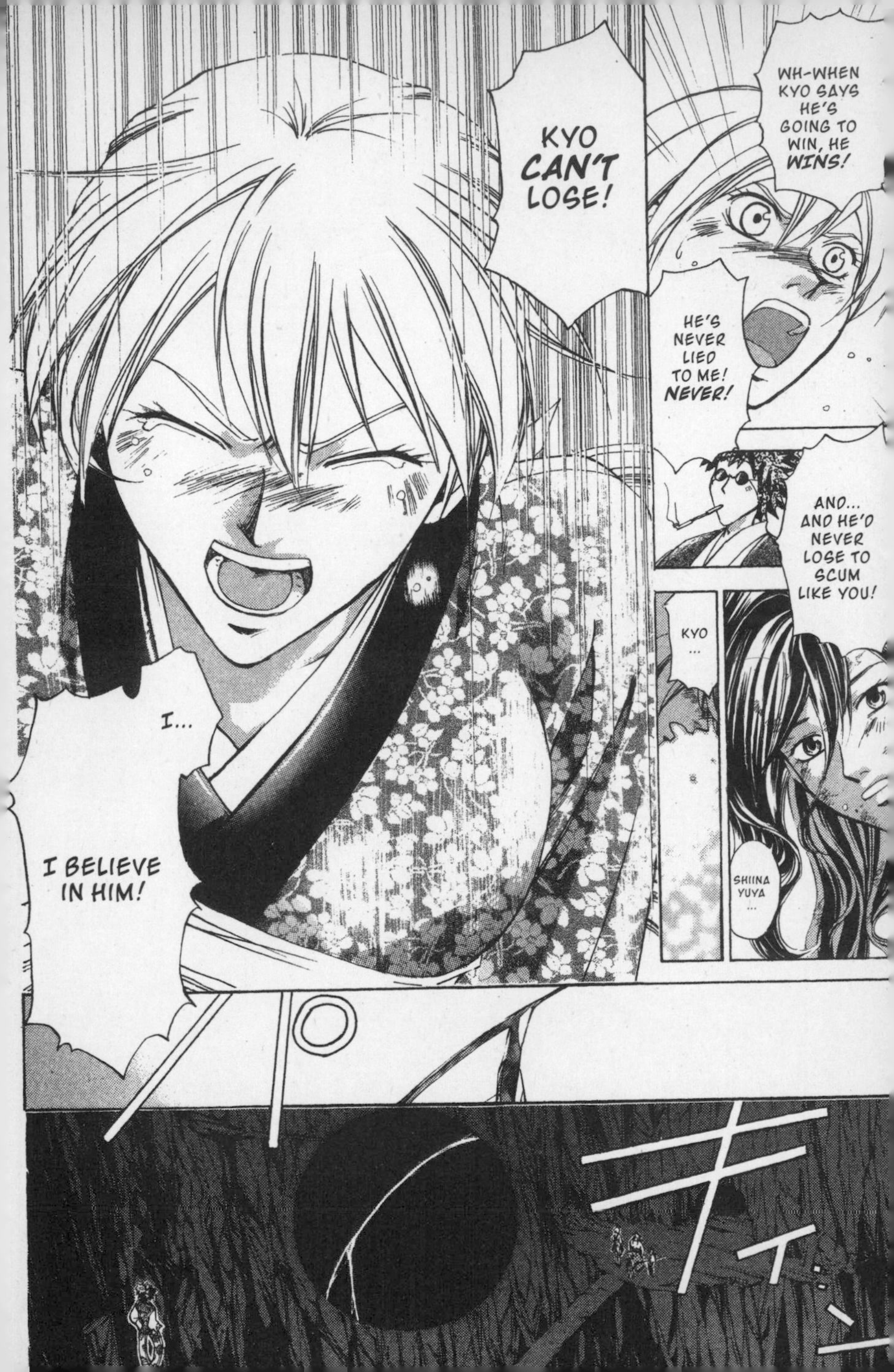
WH-WHEN KYO SAYS HE'S GOING TO WIN, HE **WINS!**
HE'S NEVER LIED TO ME! **NEVER!**
AND... AND HE'D NEVER LOSE TO SCUM LIKE YOU!
KYO ...
SHIINA YUYA ...
KYO **CAN'T** LOSE!
I...
I BELIEVE IN HIM!

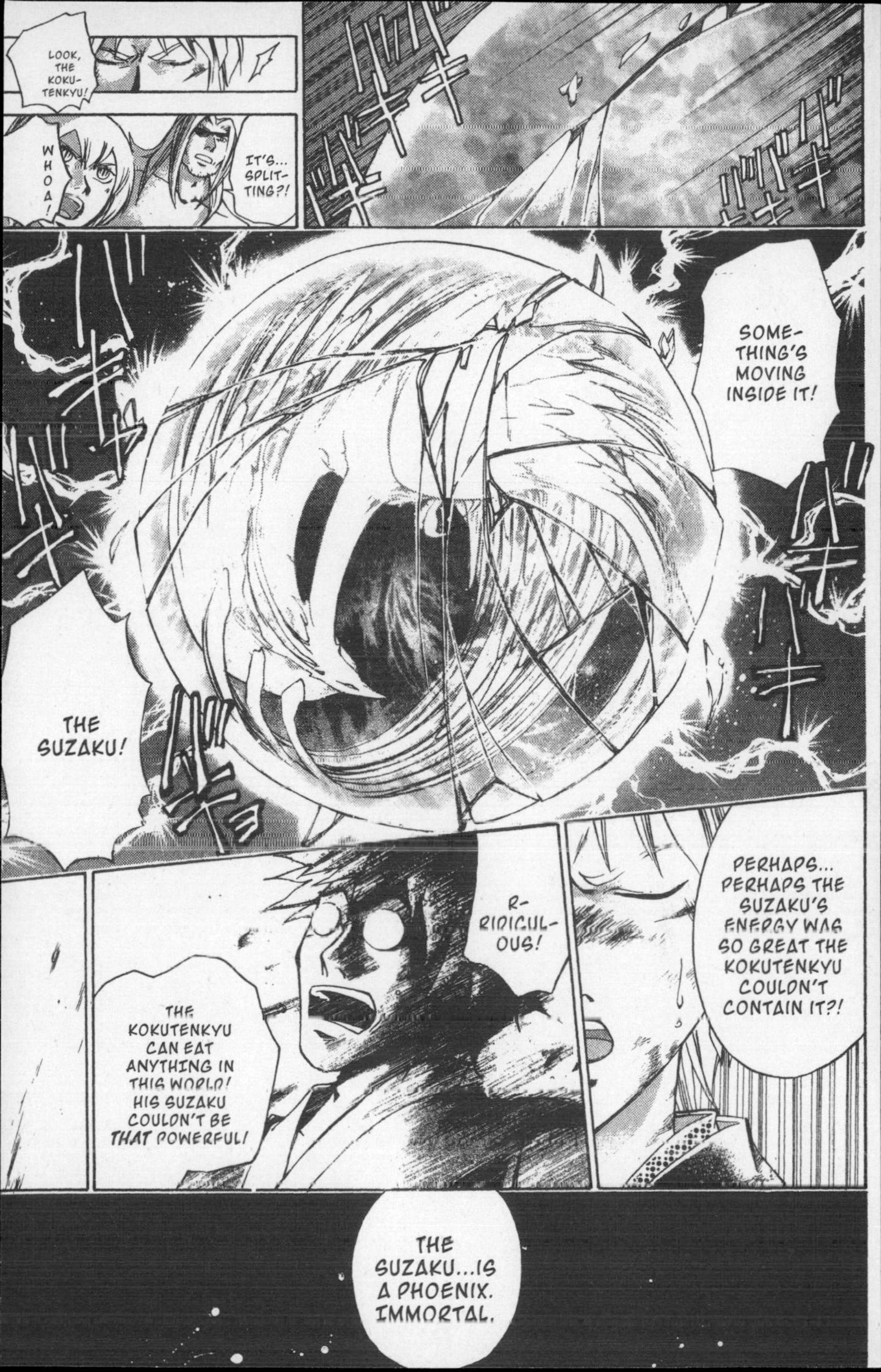
LOOK, THE KOKU-TENKYU!
IT'S... SPLIT-TING?!
WHOA!
SOME-THING'S MOVING INSIDE IT!
THE SUZAKU!
PERHAPS... PERHAPS THE SUZAKU'S ENERGY WAS SO GREAT THE KOKUTENKYU COULDN'T CONTAIN IT?!
R-RIDICUL-OUS!
THE KOKUTENKYU CAN EAT ANYTHING IN THIS WORLD! HIS SUZAKU COULDN'T BE *THAT* POWERFUL!
THE SUZAKU...IS A PHOENIX. IMMORTAL.

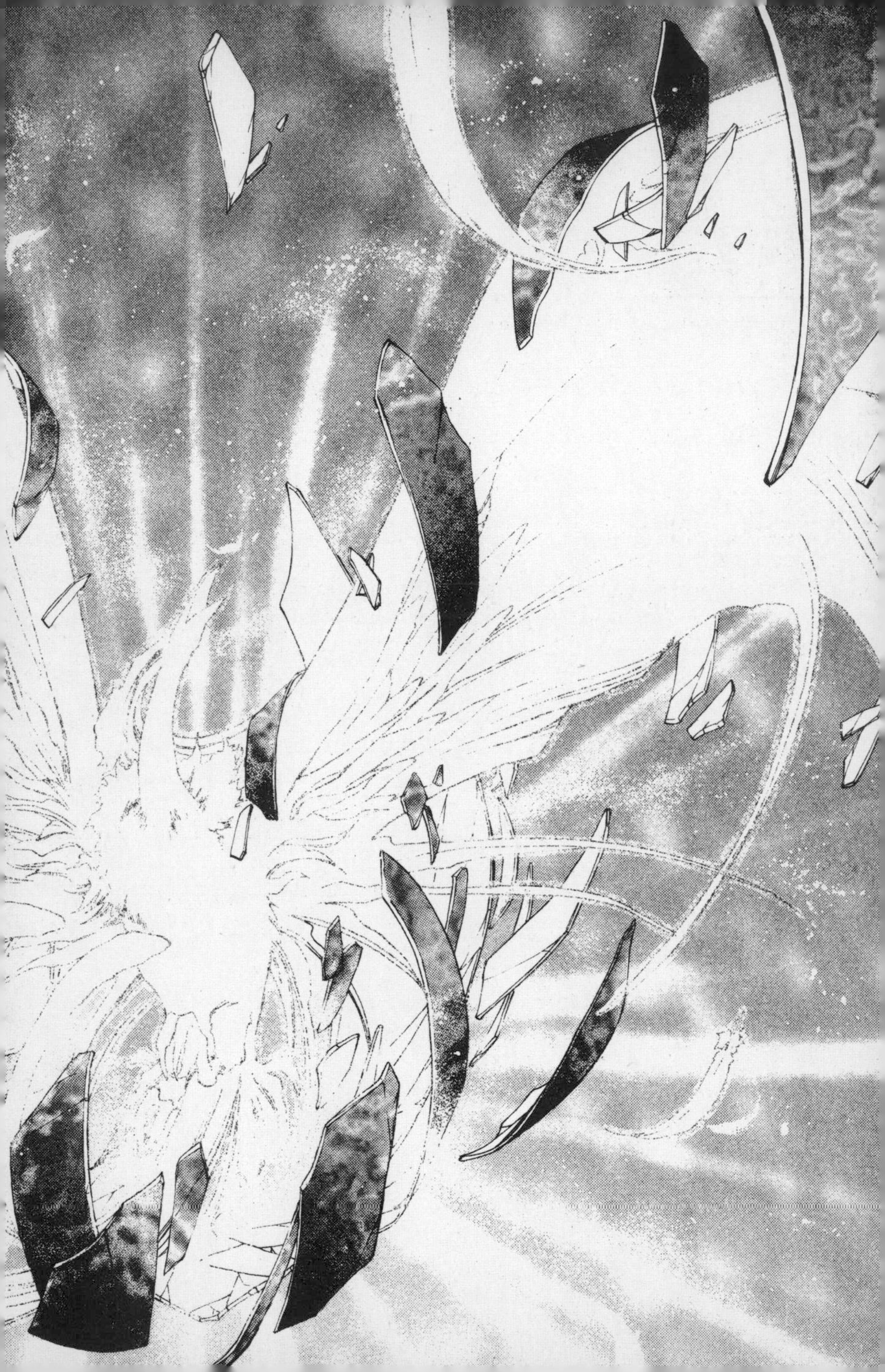

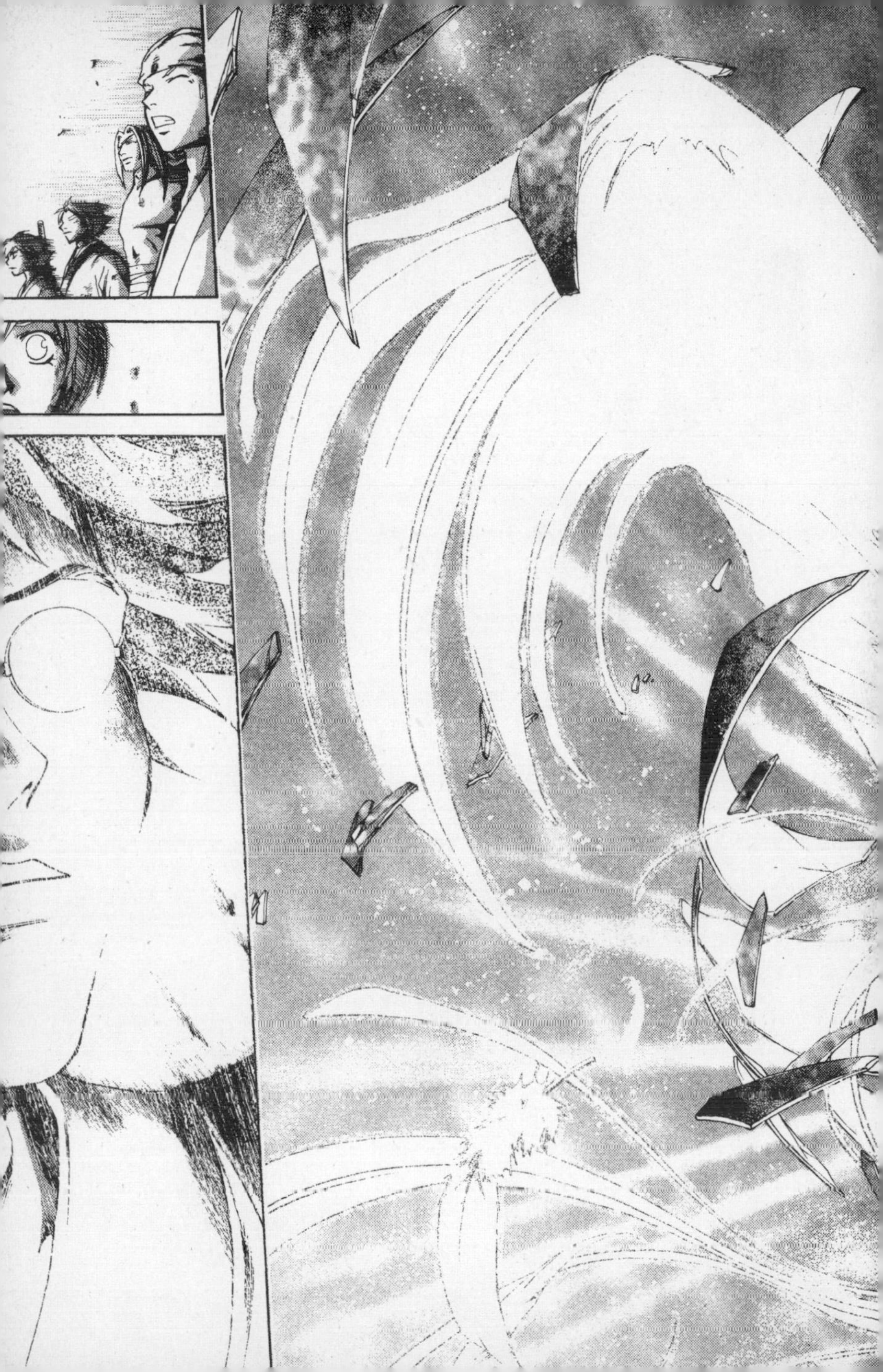

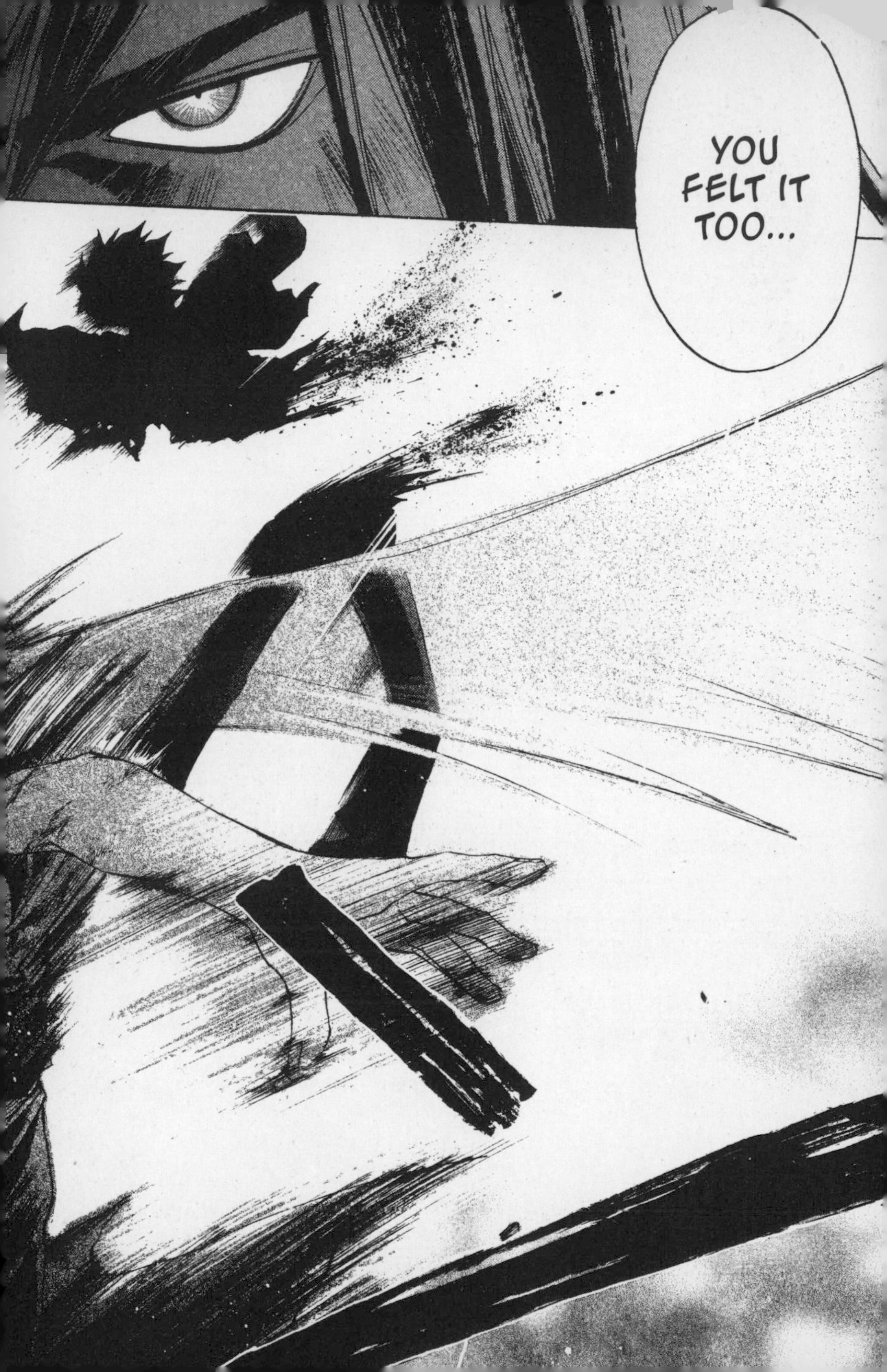
YOU FELT IT TOO...

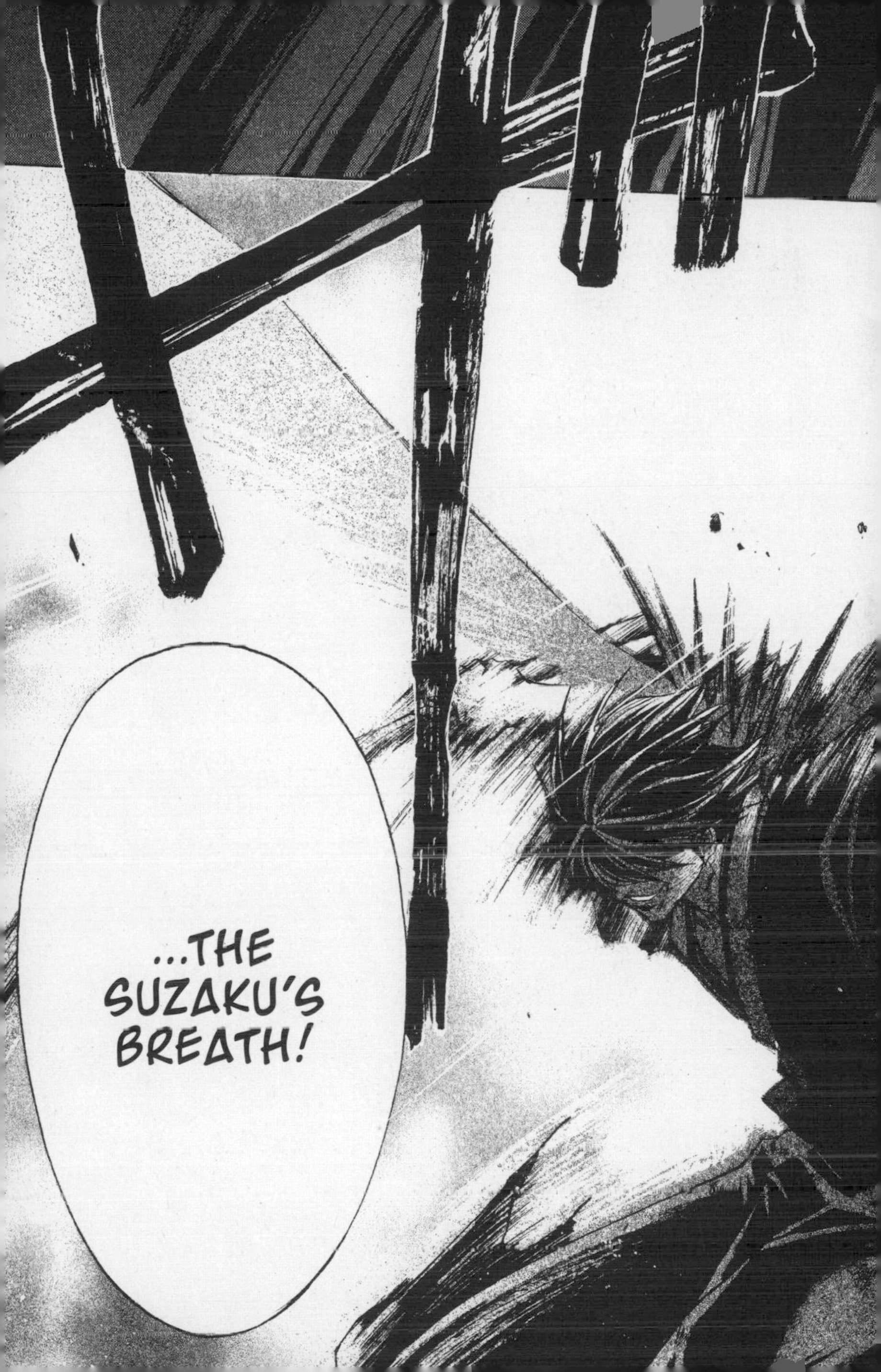
...THE SUZAKU'S BREATH!

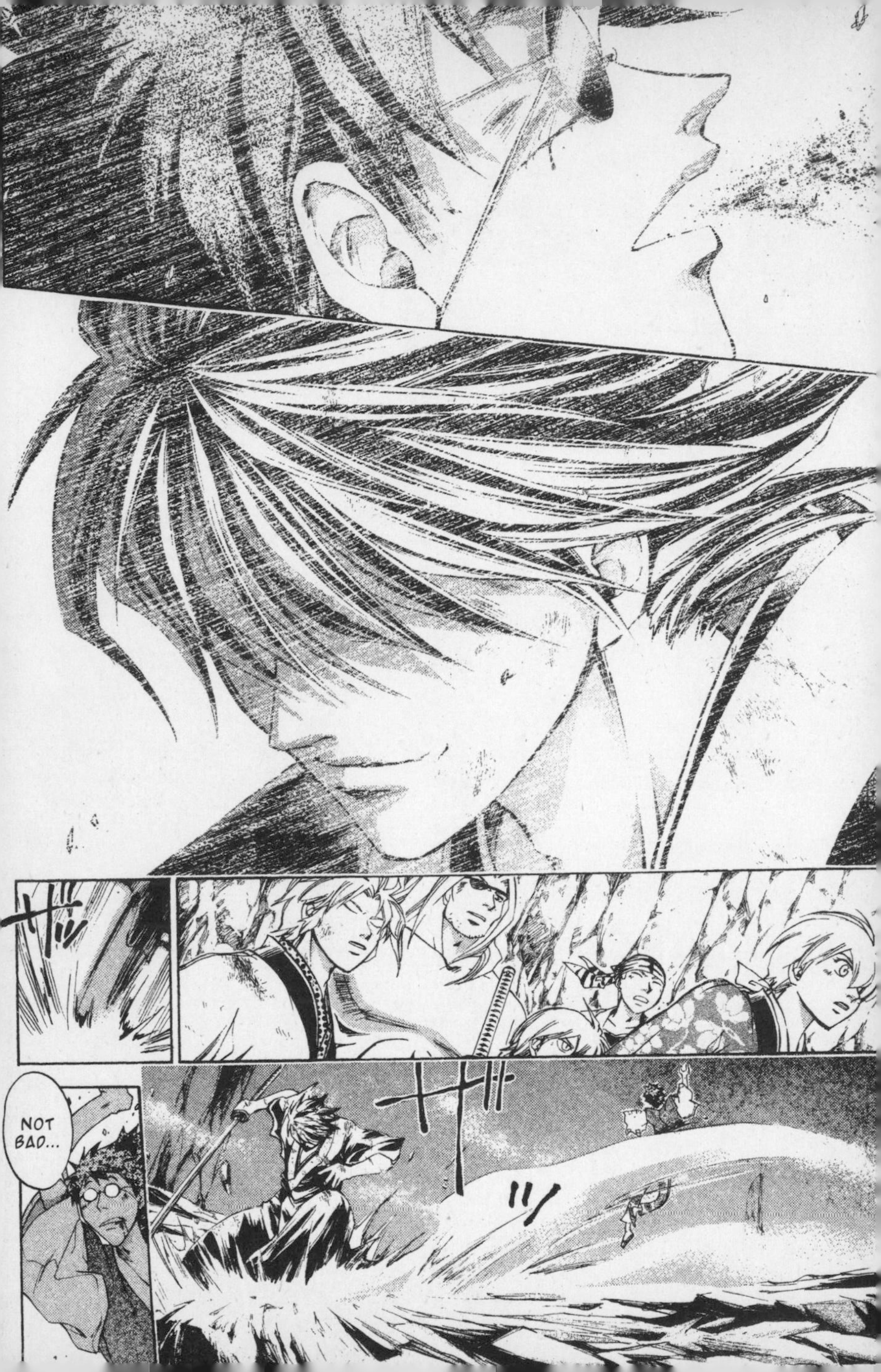
NOT BAD...

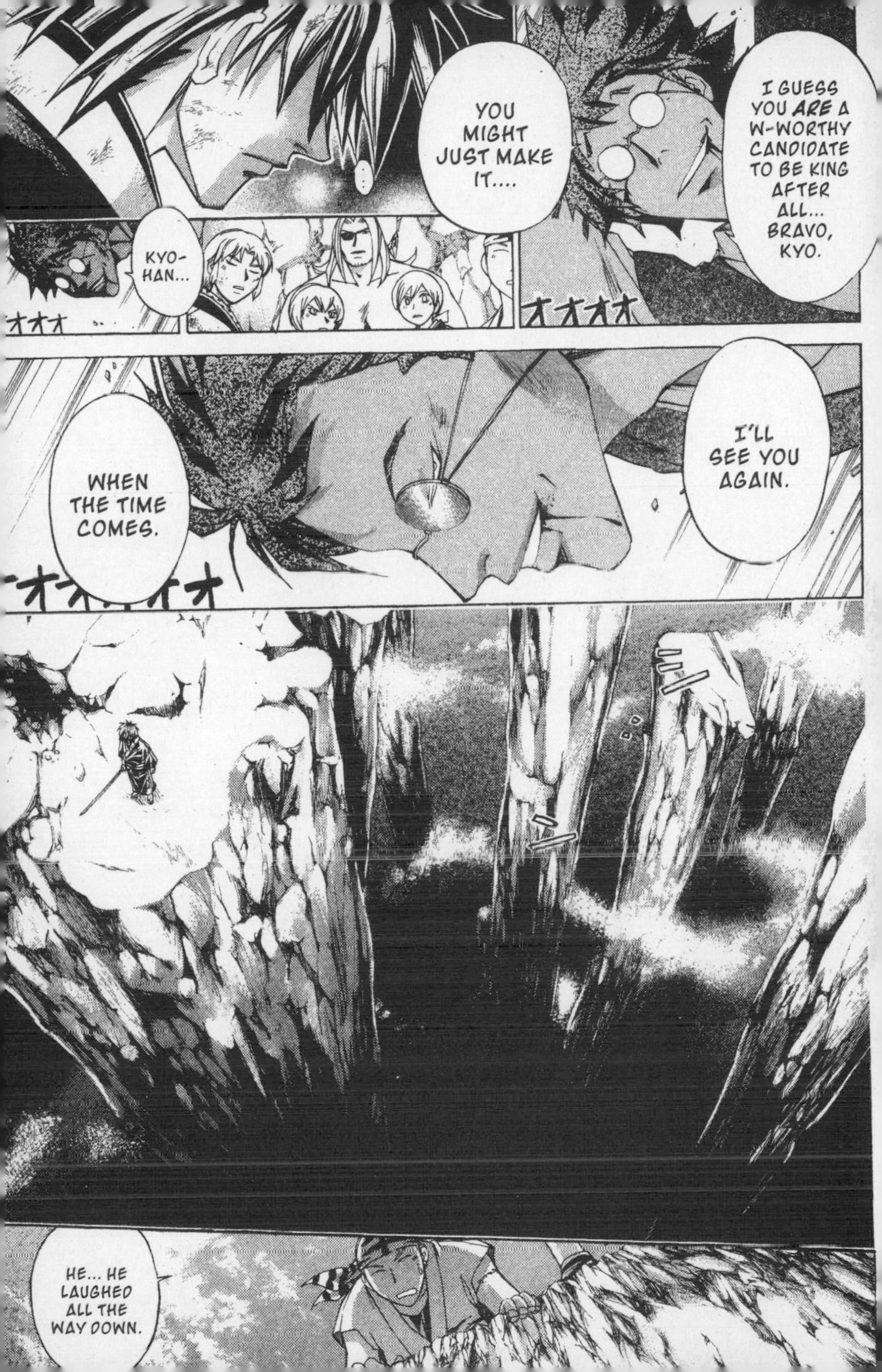
I GUESS YOU ARE A W-WORTHY CANDIDATE TO BE KING AFTER ALL... BRAVO, KYO.
オオオオ
...
YOU MIGHT JUST MAKE IT....
KYO-HAN...
オオオ
I'LL SEE YOU AGAIN.
WHEN THE TIME COMES.
オオオオオオ
HE... HE LAUGHED ALL THE WAY DOWN.

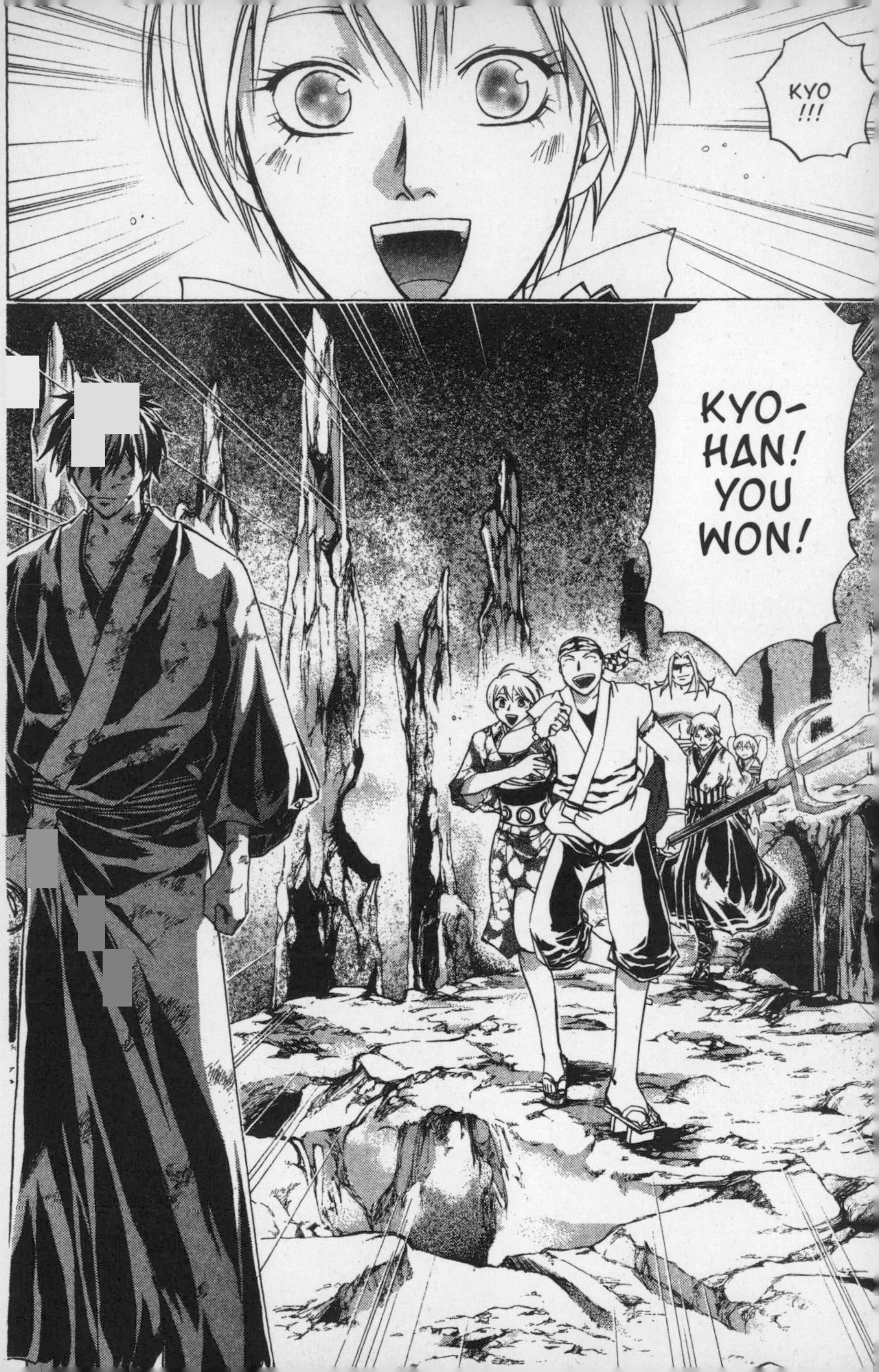
KYO !!!
KYO-HAN! YOU WON!

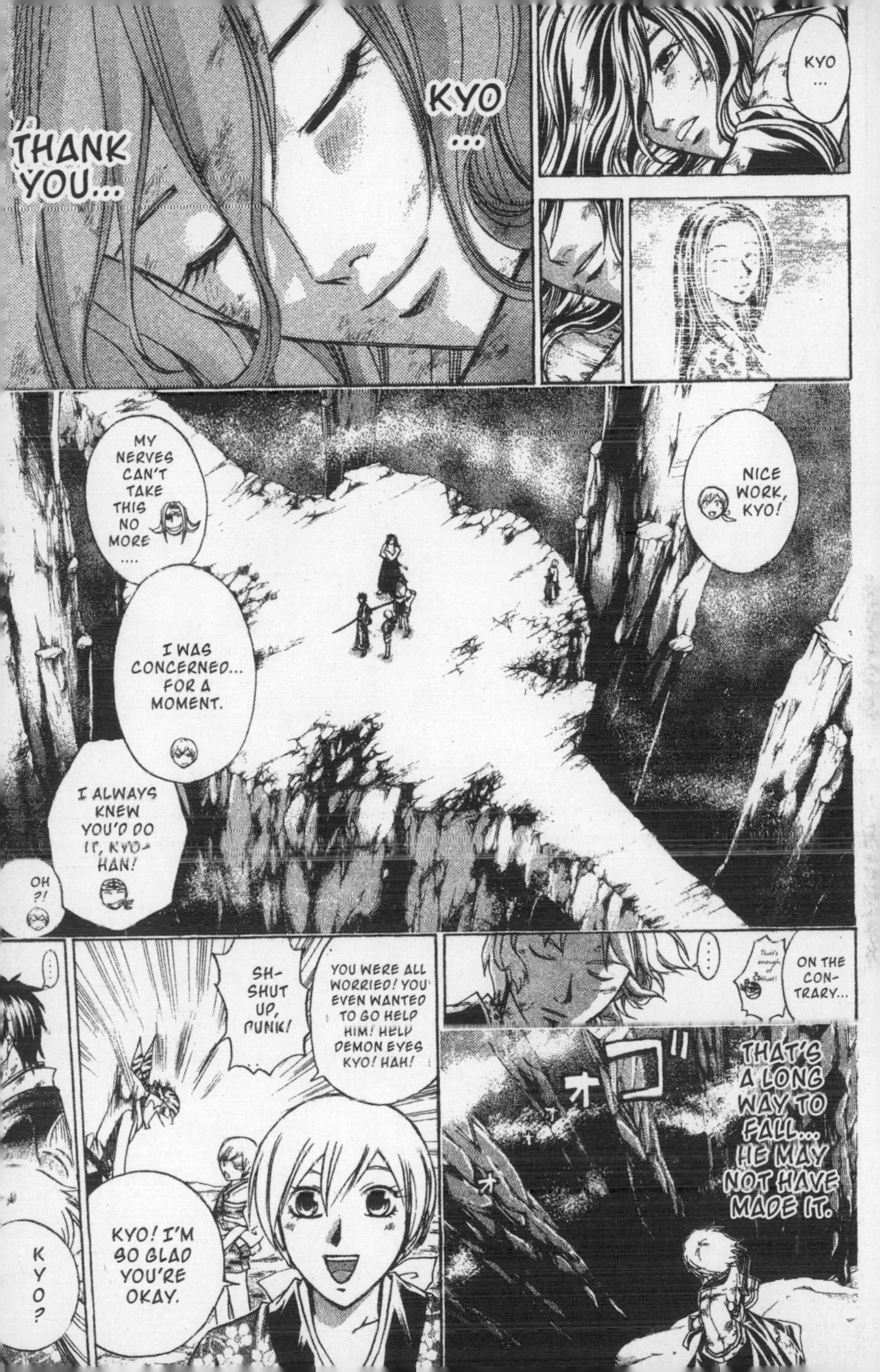
KYO ...
KYO ...
THANK YOU...
NICE WORK, KYO!
MY NERVES CAN'T TAKE THIS NO MORE ....
I WAS CONCERNED... FOR A MOMENT.
I ALWAYS KNEW YOU'D DO IT, KYO-HAN!
OH ?!
ON THE CON-TRARY...
That's enough of that!
....
THAT'S A LONG WAY TO FALL... HE MAY NOT HAVE MADE IT.
YOU WERE ALL WORRIED! YOU EVEN WANTED TO GO HELP HIM! HELP DEMON EYES KYO! HAH!
SH-SHUT UP, PUNK!
KYO! I'M SO GLAD YOU'RE OKAY.
KYO?
....

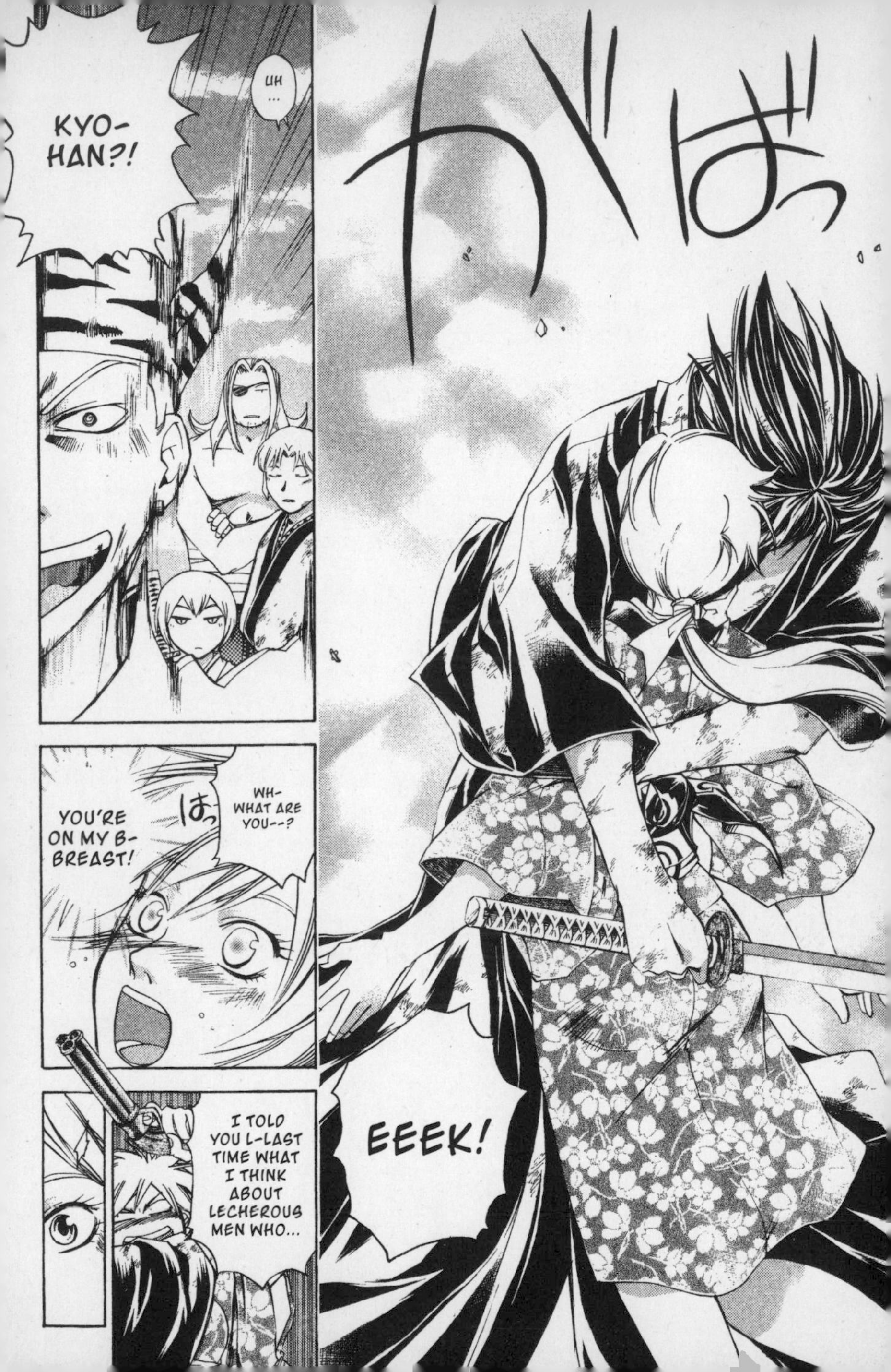

がばっ
EEEK!
UH ...
KYO-HAN?!
WH-WHAT ARE YOU--?
はっ
YOU'RE ON MY B-BREAST!
I TOLD YOU L-LAST TIME WHAT I THINK ABOUT LECHEROUS MEN WHO...

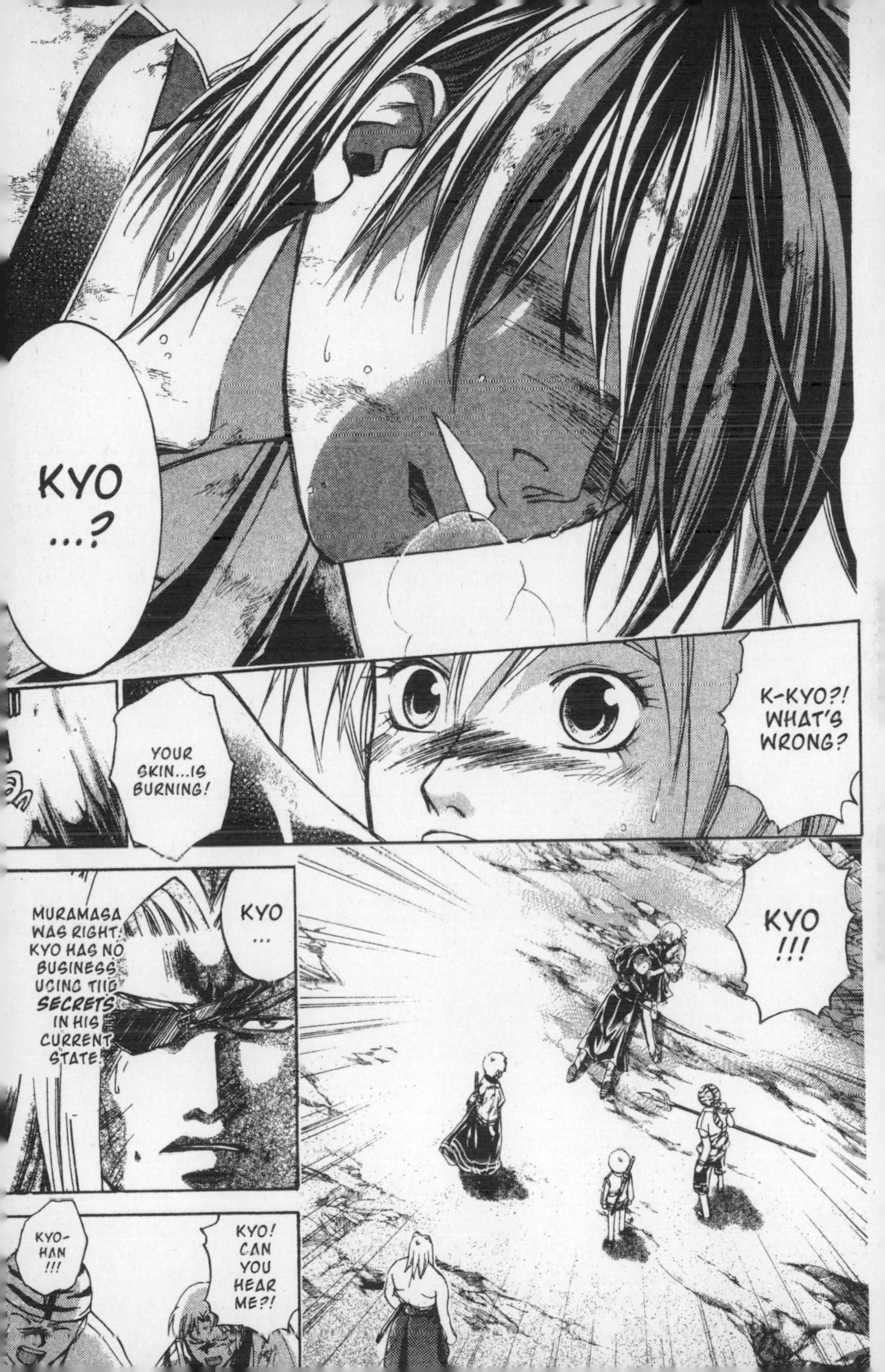

KYO ...?
K-KYO?! WHAT'S WRONG?
YOUR SKIN...IS BURNING!
KYO !!!
KYO ...
MURAMASA WAS RIGHT. KYO HAS NO BUSINESS USING THE SECRETS IN HIS CURRENT STATE.
KYO! CAN YOU HEAR ME?!
KYO-HAN !!!

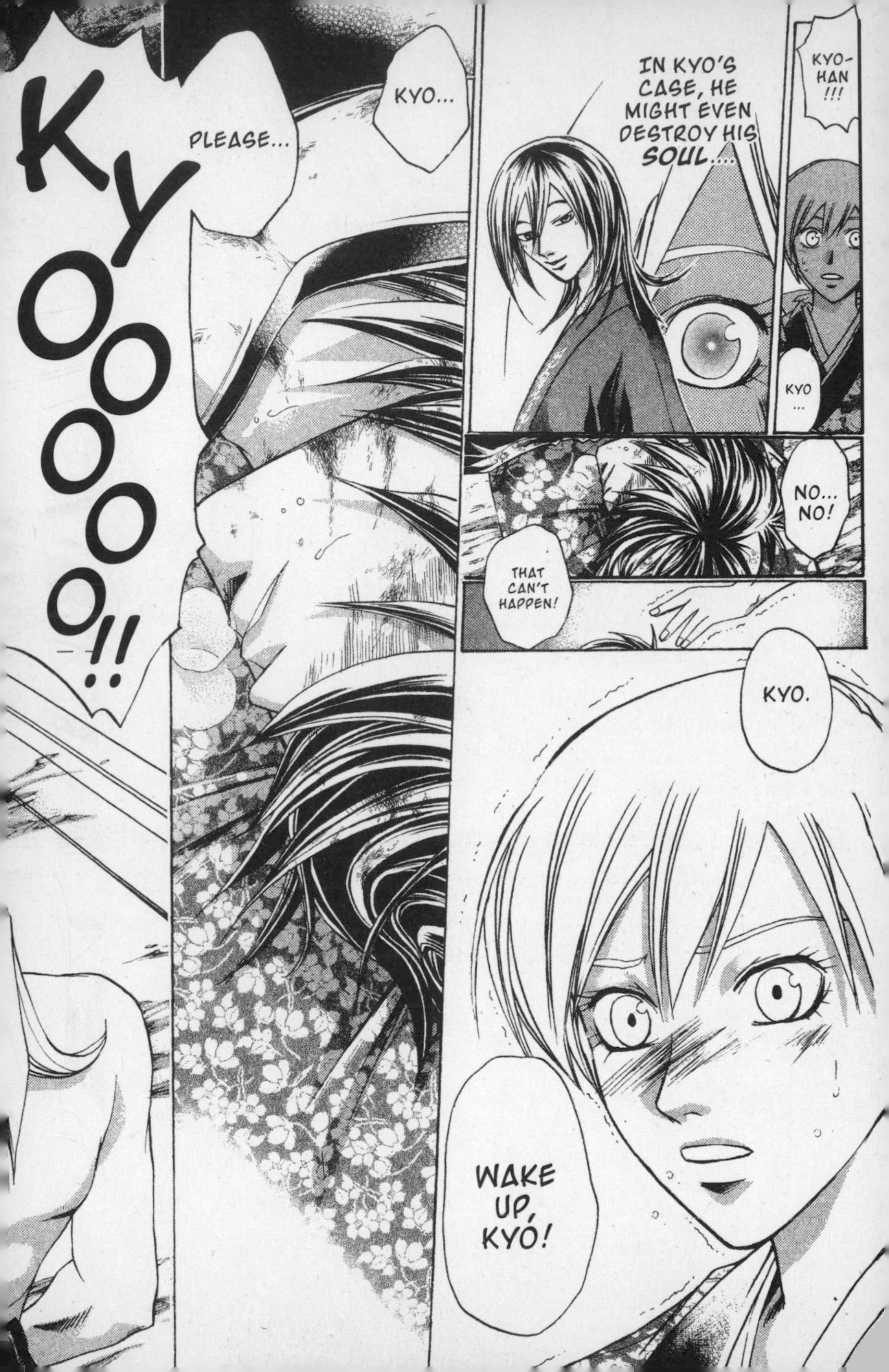
KYO-HAN!!!
KYO...
IN KYO'S CASE, HE MIGHT EVEN DESTROY HIS SOUL....
NO... NO!
THAT CAN'T HAPPEN!
KYO.
WAKE UP, KYO!
KYO...
PLEASE...
KYOOOOOO!!

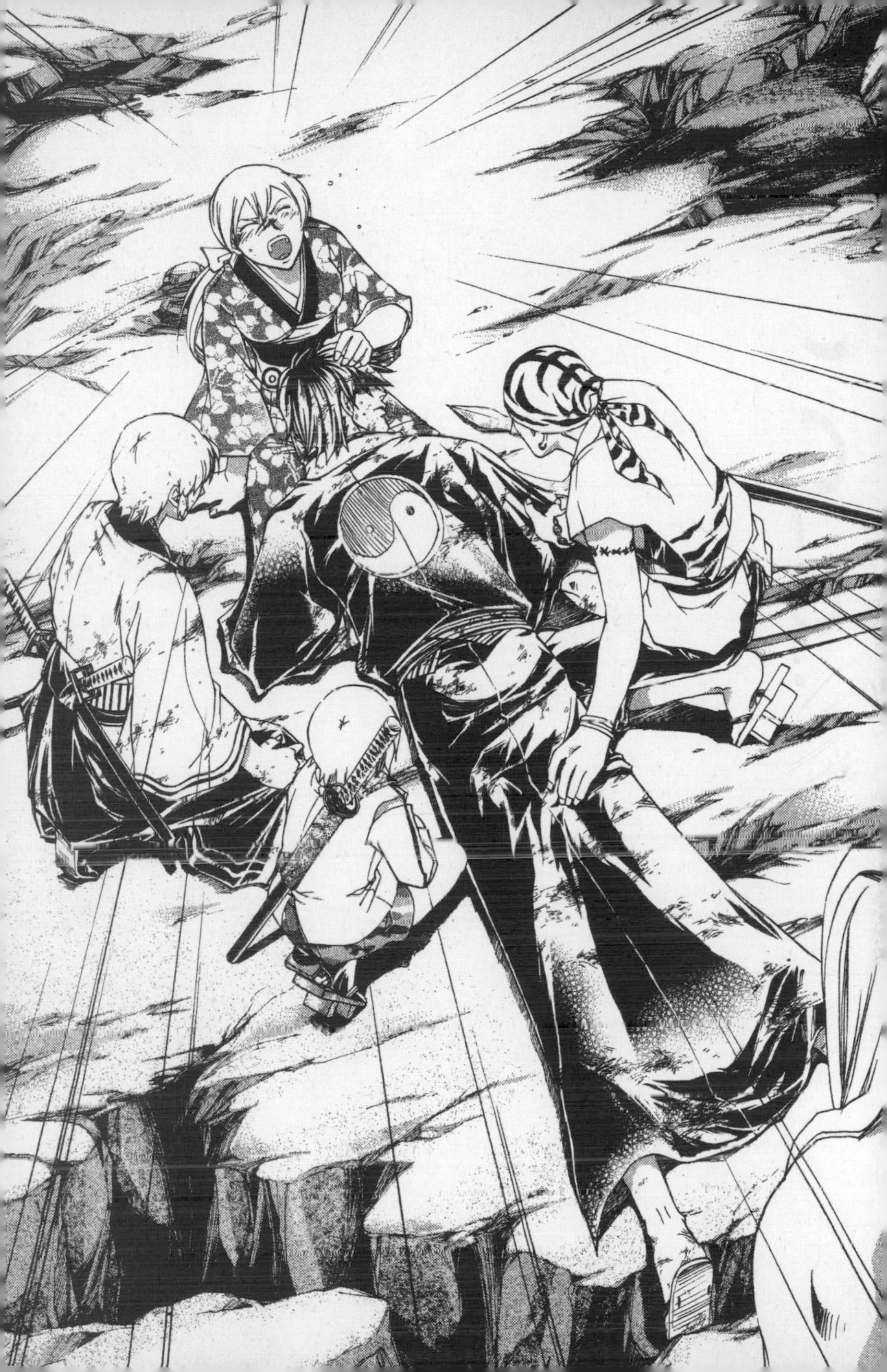

It's Gallery Time!

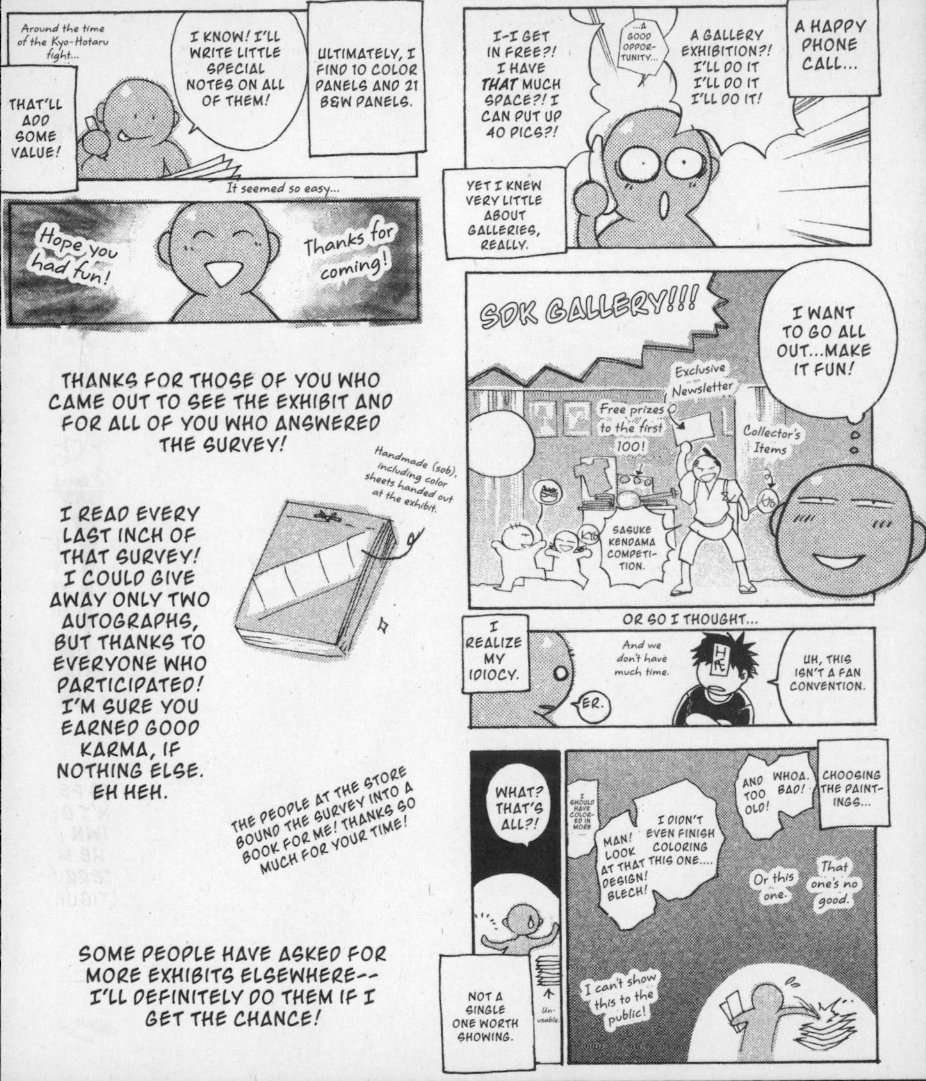
A HAPPY PHONE CALL...
A GALLERY EXHIBITION?! I'LL DO IT I'LL DO IT I'LL DO IT!
...A GOOD OPPORTUNITY...
I-I GET IN FREE?! I HAVE THAT MUCH SPACE?! I CAN PUT UP 40 PICS?!
YET I KNEW VERY LITTLE ABOUT GALLERIES, REALLY.
ULTIMATELY, I FIND 10 COLOR PANELS AND 21 B&W PANELS.
I KNOW! I'LL WRITE LITTLE SPECIAL NOTES ON ALL OF THEM!
Around the time of the Kyo-Hotaru fight...
THAT'LL ADD SOME VALUE!
It seemed so easy...
Thanks for coming!
Hope you had fun!
I WANT TO GO ALL OUT...MAKE IT FUN!
SDK GALLERY!!!
Exclusive Newsletter
Free prizes to the first 100!
Collector's Items
SASUKE KENDAMA COMPETITION.
OR SO I THOUGHT...
UH, THIS ISN'T A FAN CONVENTION.
And we don't have much time.
I REALIZE MY IDIOCY.
ER.
CHOOSING THE PAINTINGS...
WHOA. BAD!
AND TOO OLD!
That one's no good.
Or this one.
I DIDN'T EVEN FINISH COLORING THIS ONE....
MAN! LOOK AT THAT DESIGN! BLECH!
I SHOULD HAVE COLORED IN MORE....
I can't show this to the public!
WHAT? THAT'S ALL?!
Unusable.
NOT A SINGLE ONE WORTH SHOWING.
THANKS FOR THOSE OF YOU WHO CAME OUT TO SEE THE EXHIBIT AND FOR ALL OF YOU WHO ANSWERED THE SURVEY!
Handmade (sob), including color sheets handed out at the exhibit.
I READ EVERY LAST INCH OF THAT SURVEY! I COULD GIVE AWAY ONLY TWO AUTOGRAPHS, BUT THANKS TO EVERYONE WHO PARTICIPATED! I'M SURE YOU EARNED GOOD KARMA, IF NOTHING ELSE. EH HEH.
THE PEOPLE AT THE STORE BOUND THE SURVEY INTO A BOOK FOR ME! THANKS SO MUCH FOR YOUR TIME!
SOME PEOPLE HAVE ASKED FOR MORE EXHIBITS ELSEWHERE--I'LL DEFINITELY DO THEM IF I GET THE CHANCE!

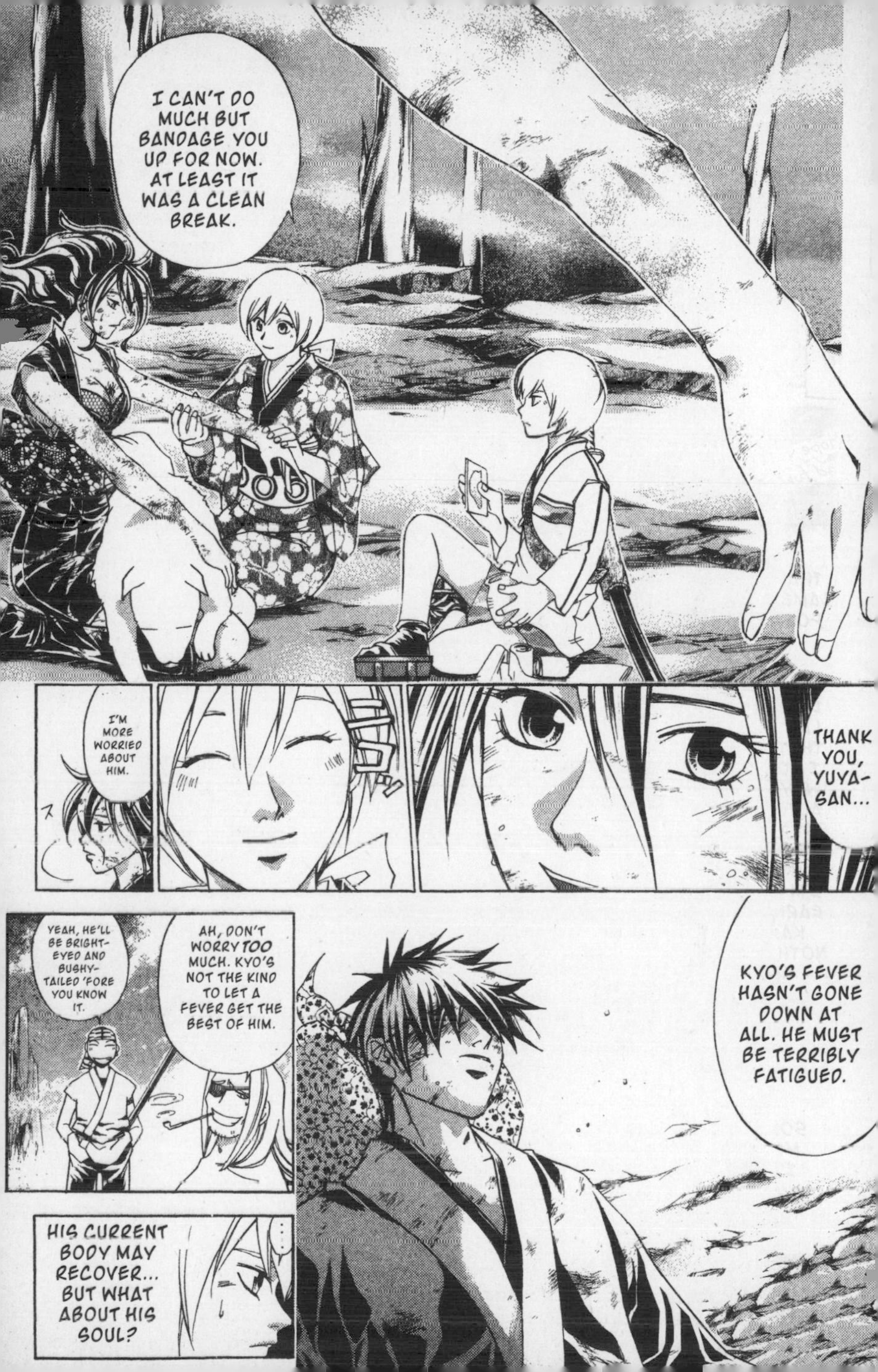
I CAN'T DO MUCH BUT BANDAGE YOU UP FOR NOW. AT LEAST IT WAS A CLEAN BREAK.
THANK YOU, YUYA-SAN...
I'M MORE WORRIED ABOUT HIM.
KYO'S FEVER HASN'T GONE DOWN AT ALL. HE MUST BE TERRIBLY FATIGUED.
AH, DON'T WORRY TOO MUCH. KYO'S NOT THE KIND TO LET A FEVER GET THE BEST OF HIM.
YEAH, HE'LL BE BRIGHT-EYED AND BUSHY-TAILED 'FORE YOU KNOW IT.
HIS CURRENT BODY MAY RECOVER... BUT WHAT ABOUT HIS SOUL?

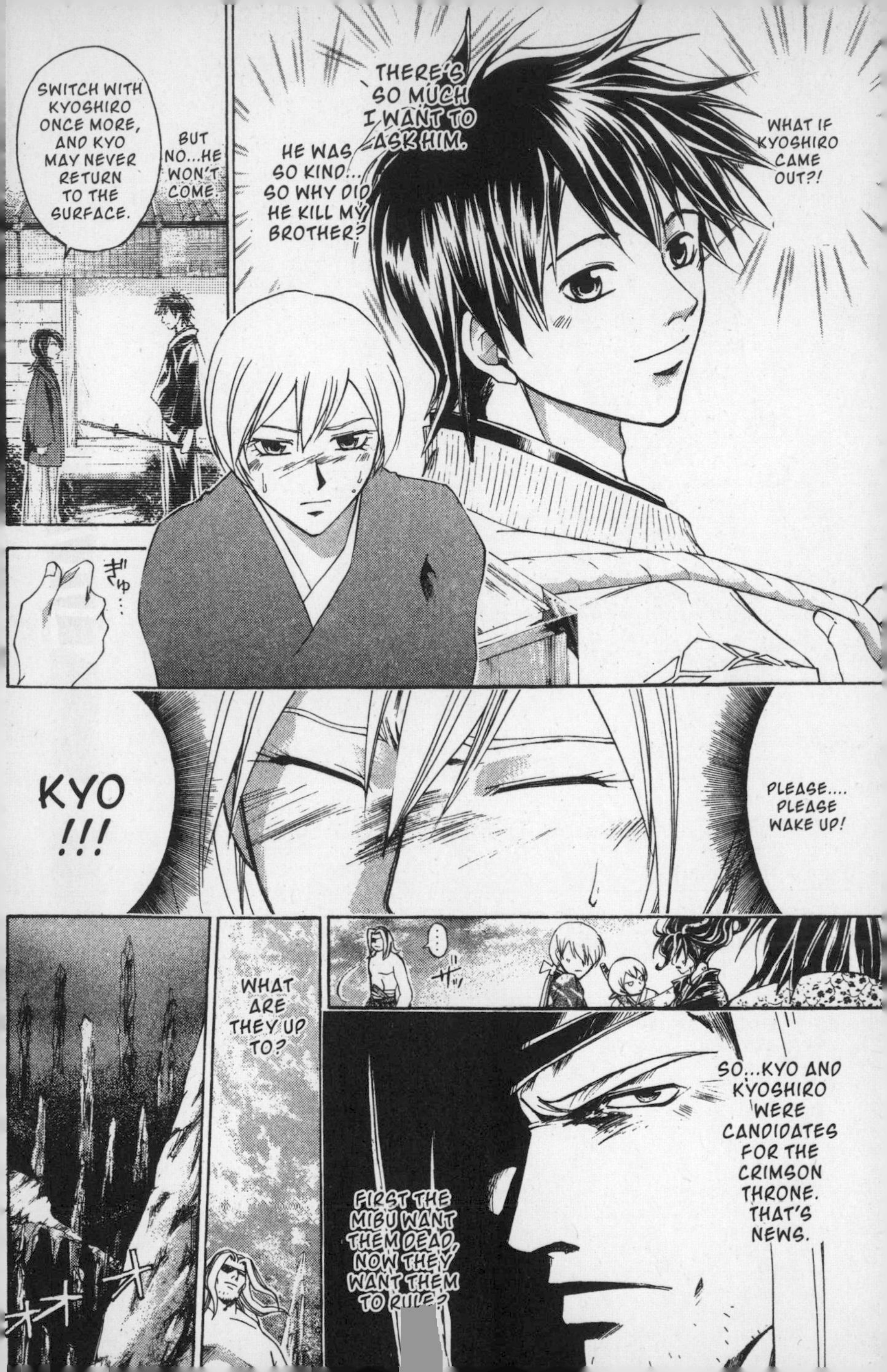
WHAT IF KYOSHIRO CAME OUT?!
THERE'S SO MUCH I WANT TO ASK HIM.
HE WAS SO KIND... SO WHY DID HE KILL MY BROTHER?
BUT NO...HE WON'T COME.
SWITCH WITH KYOSHIRO ONCE MORE, AND KYO MAY NEVER RETURN TO THE SURFACE.
ぎゅ…
PLEASE.... PLEASE WAKE UP!
KYO !!!
...
ザッ
SO...KYO AND KYOSHIRO WERE CANDIDATES FOR THE CRIMSON THRONE. THAT'S NEWS.
WHAT ARE THEY UP TO?
FIRST THE MIBU WANT THEM DEAD, NOW THEY WANT THEM TO RULE?

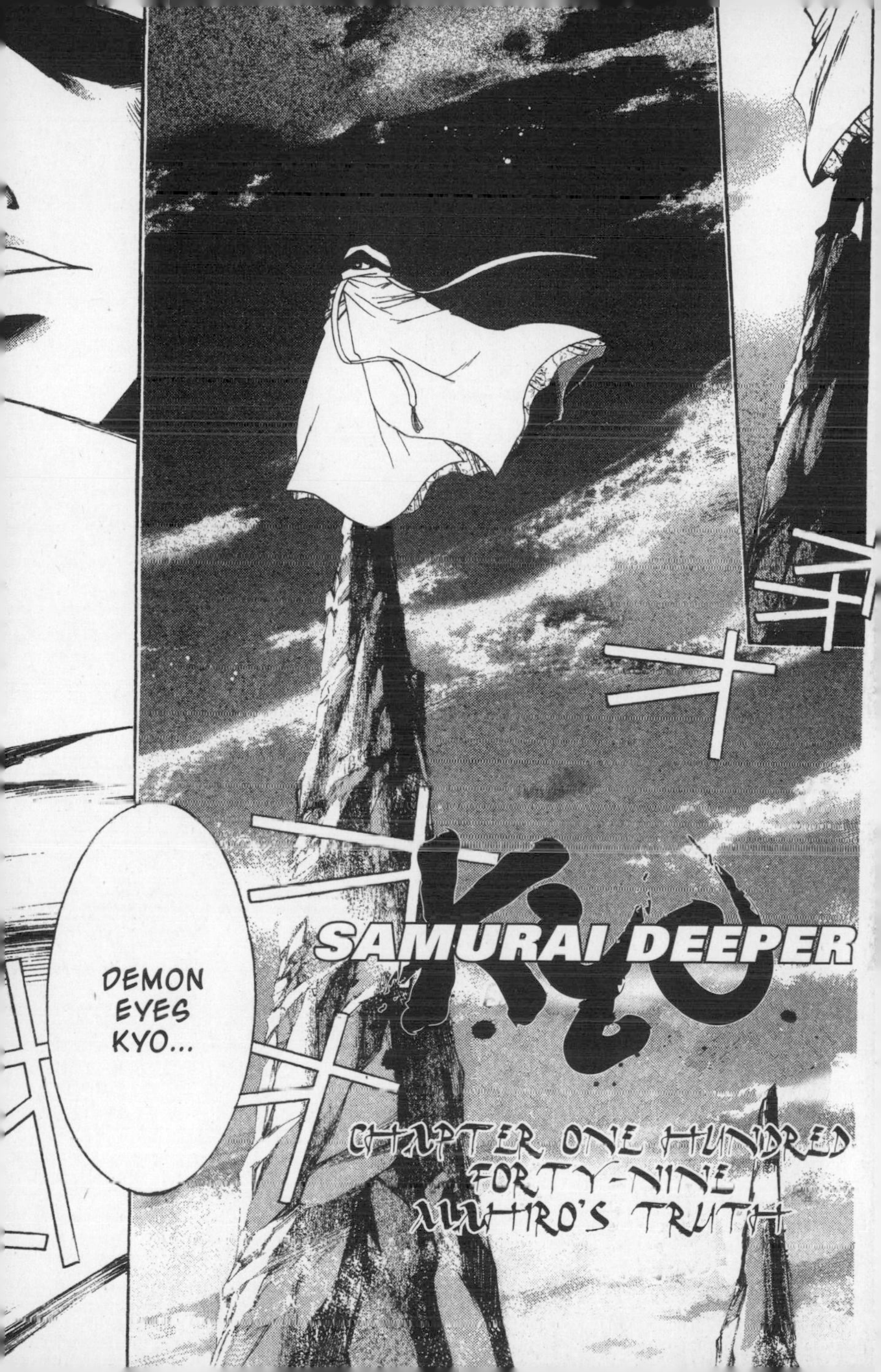
SAMURAI DEEPER KYO
CHAPTER ONE HUNDRED FORTY-NINE
AKIHIRO'S TRUTH
DEMON EYES KYO...

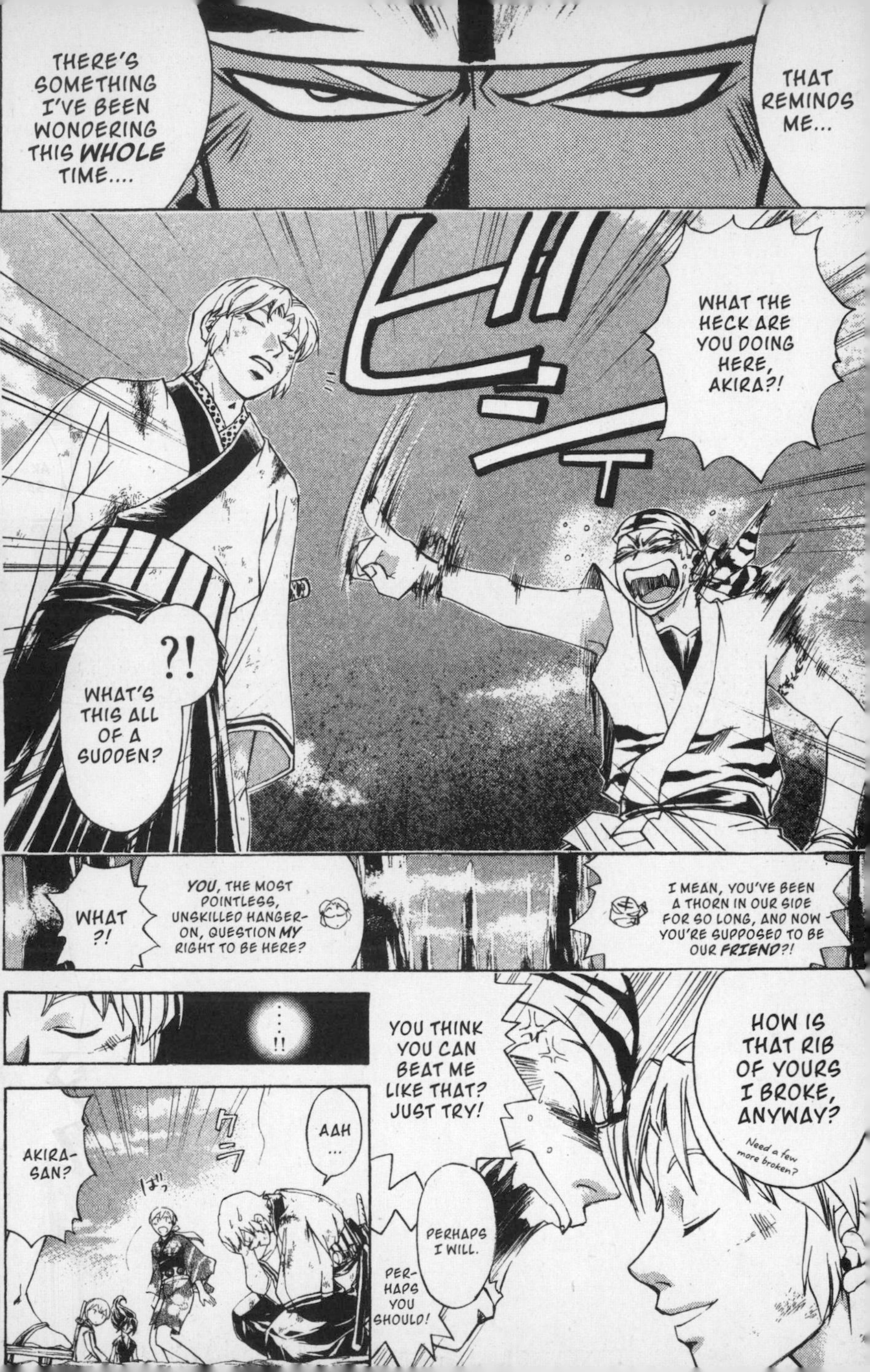
THAT REMINDS ME...
THERE'S SOMETHING I'VE BEEN WONDERING THIS *WHOLE* TIME....
WHAT THE HECK ARE YOU DOING HERE, AKIRA?!
?! WHAT'S THIS ALL OF A SUDDEN?
I MEAN, YOU'VE BEEN A THORN IN OUR SIDE FOR SO LONG, AND NOW YOU'RE SUPPOSED TO BE OUR *FRIEND*?!
YOU, THE MOST POINTLESS, UNSKILLED HANGER-ON, QUESTION *MY* RIGHT TO BE HERE?
WHAT ?!
HOW IS THAT RIB OF YOURS I BROKE, ANYWAY?
Need a few more broken?
YOU THINK YOU CAN BEAT ME LIKE THAT? JUST TRY!
PERHAPS I WILL.
PER-HAPS YOU SHOULD!
...!!
AAH ...
AKIRA-SAN?

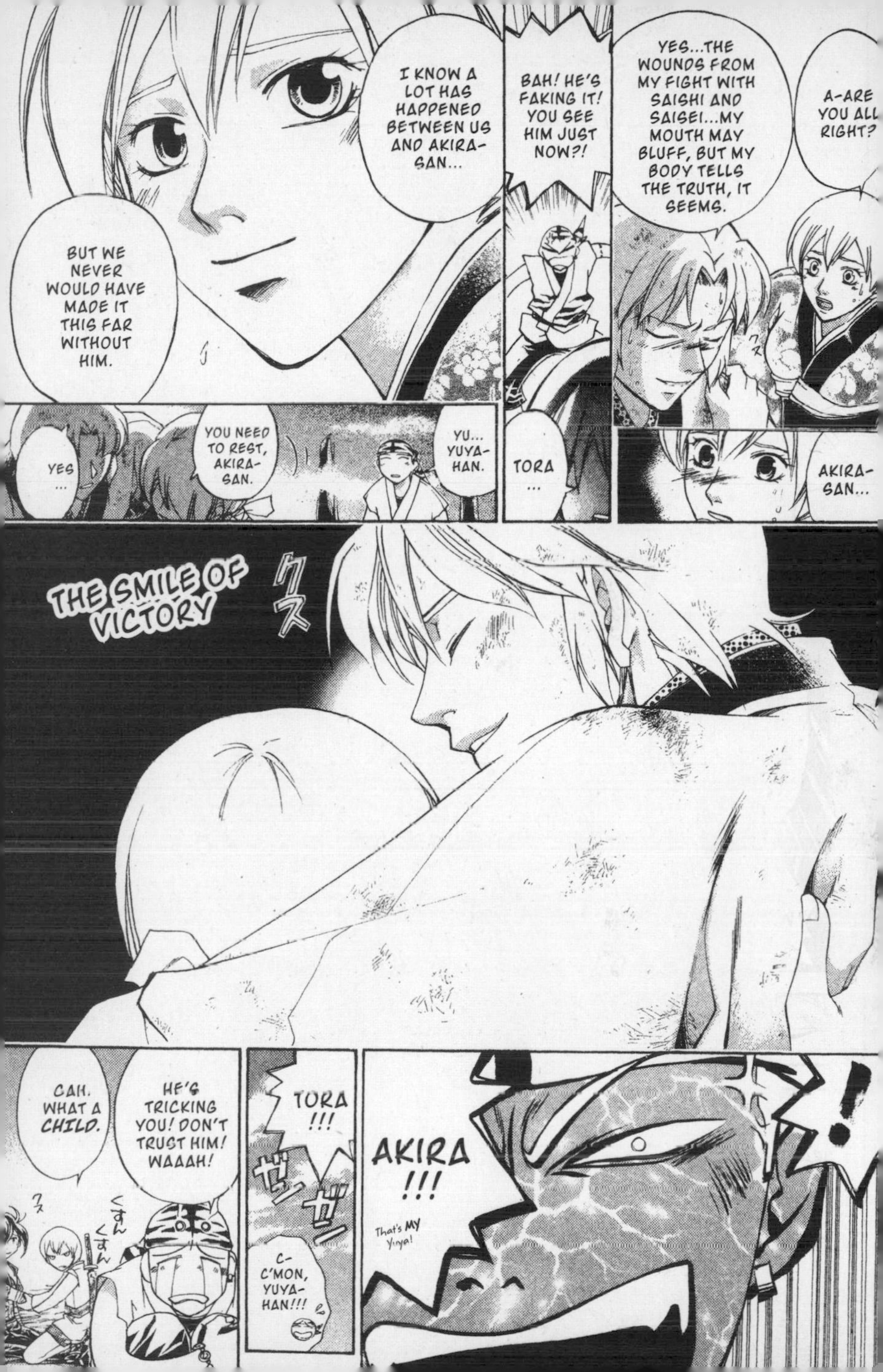
A-ARE YOU ALL RIGHT?
YES...THE WOUNDS FROM MY FIGHT WITH SAISHI AND SAISEI...MY MOUTH MAY BLUFF, BUT MY BODY TELLS THE TRUTH, IT SEEMS.
BAH! HE'S FAKING IT! YOU SEE HIM JUST NOW?!
I KNOW A LOT HAS HAPPENED BETWEEN US AND AKIRA-SAN...
BUT WE NEVER WOULD HAVE MADE IT THIS FAR WITHOUT HIM.
AKIRA-SAN...
TORA ...
YU... YUYA-HAN.
YOU NEED TO REST, AKIRA-SAN.
YES ...
THE SMILE OF VICTORY
クス
AKIRA !!!
That's MY Yuya!
TORA !!!
C- C'MON, YUYA-HAN!!!
HE'S TRICKING YOU! DON'T TRUST HIM! WAAAH!
CAH. WHAT A CHILD.
くすん くすん

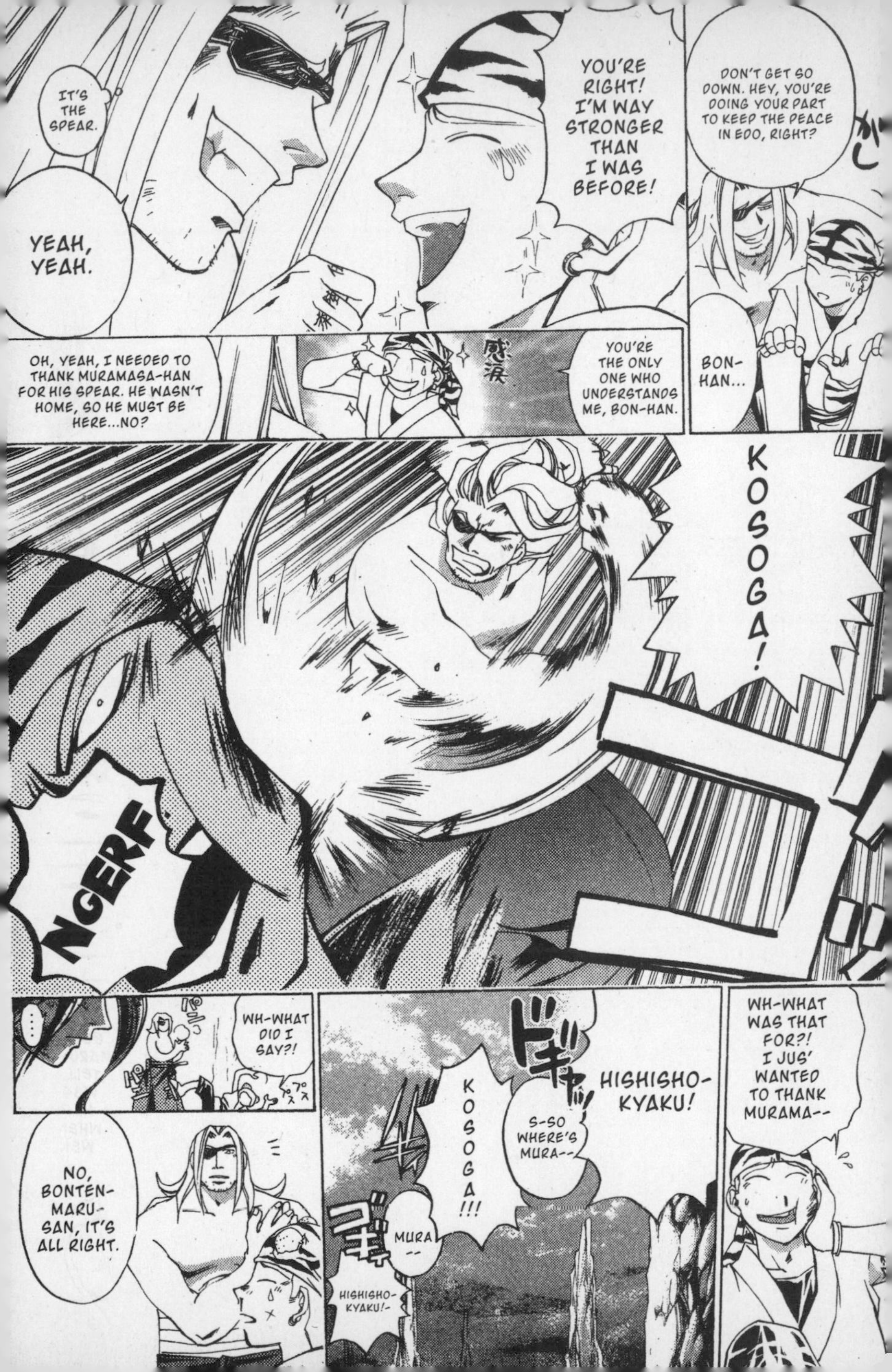
DON'T GET SO DOWN. HEY, YOU'RE DOING YOUR PART TO KEEP THE PEACE IN EDO, RIGHT?
かし
YOU'RE RIGHT! I'M WAY STRONGER THAN I WAS BEFORE!
IT'S THE SPEAR.
YEAH, YEAH.
BON-HAN...
YOU'RE THE ONLY ONE WHO UNDERSTANDS ME, BON-HAN.
感涙
OH, YEAH, I NEEDED TO THANK MURAMASA-HAN FOR HIS SPEAR. HE WASN'T HOME, SO HE MUST BE HERE...NO?
KOSOGA!
NGERF
WH-WHAT WAS THAT FOR?! I JUS' WANTED TO THANK MURAMA--
ドギャ
HISHISHO-KYAKU!
S-SO WHERE'S MURA--
KOSOGA!!!
MURA --
ゴギィ
HISHISHO-KYAKU!-
...
WH-WHAT DID I SAY?!
NO, BONTEN-MARU-SAN, IT'S ALL RIGHT.

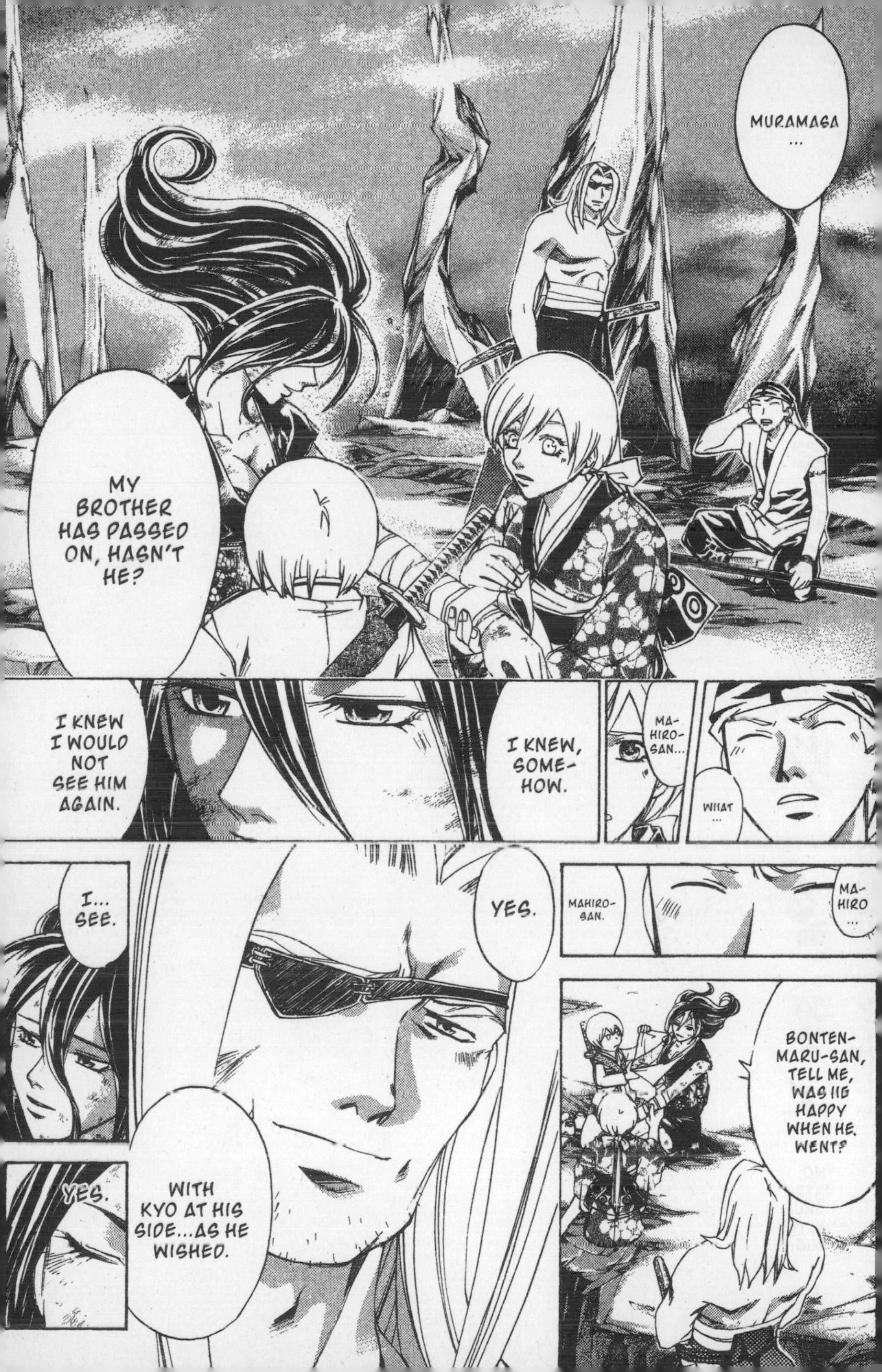
MURAMASA ...
MY BROTHER HAS PASSED ON, HASN'T HE?
MA-HIRO-SAN...
WHAT ...
I KNEW, SOME-HOW.
I KNEW I WOULD NOT SEE HIM AGAIN.
MA-HIRO ...
MAHIRO-SAN.
BONTEN-MARU-SAN, TELL ME, WAS HE HAPPY WHEN HE WENT?
YES.
WITH KYO AT HIS SIDE...AS HE WISHED.
I... SEE.
YES.

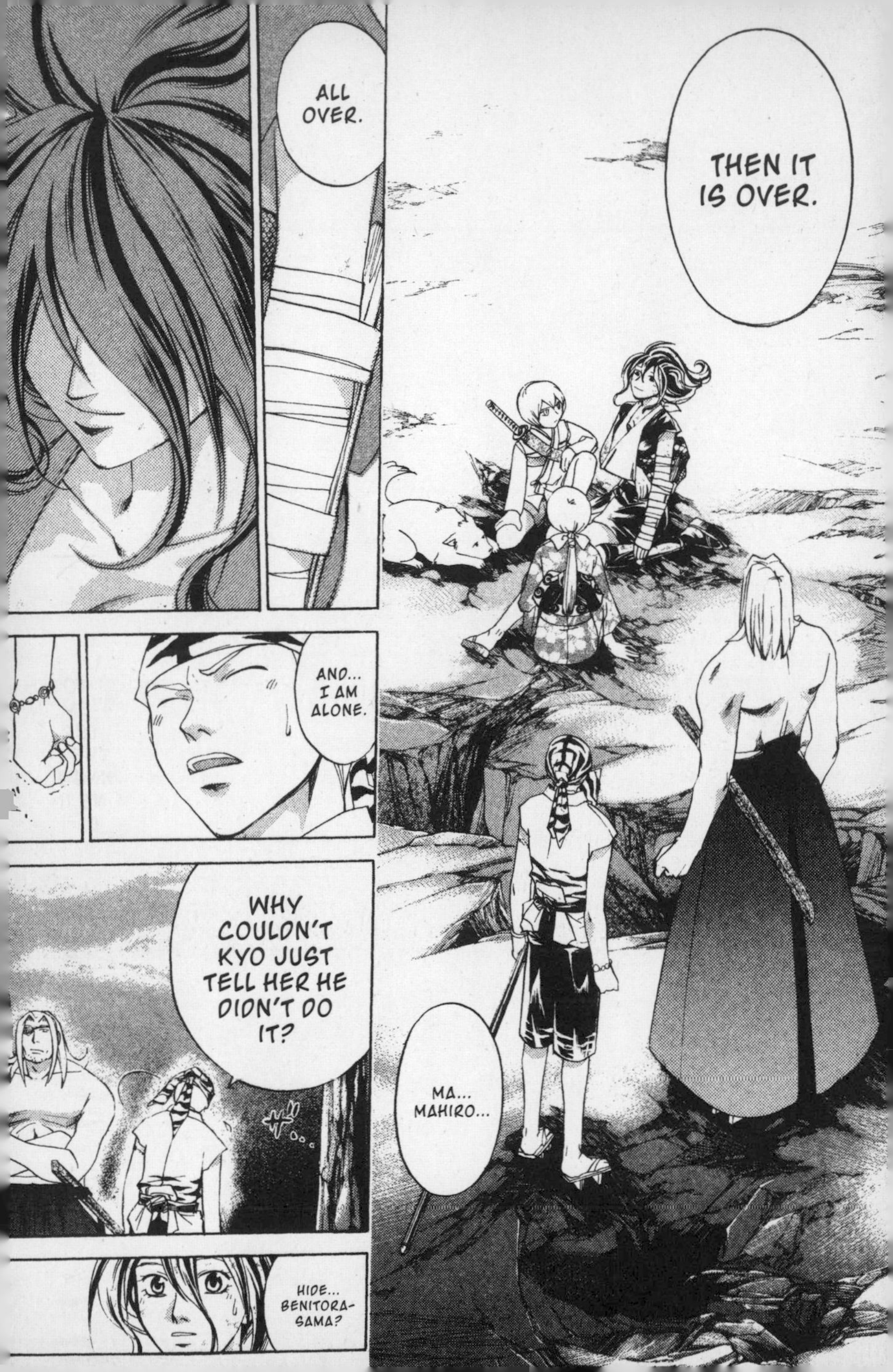
THEN IT IS OVER.
MA... MAHIRO...
ALL OVER.
AND... I AM ALONE.
WHY COULDN'T KYO JUST TELL HER HE DIDN'T DO IT?
HIDE... BENITORA-SAMA?

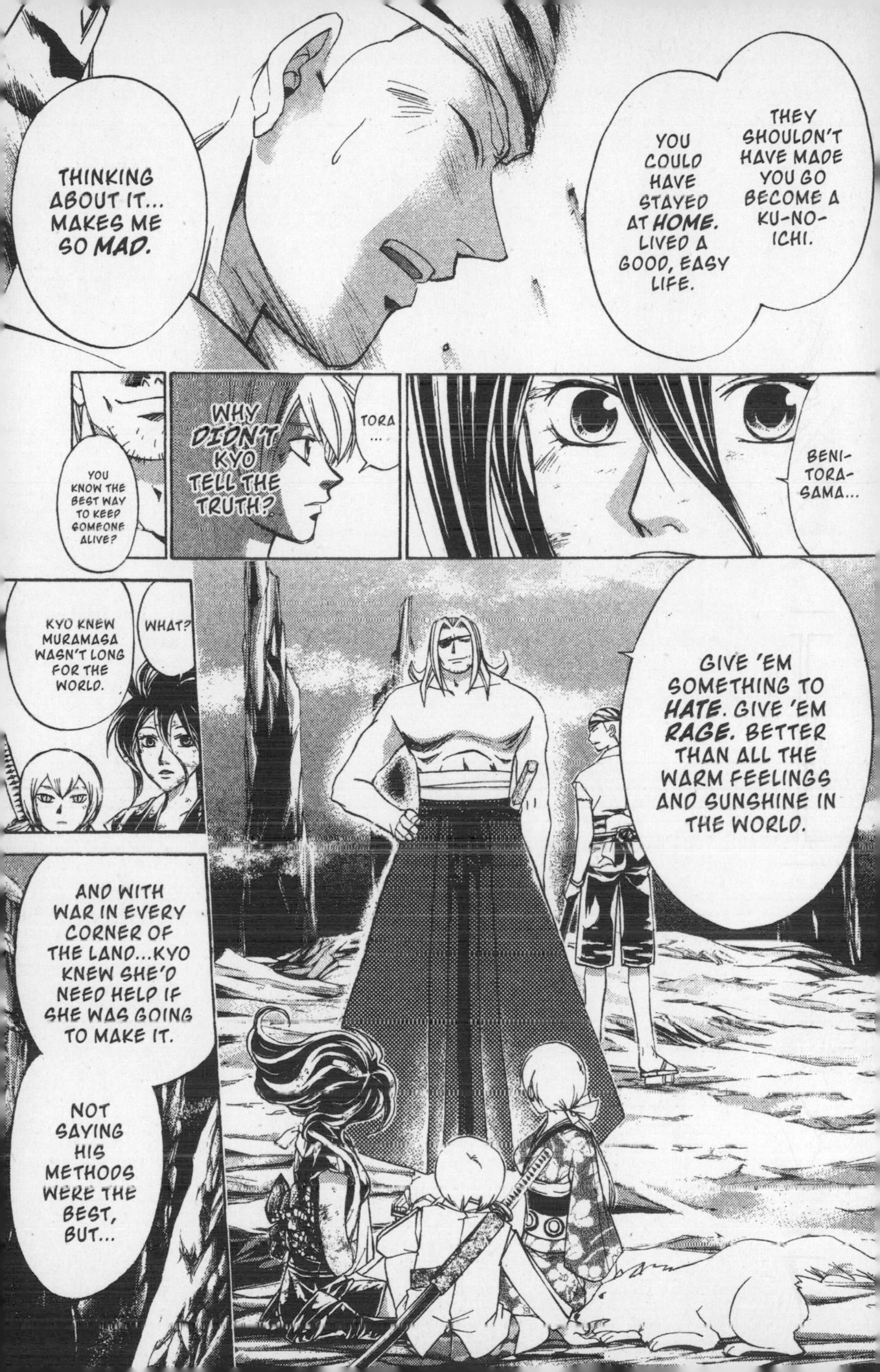
THEY SHOULDN'T HAVE MADE YOU GO BECOME A KU-NO-ICHI.
YOU COULD HAVE STAYED AT HOME. LIVED A GOOD, EASY LIFE.
THINKING ABOUT IT... MAKES ME SO MAD.
BENI-TORA-SAMA...
TORA...
WHY DIDN'T KYO TELL THE TRUTH?
YOU KNOW THE BEST WAY TO KEEP SOMEONE ALIVE?
GIVE 'EM SOMETHING TO HATE. GIVE 'EM RAGE. BETTER THAN ALL THE WARM FEELINGS AND SUNSHINE IN THE WORLD.
WHAT?
KYO KNEW MURAMASA WASN'T LONG FOR THE WORLD.
AND WITH WAR IN EVERY CORNER OF THE LAND...KYO KNEW SHE'D NEED HELP IF SHE WAS GOING TO MAKE IT.
NOT SAYING HIS METHODS WERE THE BEST, BUT...

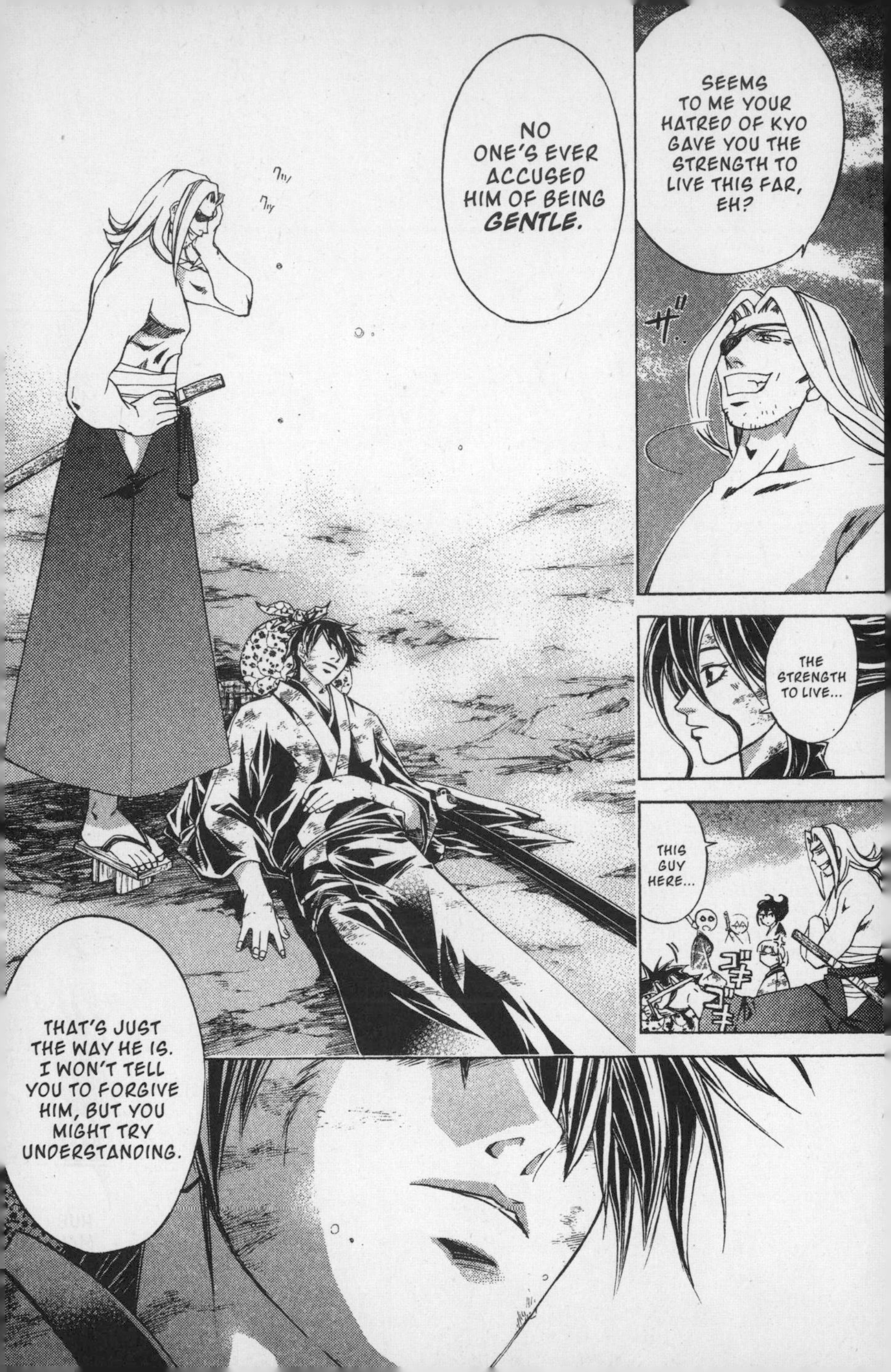
SEEMS TO ME YOUR HATRED OF KYO GAVE YOU THE STRENGTH TO LIVE THIS FAR, EH?
THE STRENGTH TO LIVE...
THIS GUY HERE...
NO ONE'S EVER ACCUSED HIM OF BEING GENTLE.
THAT'S JUST THE WAY HE IS. I WON'T TELL YOU TO FORGIVE HIM, BUT YOU MIGHT TRY UNDERSTANDING.

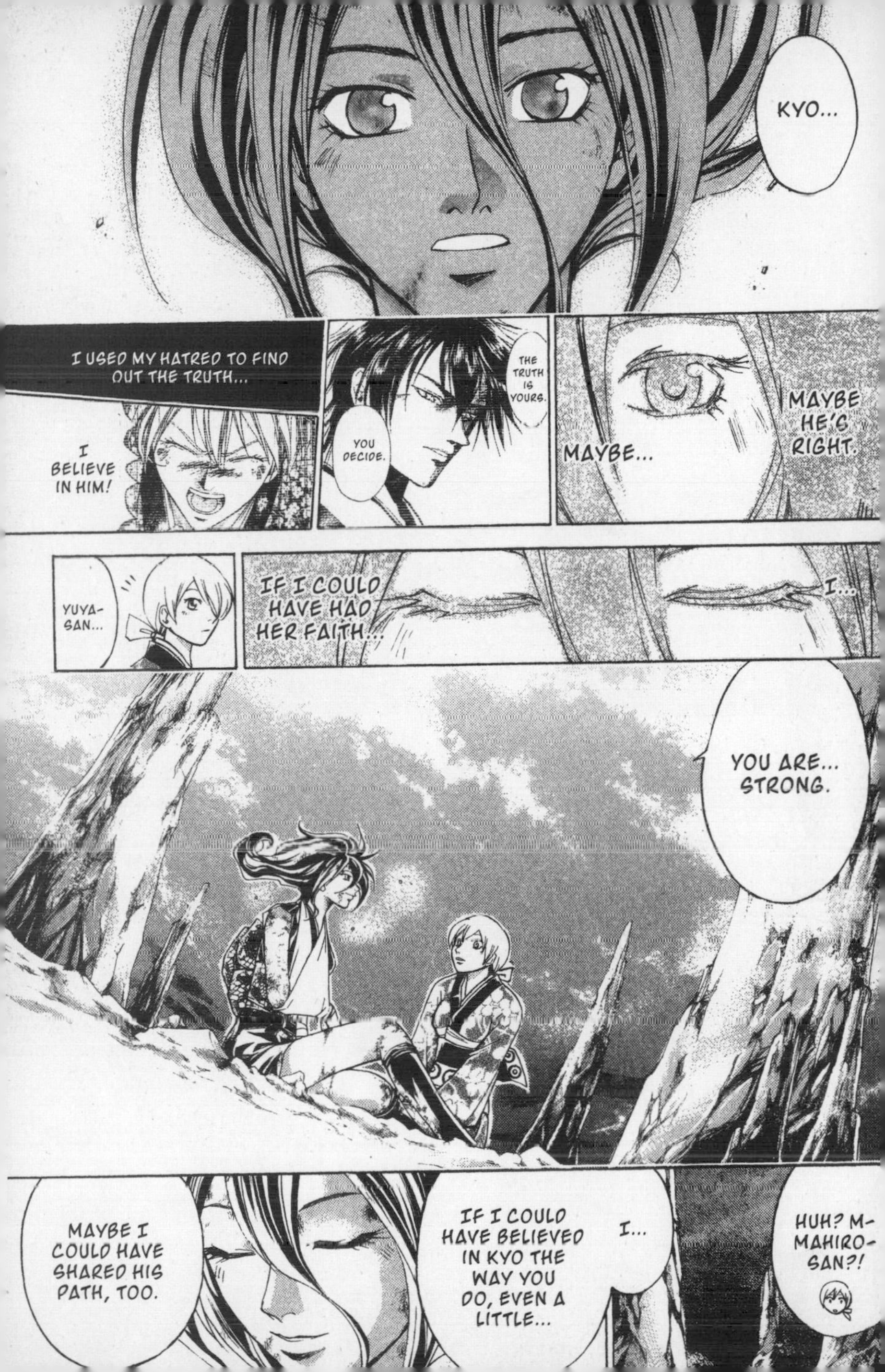
KYO...
MAYBE HE'S RIGHT.
MAYBE...
THE TRUTH IS YOURS.
YOU DECIDE.
I USED MY HATRED TO FIND OUT THE TRUTH...
I BELIEVE IN HIM!
I...
IF I COULD HAVE HAD HER FAITH...
YUYA-SAN...
YOU ARE... STRONG.
HUH? M-MAHIRO-SAN?!
I...
IF I COULD HAVE BELIEVED IN KYO THE WAY YOU DO, EVEN A LITTLE...
MAYBE I COULD HAVE SHARED HIS PATH, TOO.

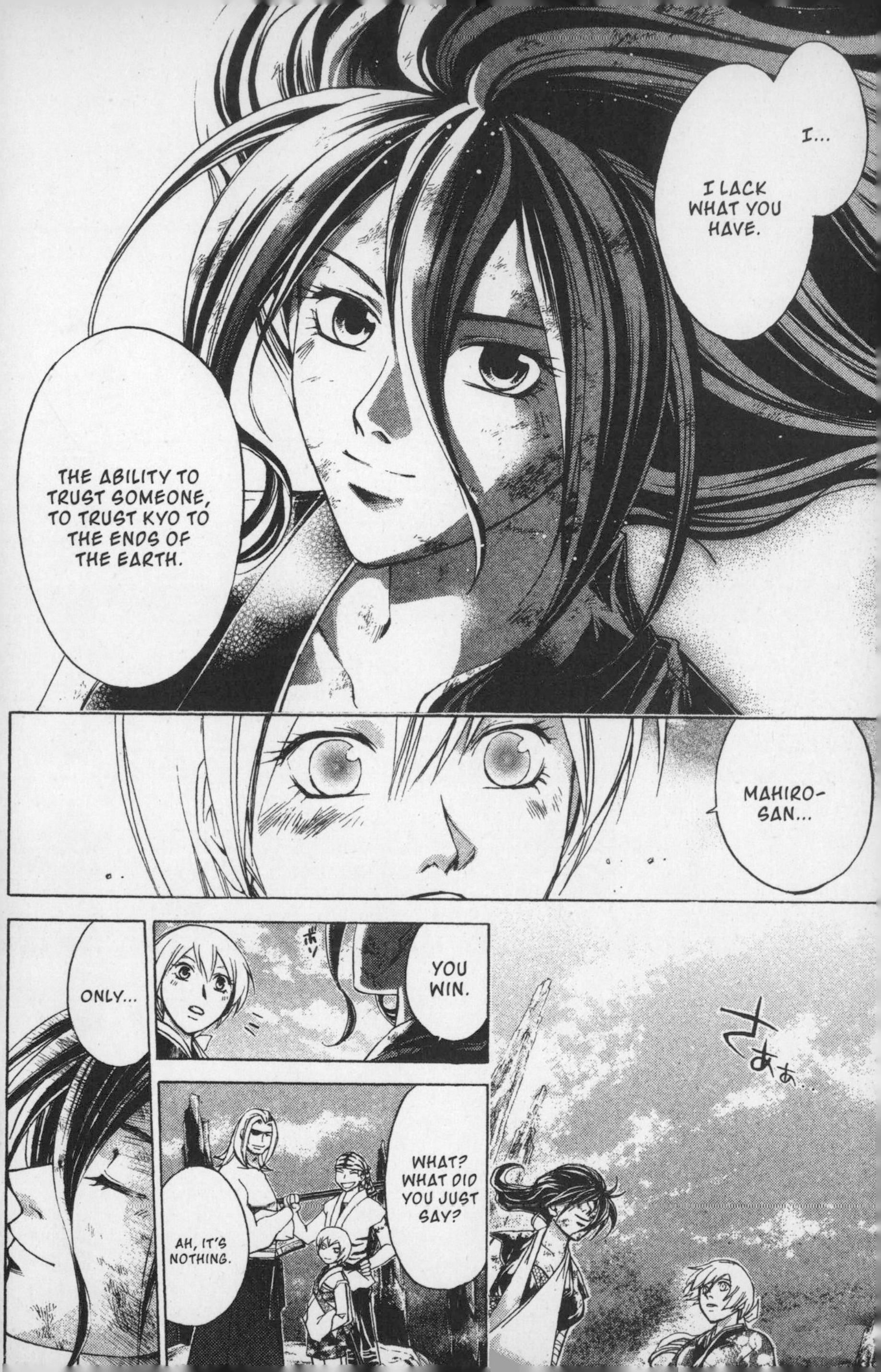
I...
I LACK WHAT YOU HAVE.
THE ABILITY TO TRUST SOMEONE, TO TRUST KYO TO THE ENDS OF THE EARTH.
MAHIRO-SAN...
さあぁ..
ボソ
YOU WIN.
WHAT? WHAT DID YOU JUST SAY?
AH, IT'S NOTHING.
ONLY...

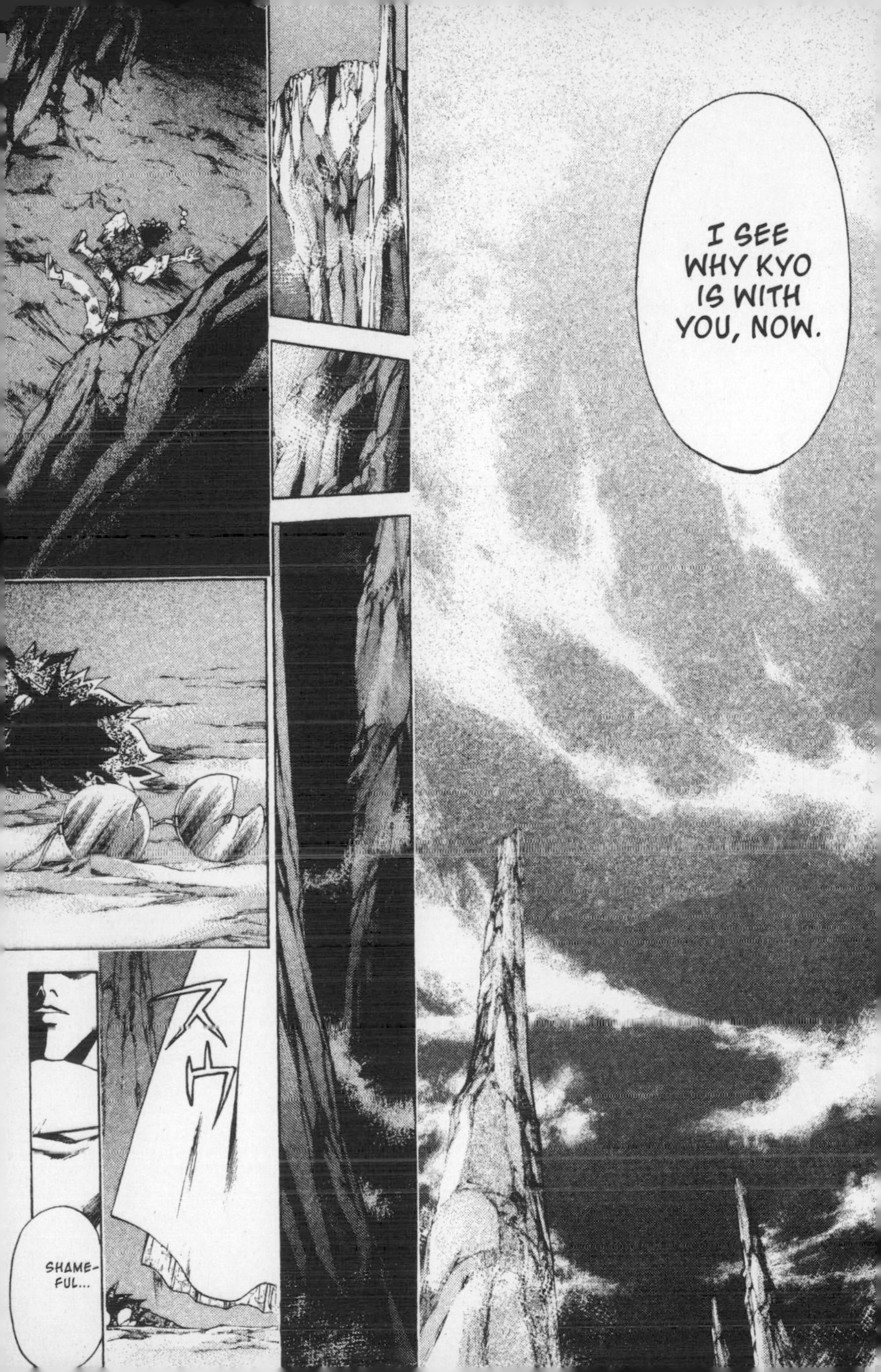
I SEE WHY KYO IS WITH YOU, NOW.
スッ
SHAME-FUL...

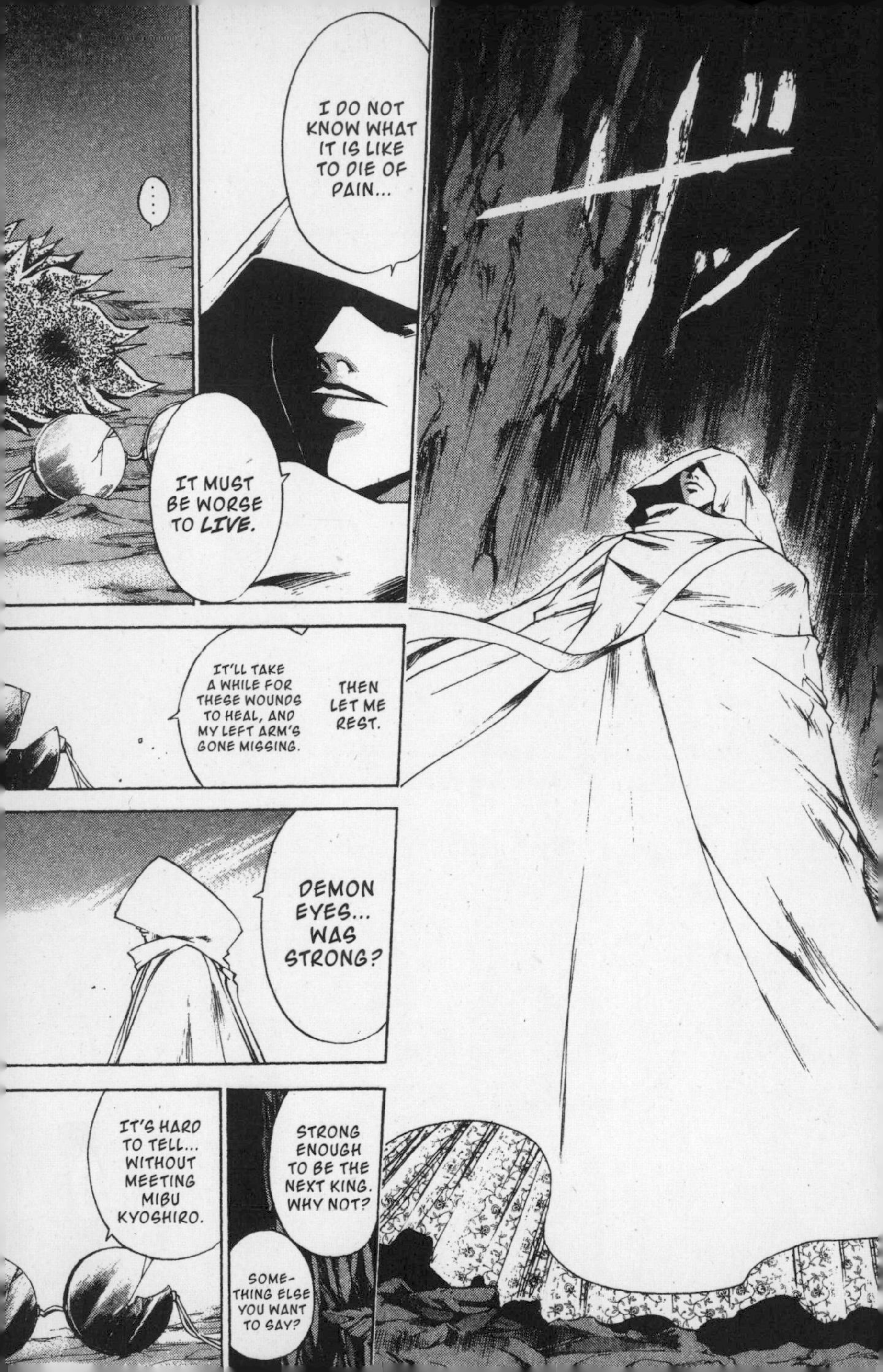
I DO NOT KNOW WHAT IT IS LIKE TO DIE OF PAIN...
IT MUST BE WORSE TO *LIVE.*
....
THEN LET ME REST.
IT'LL TAKE A WHILE FOR THESE WOUNDS TO HEAL, AND MY LEFT ARM'S GONE MISSING.
DEMON EYES... WAS STRONG?
STRONG ENOUGH TO BE THE NEXT KING. WHY NOT?
SOME-THING ELSE YOU WANT TO SAY?
IT'S HARD TO TELL... WITHOUT MEETING MIBU KYOSHIRO.

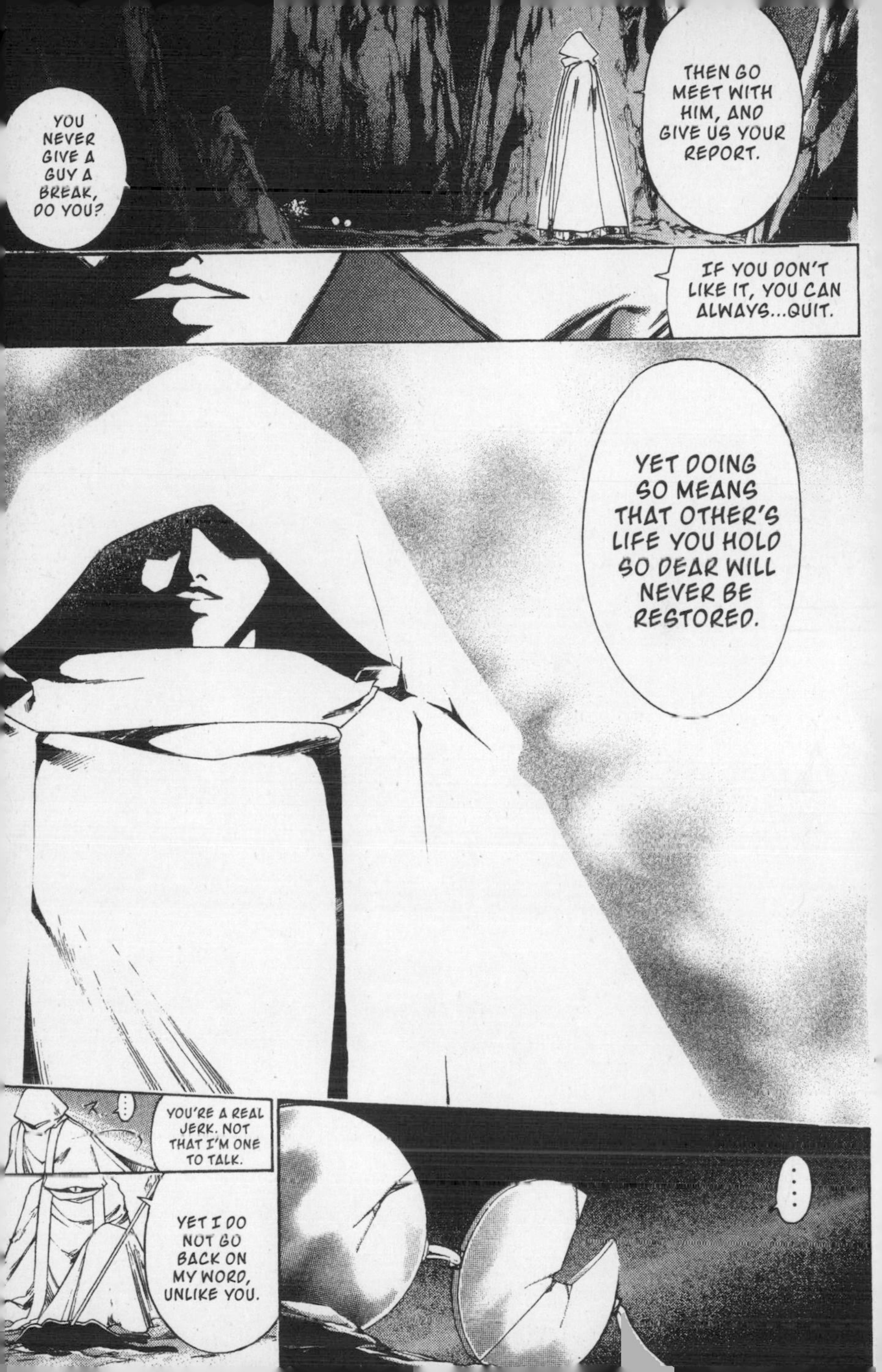
THEN GO MEET WITH HIM, AND GIVE US YOUR REPORT.
YOU NEVER GIVE A GUY A BREAK, DO YOU?
IF YOU DON'T LIKE IT, YOU CAN ALWAYS...QUIT.
YET DOING SO MEANS THAT OTHER'S LIFE YOU HOLD SO DEAR WILL NEVER BE RESTORED.
....
...
YOU'RE A REAL JERK. NOT THAT I'M ONE TO TALK.
YET I DO NOT GO BACK ON MY WORD, UNLIKE YOU.

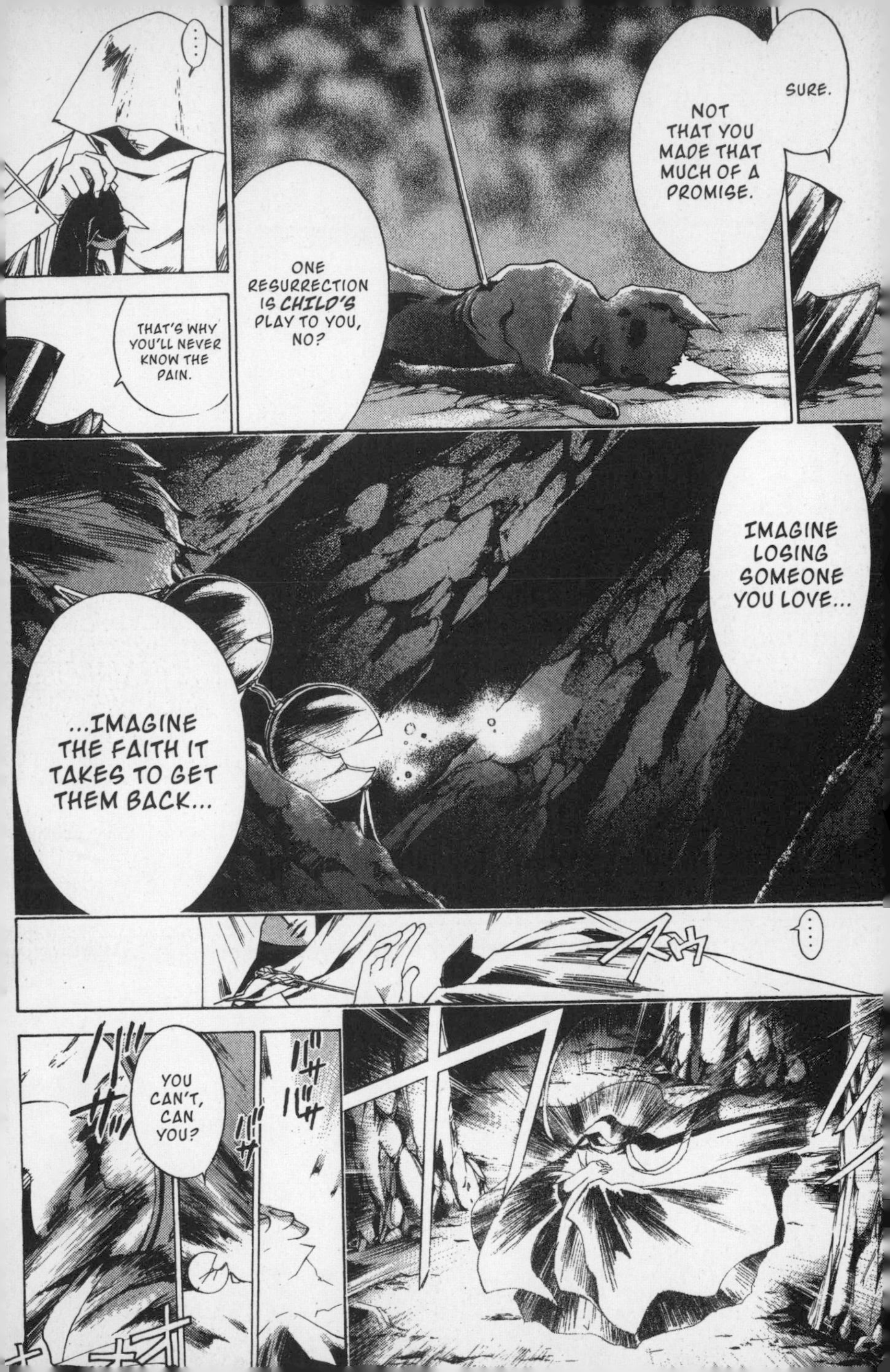
SURE.
NOT THAT YOU MADE THAT MUCH OF A PROMISE.
ONE RESURRECTION IS *CHILD'S* PLAY TO YOU, NO?
....
THAT'S WHY YOU'LL NEVER KNOW THE PAIN.
IMAGINE LOSING SOMEONE YOU LOVE...
...IMAGINE THE FAITH IT TAKES TO GET THEM BACK...
....
YOU CAN'T, CAN YOU?

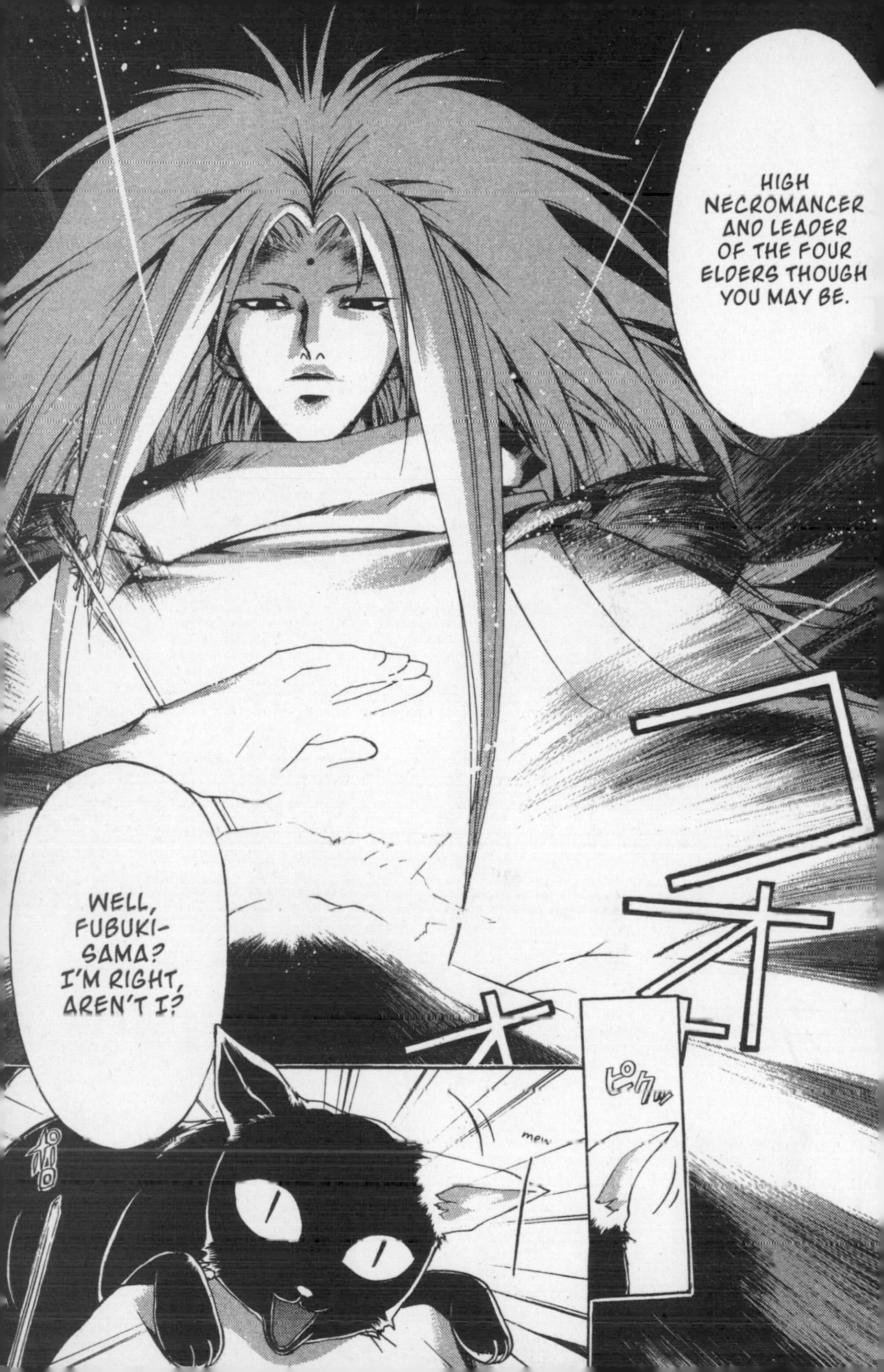
HIGH NECROMANCER AND LEADER OF THE FOUR ELDERS THOUGH YOU MAY BE.
コオオ
WELL, FUBUKI-SAMA? I'M RIGHT, AREN'T I?
ピクッ

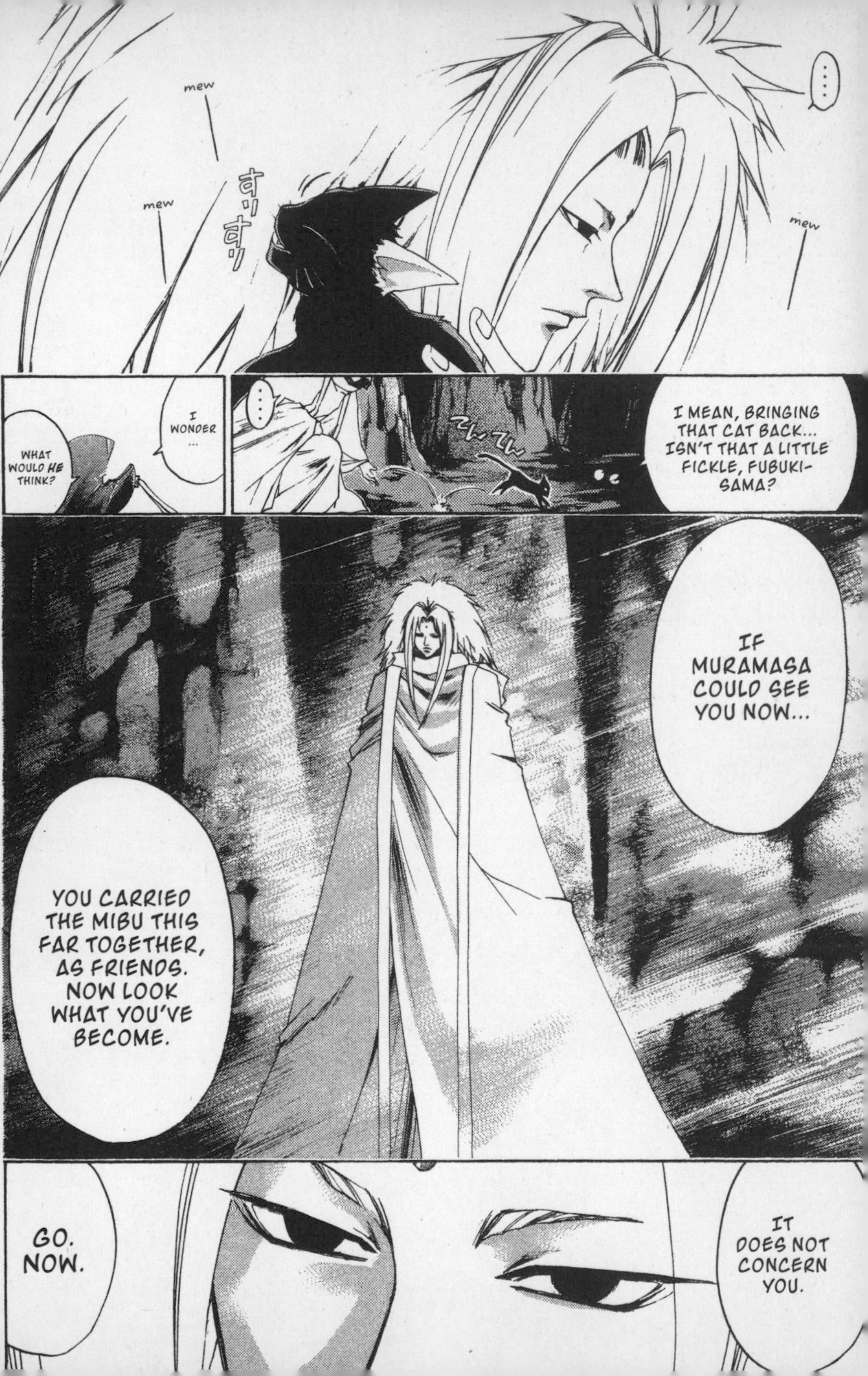
…
mew
mew
すりすり
mew
I MEAN, BRINGING THAT CAT BACK... ISN'T THAT A LITTLE FICKLE, FUBUKI-SAMA?
…
I WONDER …
WHAT WOULD HE THINK?
IF MURAMASA COULD SEE YOU NOW...
YOU CARRIED THE MIBU THIS FAR TOGETHER, AS FRIENDS. NOW LOOK WHAT YOU'VE BECOME.
IT DOES NOT CONCERN YOU.
GO. NOW.

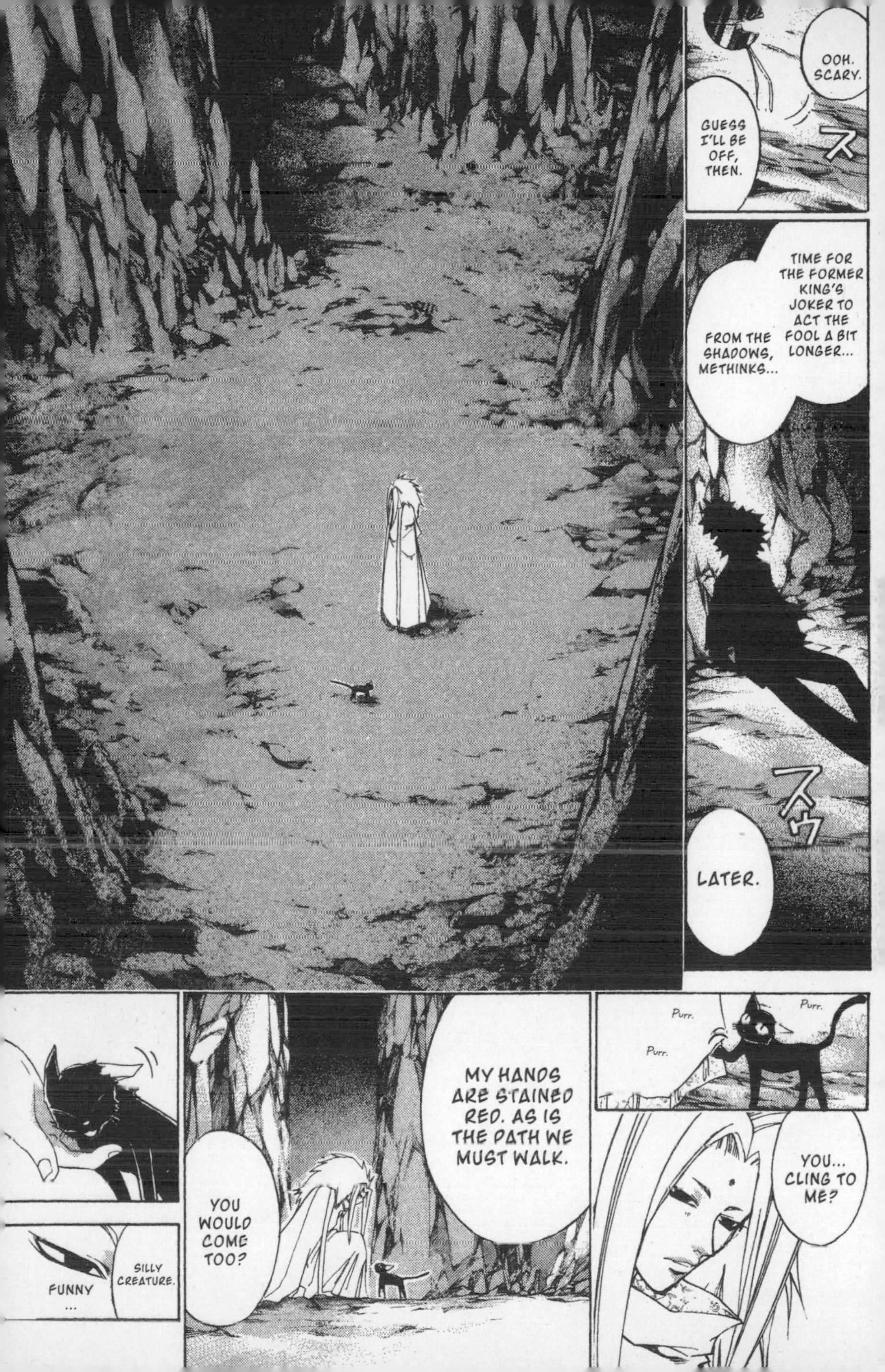
OOH. SCARY.
GUESS I'LL BE OFF, THEN.
ス
TIME FOR THE FORMER KING'S JOKER TO ACT THE FOOL A BIT LONGER...
FROM THE SHADOWS, METHINKS...
スゥ
LATER.
Purr.
Purr.
Purr.
YOU... CLING TO ME?
MY HANDS ARE STAINED RED. AS IS THE PATH WE MUST WALK.
YOU WOULD COME TOO?
SILLY CREATURE.
FUNNY ...

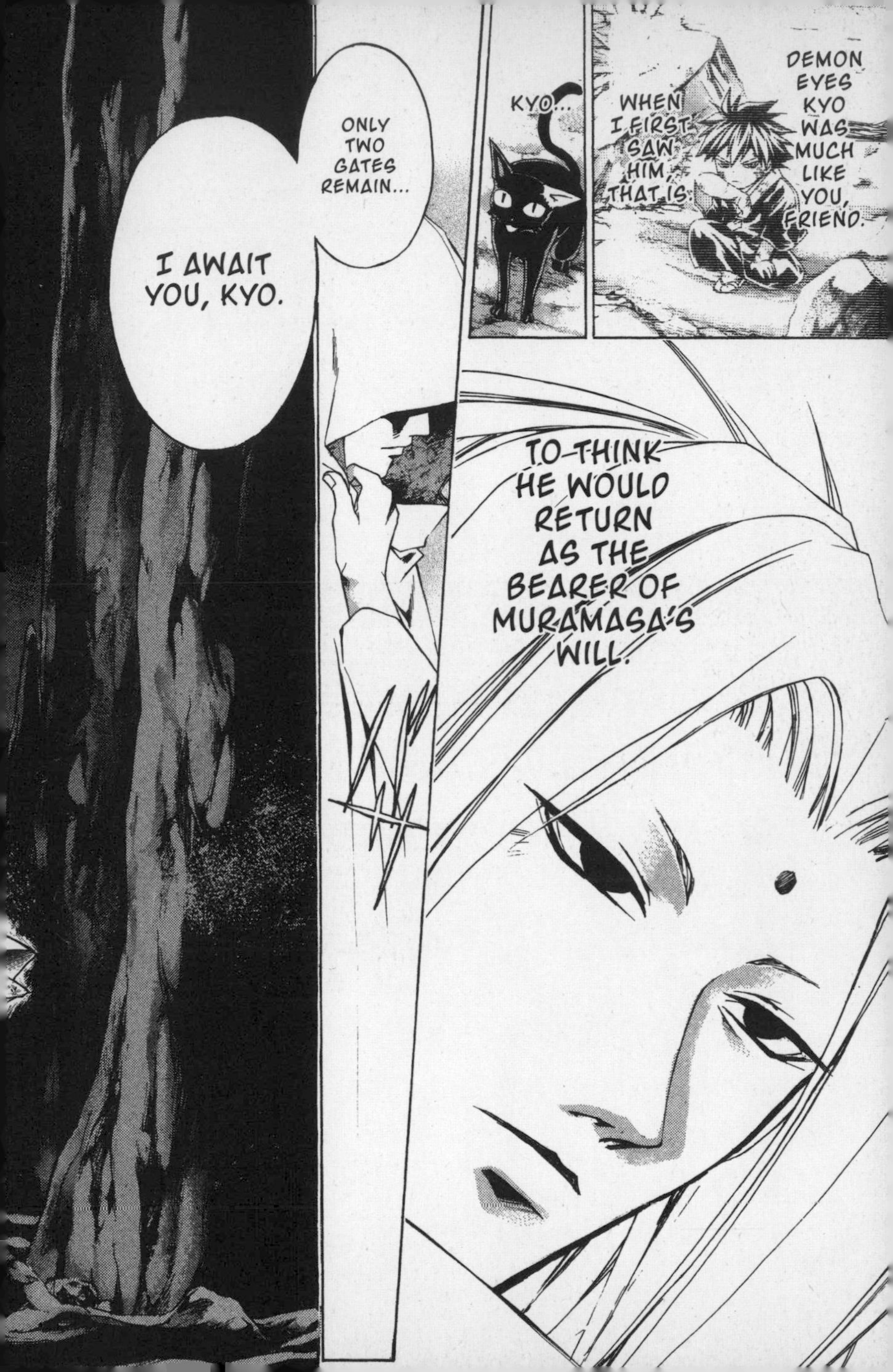
DEMON EYES KYO WAS MUCH LIKE YOU, FRIEND.
WHEN I FIRST SAW HIM THAT IS.
KYO...
TO THINK HE WOULD RETURN AS THE BEARER OF MURAMASA'S WILL.
ONLY TWO GATES REMAIN...
I AWAIT YOU, KYO.

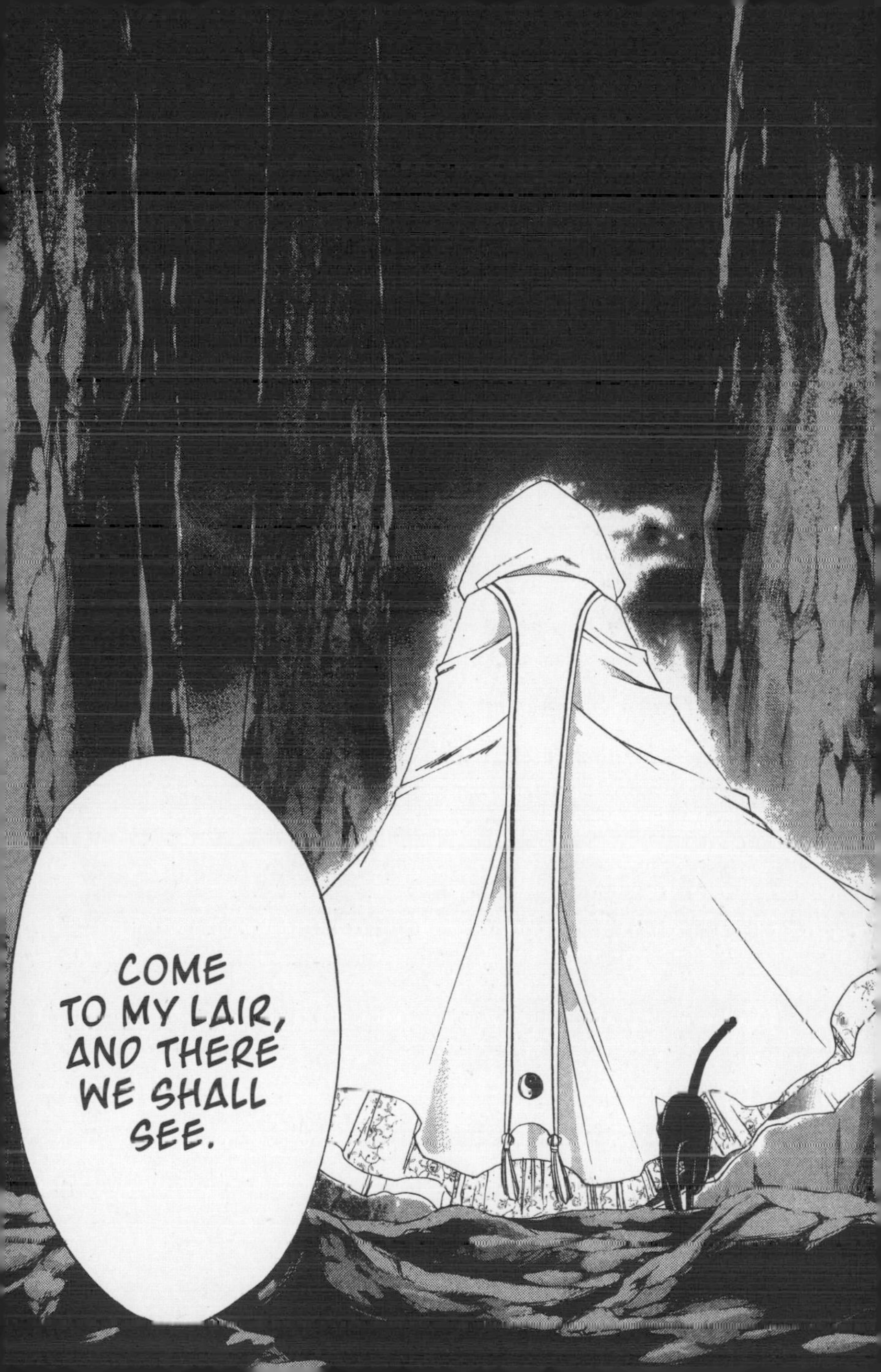
COME TO MY LAIR, AND THERE WE SHALL SEE.

Q&A CORNER

CHARACTERS

Q: How does Mahiro get her hair to stick up like that?

A: Mahiro power! :) Incidentally, rage and hatred increase Mahiro's power, and when she's happy, it fades.

Q: When Kyo and Muramasa draw swords, where do the scabbards go?

A: They throw them off frame so fast that it can't be seen in the manga!

Q: What about Kyo's tattered kimono? Where does he get new ones?

A: He has new kimono in his traveling gear, but he does try to fix the ones he's wearing after a fight. It's tough being poor! :)

Q: Why does Sasuke always carry around that stupid kendama ball?

A: It's his style. You should try!

Q: Is Kyoshiro really a bad person?

A: You'll have to keep reading *SDK* and judge for yourself!

Q: Why doesn't Kyo call Yuya by her name?

A: I wonder. Maybe he will...someday. Hee hee hee.

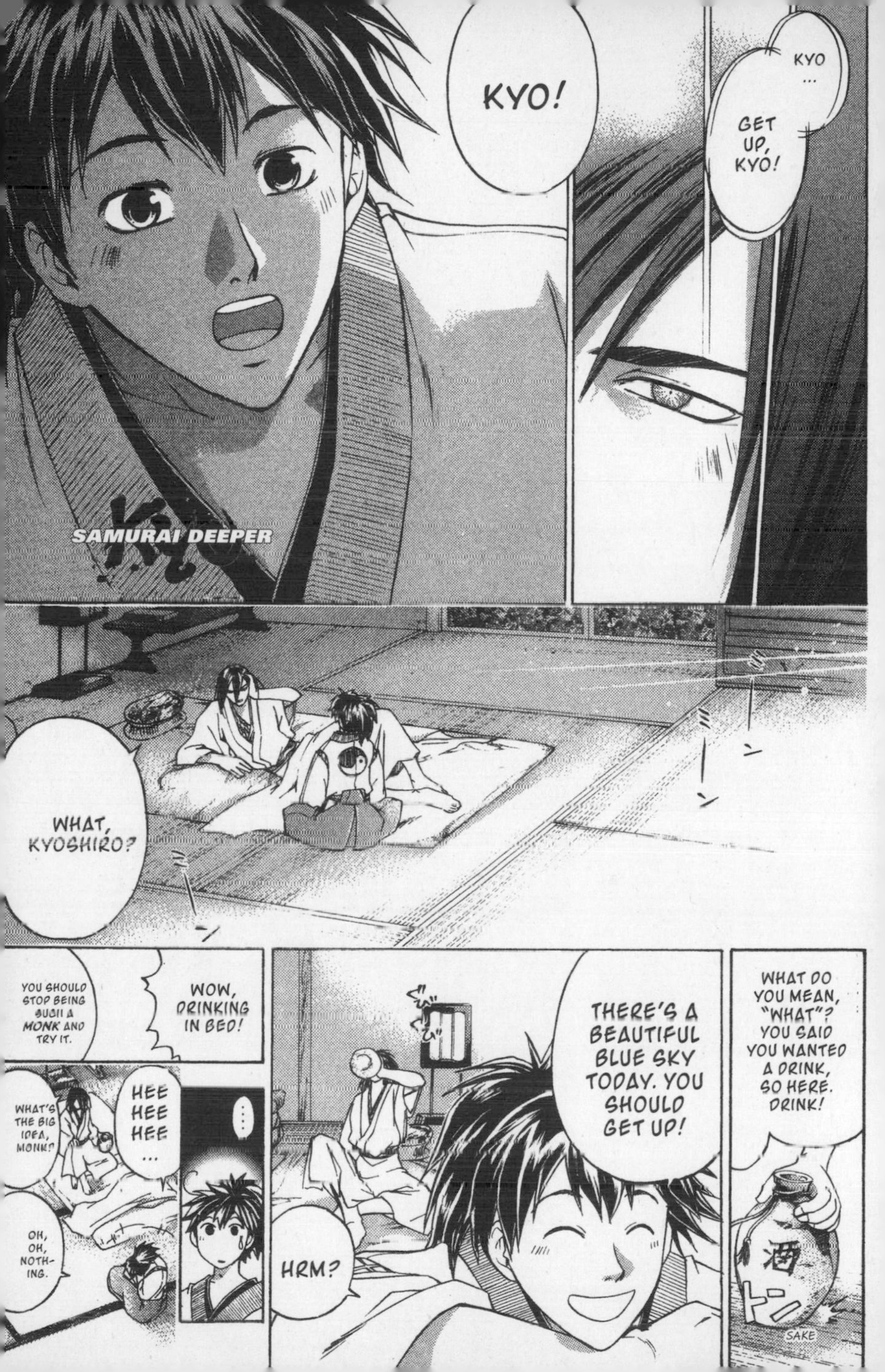
KYO ...
GET UP, KYO!
KYO!
SAMURAI DEEPER
WHAT, KYOSHIRO?
WHAT DO YOU MEAN, "WHAT"? YOU SAID YOU WANTED A DRINK, SO HERE. DRINK!
SAKE
THERE'S A BEAUTIFUL BLUE SKY TODAY. YOU SHOULD GET UP!
HRM?
WOW, DRINKING IN BED!
YOU SHOULD STOP BEING SUCH A MONK AND TRY IT.
...
HEE HEE HEE ...
WHAT'S THE BIG IDEA, MONK?
OH, OH, NOTHING.

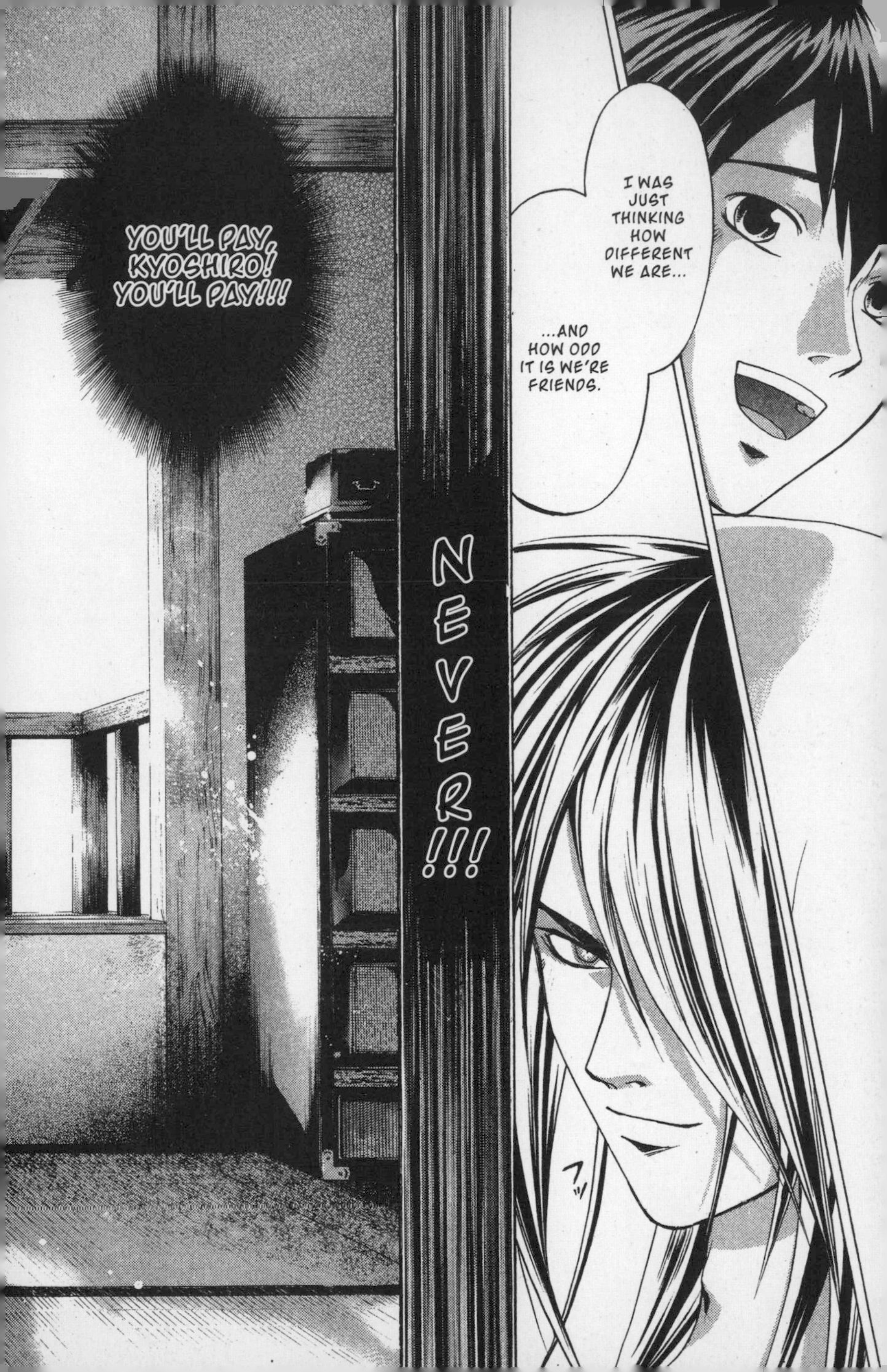
I WAS JUST THINKING HOW DIFFERENT WE ARE...
...AND HOW ODD IT IS WE'RE FRIENDS.
フッ
NEVER!!!
YOU'LL PAY, KYOSHIRO! YOU'LL PAY!!!

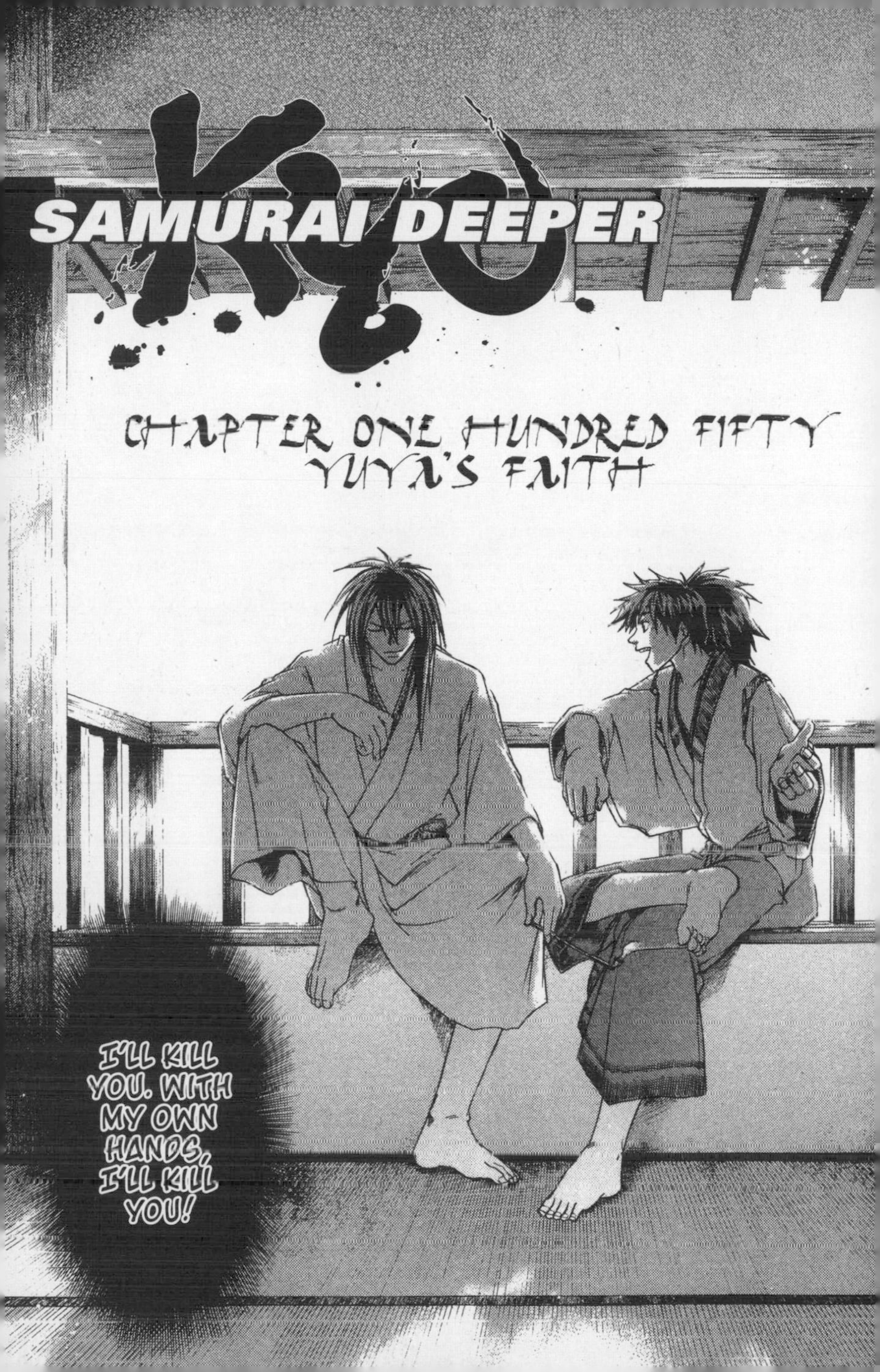
SAMURAI DEEPER KYO
CHAPTER ONE HUNDRED FIFTY
YUYA'S FAITH
I'LL KILL YOU. WITH MY OWN HANDS, I'LL KILL YOU!

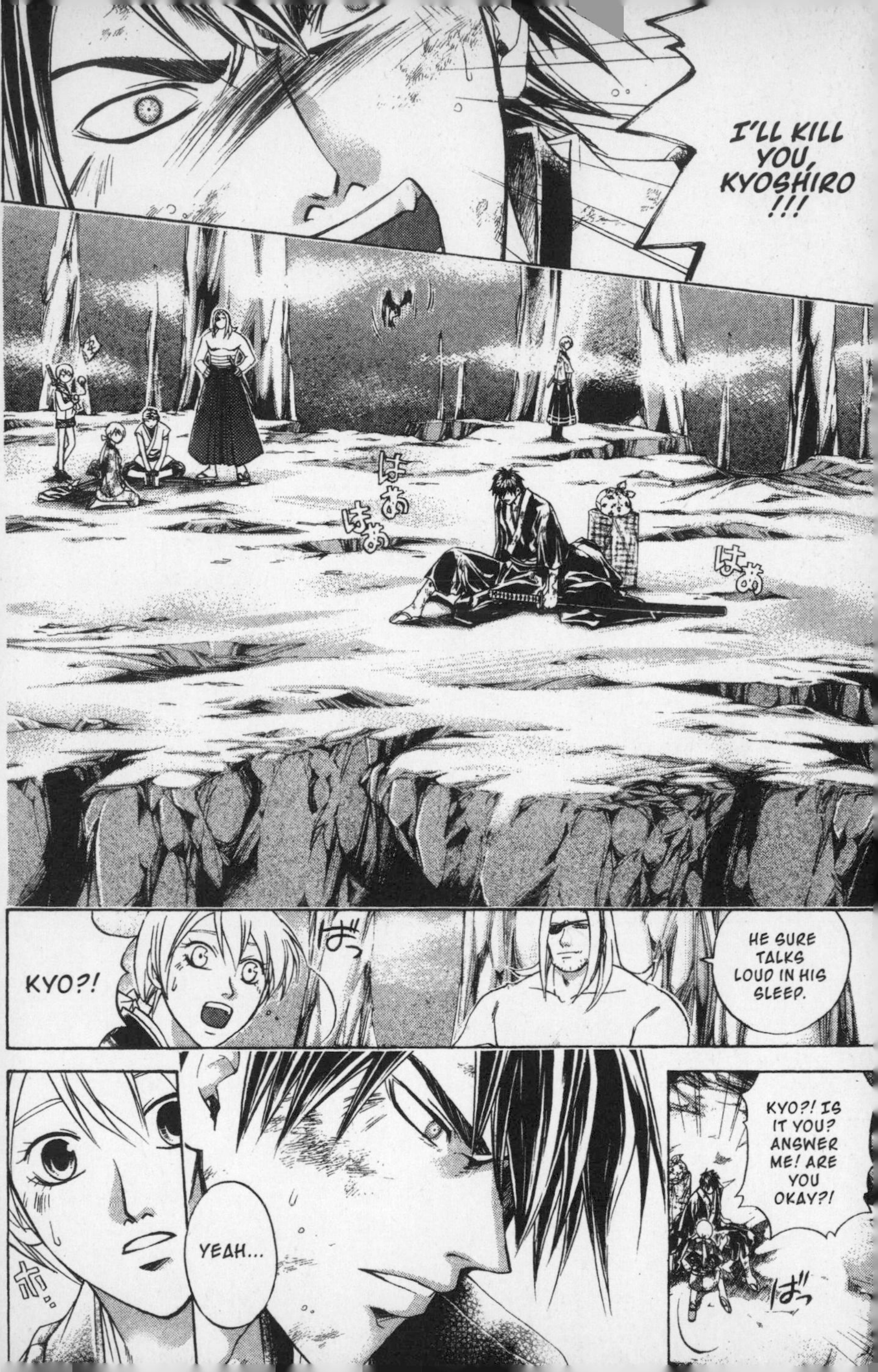
I'LL KILL YOU, KYOSHIRO!!!
はあ
はあ はあ
HE SURE TALKS LOUD IN HIS SLEEP.
ばっ
KYO?!
KYO?! IS IT YOU? ANSWER ME! ARE YOU OKAY?!
ばっ
YEAH...
ホッ

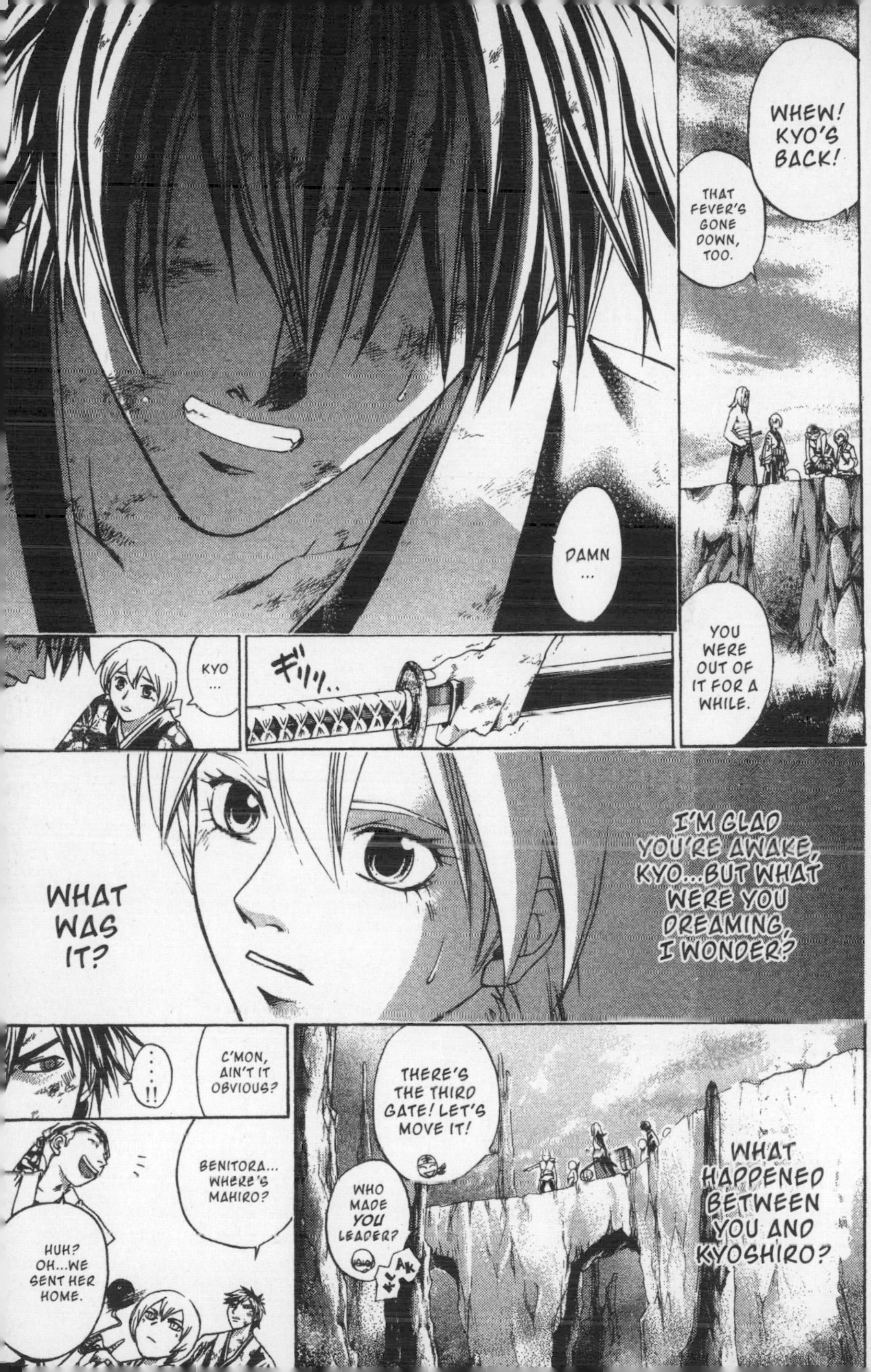
WHEW! KYO'S BACK!
THAT FEVER'S GONE DOWN, TOO.
YOU WERE OUT OF IT FOR A WHILE.
DAMN ...
ギリリ..
KYO ...
I'M GLAD YOU'RE AWAKE, KYO...BUT WHAT WERE YOU DREAMING, I WONDER?
WHAT WAS IT?
WHAT HAPPENED BETWEEN YOU AND KYOSHIRO?
THERE'S THE THIRD GATE! LET'S MOVE IT!
WHO MADE *YOU* LEADER?
C'MON, AIN'T IT OBVIOUS?
...!!
BENITORA... WHERE'S MAHIRO?
HUH? OH...WE SENT HER HOME.

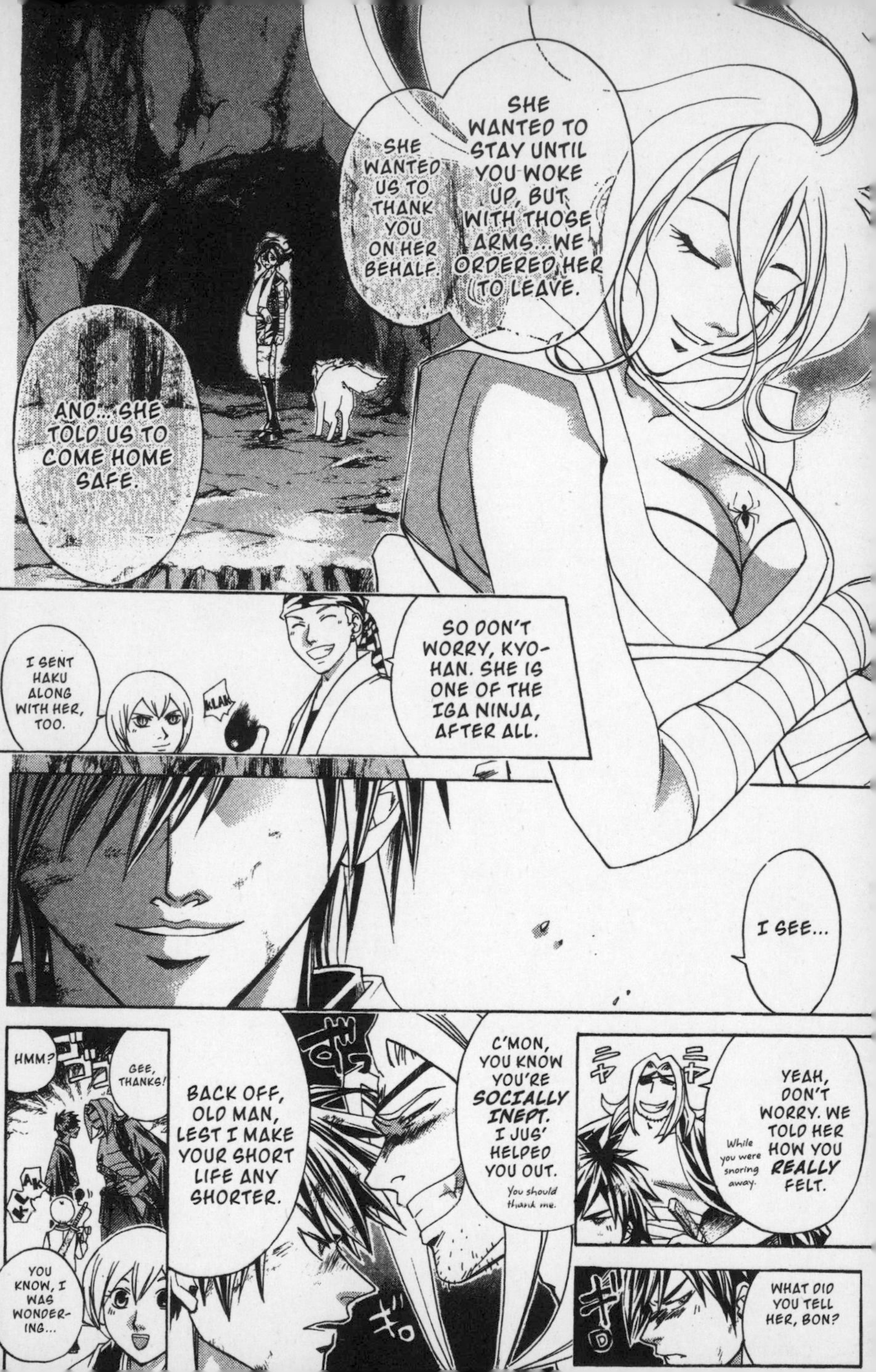
SHE WANTED TO STAY UNTIL YOU WOKE UP, BUT WITH THOSE ARMS...WE ORDERED HER TO LEAVE.
SHE WANTED US TO THANK YOU ON HER BEHALF.
AND... SHE TOLD US TO COME HOME SAFE.
SO DON'T WORRY, KYO-HAN. SHE IS ONE OF THE IGA NINJA, AFTER ALL.
KLAK
I SENT HAKU ALONG WITH HER, TOO.
I SEE...
YEAH, DON'T WORRY. WE TOLD HER HOW YOU **REALLY** FELT.
While you were snoring away.
WHAT DID YOU TELL HER, BON?
C'MON, YOU KNOW YOU'RE **SOCIALLY INEPT.** I JUS' HELPED YOU OUT.
You should thank me.
BACK OFF, OLD MAN, LEST I MAKE YOUR SHORT LIFE ANY SHORTER.
GEE, THANKS!
HMM?
AK
KL
YOU KNOW, I WAS WONDER-ING...

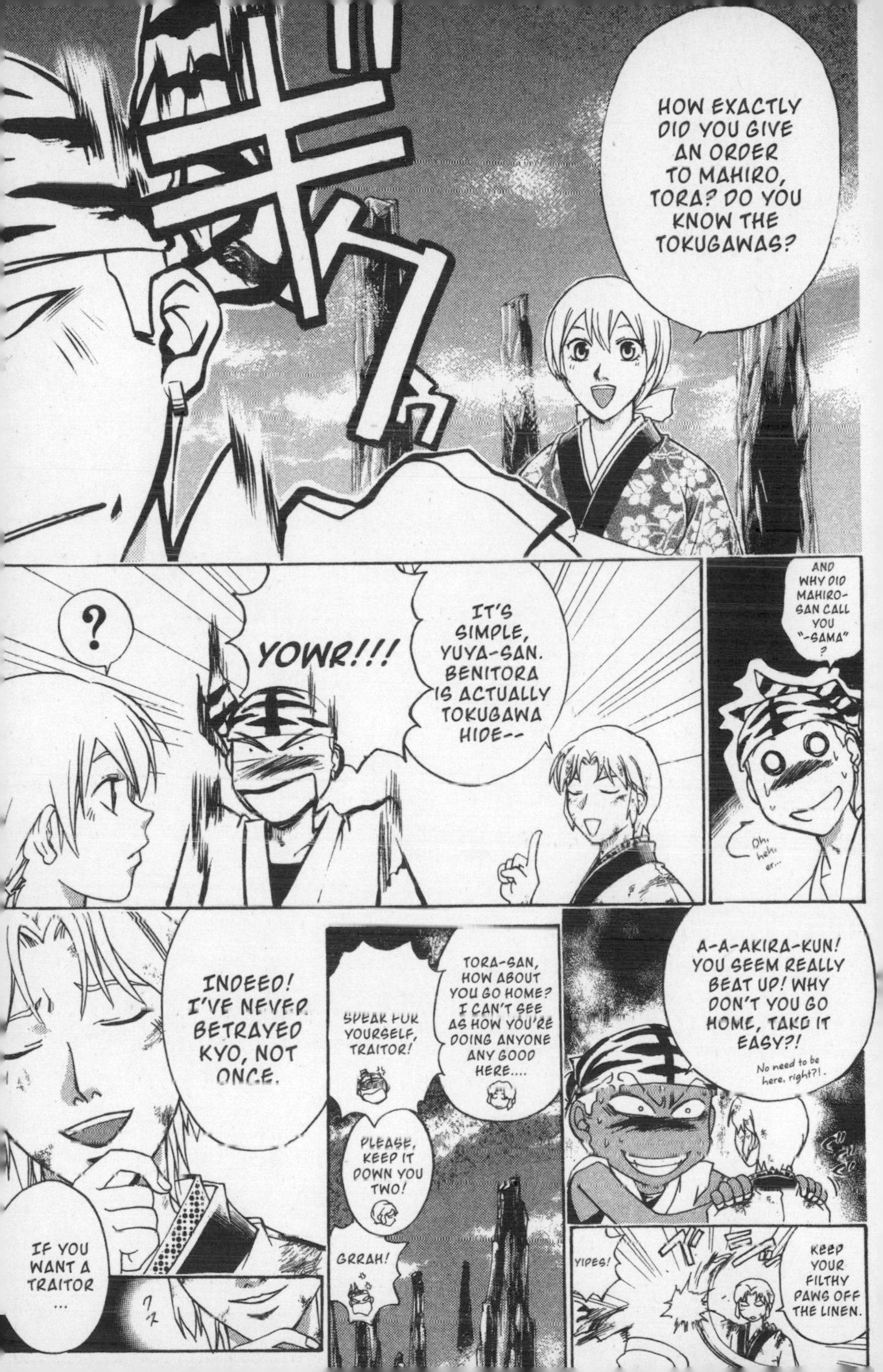
HOW EXACTLY DID YOU GIVE AN ORDER TO MAHIRO, TORA? DO YOU KNOW THE TOKUGAWAS?
AND WHY DID MAHIRO-SAN CALL YOU "-SAMA"?
Oh, heh, er...
IT'S SIMPLE, YUYA-SAN. BENITORA IS ACTUALLY TOKUGAWA HIDE--
YOWR!!!
?
A-A-AKIRA-KUN! YOU SEEM REALLY BEAT UP! WHY DON'T YOU GO HOME, TAKE IT EASY?!
No need to be here, right?!.
KEEP YOUR FILTHY PAWS OFF THE LINEN.
YIPES!
TORA-SAN, HOW ABOUT YOU GO HOME? I CAN'T SEE AS HOW YOU'RE DOING ANYONE ANY GOOD HERE....
SPEAK FOR YOURSELF, TRAITOR!
PLEASE, KEEP IT DOWN YOU TWO!
GRRAH!
INDEED! I'VE NEVER BETRAYED KYO, NOT ONCE.
IF YOU WANT A TRAITOR ...

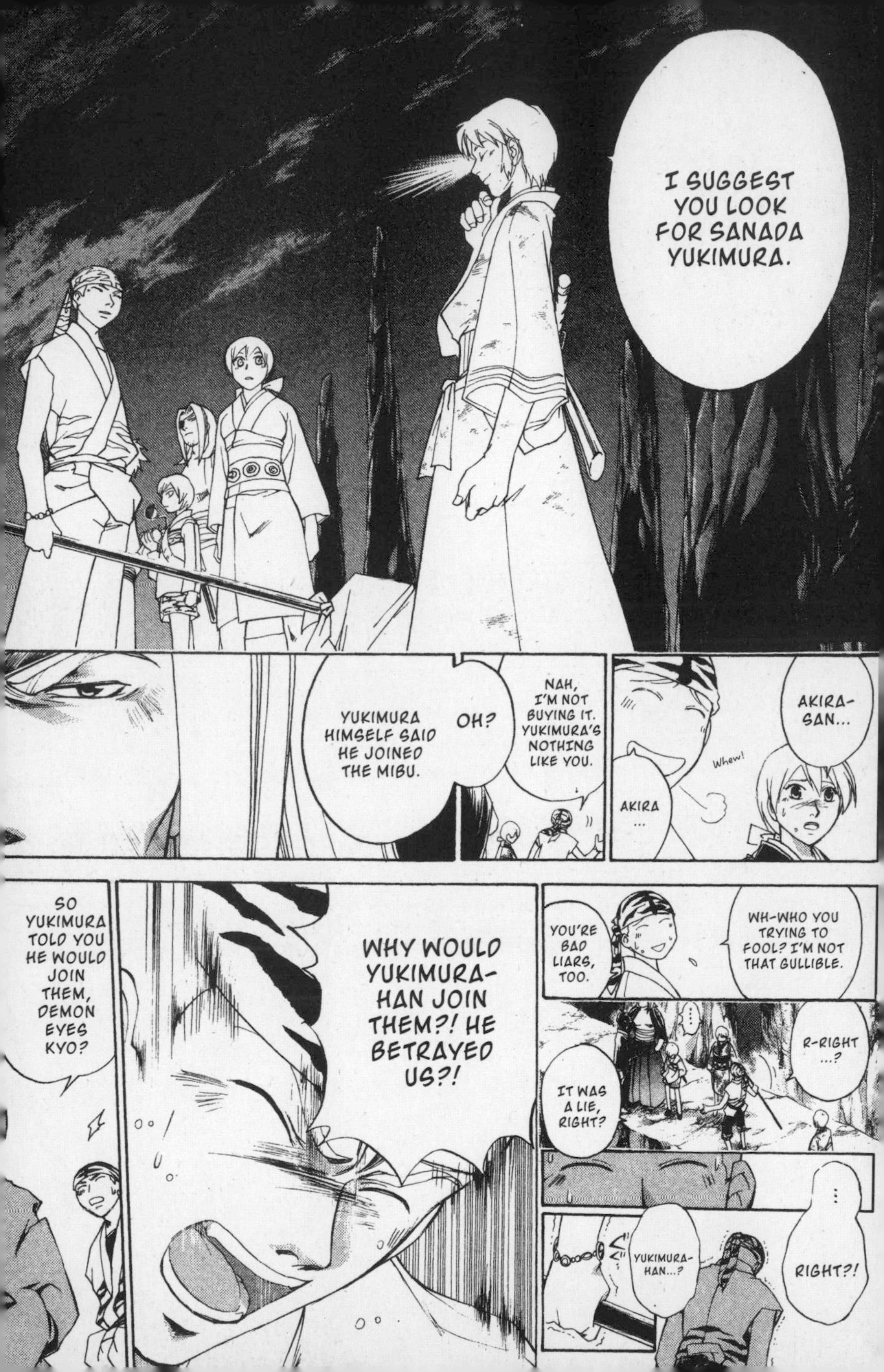
I SUGGEST YOU LOOK FOR SANADA YUKIMURA.
AKIRA-SAN...
Whew!
AKIRA ...
NAH, I'M NOT BUYING IT. YUKIMURA'S NOTHING LIKE YOU.
OH?
YUKIMURA HIMSELF SAID HE JOINED THE MIBU.
WH-WHO YOU TRYING TO FOOL? I'M NOT THAT GULLIBLE.
YOU'RE BAD LIARS, TOO.
R-RIGHT ...?
IT WAS A LIE, RIGHT?
...
...
RIGHT?!
YUKIMURA-HAN...?
WHY WOULD YUKIMURA-HAN JOIN THEM?! HE BETRAYED US?!
SO YUKIMURA TOLD YOU HE WOULD JOIN THEM, DEMON EYES KYO?

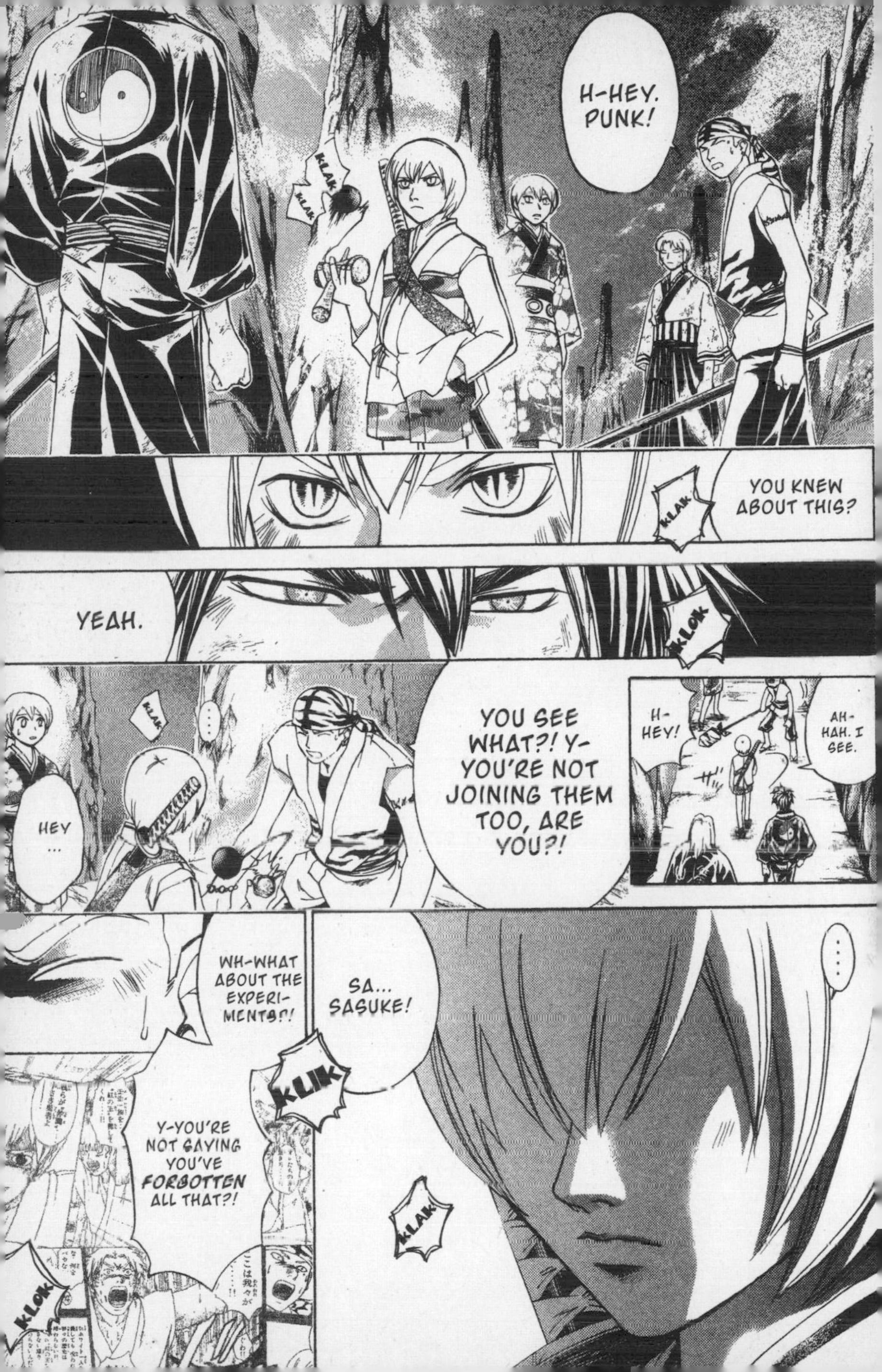
H-HEY. PUNK!
KLAK
KLAK
YOU KNEW ABOUT THIS?
KLAK
KLOK
YEAH.
AH-HAH. I SEE.
H-HEY!
YOU SEE WHAT?! Y-YOU'RE NOT JOINING THEM TOO, ARE YOU?!
KLAK
....
HEY ...
....
SA... SASUKE!
KLAK
WH-WHAT ABOUT THE EXPERIMENTS?!
KLIK
Y-YOU'RE NOT SAYING YOU'VE **FORGOTTEN** ALL THAT?!
KLOK

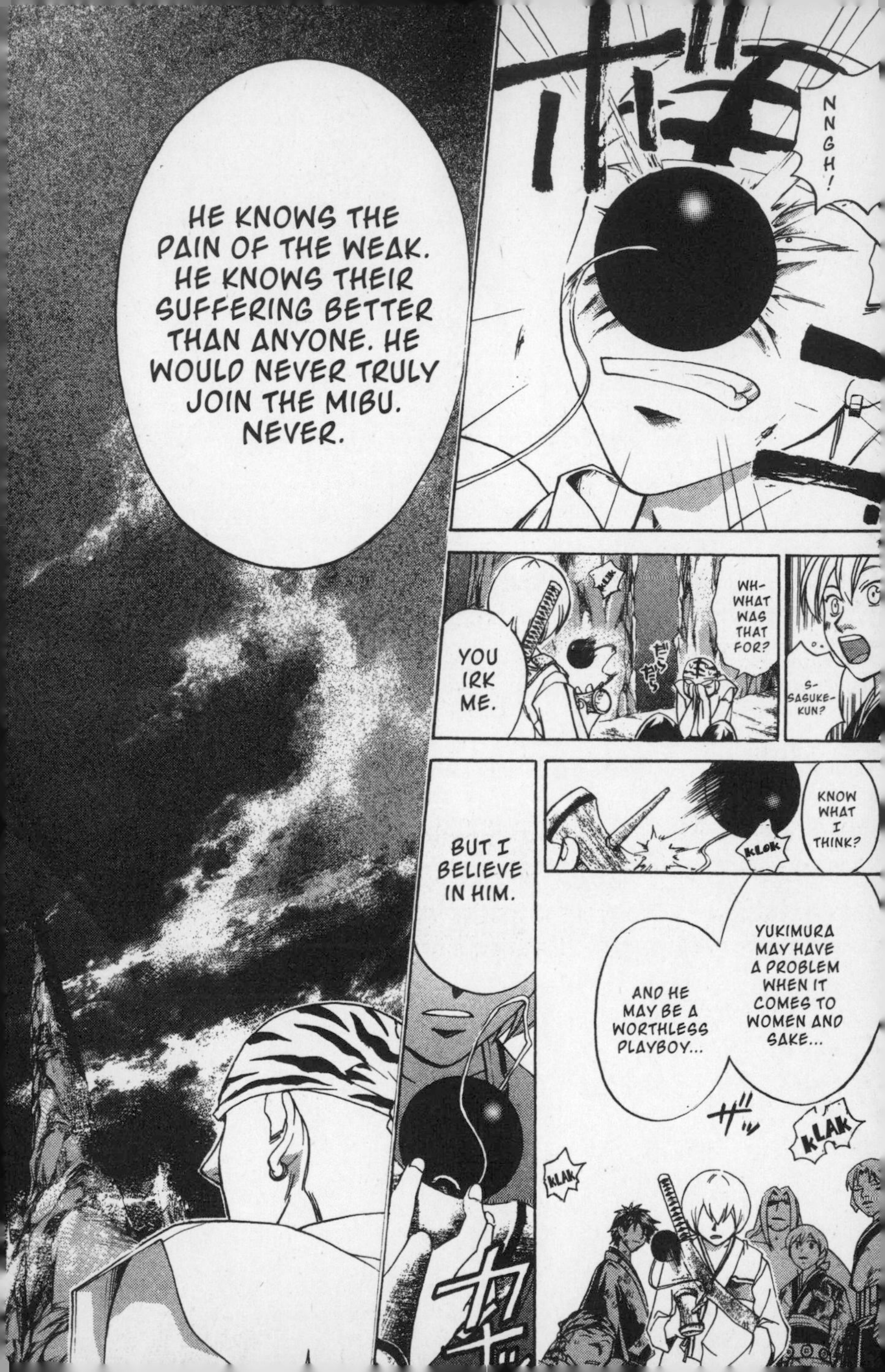
NNGH!
WH-WHAT WAS THAT FOR?
S-SASUKE-KUN?
KLAK
YOU IRK ME.
KNOW WHAT I THINK?
KLOK
YUKIMURA MAY HAVE A PROBLEM WHEN IT COMES TO WOMEN AND SAKE...
AND HE MAY BE A WORTHLESS PLAYBOY...
KLAK
KLAK
BUT I BELIEVE IN HIM.
HE KNOWS THE PAIN OF THE WEAK. HE KNOWS THEIR SUFFERING BETTER THAN ANYONE. HE WOULD NEVER TRULY JOIN THE MIBU. NEVER.

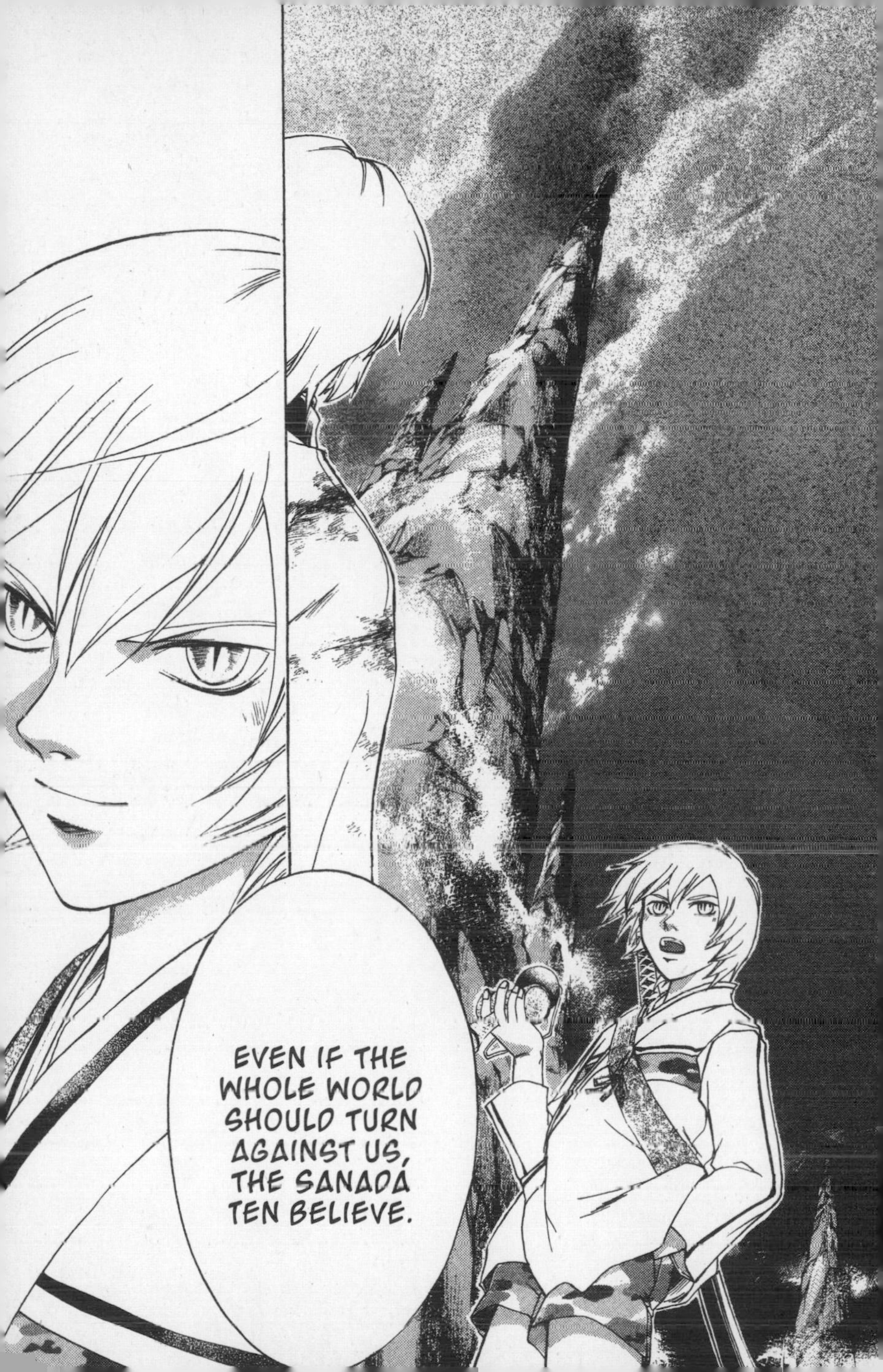
EVEN IF THE WHOLE WORLD SHOULD TURN AGAINST US, THE SANADA TEN BELIEVE.

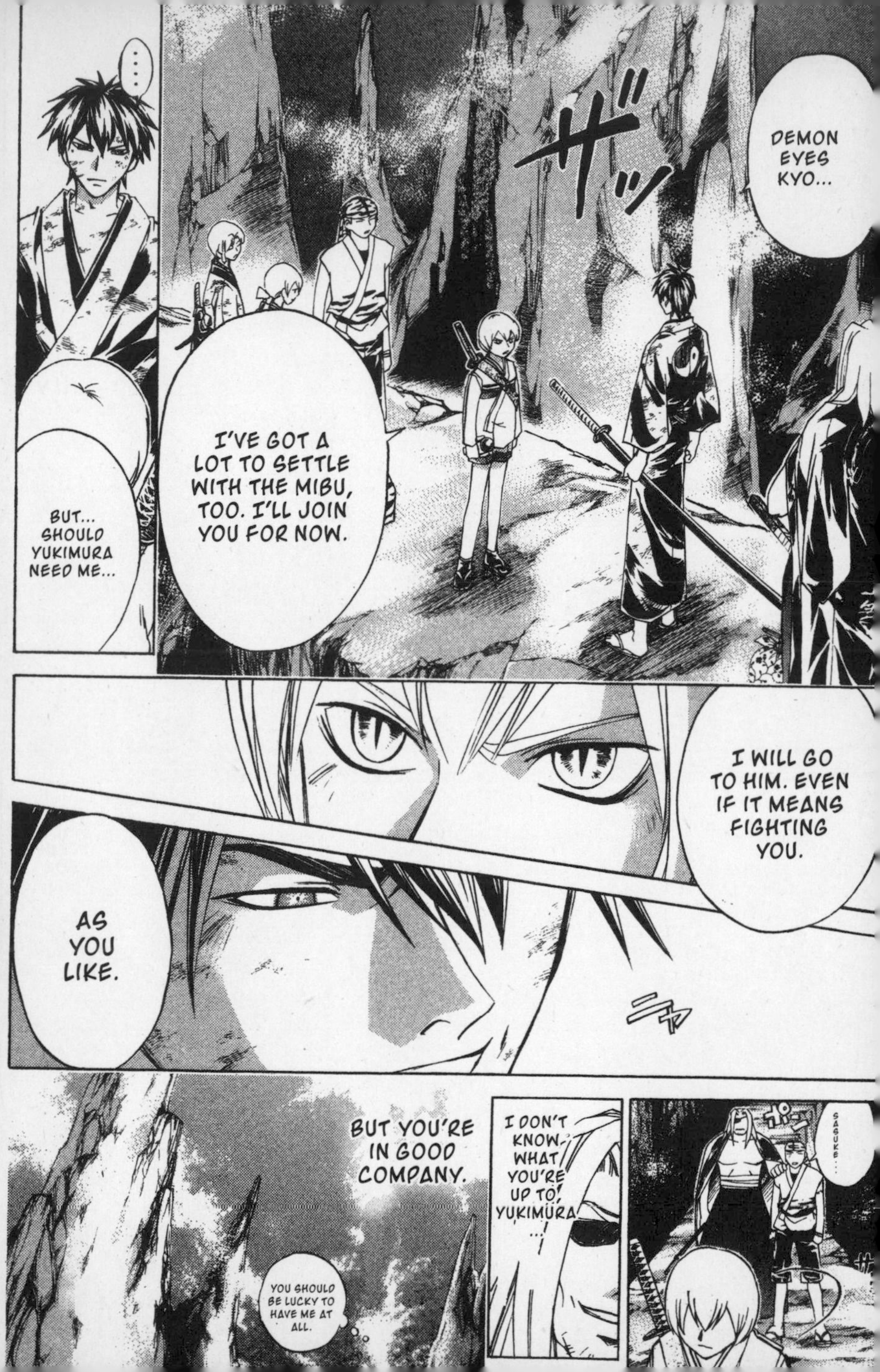
DEMON EYES KYO...
ザッ
I'VE GOT A LOT TO SETTLE WITH THE MIBU, TOO. I'LL JOIN YOU FOR NOW.
...
BUT... SHOULD YUKIMURA NEED ME...
I WILL GO TO HIM. EVEN IF IT MEANS FIGHTING YOU.
AS YOU LIKE.
ニヤ
SASUKE...
I DON'T KNOW WHAT YOU'RE UP TO, YUKIMURA...!
BUT YOU'RE IN GOOD COMPANY.
YOU SHOULD BE LUCKY TO HAVE ME AT ALL.

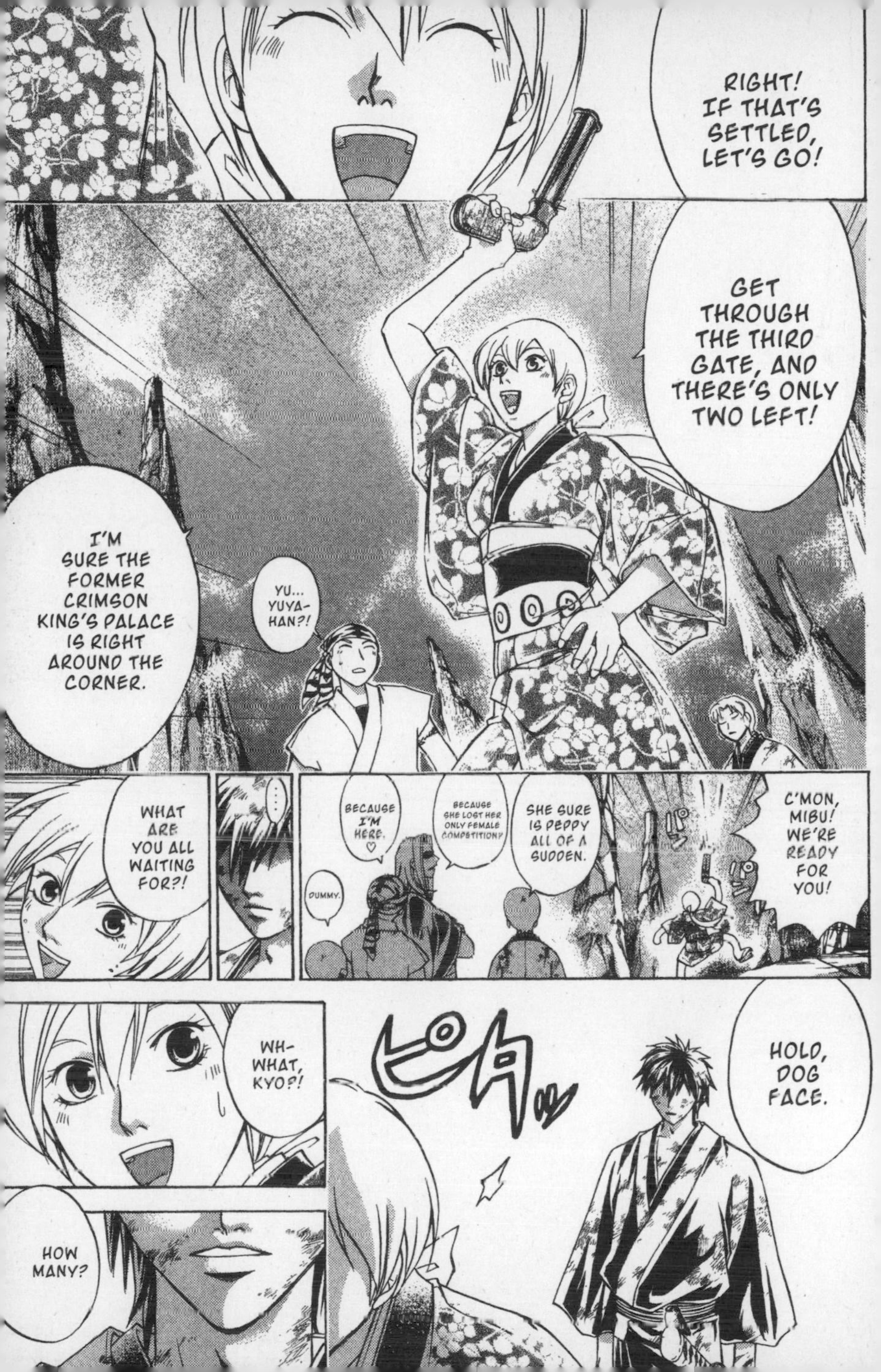
RIGHT! IF THAT'S SETTLED, LET'S GO!
GET THROUGH THE THIRD GATE, AND THERE'S ONLY TWO LEFT!
YU... YUYA-HAN?!
I'M SURE THE FORMER CRIMSON KING'S PALACE IS RIGHT AROUND THE CORNER.
C'MON, MIBU! WE'RE READY FOR YOU!
SHE SURE IS PEPPY ALL OF A SUDDEN.
BECAUSE SHE LOST HER ONLY FEMALE COMPETITION?
BECAUSE I'M HERE. ♡
DUMMY.
...
WHAT ARE YOU ALL WAITING FOR?!
HOLD, DOG FACE.
ピタッ
WH-WHAT, KYO?!
HOW MANY?

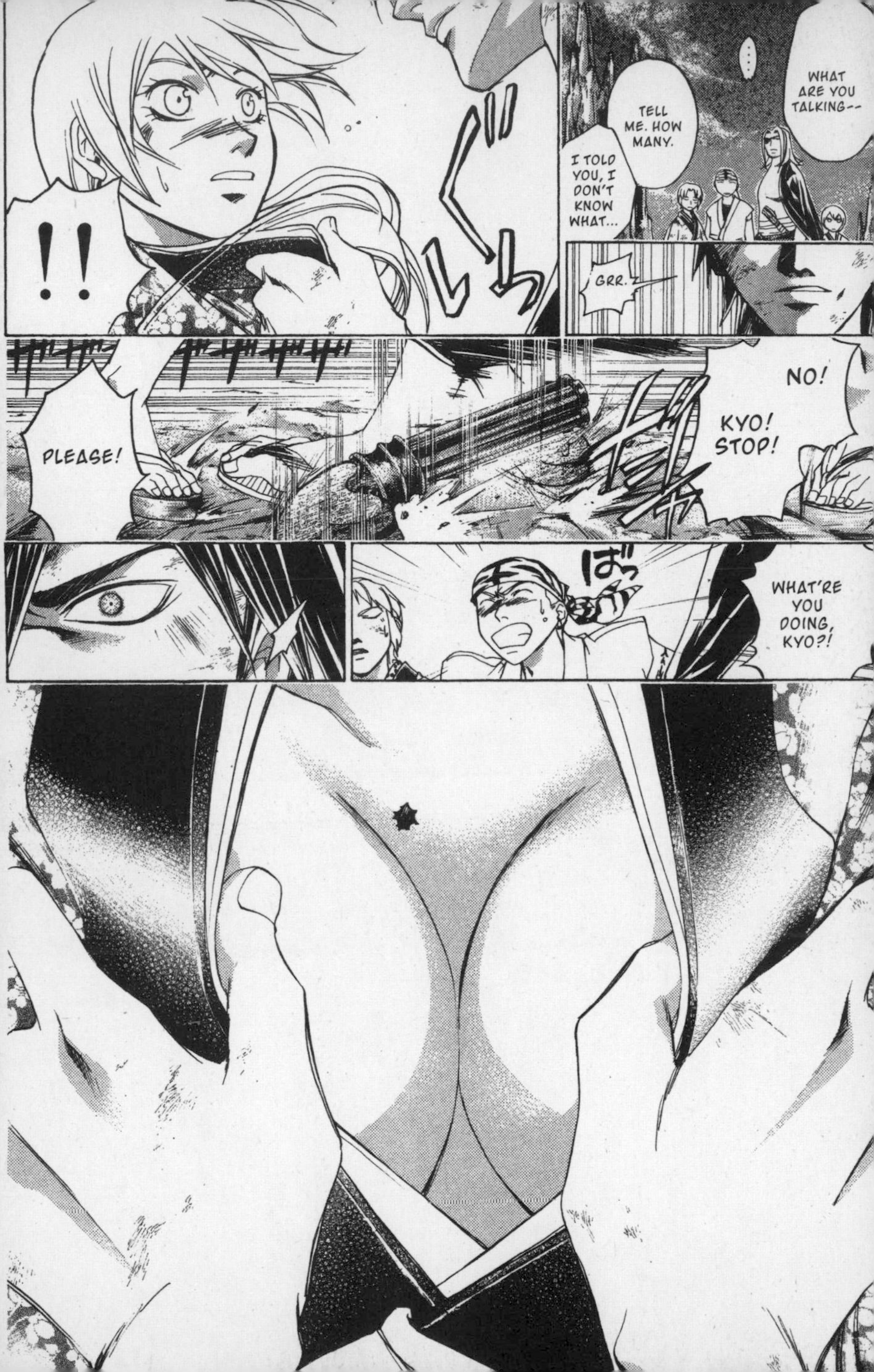
WHAT ARE YOU TALKING--
...
TELL ME. HOW MANY.
I TOLD YOU, I DON'T KNOW WHAT...
GRR.
!!
NO!
KYO! STOP!
PLEASE!
WHAT'RE YOU DOING, KYO?!
ばっ

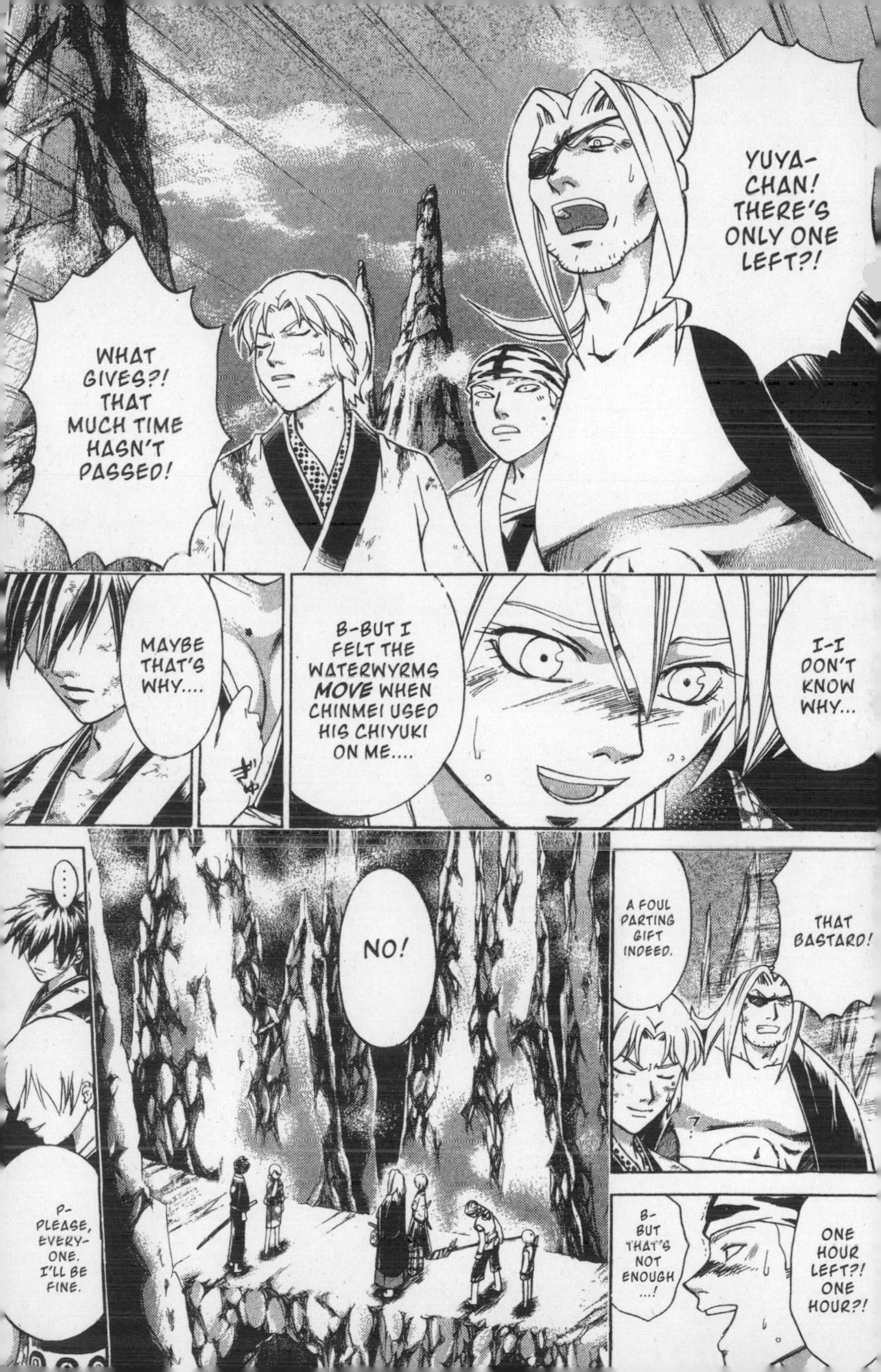
YUYA-CHAN! THERE'S ONLY ONE LEFT?!
WHAT GIVES?! THAT MUCH TIME HASN'T PASSED!
I-I DON'T KNOW WHY...
B-BUT I FELT THE WATERWYRMS *MOVE* WHEN CHINMEI USED HIS CHIYUKI ON ME....
MAYBE THAT'S WHY....
THAT BASTARD!
A FOUL PARTING GIFT INDEED.
ONE HOUR LEFT?! ONE HOUR?!
B-BUT THAT'S NOT ENOUGH...!
NO!
....
P-PLEASE, EVERYONE. I'LL BE FINE.

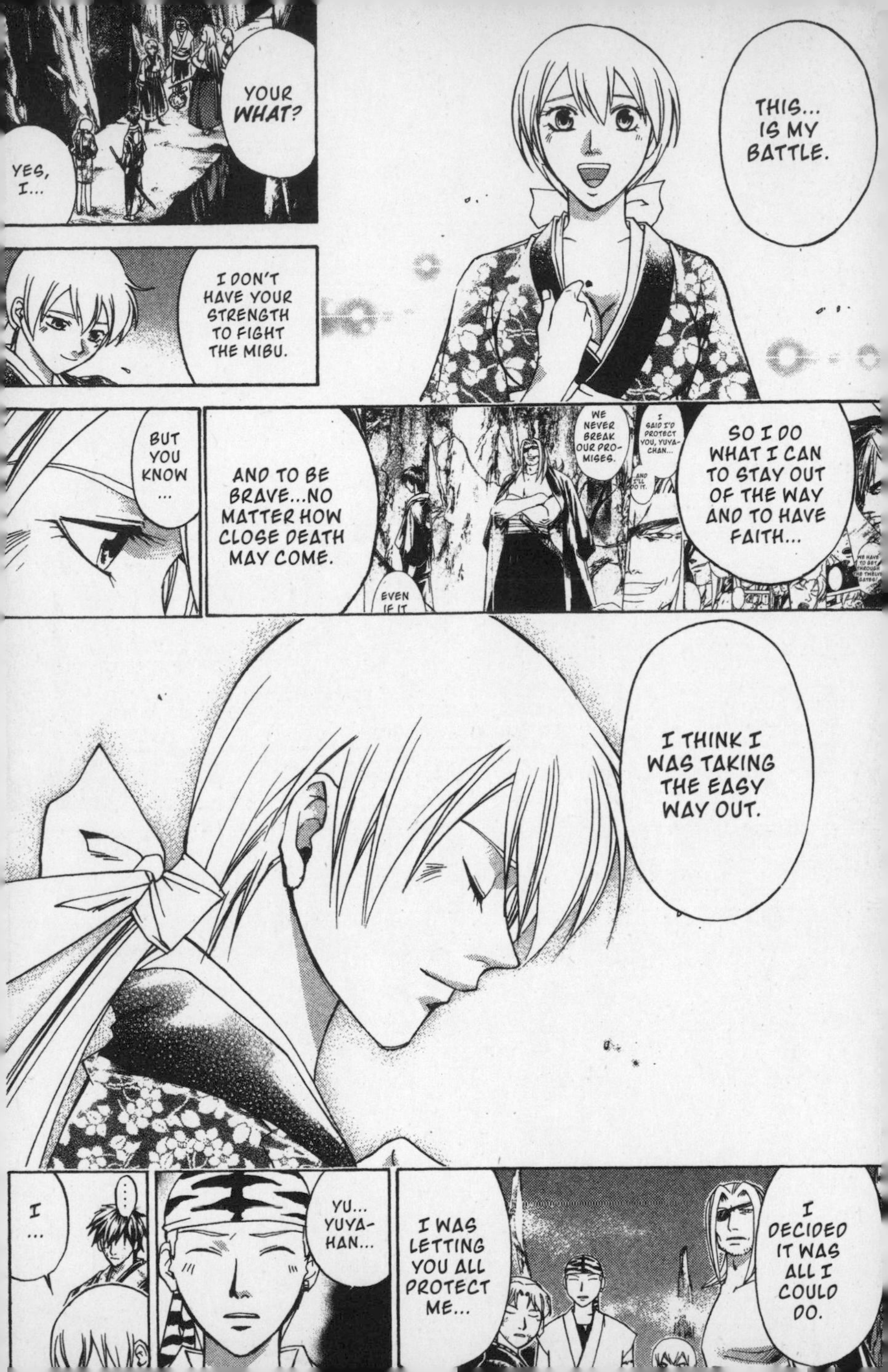
THIS... IS MY BATTLE.
YOUR WHAT?
YES, I...
I DON'T HAVE YOUR STRENGTH TO FIGHT THE MIBU.
SO I DO WHAT I CAN TO STAY OUT OF THE WAY AND TO HAVE FAITH...
I SAID I'D PROTECT YOU, YUYA-CHAN...
AND I'LL DO IT.
WE NEVER BREAK OUR PROMISES.
EVEN IF IT
AND TO BE BRAVE...NO MATTER HOW CLOSE DEATH MAY COME.
BUT YOU KNOW ...
I THINK I WAS TAKING THE EASY WAY OUT.
I DECIDED IT WAS ALL I COULD DO.
I WAS LETTING YOU ALL PROTECT ME...
YU... YUYA-HAN...
...
I ...

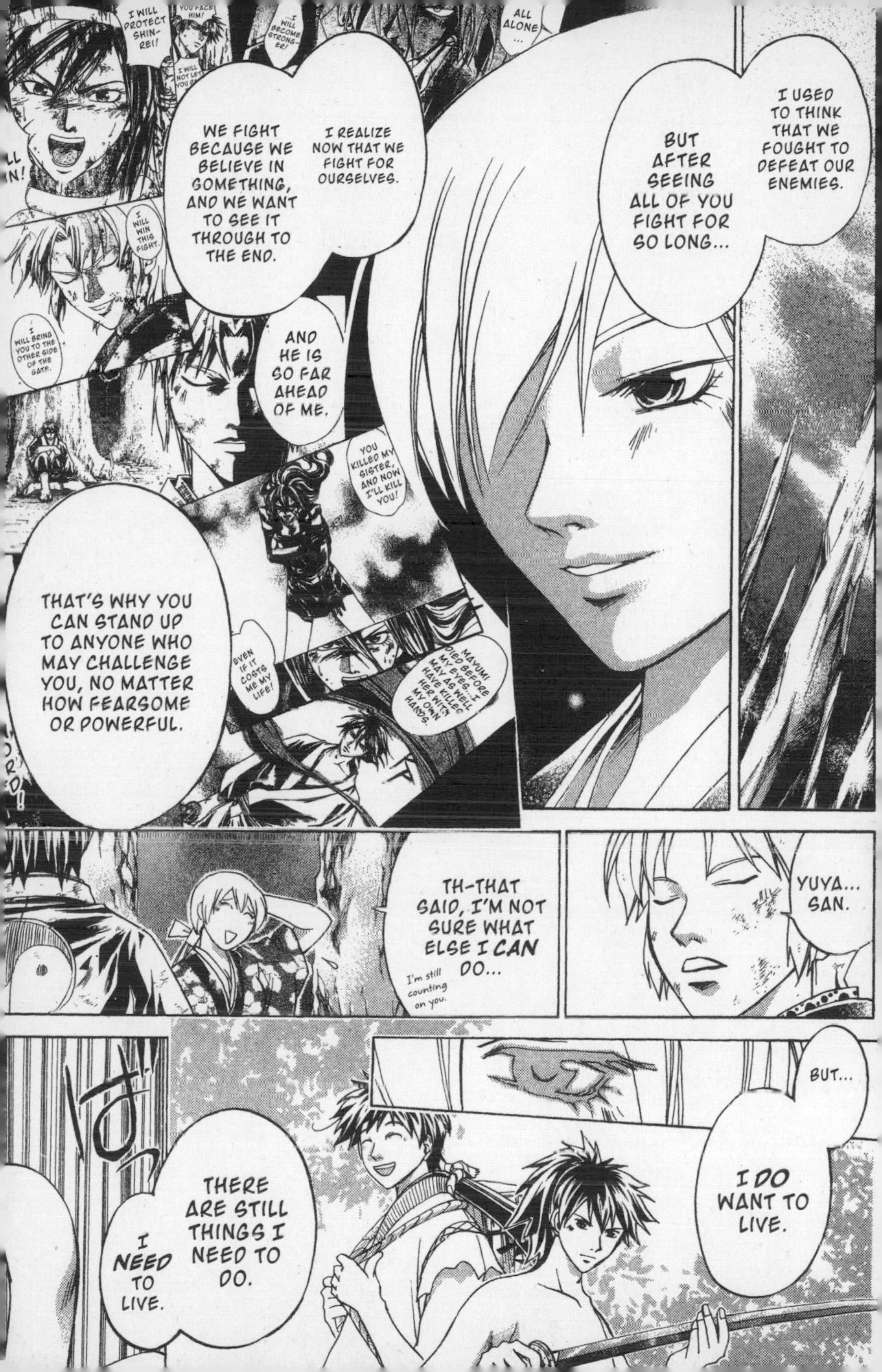
ALL ALONE ...
...I WILL BECOME STRONGER!
YOU FACE HIM!
I WILL NOT LET YOU GO
I WILL PROTECT SHIN-REI!
I USED TO THINK THAT WE FOUGHT TO DEFEAT OUR ENEMIES.
BUT AFTER SEEING ALL OF YOU FIGHT FOR SO LONG...
I REALIZE NOW THAT WE FIGHT FOR OURSELVES.
WE FIGHT BECAUSE WE BELIEVE IN SOMETHING, AND WE WANT TO SEE IT THROUGH TO THE END.
I WILL WIN THIS FIGHT.
AND HE IS SO FAR AHEAD OF ME.
I WILL BRING YOU TO THE OTHER SIDE OF THE GATE.
YOU KILLED MY SISTER, AND NOW I'LL KILL YOU!
MAYUMI DIED BEFORE MY EYES... I MAY AS WELL HAVE KILLED HER WITH MY OWN HANDS.
EVEN IF IT COSTS ME MY LIFE!
THAT'S WHY YOU CAN STAND UP TO ANYONE WHO MAY CHALLENGE YOU, NO MATTER HOW FEARSOME OR POWERFUL.
YUYA... SAN.
TH-THAT SAID, I'M NOT SURE WHAT ELSE I CAN DO...
I'm still counting on you.
BUT...
I DO WANT TO LIVE.
THERE ARE STILL THINGS I NEED TO DO.
I NEED TO LIVE.
はっ

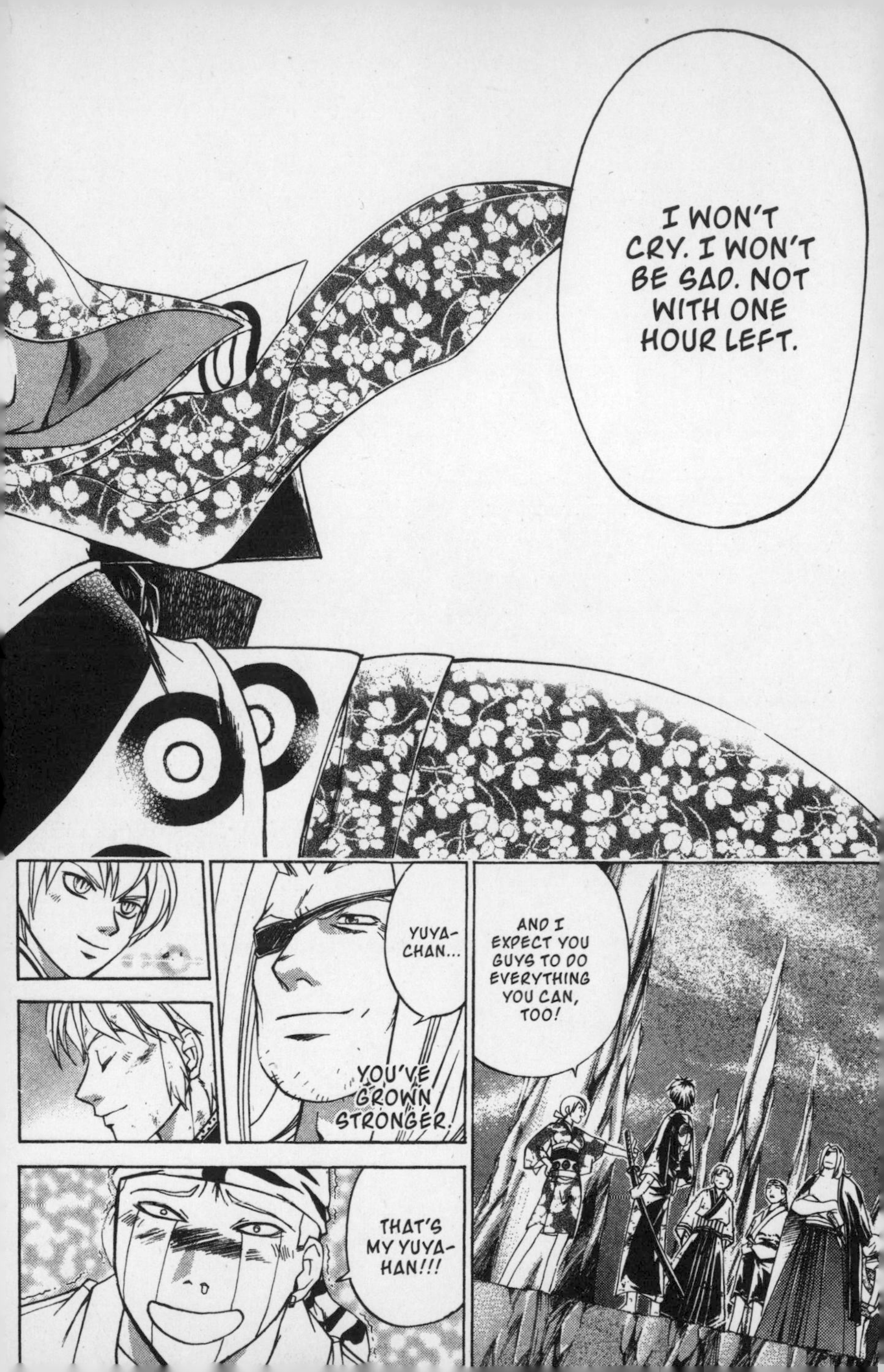
I WON'T CRY. I WON'T BE SAD. NOT WITH ONE HOUR LEFT.
AND I EXPECT YOU GUYS TO DO EVERYTHING YOU CAN, TOO!
YUYA-CHAN...
YOU'VE GROWN STRONGER.
THAT'S MY YUYA-HAN!!!

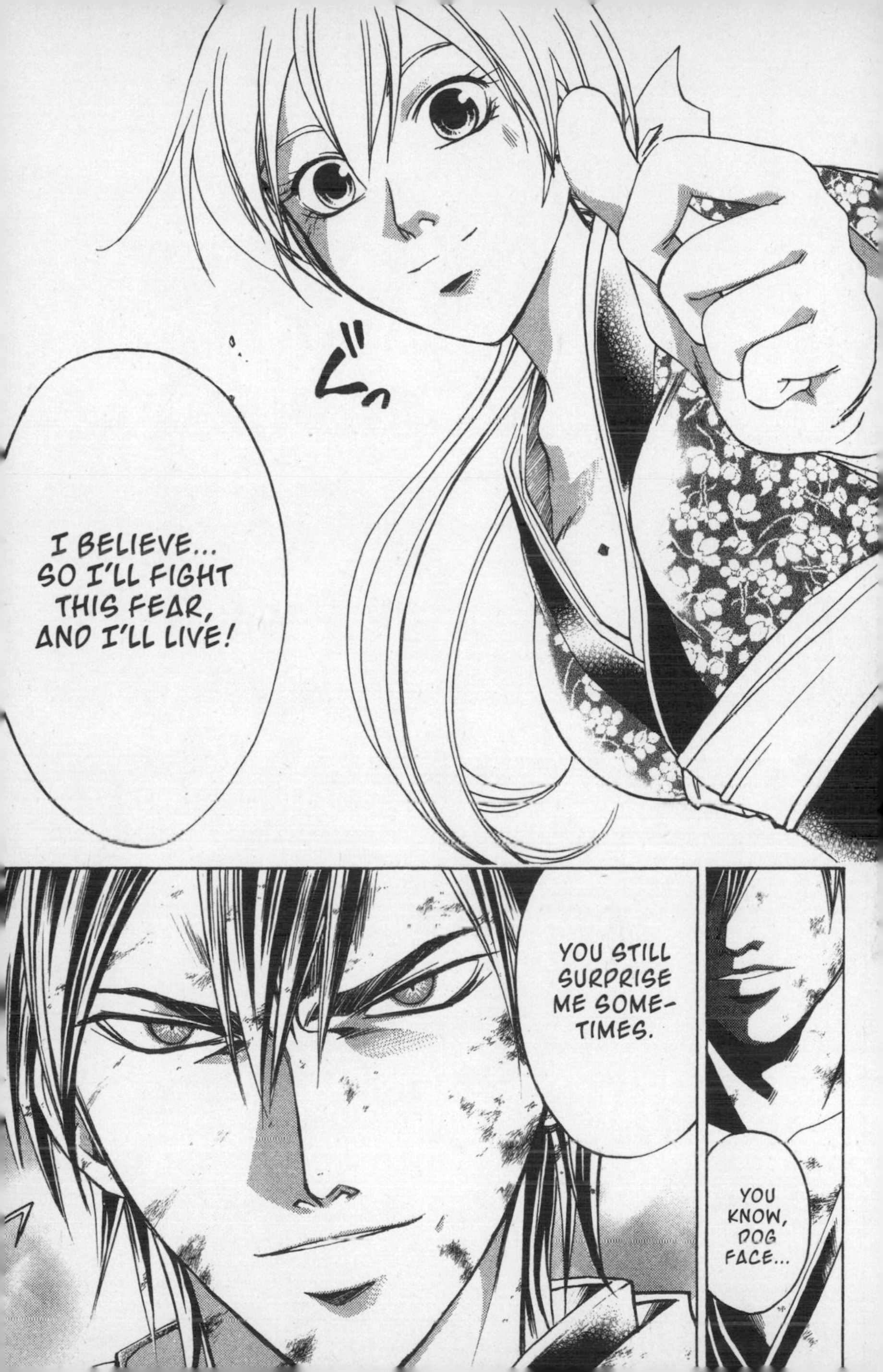
ぐっ
I BELIEVE... SO I'LL FIGHT THIS FEAR, AND I'LL LIVE!
YOU KNOW, DOG FACE...
YOU STILL SURPRISE ME SOME-TIMES.

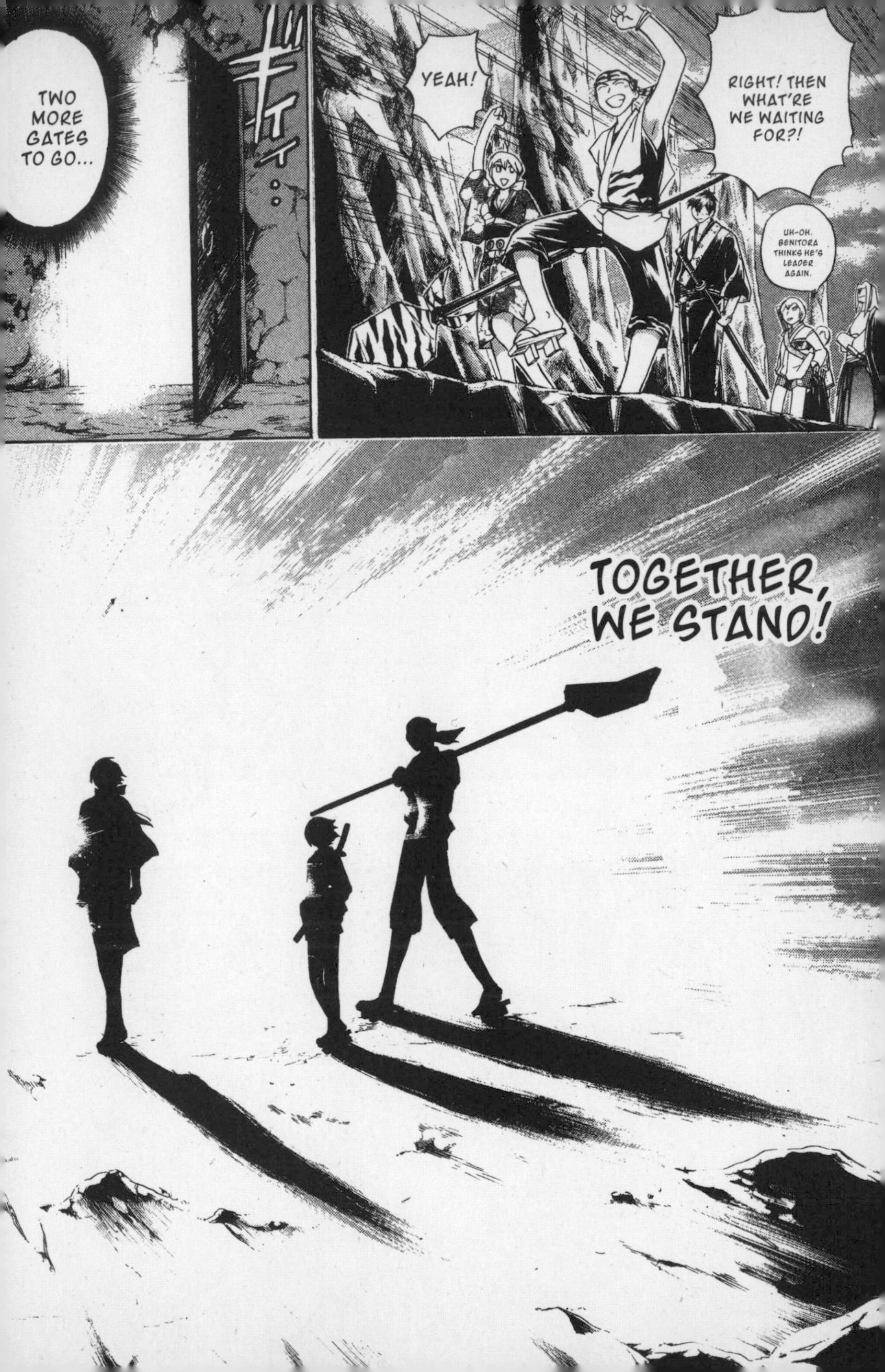
RIGHT! THEN WHAT'RE WE WAITING FOR?!
YEAH!
UH-OH. BENITORA THINKS HE'S LEADER AGAIN.
TWO MORE GATES TO GO...
TOGETHER, WE STAND!

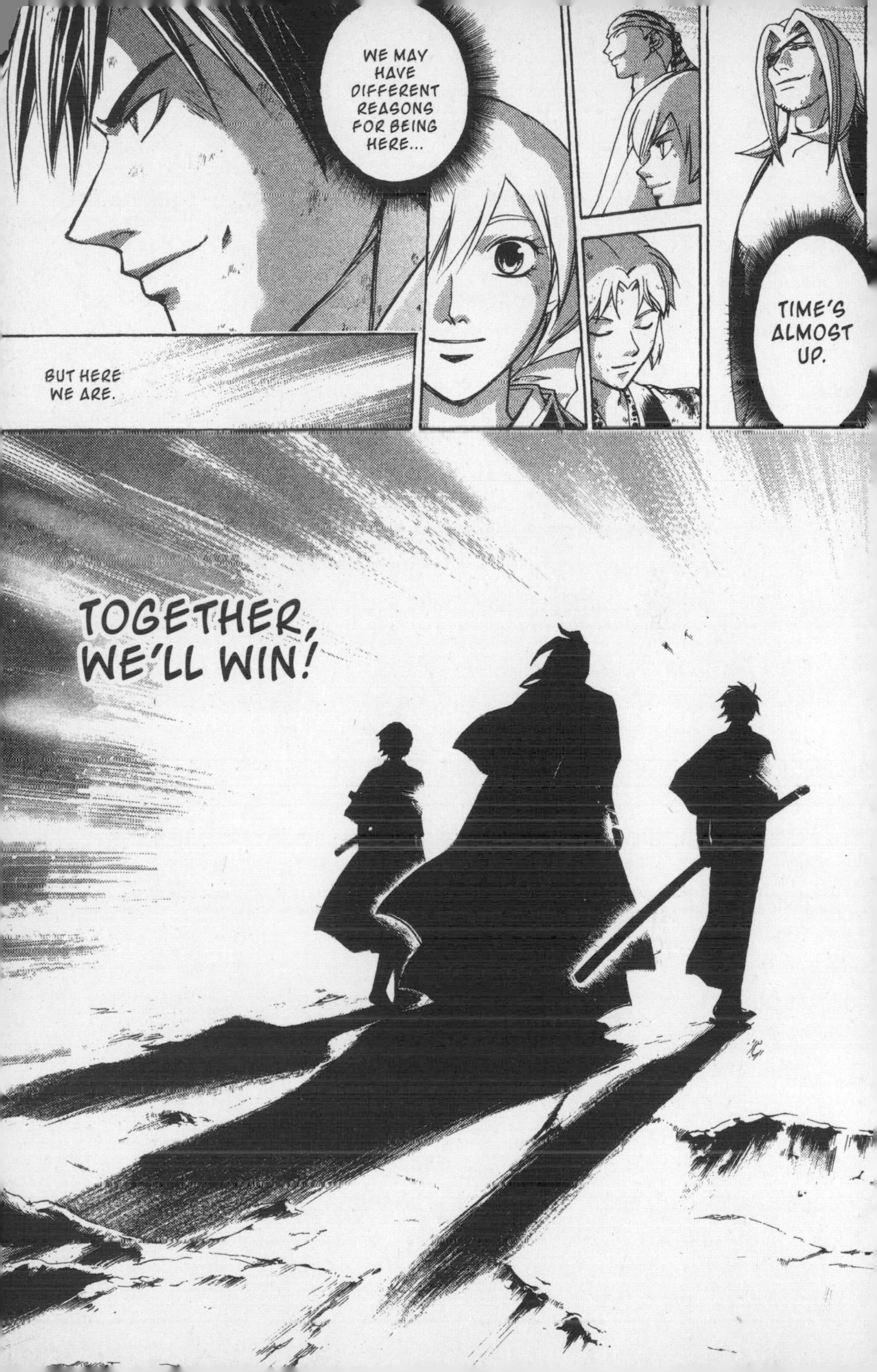
TIME'S ALMOST UP.
WE MAY HAVE DIFFERENT REASONS FOR BEING HERE...
BUT HERE WE ARE.
TOGETHER, WE'LL WIN!

Q&A CORNER

SDK

Q: Do you choose the chapter titles, Kamijyo-sensei?

A: Of course! My favorite so far is from Chapter 18: Cherry Blossoms in Full Bloom, Flying Crows Keeps Singing Quietly...

Q: When the attacks are going so fast they can't be seen, why does everyone say "he hit 'im three, no, five times!"

A: Because that's the number they could see! :)

Q: When Bontenmaru and Tokito were fighting in the Chamber of Time in Chapter One Hundred Nineteen, "Threads of Fate," didn't they break or at least put out a ton of candles? And doesn't that mean they killed a lot of people?!

A: C'mon, this is one of the Four Emperors and one of the Four Elders you're talking about! They could fight with one arm tied behind their backs and STILL not put out any candles! So, nobody died. :)

Q: I've been a member of the Mibu Clan for three years now, so you can imagine my surprise when I saw the "members wanted" add on the back flap of Volume 12. I had to buy my own costume (at the Mibu Dept. Store), and I didn't get no biannual bonus!

A: As you surely know, the Mibu can't have children. With the population dwindling, they've been forced to offer incentives to encourage people to join! In fact, you should be getting your friends to join, too! Of course, Kyo and friends might come along and kill you, so I can't guarantee your safety.

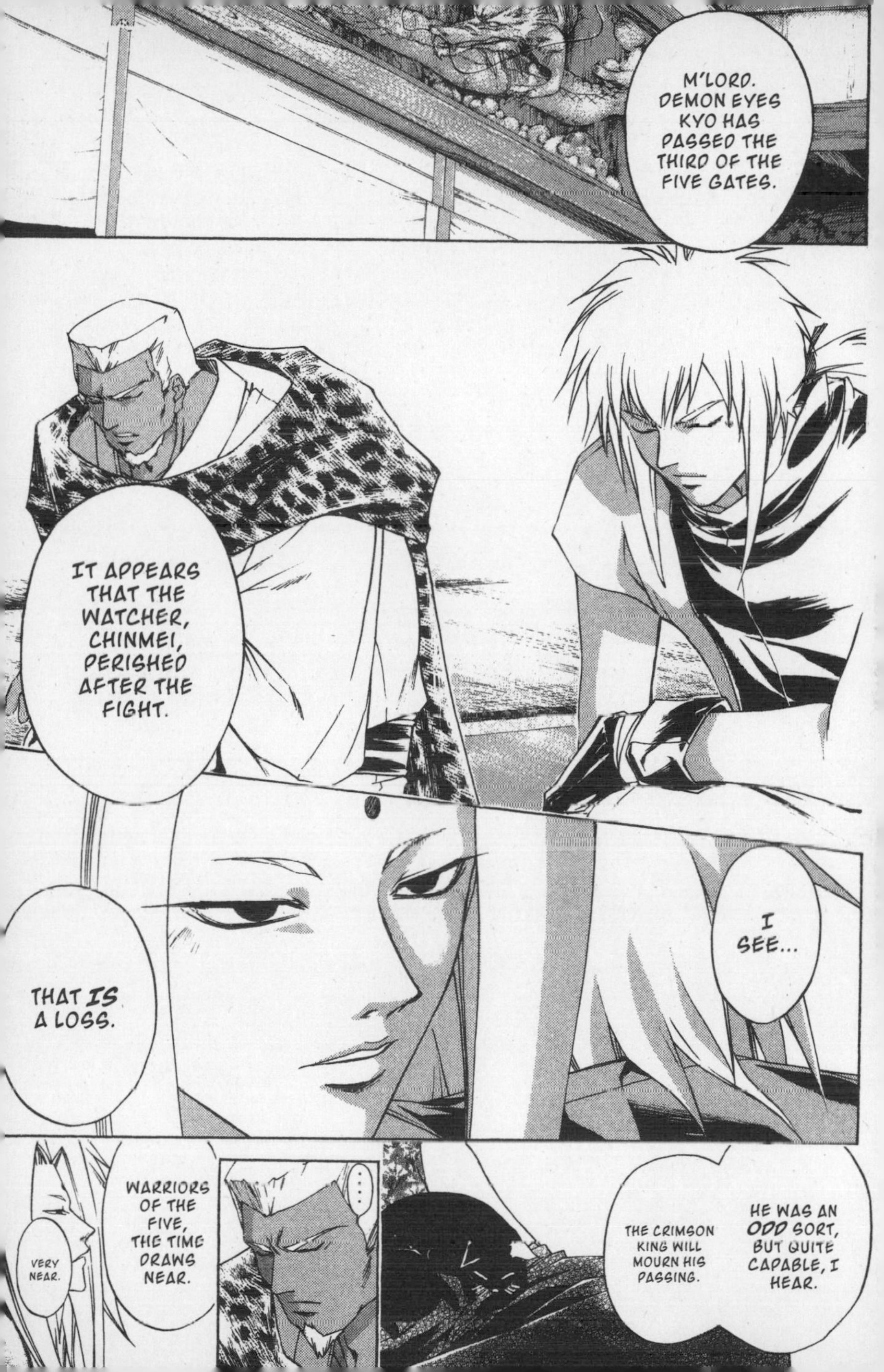
M'LORD. DEMON EYES KYO HAS PASSED THE THIRD OF THE FIVE GATES.
IT APPEARS THAT THE WATCHER, CHINMEI, PERISHED AFTER THE FIGHT.
I SEE...
THAT *IS* A LOSS.
HE WAS AN *ODD* SORT, BUT QUITE CAPABLE, I HEAR.
THE CRIMSON KING WILL MOURN HIS PASSING.
....
WARRIORS OF THE FIVE, THE TIME DRAWS NEAR.
VERY NEAR.

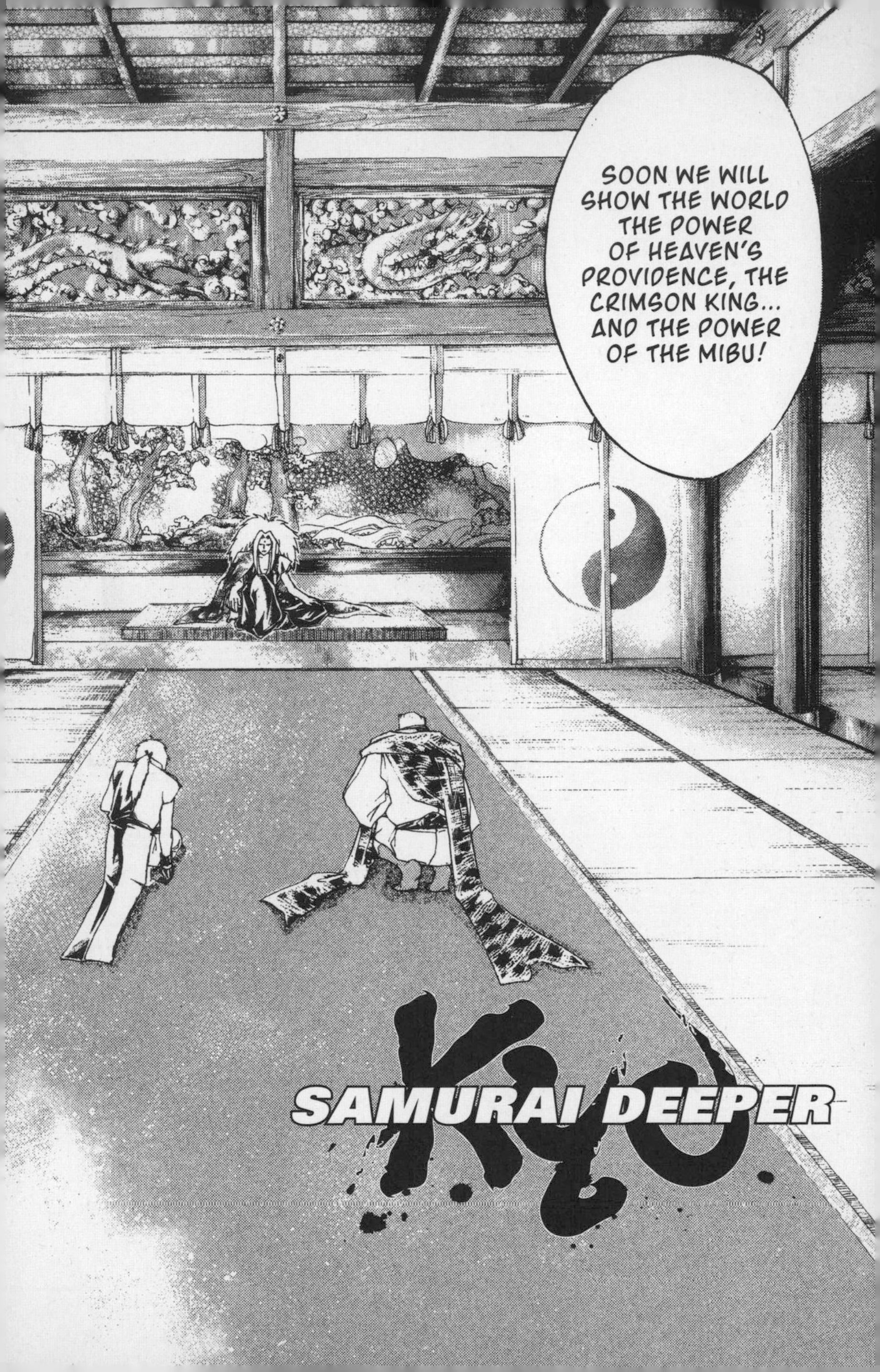
SOON WE WILL SHOW THE WORLD THE POWER OF HEAVEN'S PROVIDENCE, THE CRIMSON KING... AND THE POWER OF THE MIBU!
SAMURAI DEEPER KYO

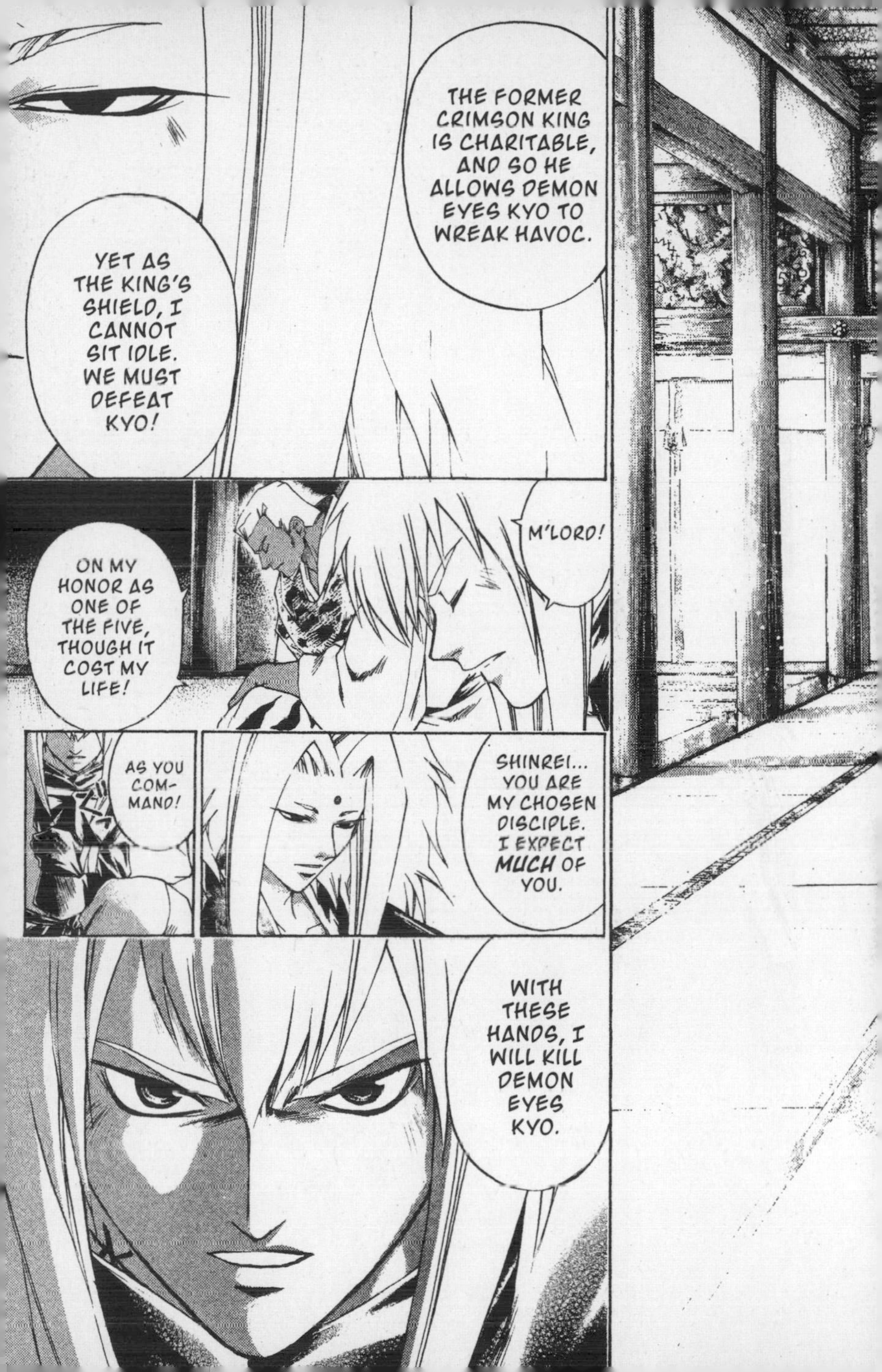
THE FORMER CRIMSON KING IS CHARITABLE, AND SO HE ALLOWS DEMON EYES KYO TO WREAK HAVOC.
YET AS THE KING'S SHIELD, I CANNOT SIT IDLE. WE MUST DEFEAT KYO!
M'LORD!
ON MY HONOR AS ONE OF THE FIVE, THOUGH IT COST MY LIFE!
SHINREI... YOU ARE MY CHOSEN DISCIPLE. I EXPECT *MUCH* OF YOU.
AS YOU COM-MAND!
WITH THESE HANDS, I WILL KILL DEMON EYES KYO.

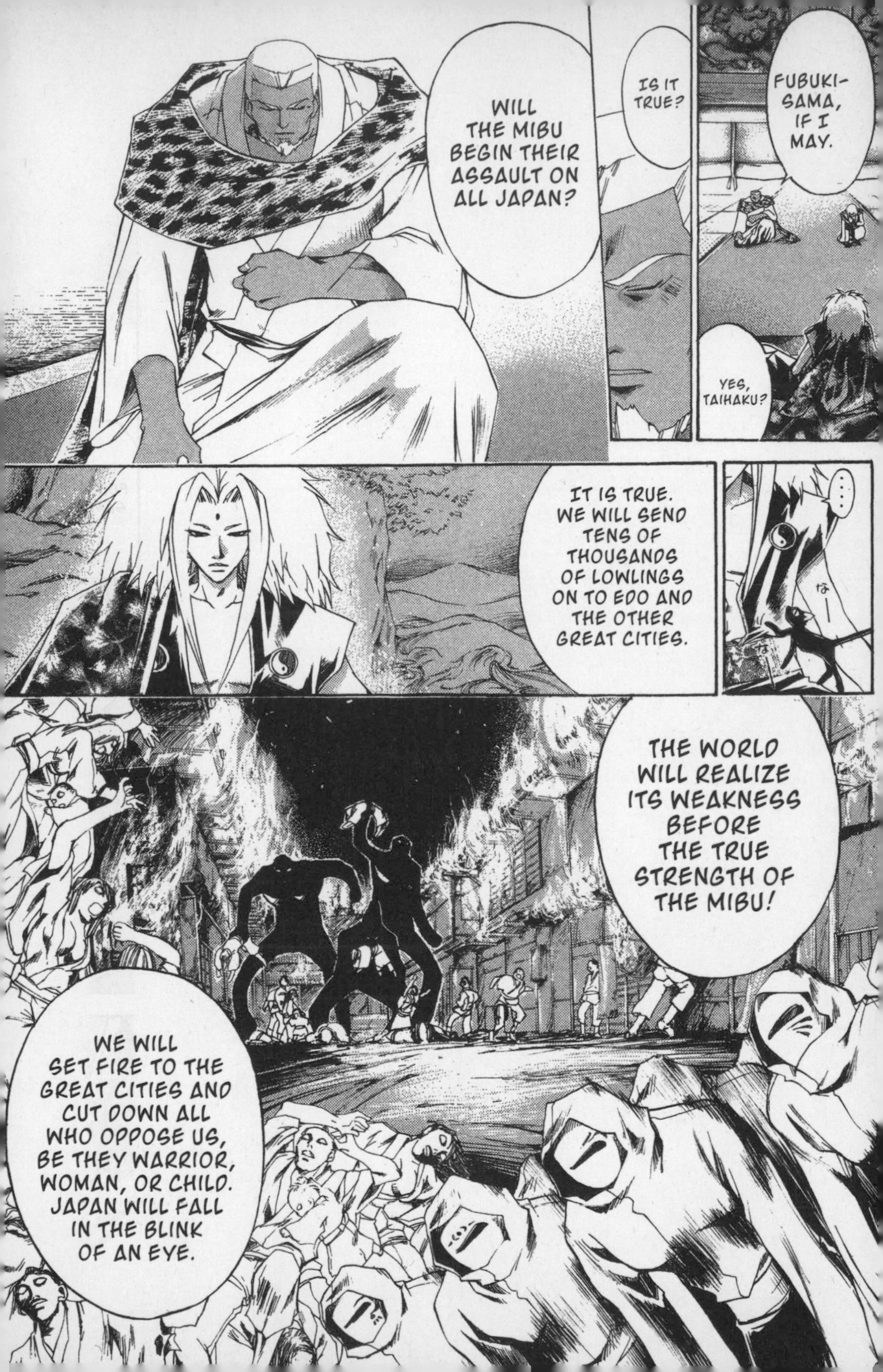
FUBUKI-SAMA, IF I MAY.
YES, TAIHAKU?
IS IT TRUE?
WILL THE MIBU BEGIN THEIR ASSAULT ON ALL JAPAN?
...
な
IT IS TRUE. WE WILL SEND TENS OF THOUSANDS OF LOWLINGS ON TO EDO AND THE OTHER GREAT CITIES.
THE WORLD WILL REALIZE ITS WEAKNESS BEFORE THE TRUE STRENGTH OF THE MIBU!
WE WILL SET FIRE TO THE GREAT CITIES AND CUT DOWN ALL WHO OPPOSE US, BE THEY WARRIOR, WOMAN, OR CHILD. JAPAN WILL FALL IN THE BLINK OF AN EYE.

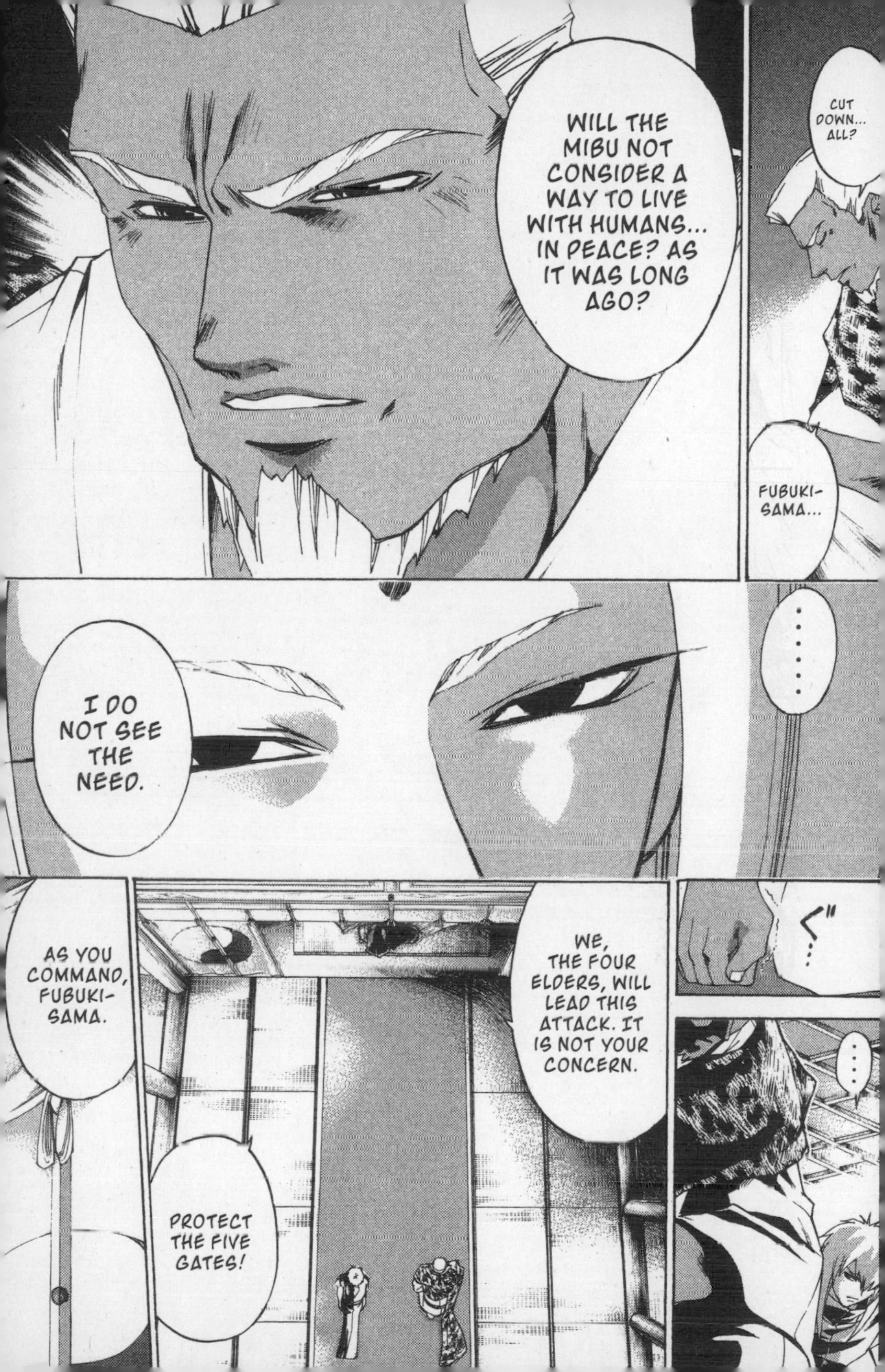
CUT DOWN... ALL?
FUBUKI-SAMA...
WILL THE MIBU NOT CONSIDER A WAY TO LIVE WITH HUMANS... IN PEACE? AS IT WAS LONG AGO?
......
I DO NOT SEE THE NEED.
....
WE, THE FOUR ELDERS, WILL LEAD THIS ATTACK. IT IS NOT YOUR CONCERN.
PROTECT THE FIVE GATES!
AS YOU COMMAND, FUBUKI-SAMA.

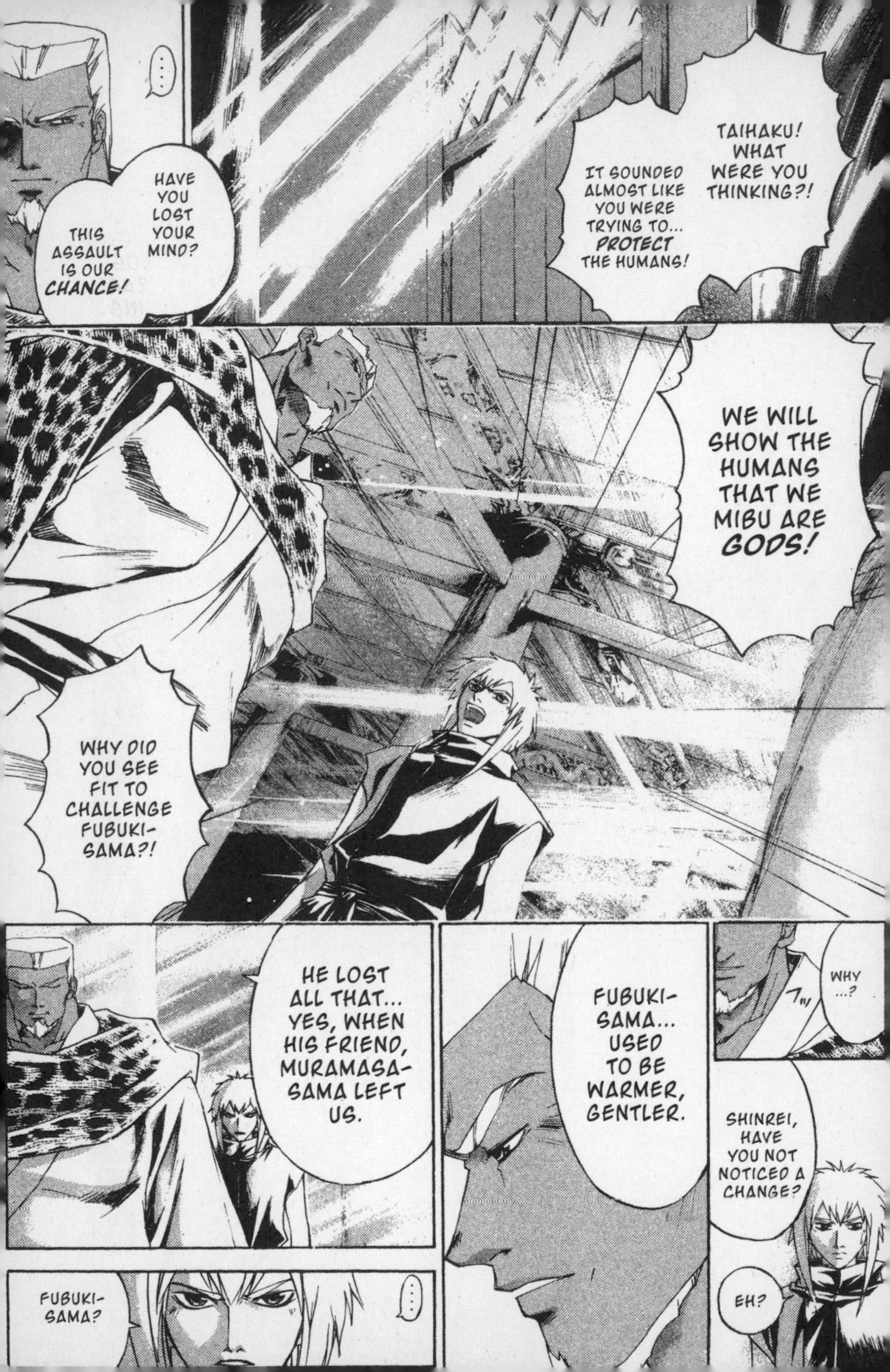
TAIHAKU! WHAT WERE YOU THINKING?!
IT SOUNDED ALMOST LIKE YOU WERE TRYING TO... PROTECT THE HUMANS!
. . . .
HAVE YOU LOST YOUR MIND?
THIS ASSAULT IS OUR CHANCE!
WE WILL SHOW THE HUMANS THAT WE MIBU ARE GODS!
WHY DID YOU SEE FIT TO CHALLENGE FUBUKI-SAMA?!
WHY ...?
SHINREI, HAVE YOU NOT NOTICED A CHANGE?
EH?
FUBUKI-SAMA... USED TO BE WARMER, GENTLER.
HE LOST ALL THAT... YES, WHEN HIS FRIEND, MURAMASA-SAMA LEFT US.
. . . .
FUBUKI-SAMA?

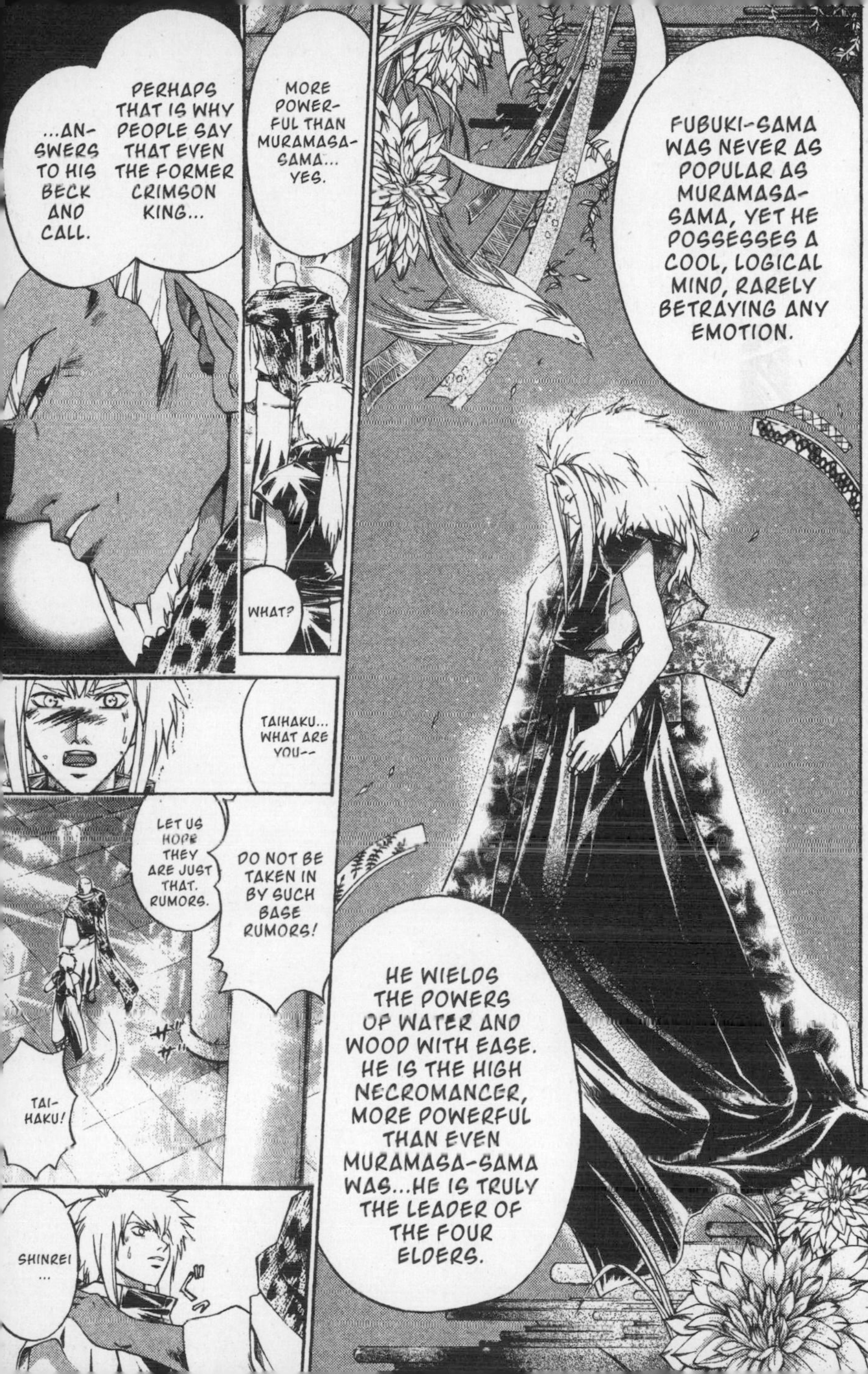
FUBUKI-SAMA WAS NEVER AS POPULAR AS MURAMASA-SAMA, YET HE POSSESSES A COOL, LOGICAL MIND, RARELY BETRAYING ANY EMOTION.
HE WIELDS THE POWERS OF WATER AND WOOD WITH EASE. HE IS THE HIGH NECROMANCER, MORE POWERFUL THAN EVEN MURAMASA-SAMA WAS...HE IS TRULY THE LEADER OF THE FOUR ELDERS.
MORE POWER-FUL THAN MURAMASA-SAMA... YES.
WHAT?
PERHAPS THAT IS WHY PEOPLE SAY THAT EVEN THE FORMER CRIMSON KING...
...AN-SWERS TO HIS BECK AND CALL.
TAIHAKU... WHAT ARE YOU--
DO NOT BE TAKEN IN BY SUCH BASE RUMORS!
LET US HOPE THEY ARE JUST THAT. RUMORS.
TAI-HAKU!
SHINREI ...

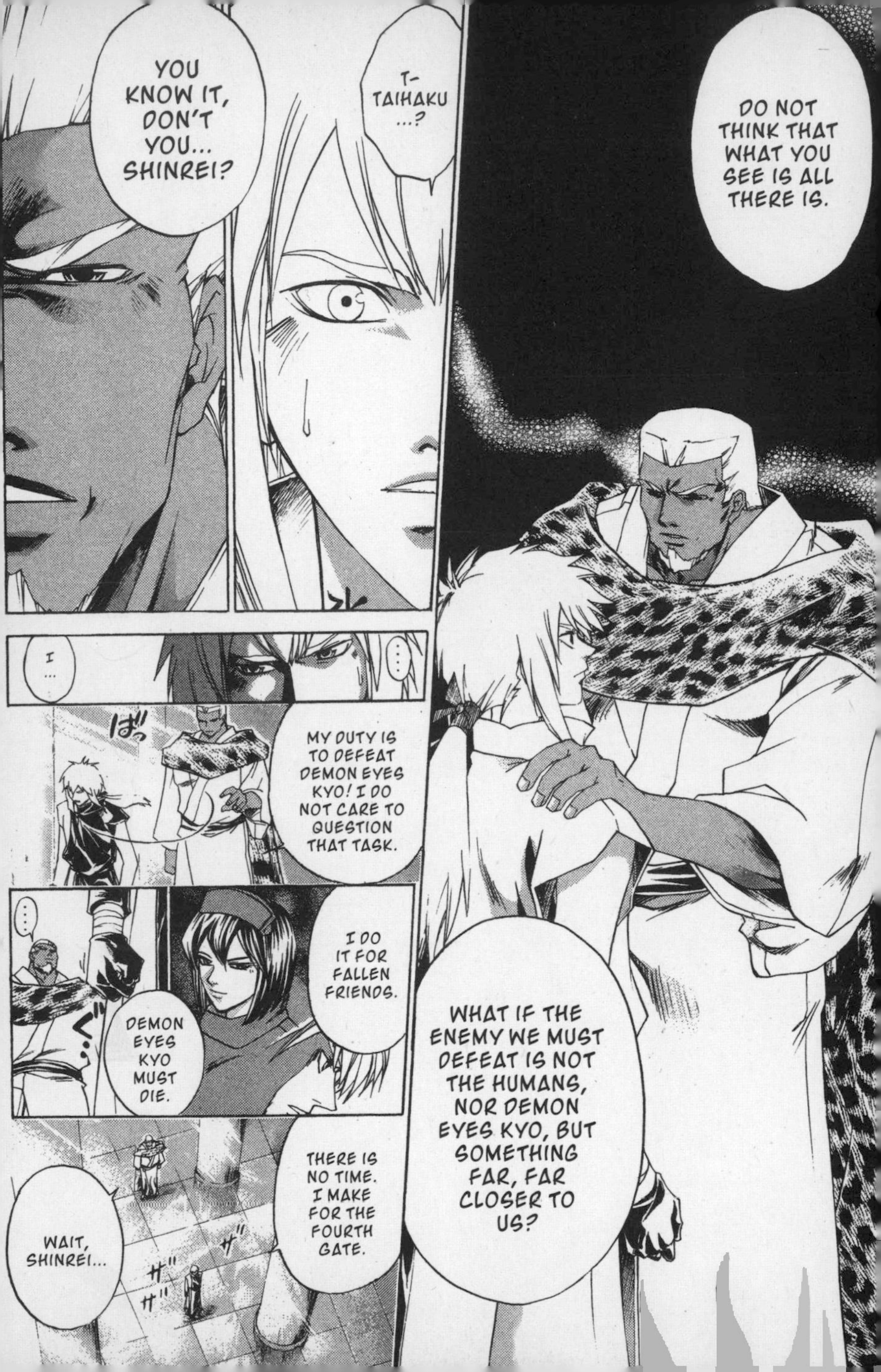
DO NOT THINK THAT WHAT YOU SEE IS ALL THERE IS.
WHAT IF THE ENEMY WE MUST DEFEAT IS NOT THE HUMANS, NOR DEMON EYES KYO, BUT SOMETHING FAR, FAR CLOSER TO US?
T-TAIHAKU ...?
YOU KNOW IT, DON'T YOU... SHINREI?
...
I ...
ばっ
MY DUTY IS TO DEFEAT DEMON EYES KYO! I DO NOT CARE TO QUESTION THAT TASK.
I DO IT FOR FALLEN FRIENDS.
DEMON EYES KYO MUST DIE.
...
THERE IS NO TIME. I MAKE FOR THE FOURTH GATE.
WAIT, SHINREI...

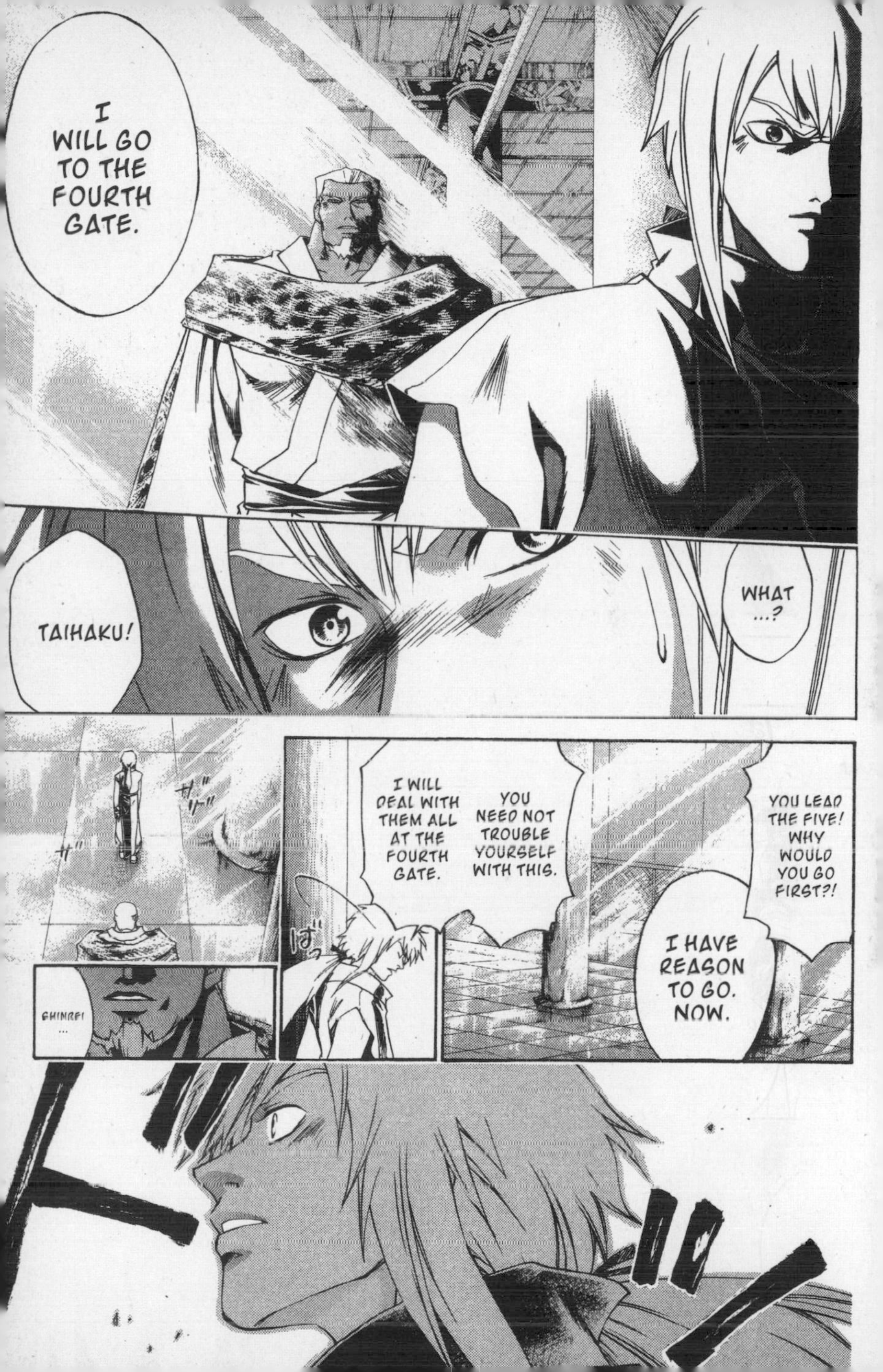
I WILL GO TO THE FOURTH GATE.
WHAT ...?
TAIHAKU!
YOU LEAD THE FIVE! WHY WOULD YOU GO FIRST?!
I HAVE REASON TO GO. NOW.
YOU NEED NOT TROUBLE YOURSELF WITH THIS.
I WILL DEAL WITH THEM ALL AT THE FOURTH GATE.
ばっ
SHINREI ...

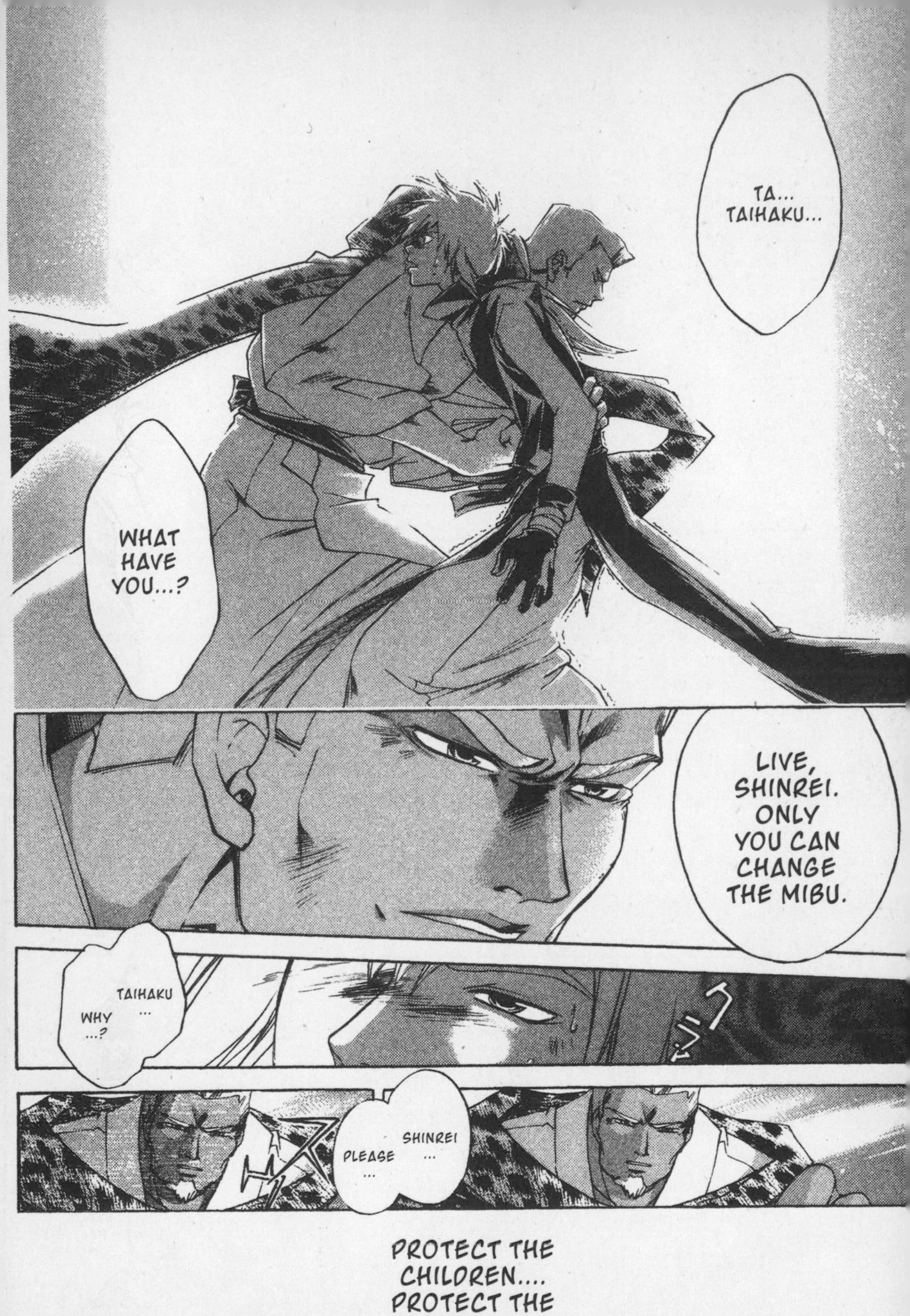
TA... TAIHAKU...
WHAT HAVE YOU...?
LIVE, SHINREI. ONLY YOU CAN CHANGE THE MIBU.
TAIHAKU... WHY...?
SHINREI... PLEASE...
PROTECT THE CHILDREN.... PROTECT THE MIBU.

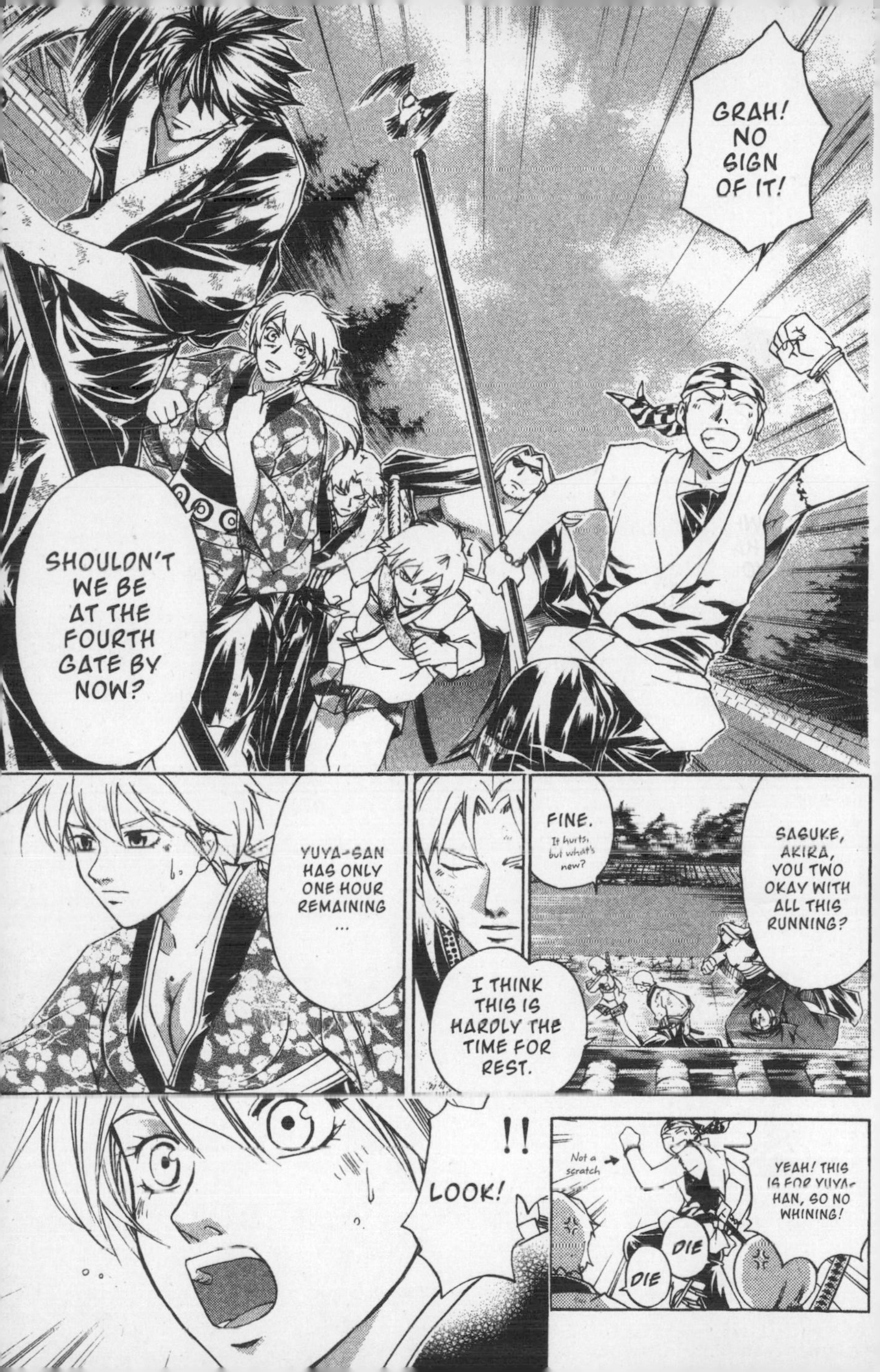
GRAH! NO SIGN OF IT!
SHOULDN'T WE BE AT THE FOURTH GATE BY NOW?
SASUKE, AKIRA, YOU TWO OKAY WITH ALL THIS RUNNING?
FINE.
It hurts, but what's new?
I THINK THIS IS HARDLY THE TIME FOR REST.
YUYA-SAN HAS ONLY ONE HOUR REMAINING ...
YEAH! THIS IS FOR YUYA-HAN, SO NO WHINING!
Not a scratch
DIE
DIE
!!
LOOK!

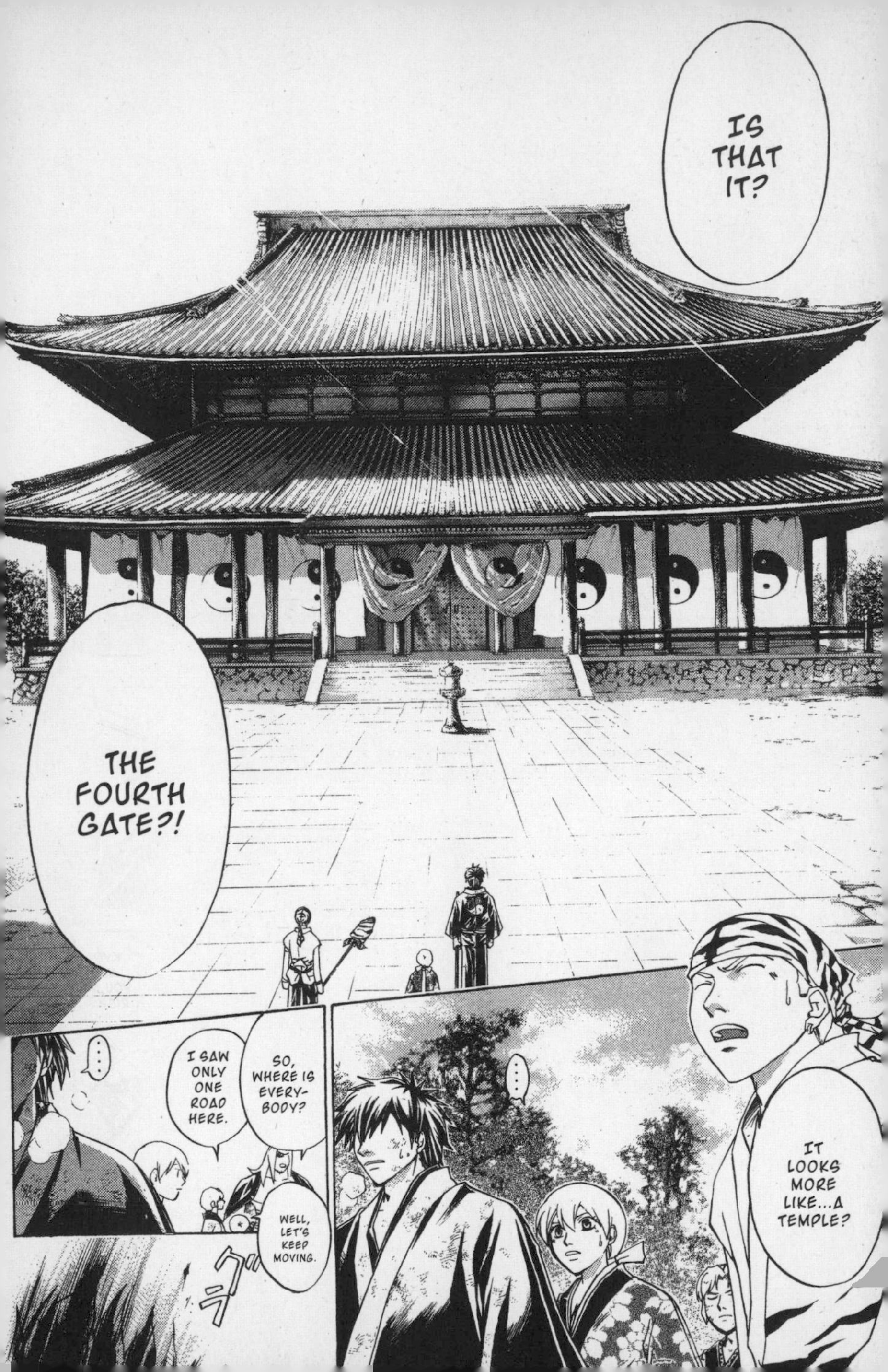
IS THAT IT?
THE FOURTH GATE?!
IT LOOKS MORE LIKE...A TEMPLE?
....
SO, WHERE IS EVERYBODY?
I SAW ONLY ONE ROAD HERE.
....
WELL, LET'S KEEP MOVING.

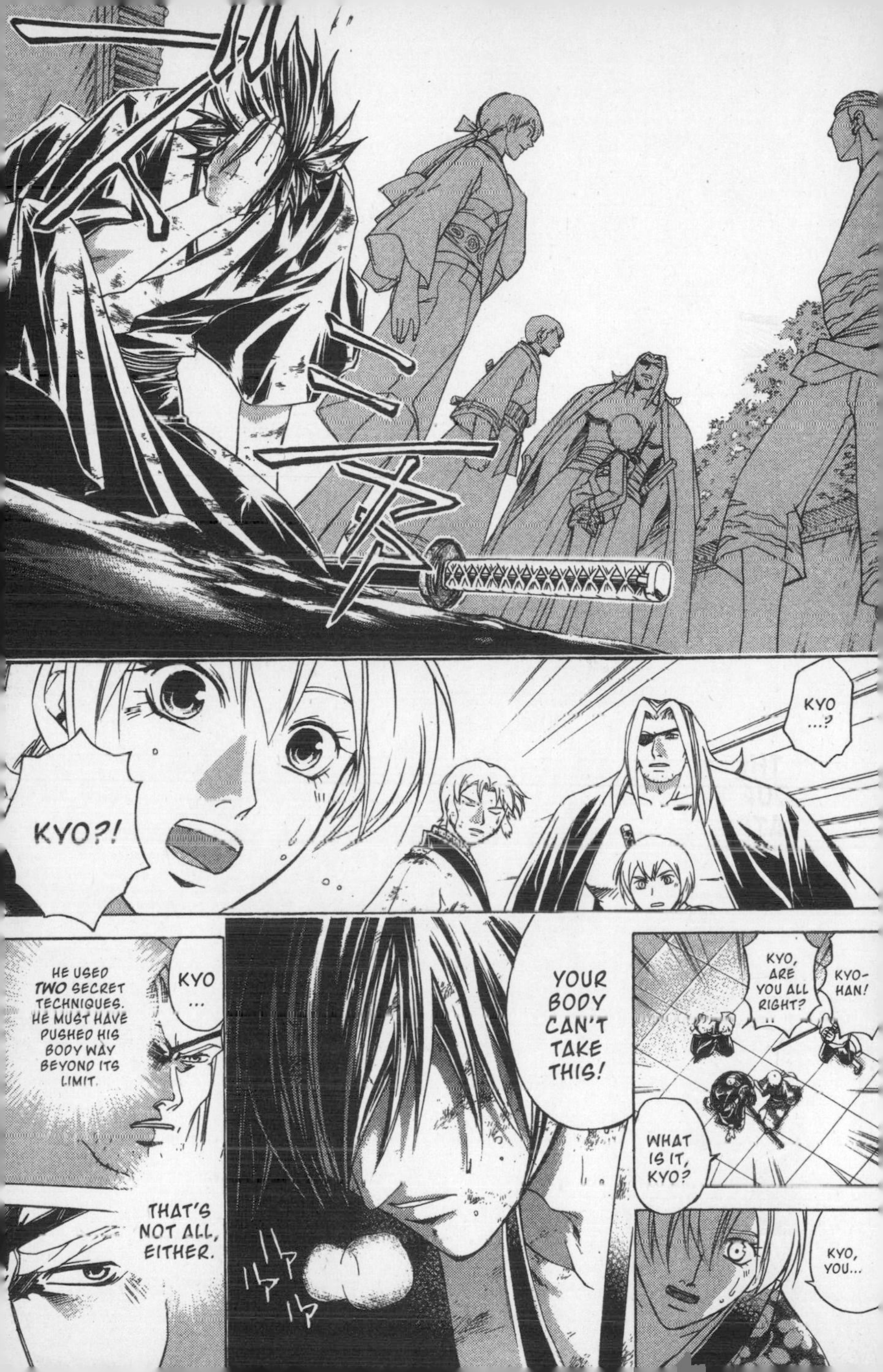
KYO ...?
KYO?!
KYO-HAN!
KYO, ARE YOU ALL RIGHT?
WHAT IS IT, KYO?
KYO, YOU...
YOUR BODY CAN'T TAKE THIS!
KYO ...
HE USED TWO SECRET TECHNIQUES. HE MUST HAVE PUSHED HIS BODY WAY BEYOND ITS LIMIT.
THAT'S NOT ALL, EITHER.

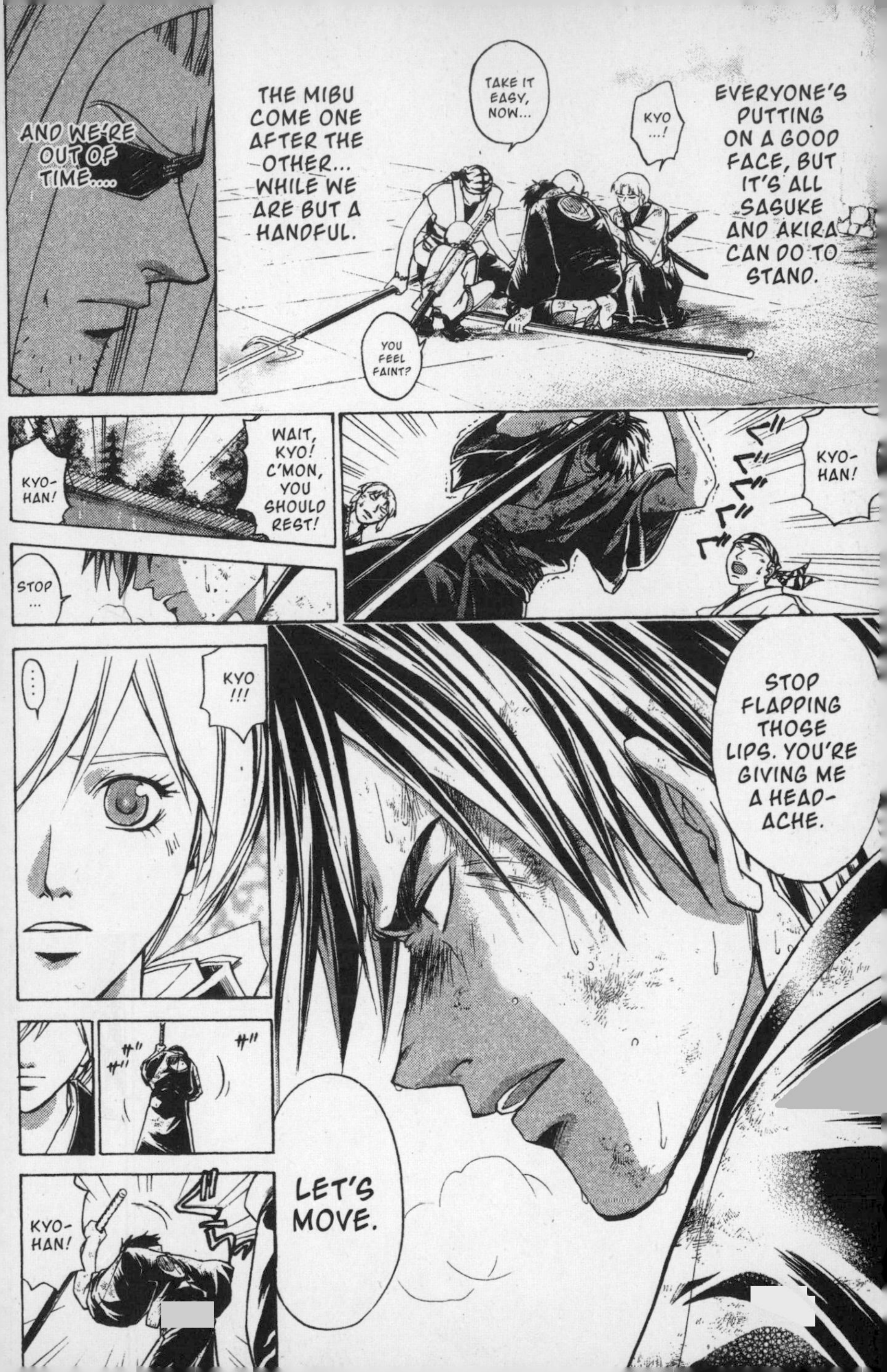
EVERYONE'S PUTTING ON A GOOD FACE, BUT IT'S ALL SASUKE AND AKIRA CAN DO TO STAND.
KYO ...!
TAKE IT EASY, NOW...
THE MIBU COME ONE AFTER THE OTHER... WHILE WE ARE BUT A HANDFUL.
YOU FEEL FAINT?
AND WE'RE OUT OF TIME....
KYO-HAN!
WAIT, KYO! C'MON, YOU SHOULD REST!
KYO-HAN!
STOP ...
STOP FLAPPING THOSE LIPS. YOU'RE GIVING ME A HEAD-ACHE.
LET'S MOVE.
KYO !!!
....
KYO-HAN!

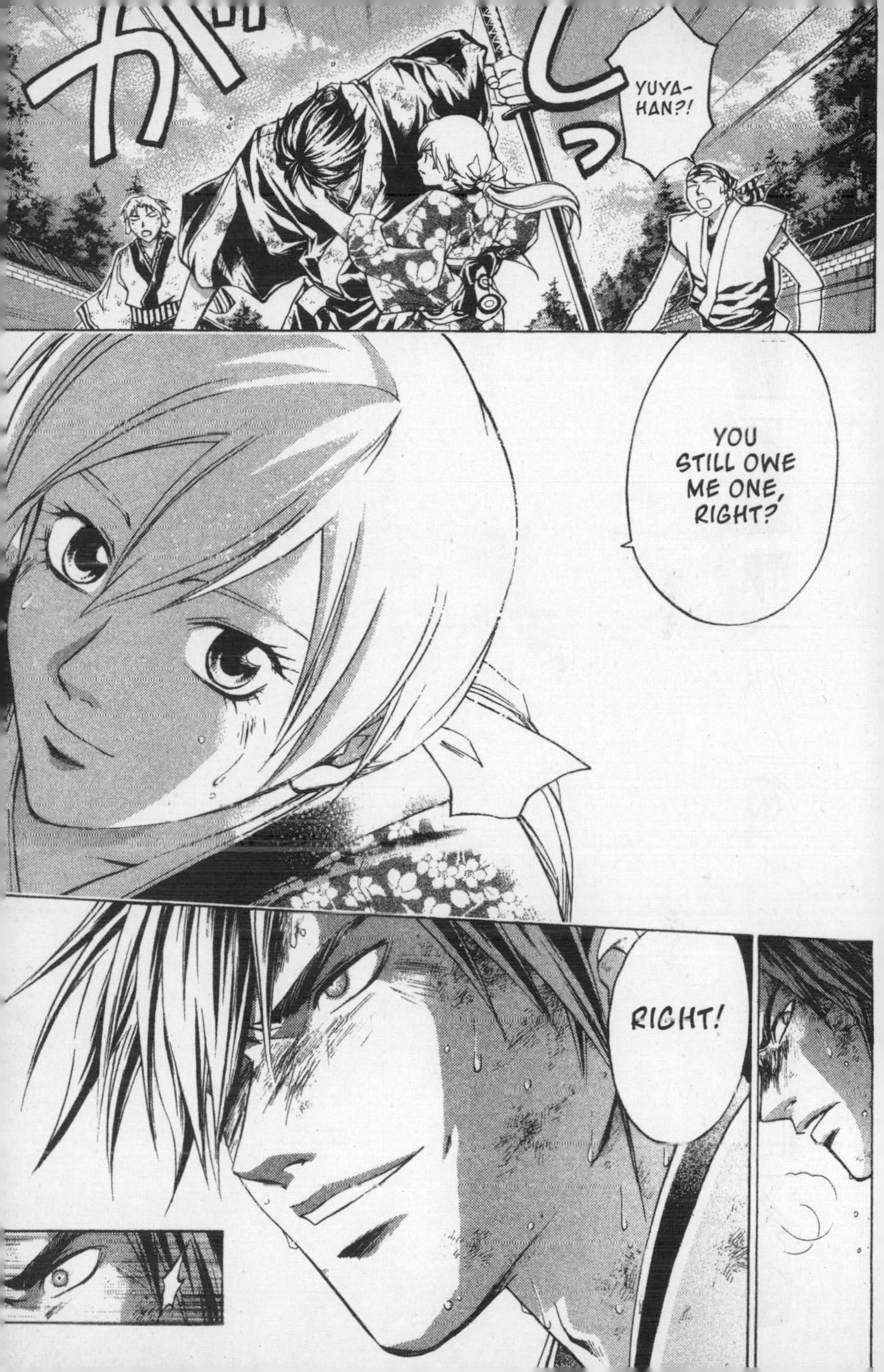
YUYA-HAN?!
がしっ
YOU STILL OWE ME ONE, RIGHT?
RIGHT!

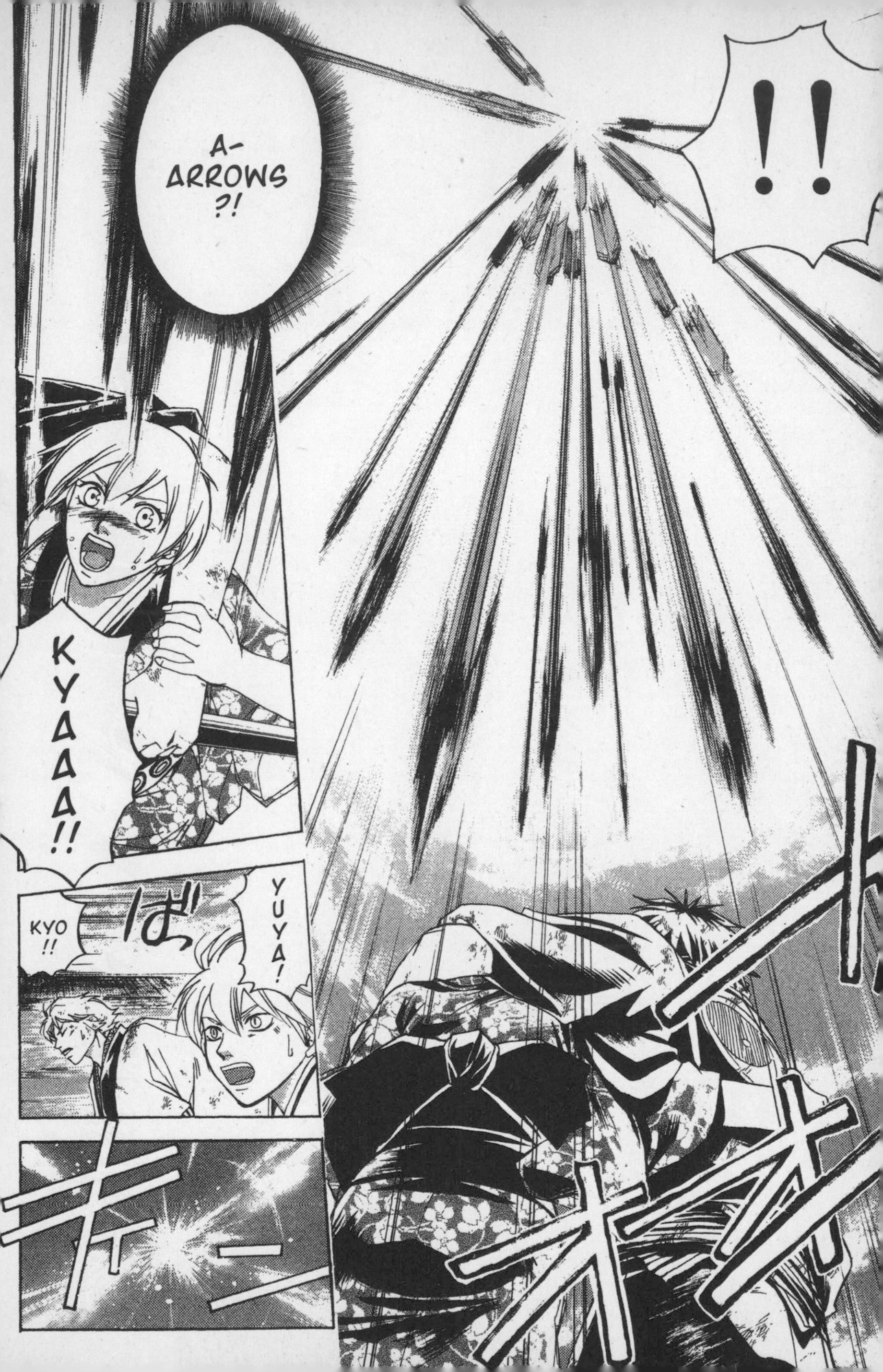
!!
A-ARROWS ?!
KYAAAA!!
YUYA!
KYO !!

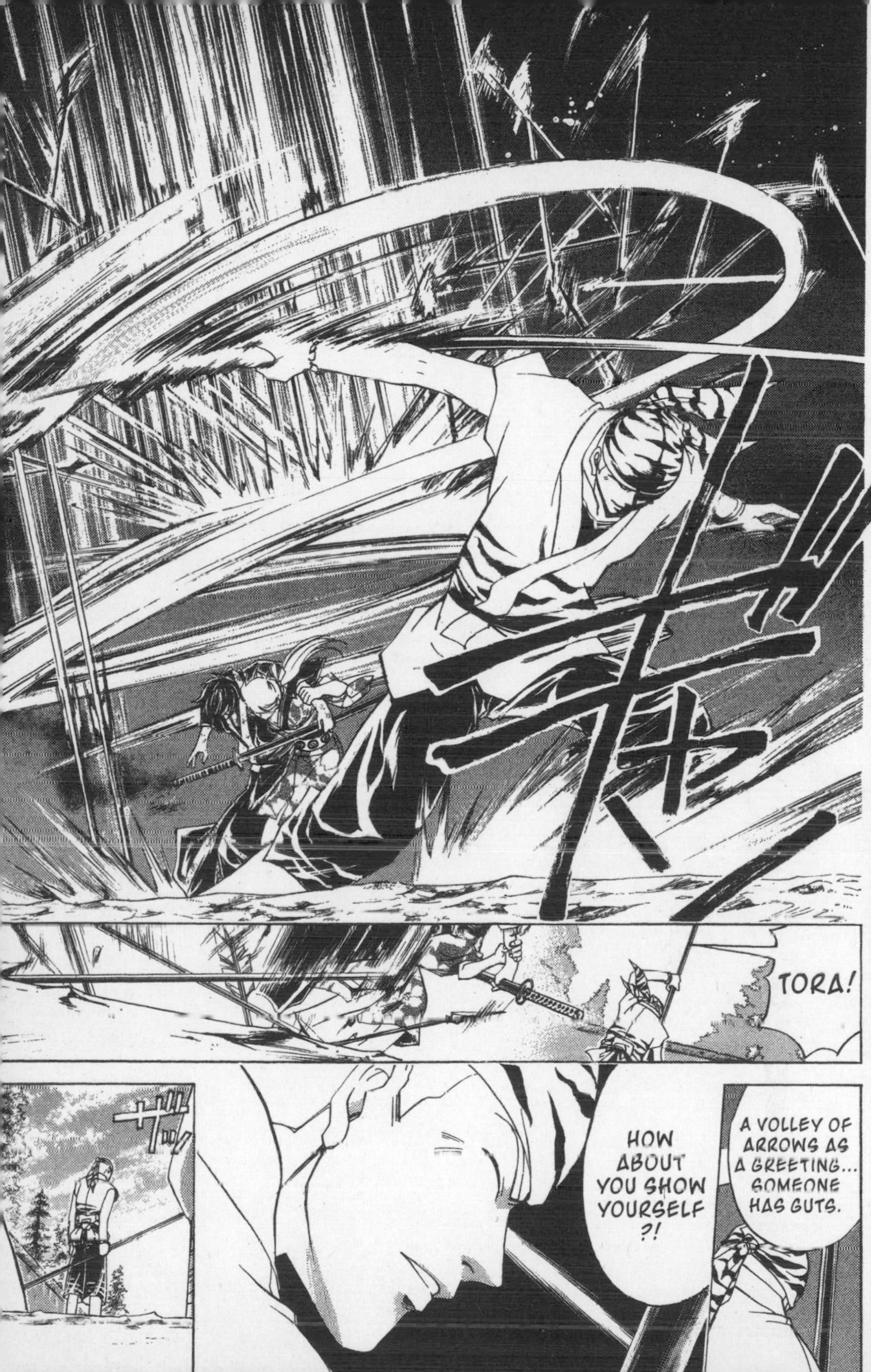
TORA!
A VOLLEY OF ARROWS AS A GREETING... SOMEONE HAS GUTS.
HOW ABOUT YOU SHOW YOURSELF ?!

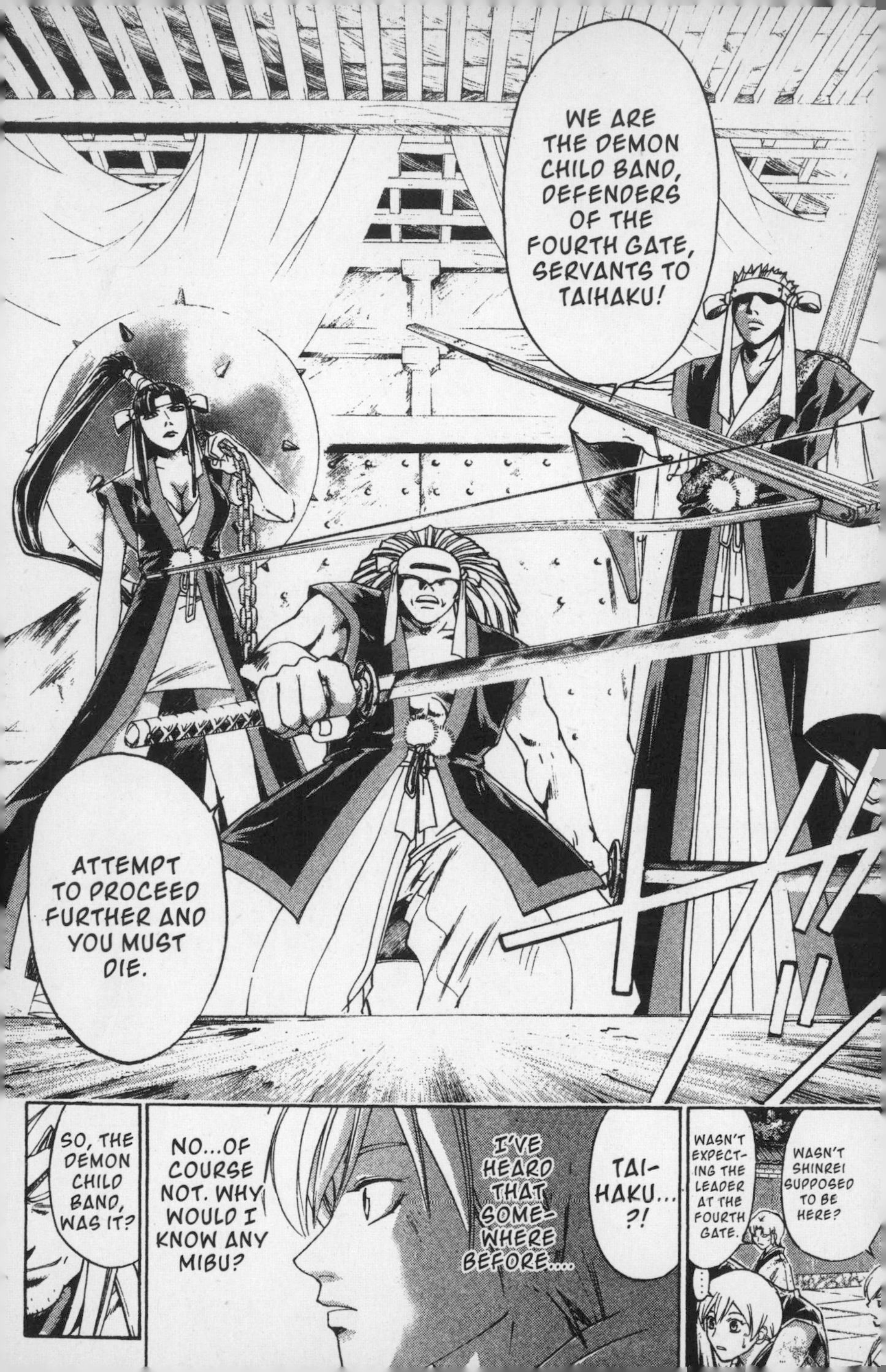
WE ARE THE DEMON CHILD BAND, DEFENDERS OF THE FOURTH GATE, SERVANTS TO TAIHAKU!
ATTEMPT TO PROCEED FURTHER AND YOU MUST DIE.
WASN'T SHINREI SUPPOSED TO BE HERE?
WASN'T EXPECTING THE LEADER AT THE FOURTH GATE.
...
TAI-HAKU...?!
I'VE HEARD THAT SOME-WHERE BEFORE....
NO...OF COURSE NOT. WHY WOULD I KNOW ANY MIBU?
SO, THE DEMON CHILD BAND, WAS IT?

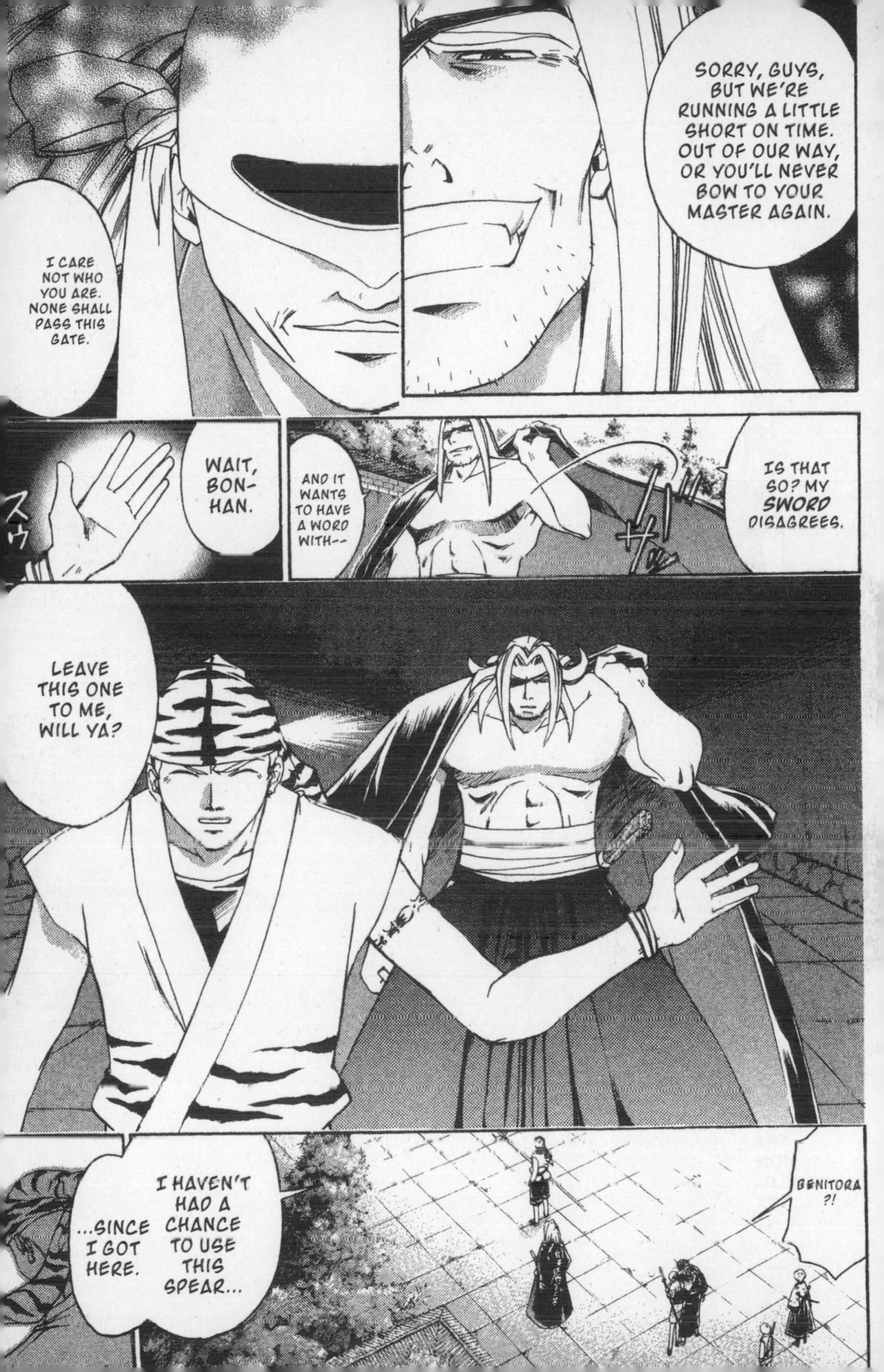
SORRY, GUYS, BUT WE'RE RUNNING A LITTLE SHORT ON TIME. OUT OF OUR WAY, OR YOU'LL NEVER BOW TO YOUR MASTER AGAIN.
I CARE NOT WHO YOU ARE. NONE SHALL PASS THIS GATE.
IS THAT SO? MY **SWORD** DISAGREES.
AND IT WANTS TO HAVE A WORD WITH--
WAIT, BON-HAN.
スゥ
LEAVE THIS ONE TO ME, WILL YA?
BENITORA ?!
I HAVEN'T HAD A CHANCE TO USE THIS SPEAR...
...SINCE I GOT HERE.

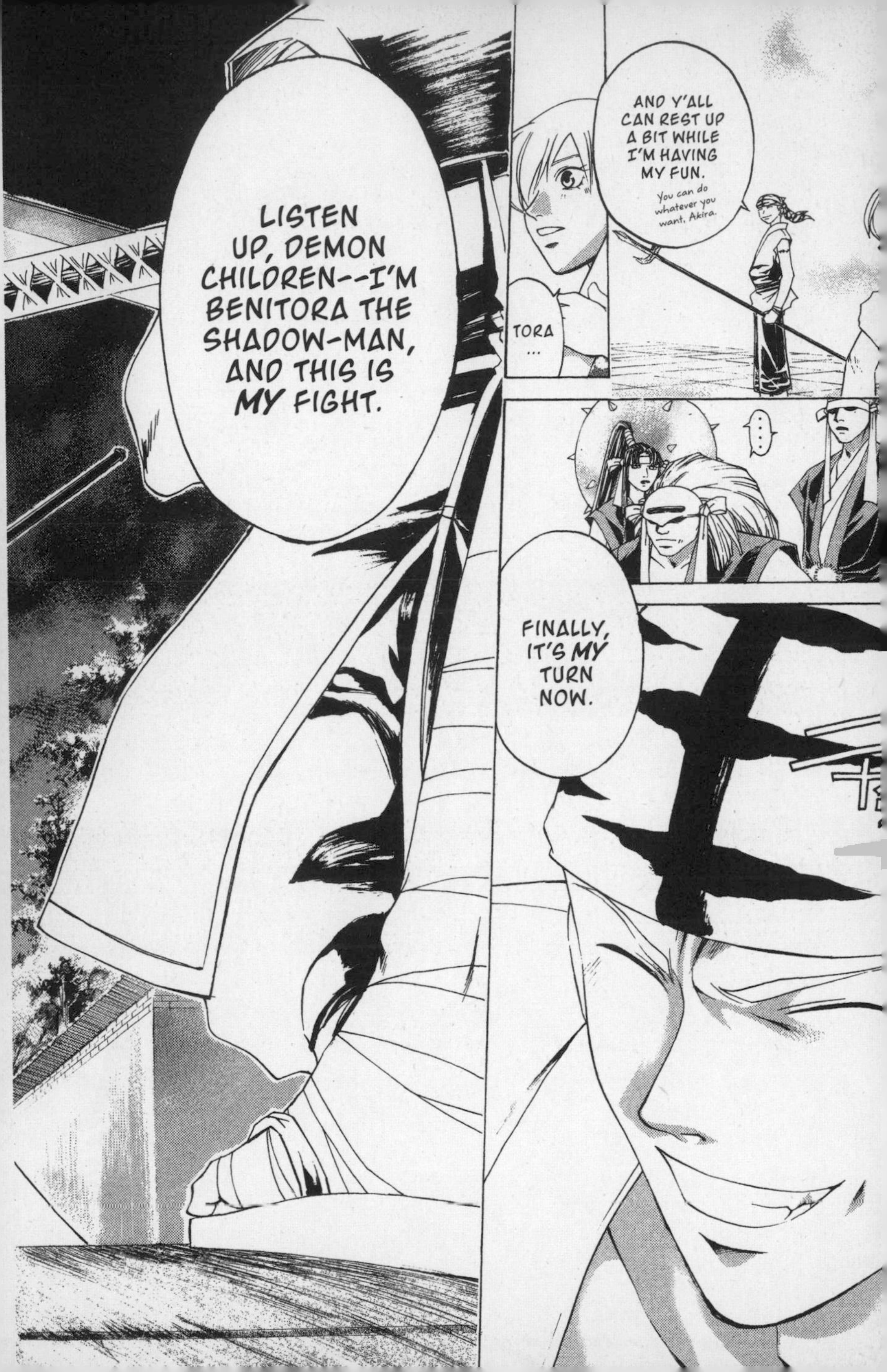
AND Y'ALL CAN REST UP A BIT WHILE I'M HAVING MY FUN.
You can do whatever you want, Akira.
TORA ...
...
FINALLY, IT'S MY TURN NOW.
LISTEN UP, DEMON CHILDREN--I'M BENITORA THE SHADOW-MAN, AND THIS IS MY FIGHT.

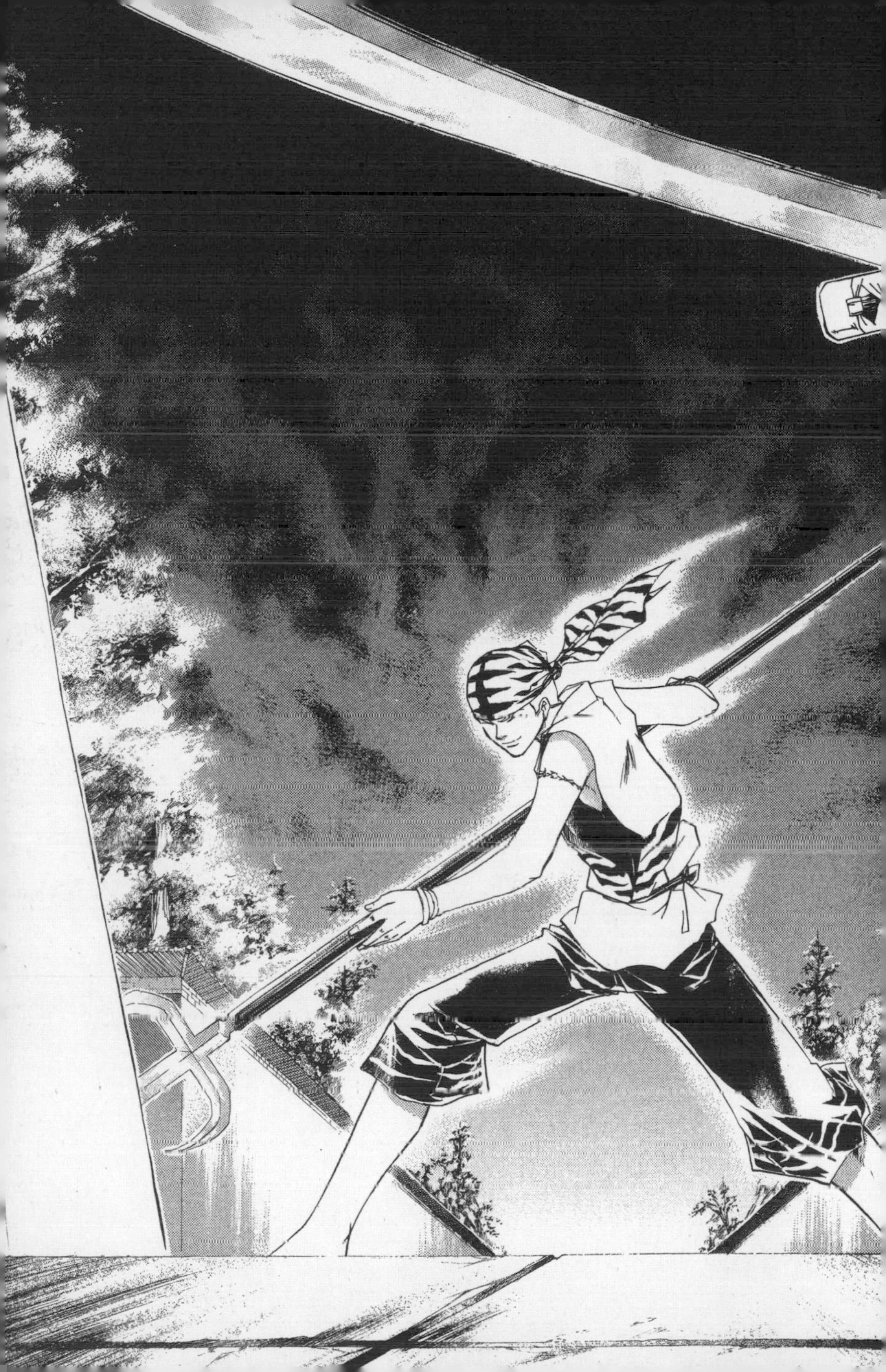

Q&A CORNER

KAMIJYO

Q: What is your favorite food?

A: Well, it's winter now, so...stew!

Q: Which is your favorite chapter?

A: I don't think I've done anything so good as to call it my "favorite"...but I'll keep trying!

Q: Don't you get bored of drawing Kyo all the time?

A: Not at all! Except...Kyo doesn't show much emotion, so he's the hardest to draw!

Q: What's the secret to drawing Hotaru and Muramasa?

A: You've got to get into their characters. When you're drawing Hotaru, you just have to go for it without thinking too much! With Muramasa you have to be calm, centered. See? You did it!

Q: Do you start trying characters from their outline, or from the details?

A: I do it any number of ways. I usually start with an outline, but depending on the scene, I might start with a hand, the sword, the sandals...

Q: When you draw yourself, you're always completely bald. Do you have hair in real life?

A: Quite a lot, actually. But once, a barber told me I'd go bald when I got older. *sob*

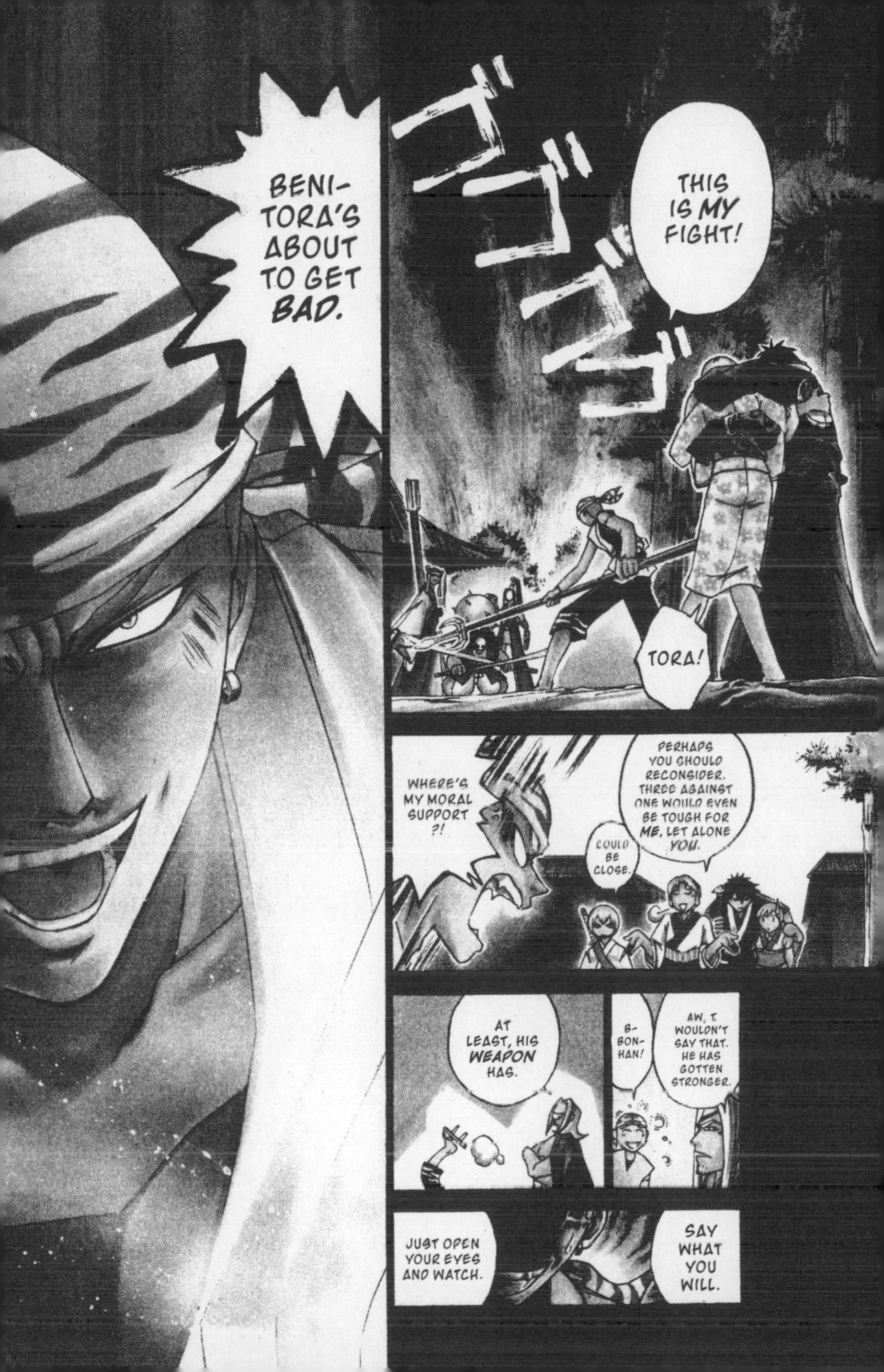
ゴゴゴゴ
THIS IS MY FIGHT!
TORA!
PERHAPS YOU SHOULD RECONSIDER. THREE AGAINST ONE WOULD EVEN BE TOUGH FOR ME, LET ALONE YOU.
COULD BE CLOSE.
WHERE'S MY MORAL SUPPORT ?!
AW, I WOULDN'T SAY THAT. HE HAS GOTTEN STRONGER.
B-BON-HAN!
AT LEAST, HIS WEAPON HAS.
SAY WHAT YOU WILL.
JUST OPEN YOUR EYES AND WATCH.
BENI-TORA'S ABOUT TO GET BAD.

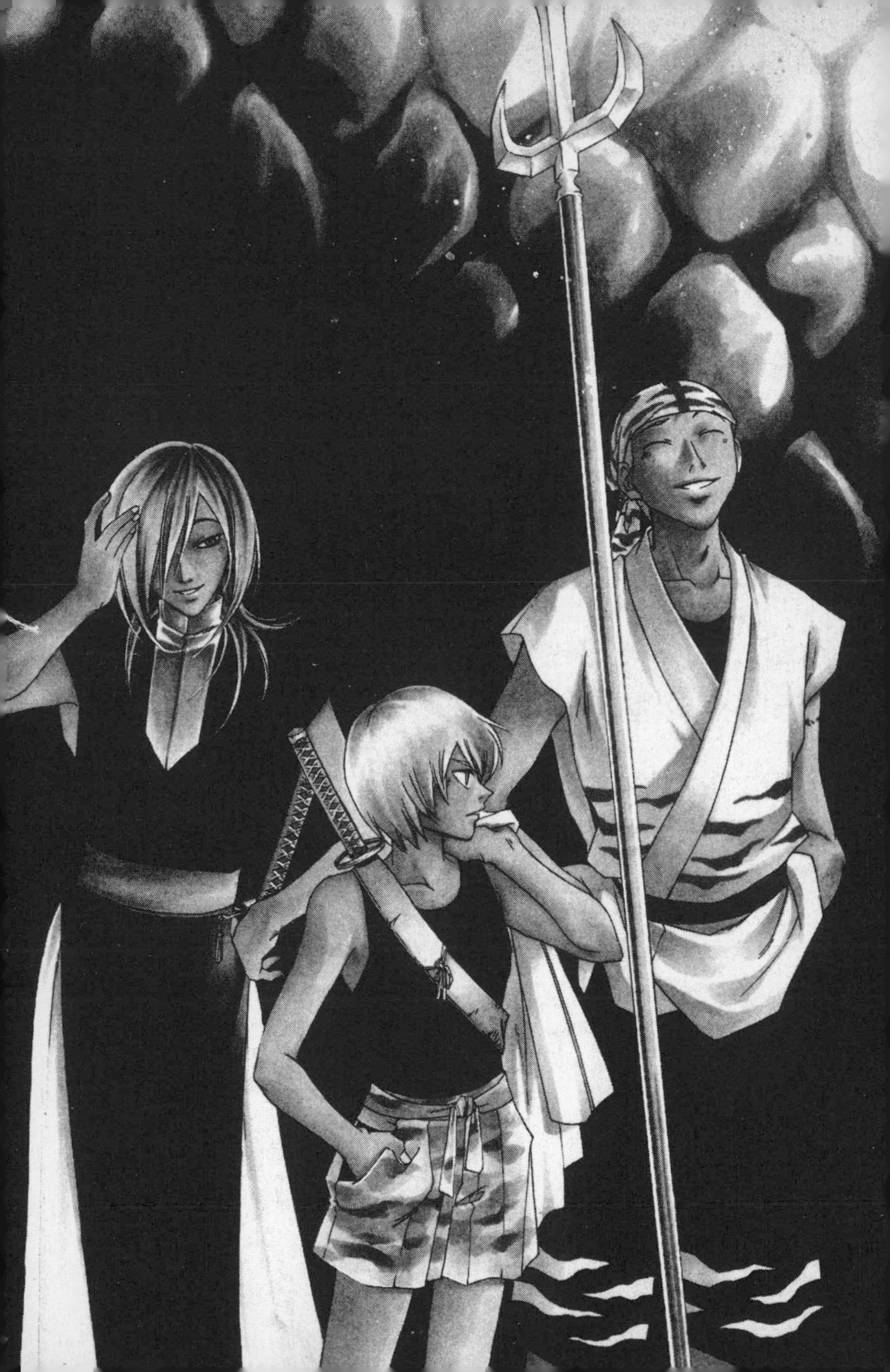

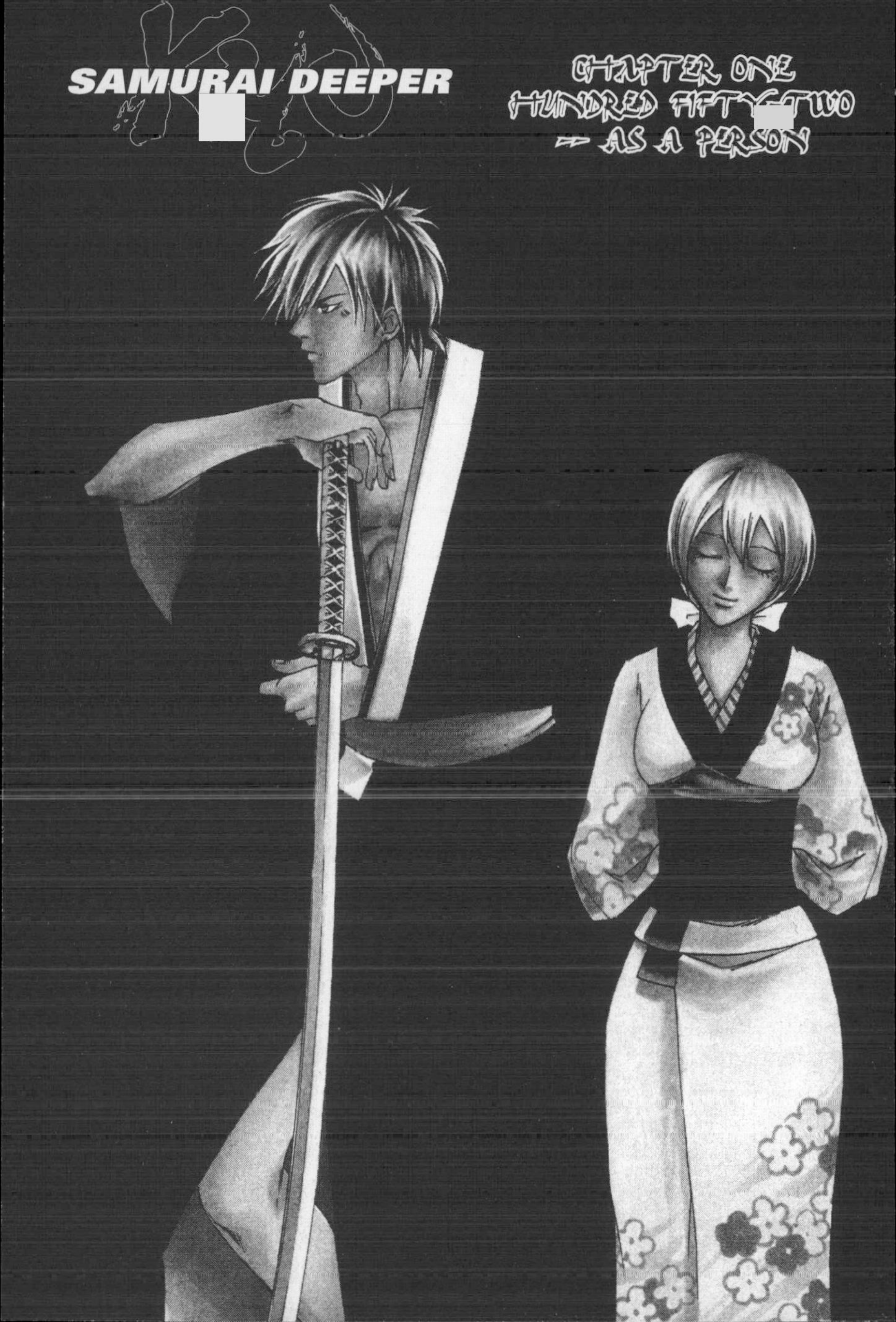
SAMURAI DEEPER
CHAPTER ONE
HUNDRED FIFTY-TWO
-- AS A PERSON

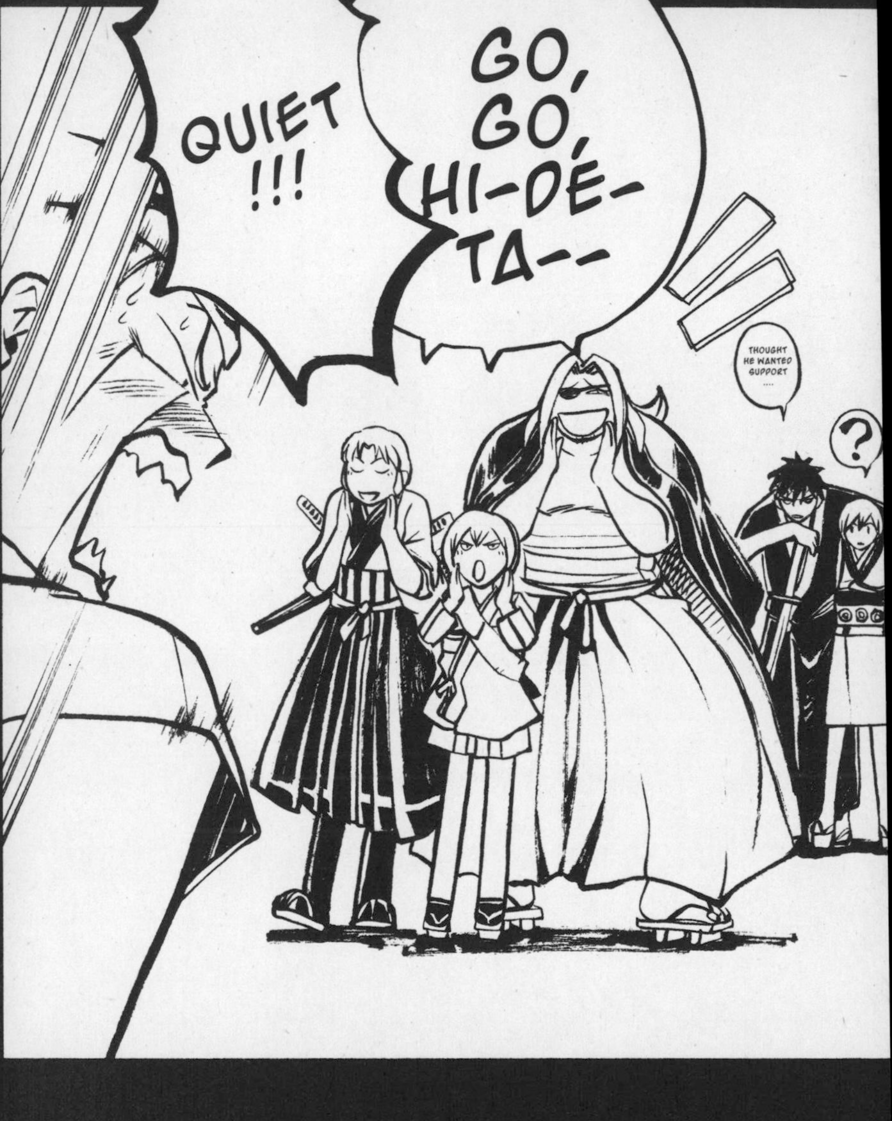
GO, GO, HI-DÉ-TA--
QUIET !!!
THOUGHT HE WANTED SUPPORT ....
?

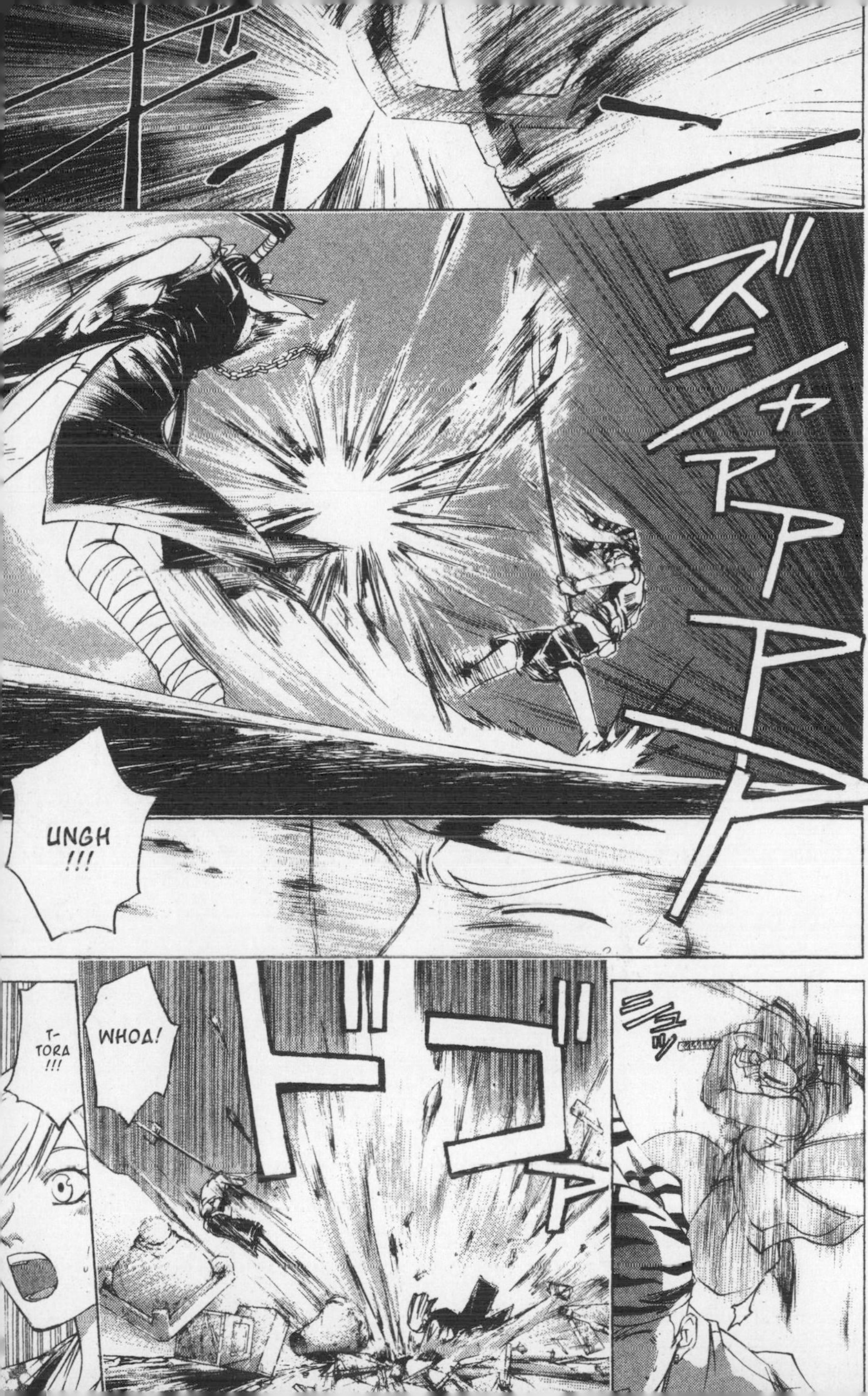
ズシャアアアア
UNGH !!!
ミシッ
ドゴァ
WHOA!
T-TORA !!!

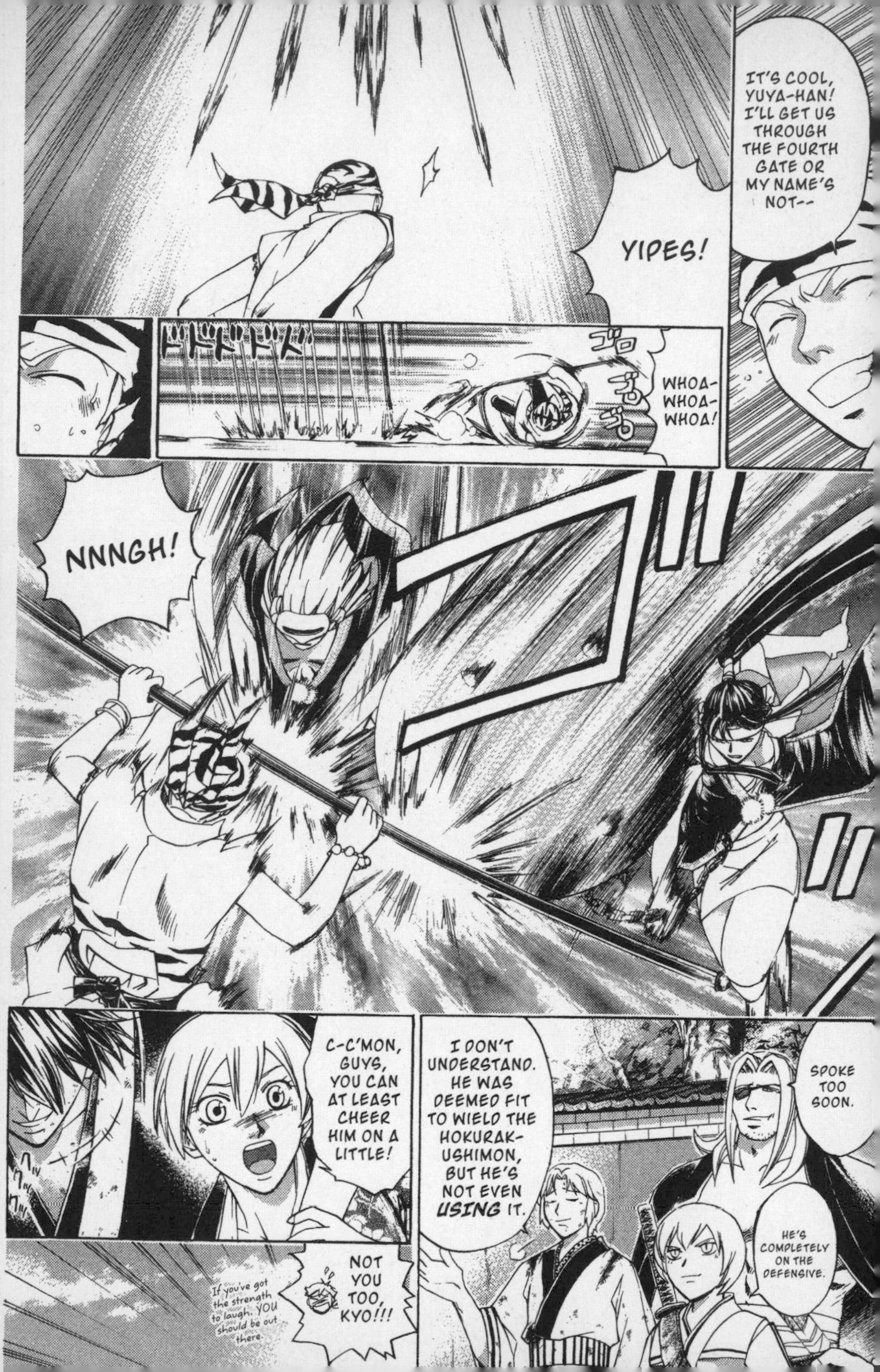
IT'S COOL, YUYA-HAN! I'LL GET US THROUGH THE FOURTH GATE OR MY NAME'S NOT--
YIPES!
WHOA-WHOA-WHOA!
ゴロゴロ
ドドドドド
NNNGH!
SPOKE TOO SOON.
I DON'T UNDERSTAND. HE WAS DEEMED FIT TO WIELD THE HOKURAK-USHIMON, BUT HE'S NOT EVEN *USING* IT.
HE'S COMPLETELY ON THE DEFENSIVE.
C-C'MON, GUYS, YOU CAN AT LEAST CHEER HIM ON A LITTLE!
NOT YOU TOO, KYO!!!
If you've got the strength to laugh, YOU should be out there.

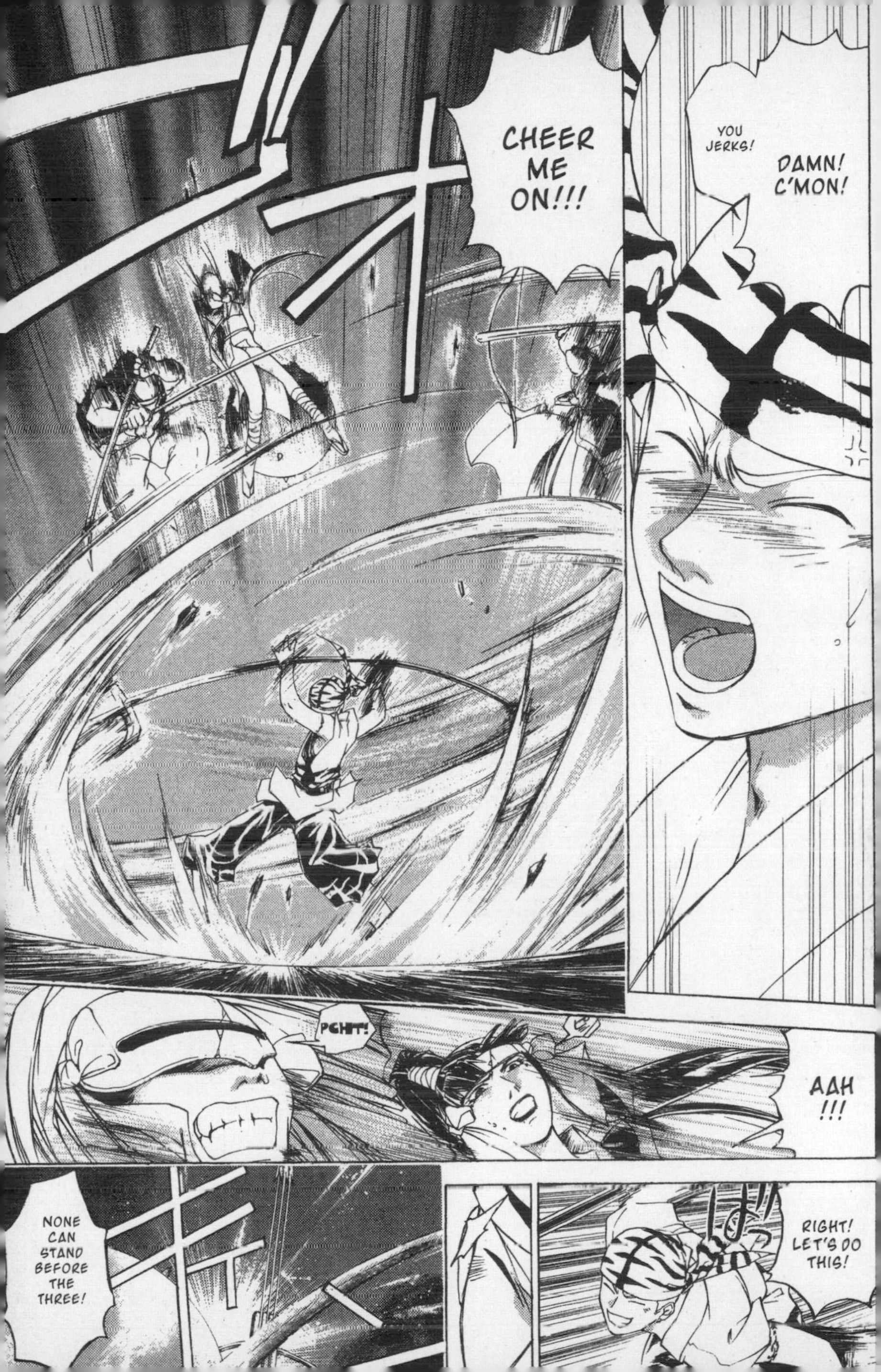
DAMN! C'MON!
YOU JERKS!
CHEER ME ON!!!
AAH!!!
PCHIT!
RIGHT! LET'S DO THIS!
NONE CAN STAND BEFORE THE THREE!

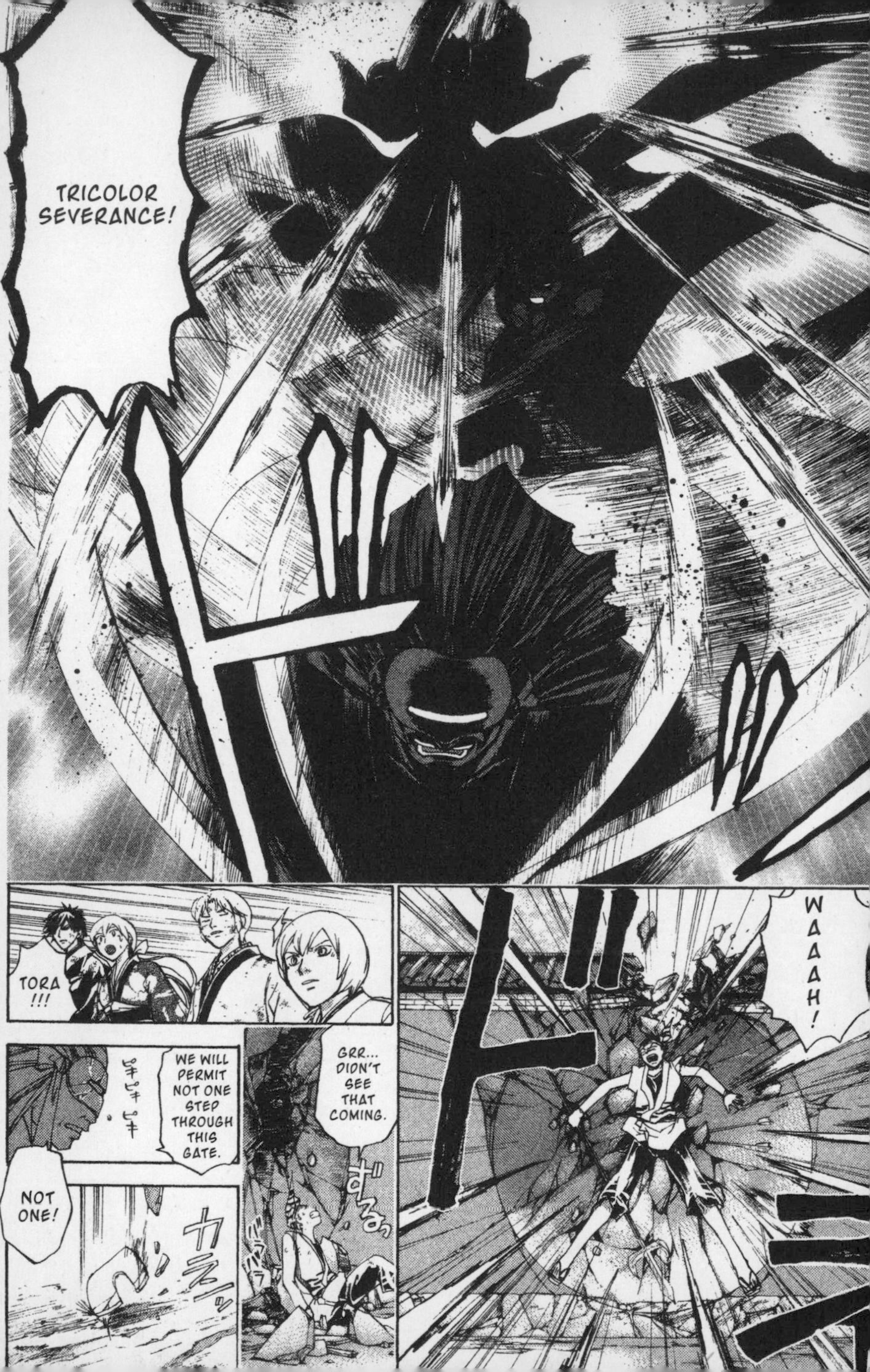
TRICOLOR SEVERANCE!
WAAAAH!
TORA!!!
GRR... DIDN'T SEE THAT COMING.
ずるっ
WE WILL PERMIT NOT ONE STEP THROUGH THIS GATE.
ピキピキ ピキ
NOT ONE!

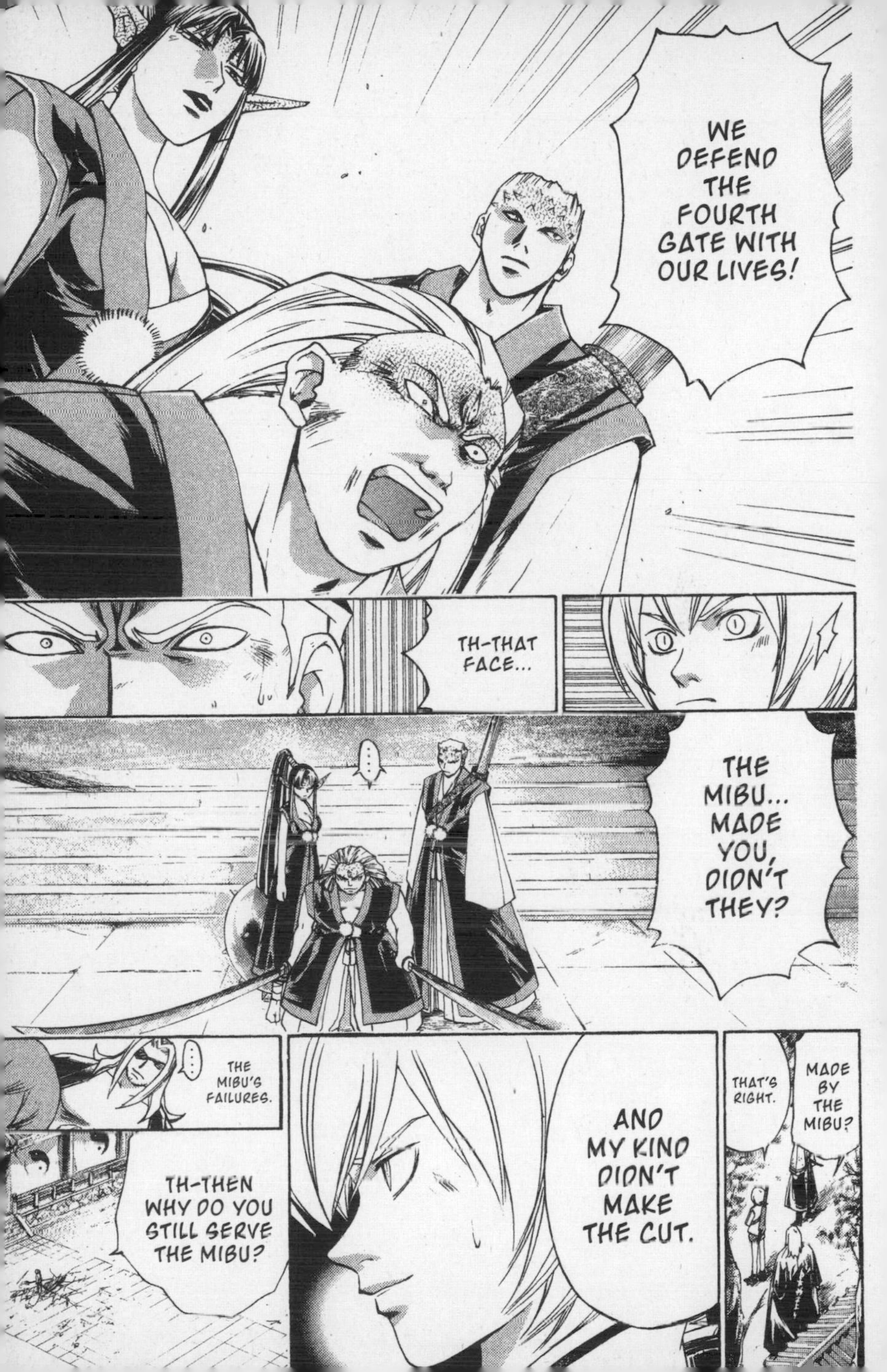
WE DEFEND THE FOURTH GATE WITH OUR LIVES!
TH-THAT FACE...
...
THE MIBU... MADE YOU, DIDN'T THEY?
MADE BY THE MIBU?
THAT'S RIGHT.
AND MY KIND DIDN'T MAKE THE CUT.
...
THE MIBU'S FAILURES.
TH-THEN WHY DO YOU STILL SERVE THE MIBU?

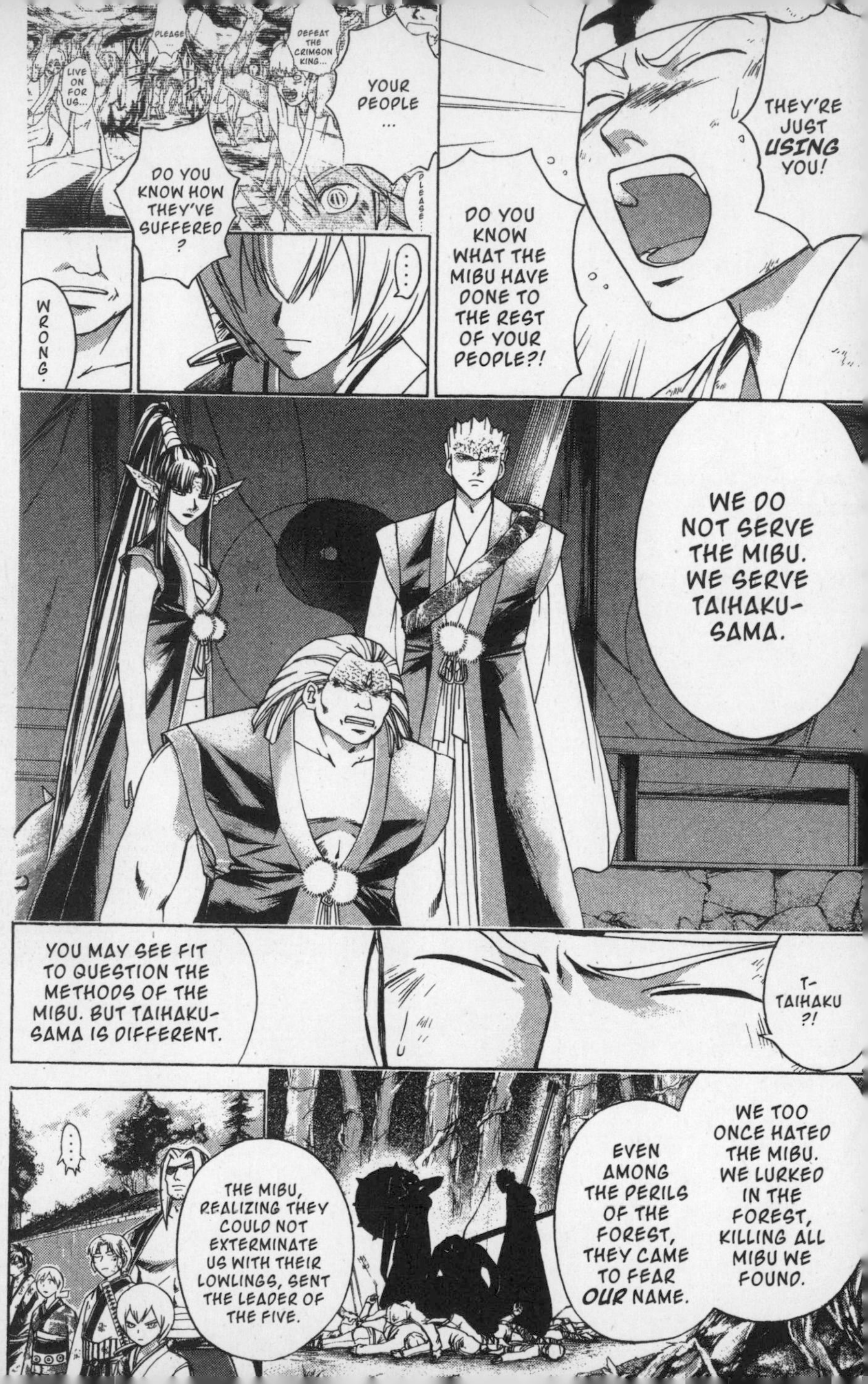
THEY'RE JUST *USING* YOU!
DO YOU KNOW WHAT THE MIBU HAVE DONE TO THE REST OF YOUR PEOPLE?!
DEFEAT THE CRIMSON KING...
YOUR PEOPLE ...
PLEASE ...
LIVE ON FOR US...
PLEASE...
DO YOU KNOW HOW THEY'VE SUFFERED ?
......
WRONG.
WE DO NOT SERVE THE MIBU. WE SERVE TAIHAKU-SAMA.
T-TAIHAKU ?!
YOU MAY SEE FIT TO QUESTION THE METHODS OF THE MIBU. BUT TAIHAKU-SAMA IS DIFFERENT.
WE TOO ONCE HATED THE MIBU. WE LURKED IN THE FOREST, KILLING ALL MIBU WE FOUND.
EVEN AMONG THE PERILS OF THE FOREST, THEY CAME TO FEAR *OUR* NAME.
THE MIBU, REALIZING THEY COULD NOT EXTERMINATE US WITH THEIR LOWLINGS, SENT THE LEADER OF THE FIVE.
......

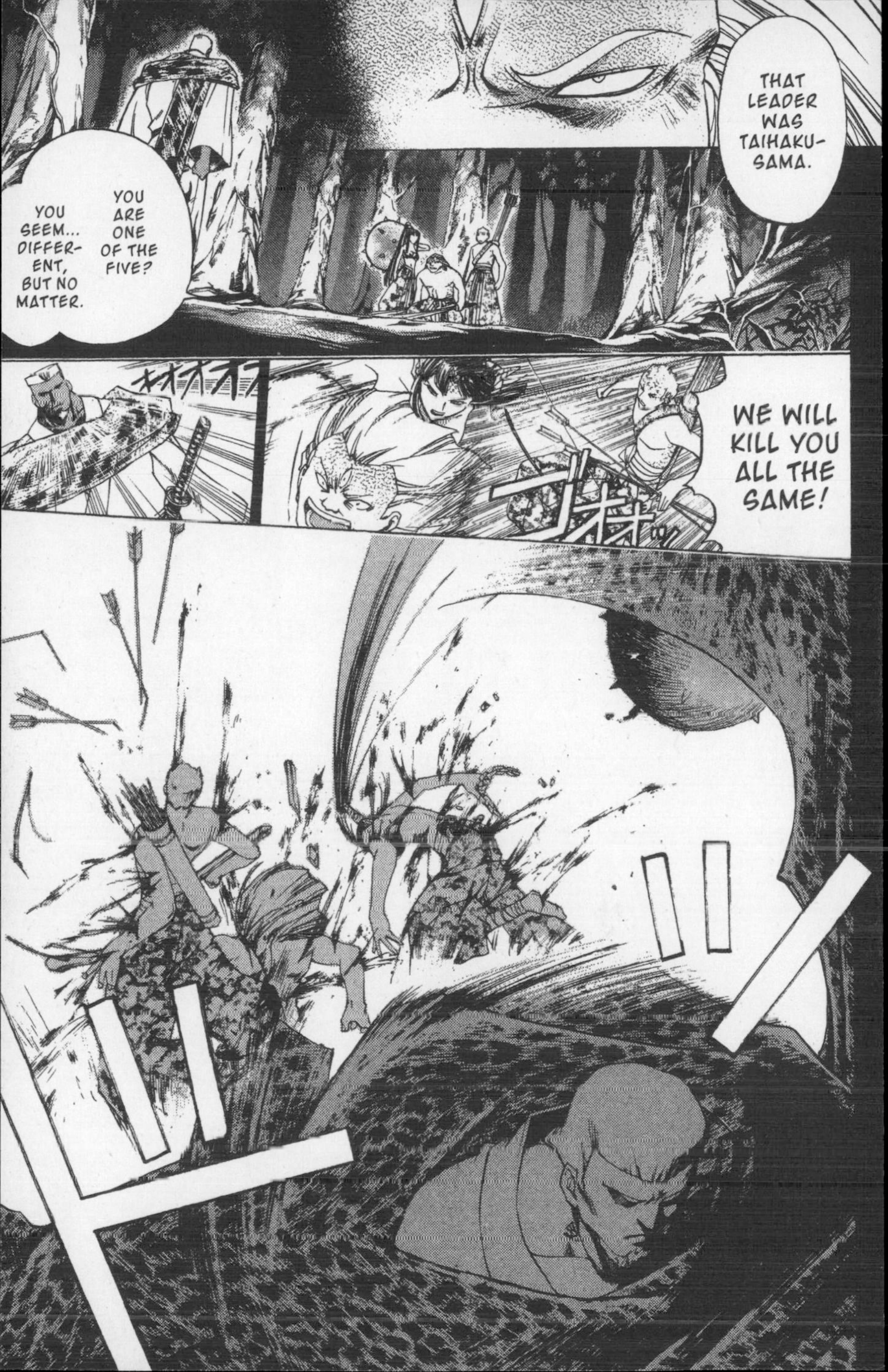
THAT LEADER WAS TAIHAKU-SAMA.
YOU ARE ONE OF THE FIVE?
YOU SEEM... DIFFER-ENT, BUT NO MATTER.
WE WILL KILL YOU ALL THE SAME!

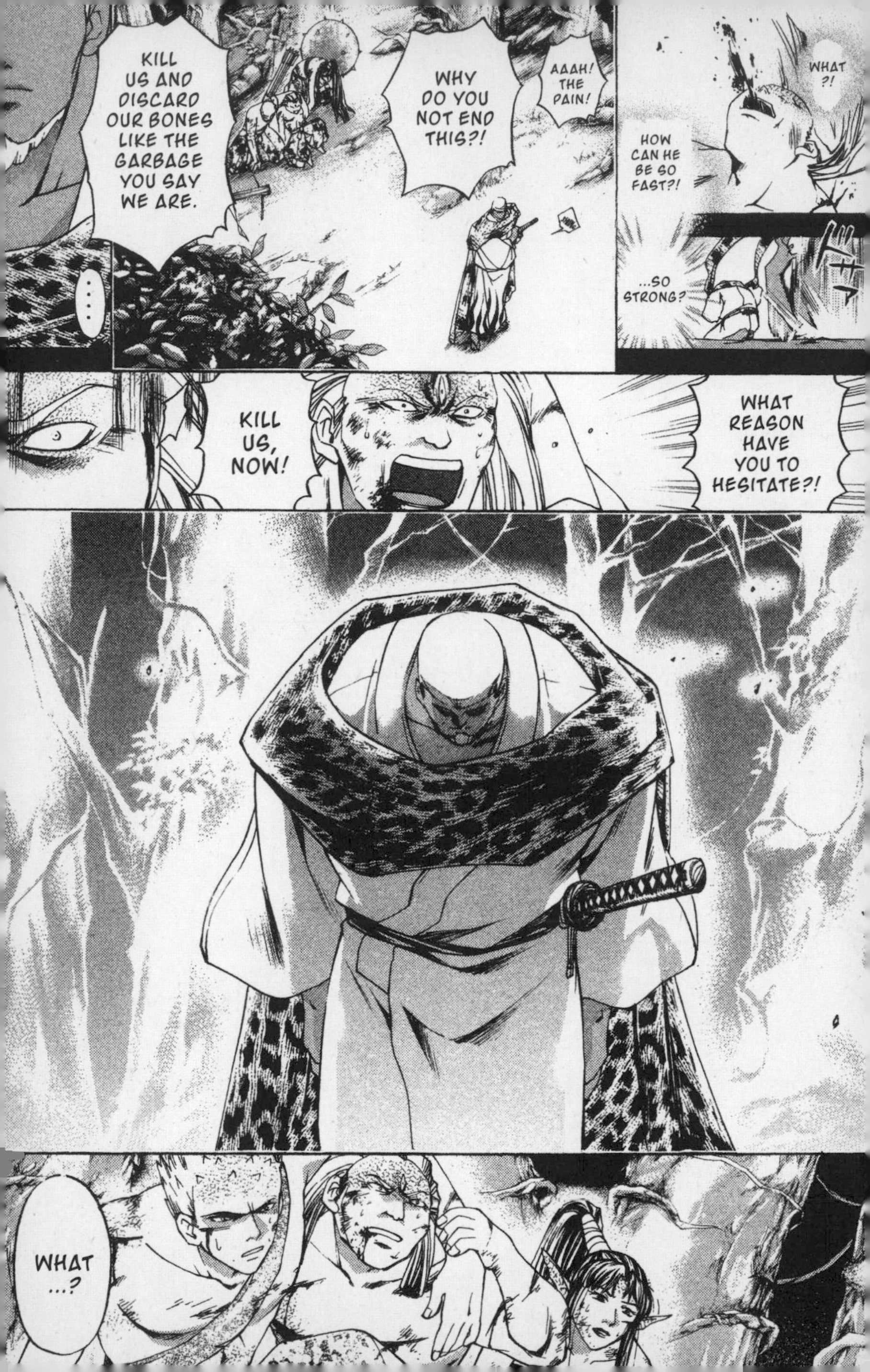
WHAT ?!
HOW CAN HE BE SO FAST?!
...SO STRONG?
AAAH! THE PAIN!
WHY DO YOU NOT END THIS?!
KILL US AND DISCARD OUR BONES LIKE THE GARBAGE YOU SAY WE ARE.
....
WHAT REASON HAVE YOU TO HESITATE?!
KILL US, NOW!
WHAT ...?

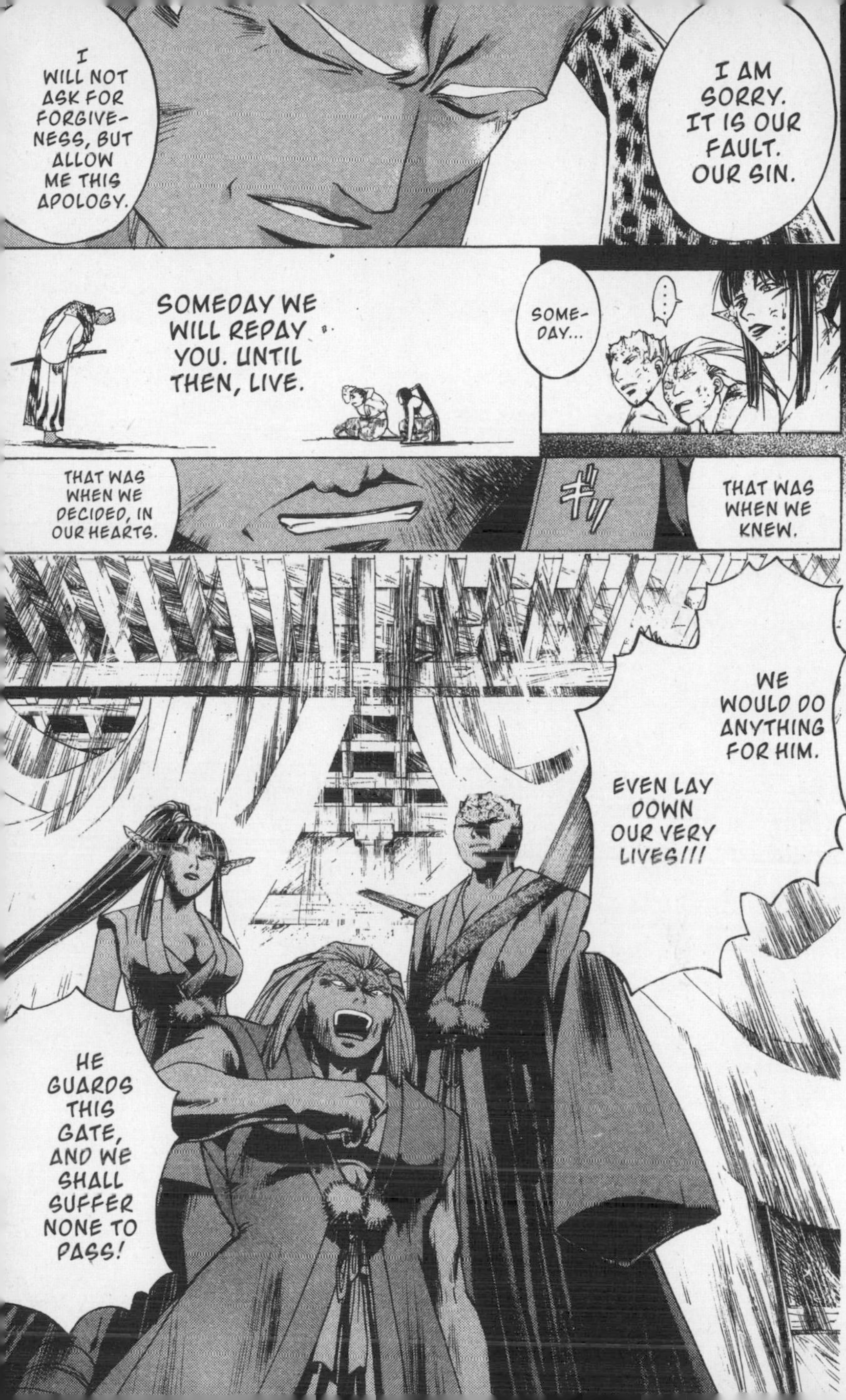
I AM SORRY. IT IS OUR FAULT. OUR SIN.
I WILL NOT ASK FOR FORGIVE-NESS, BUT ALLOW ME THIS APOLOGY.
...
SOME-DAY...
SOMEDAY WE WILL REPAY YOU. UNTIL THEN, LIVE.
THAT WAS WHEN WE KNEW.
ギリ
THAT WAS WHEN WE DECIDED, IN OUR HEARTS.
WE WOULD DO ANYTHING FOR HIM.
EVEN LAY DOWN OUR VERY LIVES!!!
HE GUARDS THIS GATE, AND WE SHALL SUFFER NONE TO PASS!

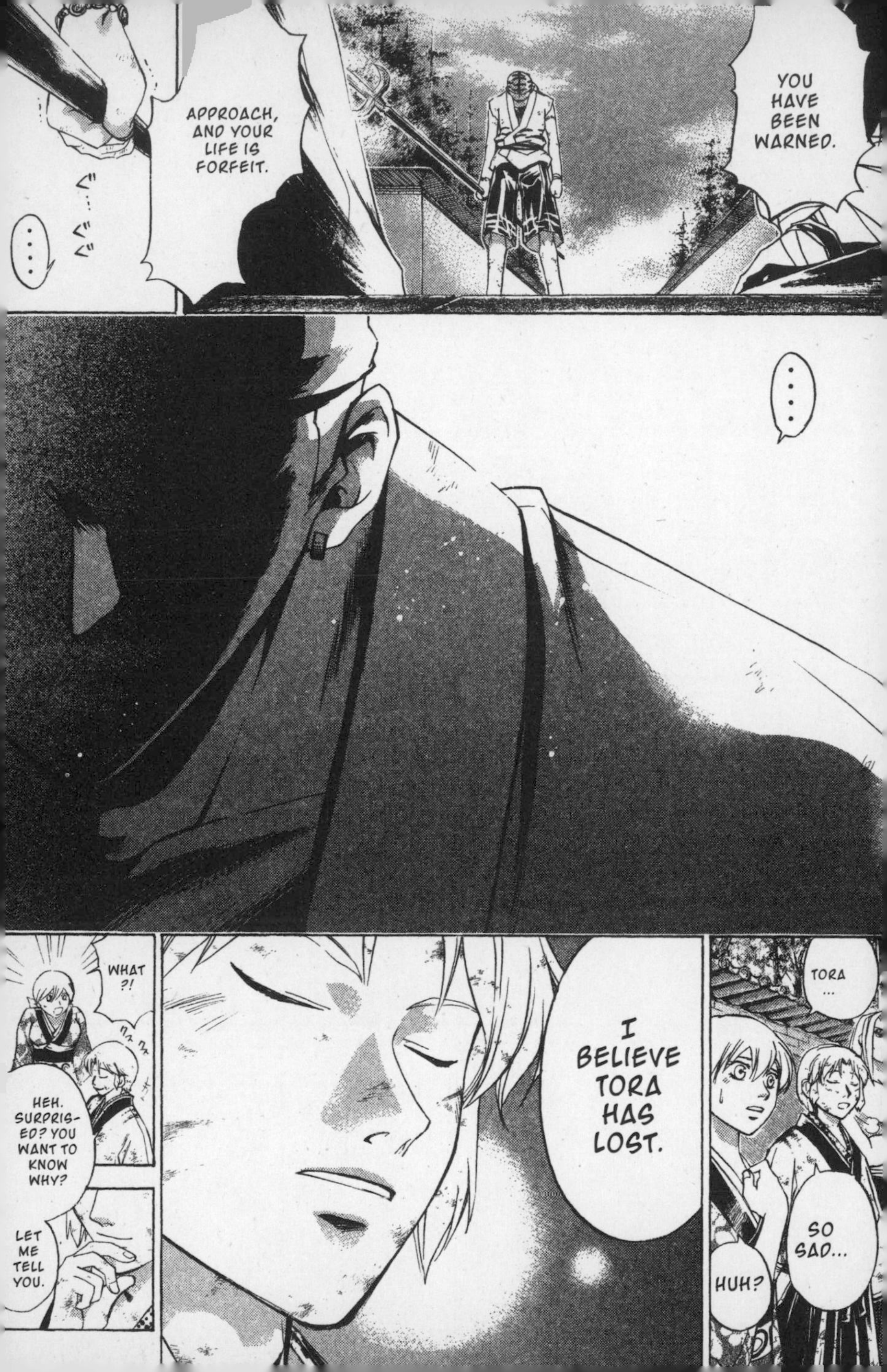

YOU HAVE BEEN WARNED.
APPROACH, AND YOUR LIFE IS FORFEIT.
...
....
TORA ...
SO SAD...
HUH?
I BELIEVE TORA HAS LOST.
WHAT?!
HEH. SURPRISED? YOU WANT TO KNOW WHY?
LET ME TELL YOU.

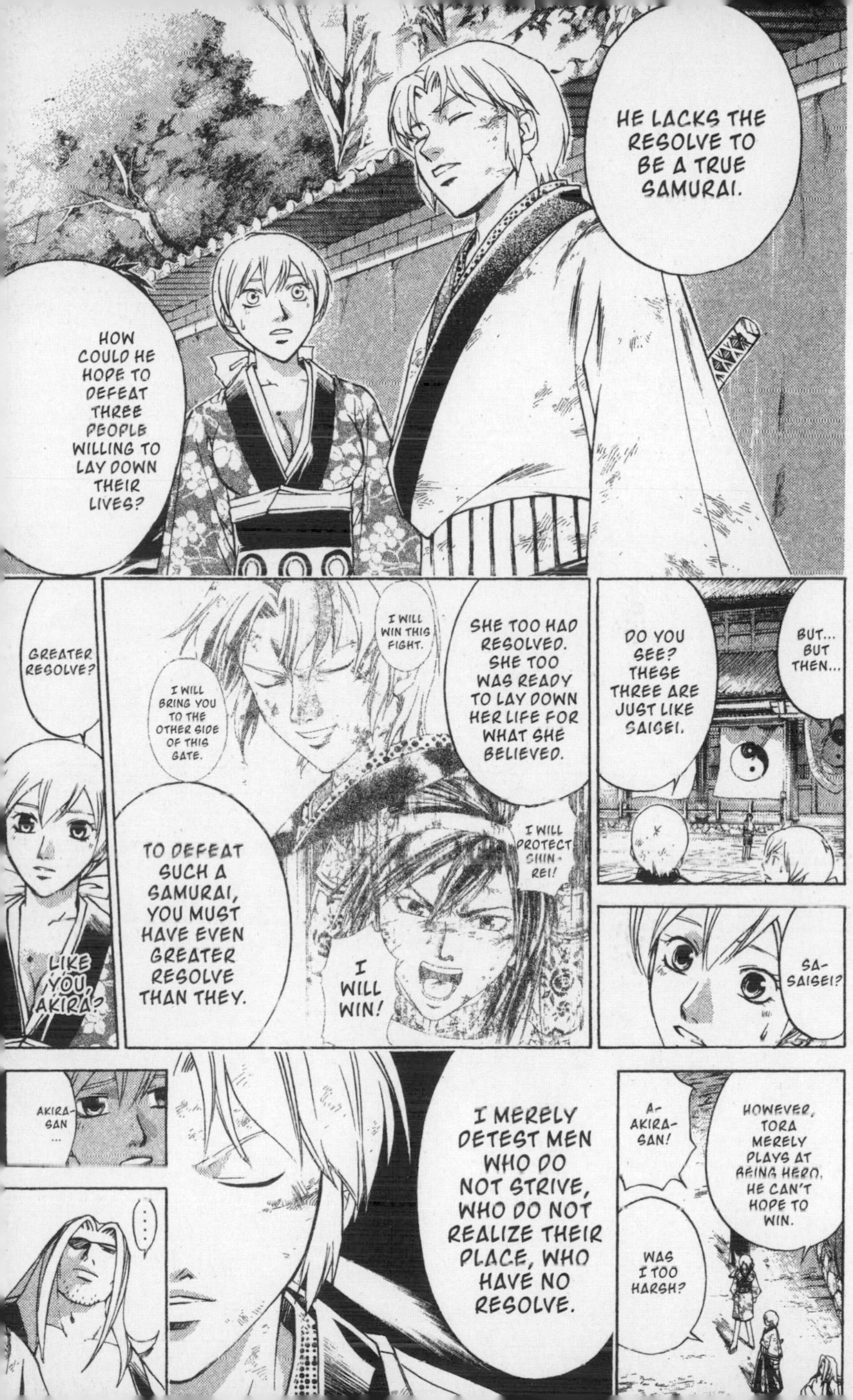
HE LACKS THE RESOLVE TO BE A TRUE SAMURAI.
HOW COULD HE HOPE TO DEFEAT THREE PEOPLE WILLING TO LAY DOWN THEIR LIVES?
BUT... BUT THEN...
DO YOU SEE? THESE THREE ARE JUST LIKE SAISEI.
SA-SAISEI?
SHE TOO HAD RESOLVED. SHE TOO WAS READY TO LAY DOWN HER LIFE FOR WHAT SHE BELIEVED.
I WILL WIN THIS FIGHT.
I WILL BRING YOU TO THE OTHER SIDE OF THIS GATE.
I WILL PROTECT SHIN-REI!
I WILL WIN!
TO DEFEAT SUCH A SAMURAI, YOU MUST HAVE EVEN GREATER RESOLVE THAN THEY.
GREATER RESOLVE?
LIKE YOU, AKIRA?
HOWEVER, TORA MERELY PLAYS AT BEING HERO. HE CAN'T HOPE TO WIN.
A-AKIRA-SAN!
WAS I TOO HARSH?
I MERELY DETEST MEN WHO DO NOT STRIVE, WHO DO NOT REALIZE THEIR PLACE, WHO HAVE NO RESOLVE.
AKIRA-SAN ...
...

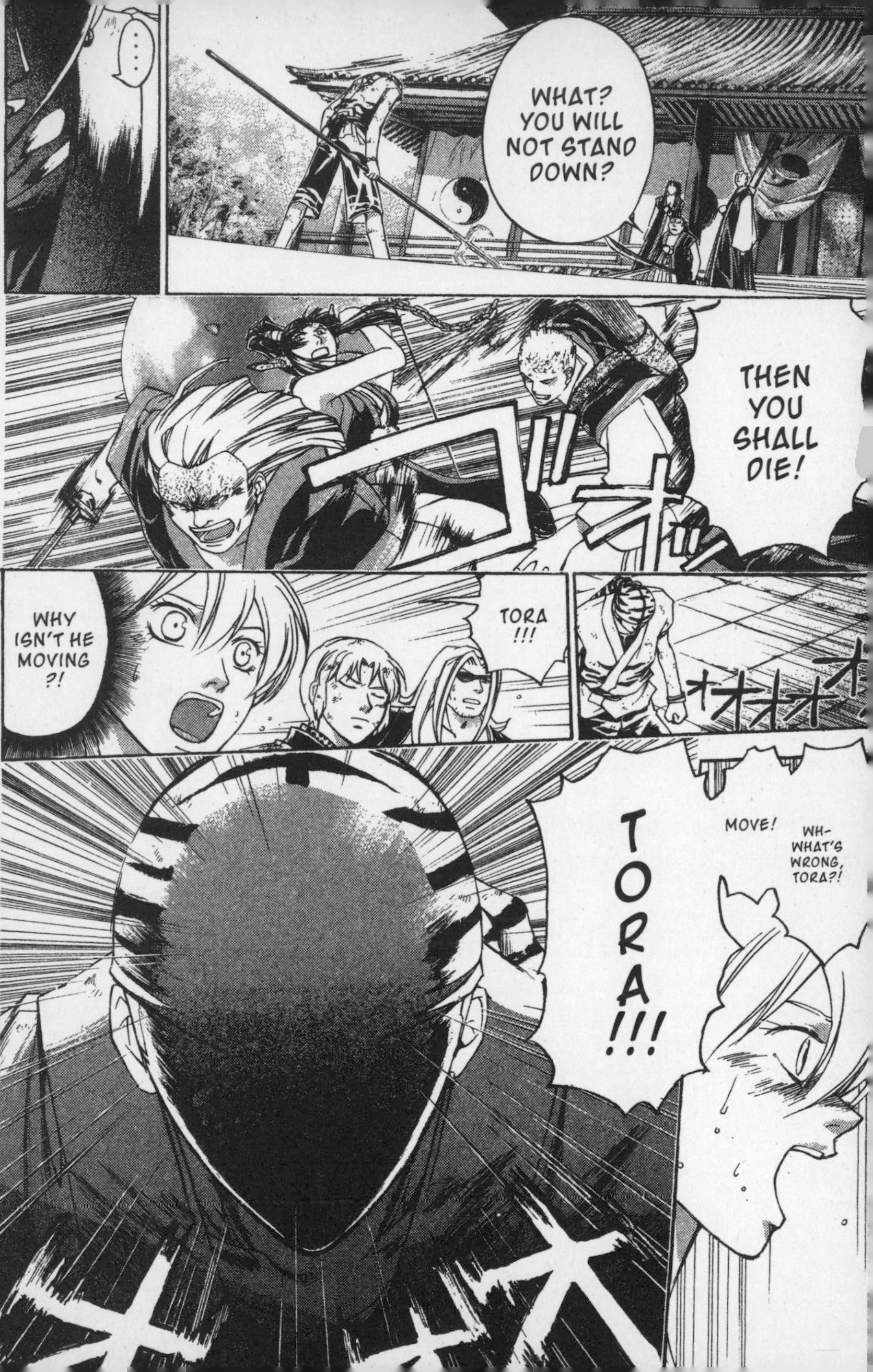
WHAT? YOU WILL NOT STAND DOWN?
....
THEN YOU SHALL DIE!
TORA !!!
WHY ISN'T HE MOVING ?!
WH- WHAT'S WRONG, TORA?!
MOVE!
TORA!!!

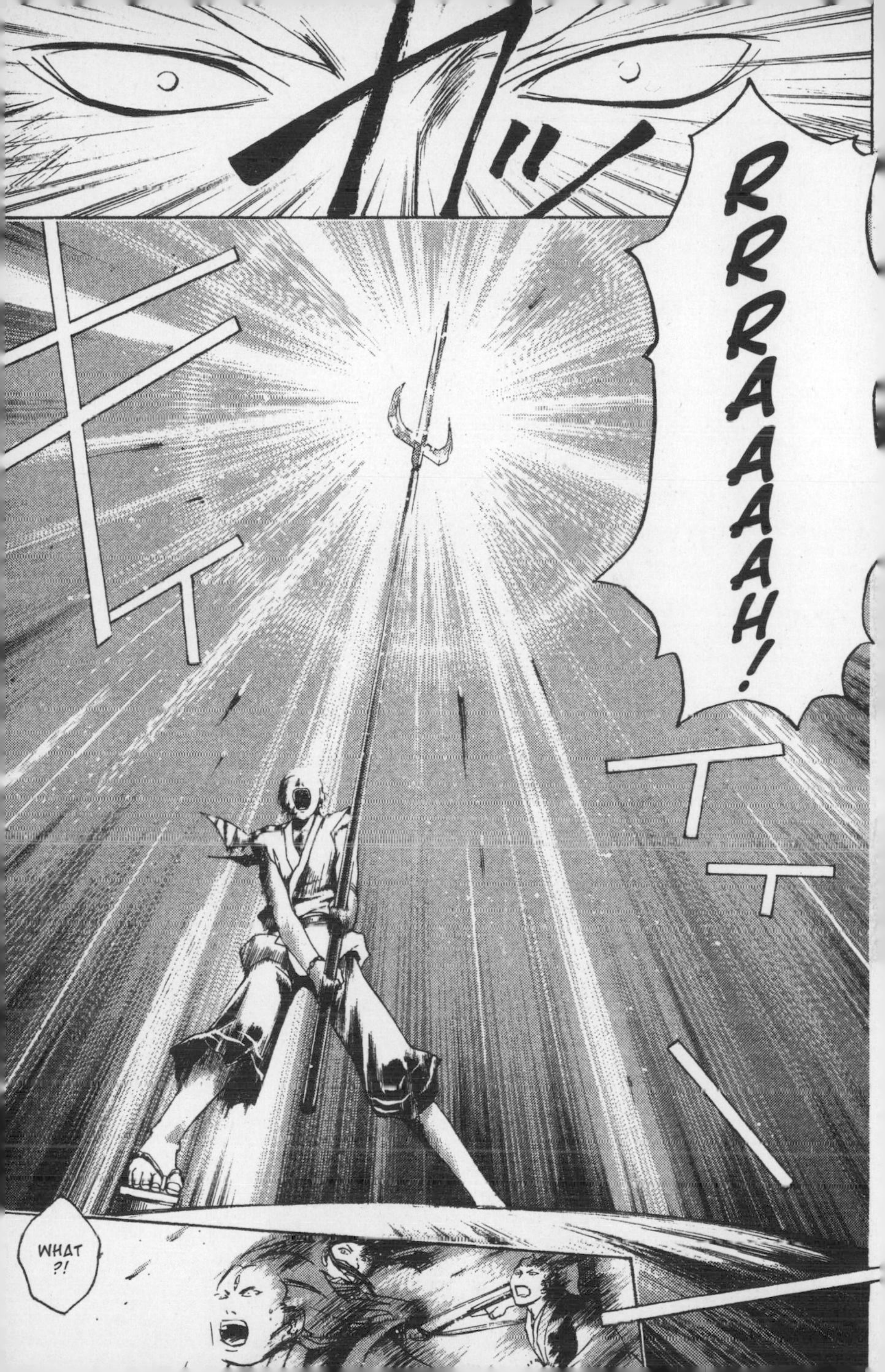
RRRAAAAH!
WHAT ?!

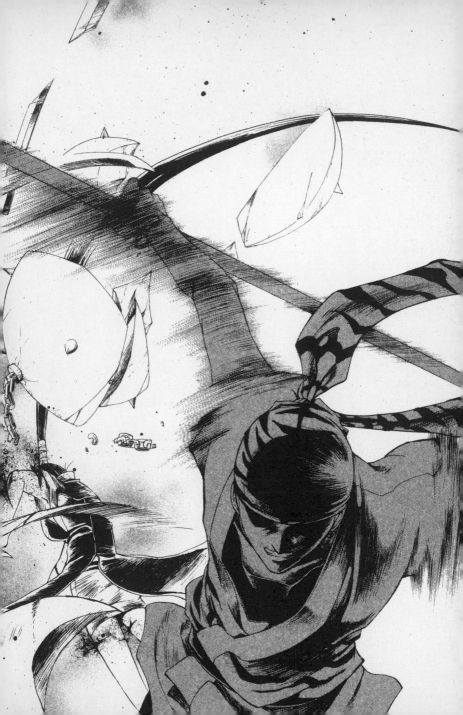

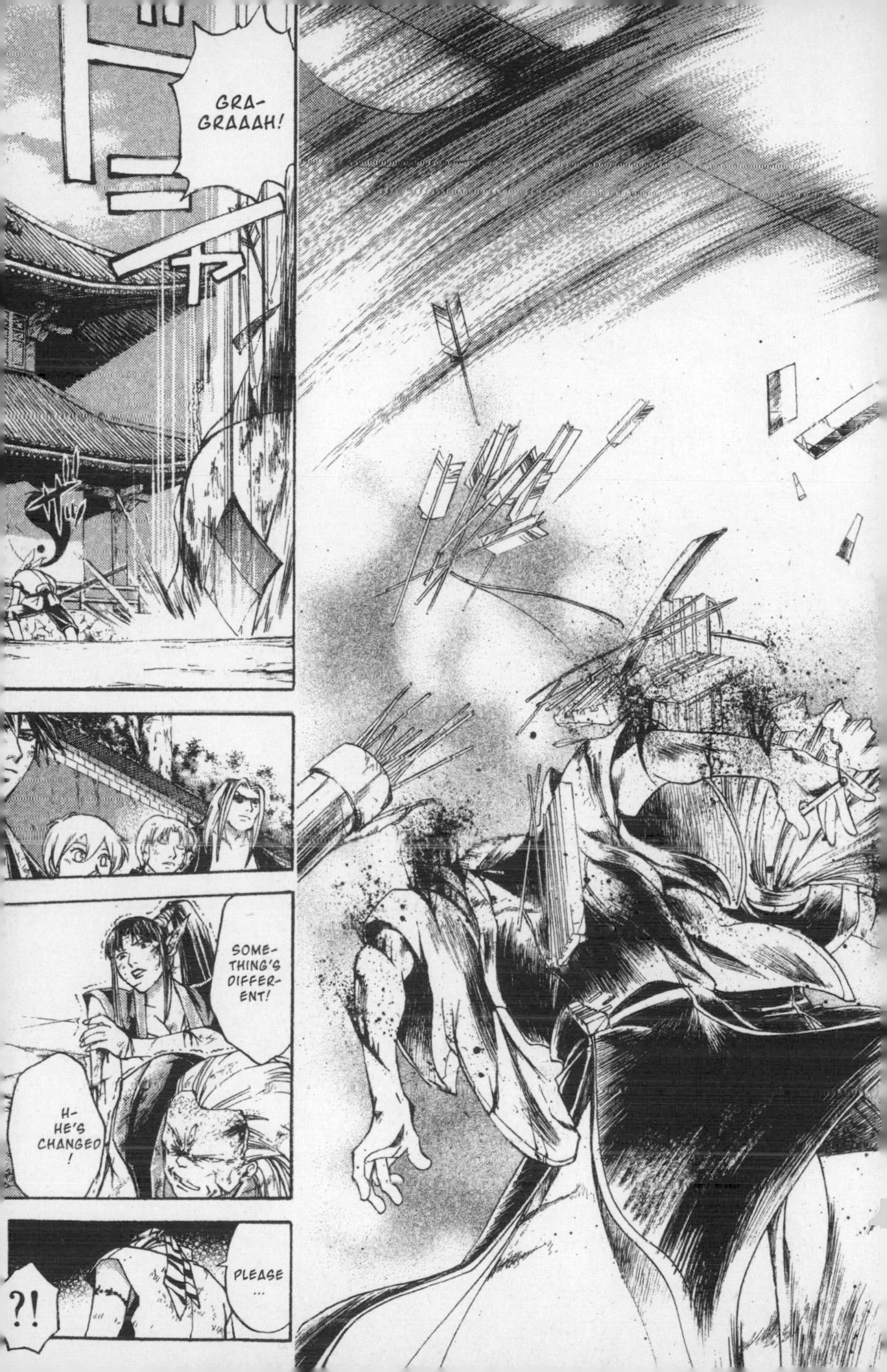
GRA-GRAAAH!
SOME-THING'S DIFFER-ENT!
H-HE'S CHANGED!
PLEASE ...
?!

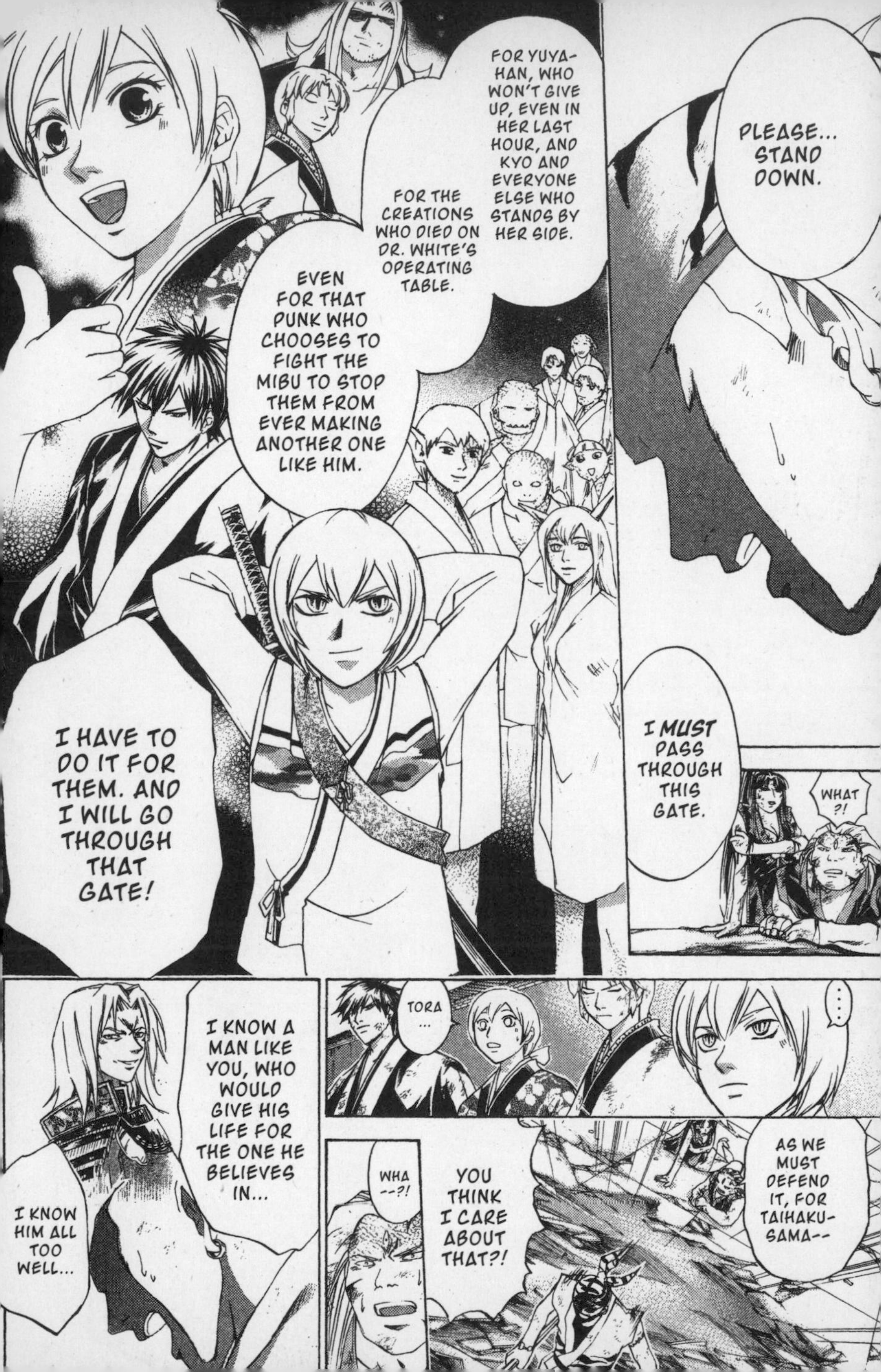
PLEASE... STAND DOWN.
I MUST PASS THROUGH THIS GATE.
WHAT ?!
FOR YUYA-HAN, WHO WON'T GIVE UP, EVEN IN HER LAST HOUR, AND KYO AND EVERYONE ELSE WHO STANDS BY HER SIDE.
FOR THE CREATIONS WHO DIED ON DR. WHITE'S OPERATING TABLE.
EVEN FOR THAT PUNK WHO CHOOSES TO FIGHT THE MIBU TO STOP THEM FROM EVER MAKING ANOTHER ONE LIKE HIM.
I HAVE TO DO IT FOR THEM. AND I WILL GO THROUGH THAT GATE!
...
TORA ...
AS WE MUST DEFEND IT, FOR TAIHAKU-SAMA--
WHA --?!
YOU THINK I CARE ABOUT THAT?!
I KNOW A MAN LIKE YOU, WHO WOULD GIVE HIS LIFE FOR THE ONE HE BELIEVES IN...
I KNOW HIM ALL TOO WELL...

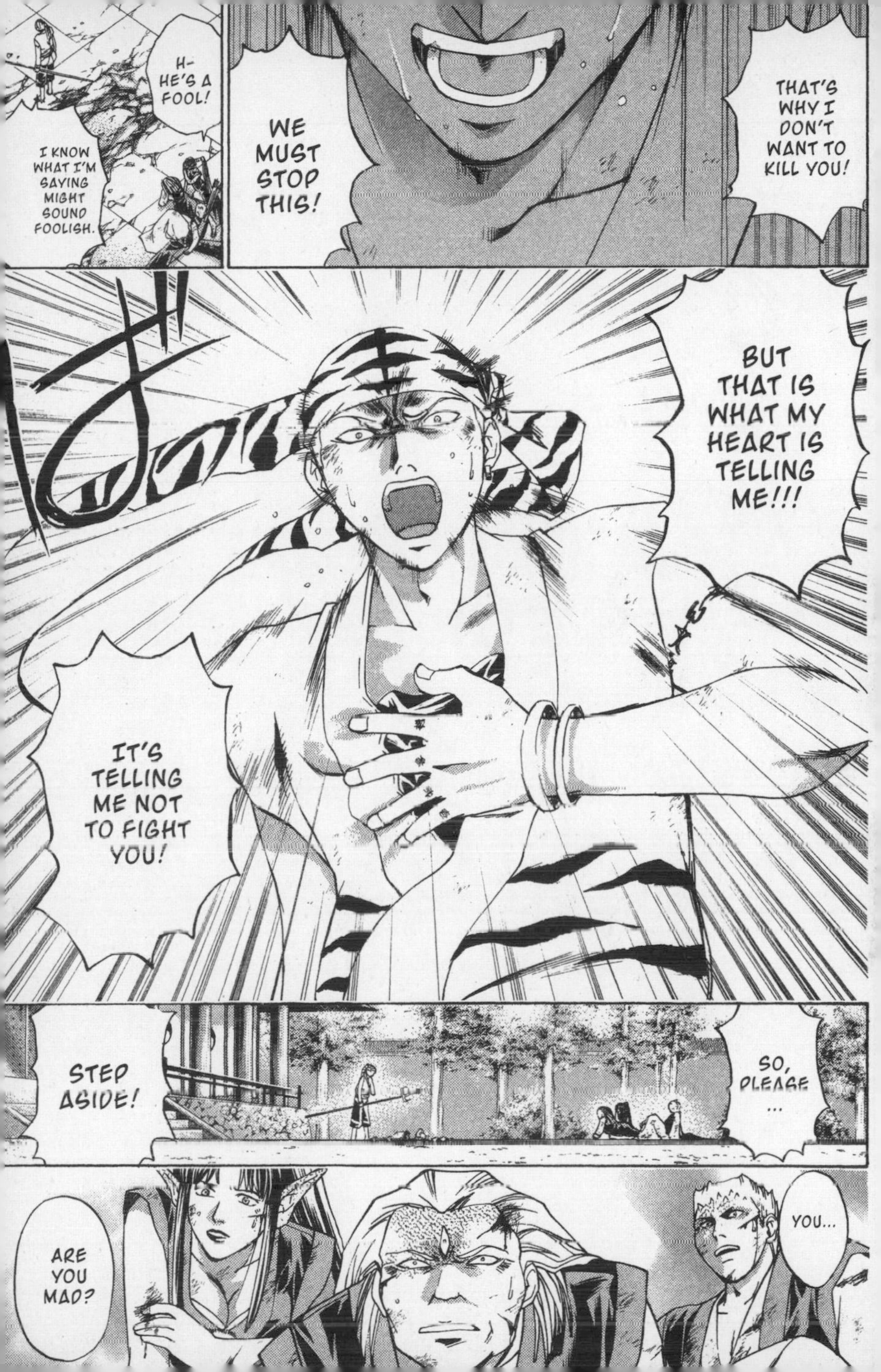
THAT'S WHY I DON'T WANT TO KILL YOU!
WE MUST STOP THIS!
H-HE'S A FOOL!
I KNOW WHAT I'M SAYING MIGHT SOUND FOOLISH.
BUT THAT IS WHAT MY HEART IS TELLING ME!!!
IT'S TELLING ME NOT TO FIGHT YOU!
SO, PLEASE ...
STEP ASIDE!
YOU...
ARE YOU MAD?

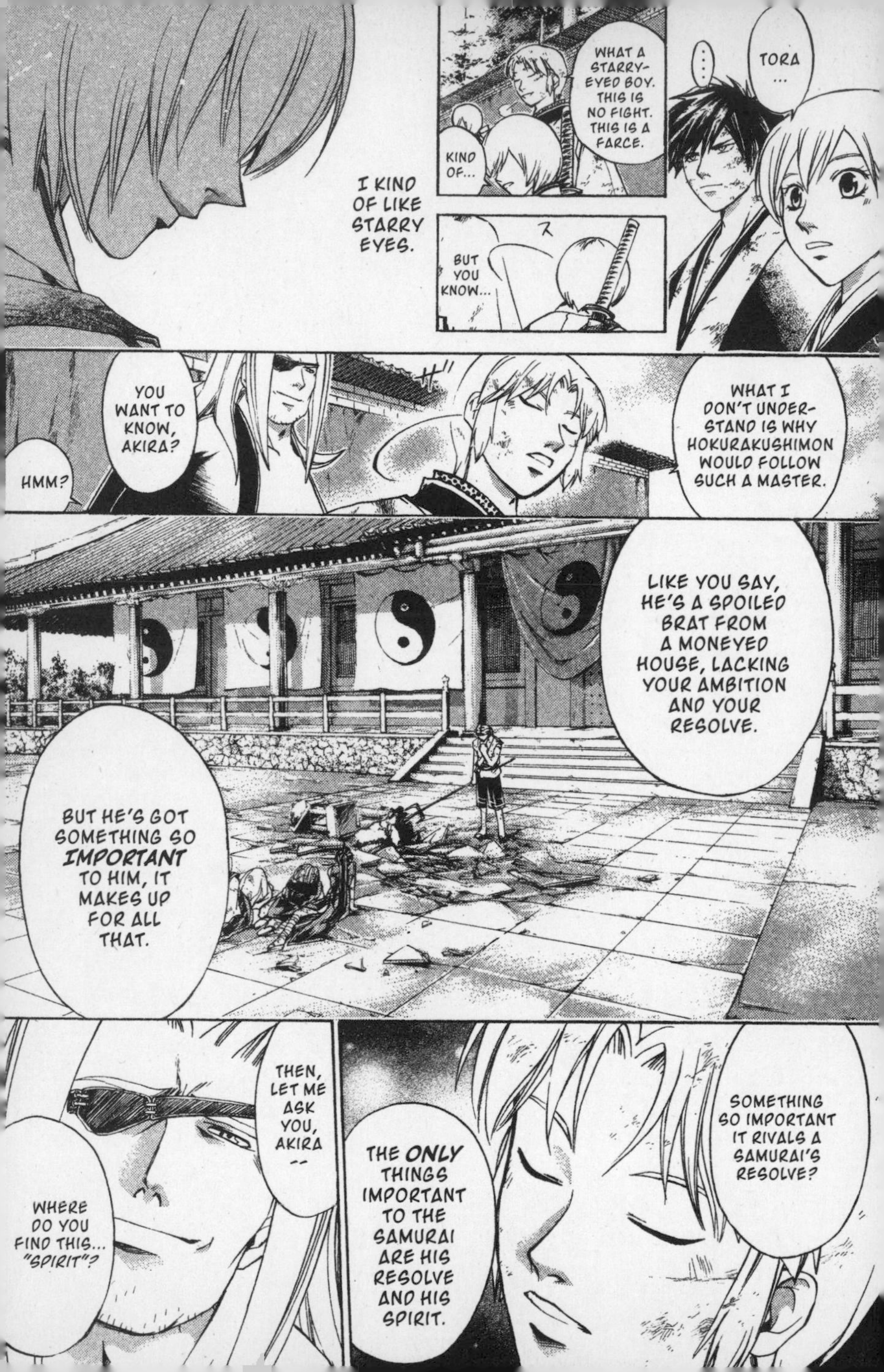
TORA ...
...
WHAT A STARRY-EYED BOY. THIS IS NO FIGHT. THIS IS A FARCE.
KIND OF...
I KIND OF LIKE STARRY EYES.
BUT YOU KNOW...
WHAT I DON'T UNDER-STAND IS WHY HOKURAKUSHIMON WOULD FOLLOW SUCH A MASTER.
YOU WANT TO KNOW, AKIRA?
HMM?
LIKE YOU SAY, HE'S A SPOILED BRAT FROM A MONEYED HOUSE, LACKING YOUR AMBITION AND YOUR RESOLVE.
BUT HE'S GOT SOMETHING SO IMPORTANT TO HIM, IT MAKES UP FOR ALL THAT.
SOMETHING SO IMPORTANT IT RIVALS A SAMURAI'S RESOLVE?
THE ONLY THINGS IMPORTANT TO THE SAMURAI ARE HIS RESOLVE AND HIS SPIRIT.
THEN, LET ME ASK YOU, AKIRA --
WHERE DO YOU FIND THIS... "SPIRIT"?

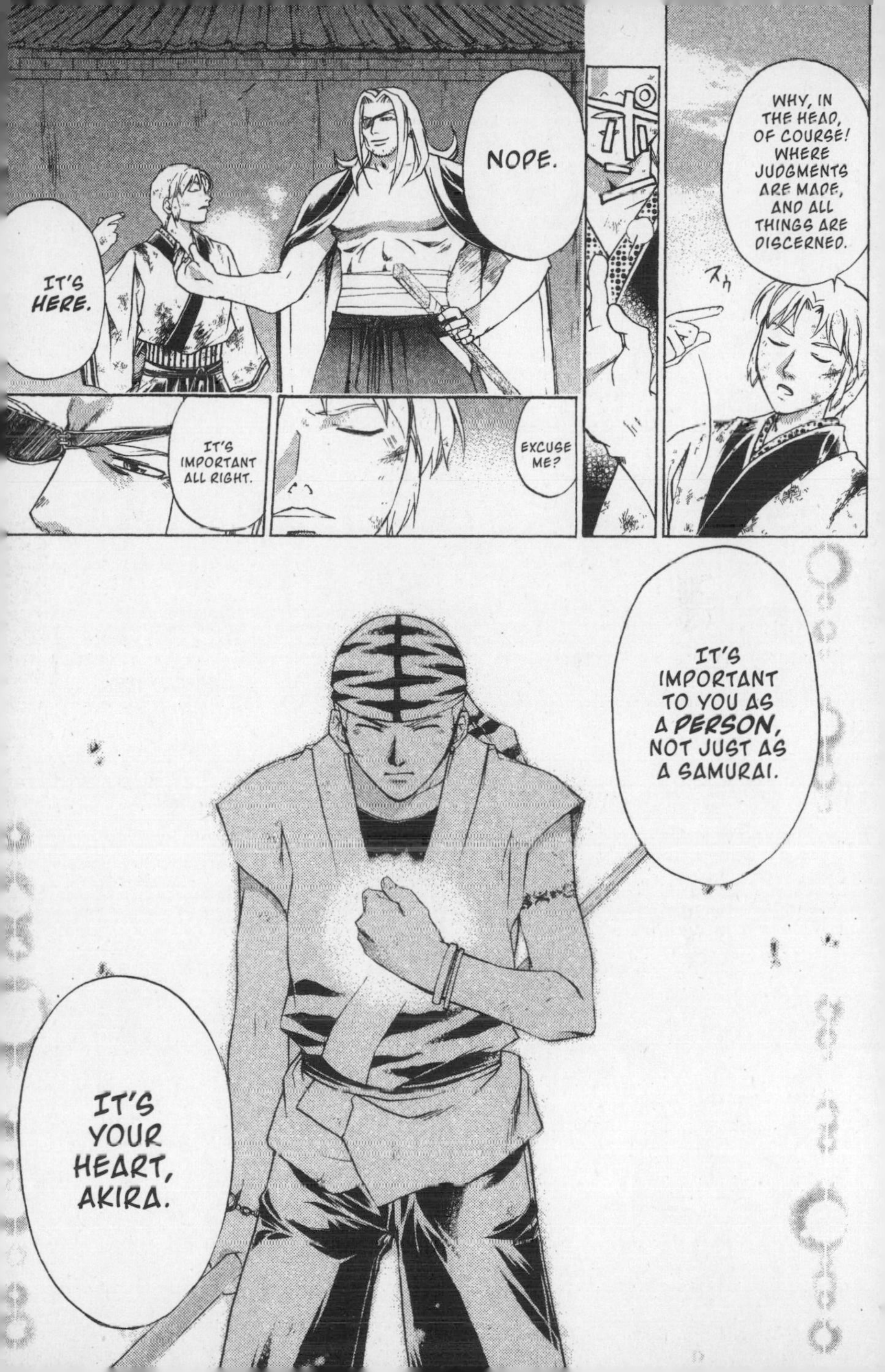
WHY, IN THE HEAD, OF COURSE! WHERE JUDGMENTS ARE MADE, AND ALL THINGS ARE DISCERNED.
スッ
NOPE.
IT'S HERE.
EXCUSE ME?
IT'S IMPORTANT ALL RIGHT.
IT'S IMPORTANT TO YOU AS A *PERSON*, NOT JUST AS A SAMURAI.
IT'S YOUR HEART, AKIRA.

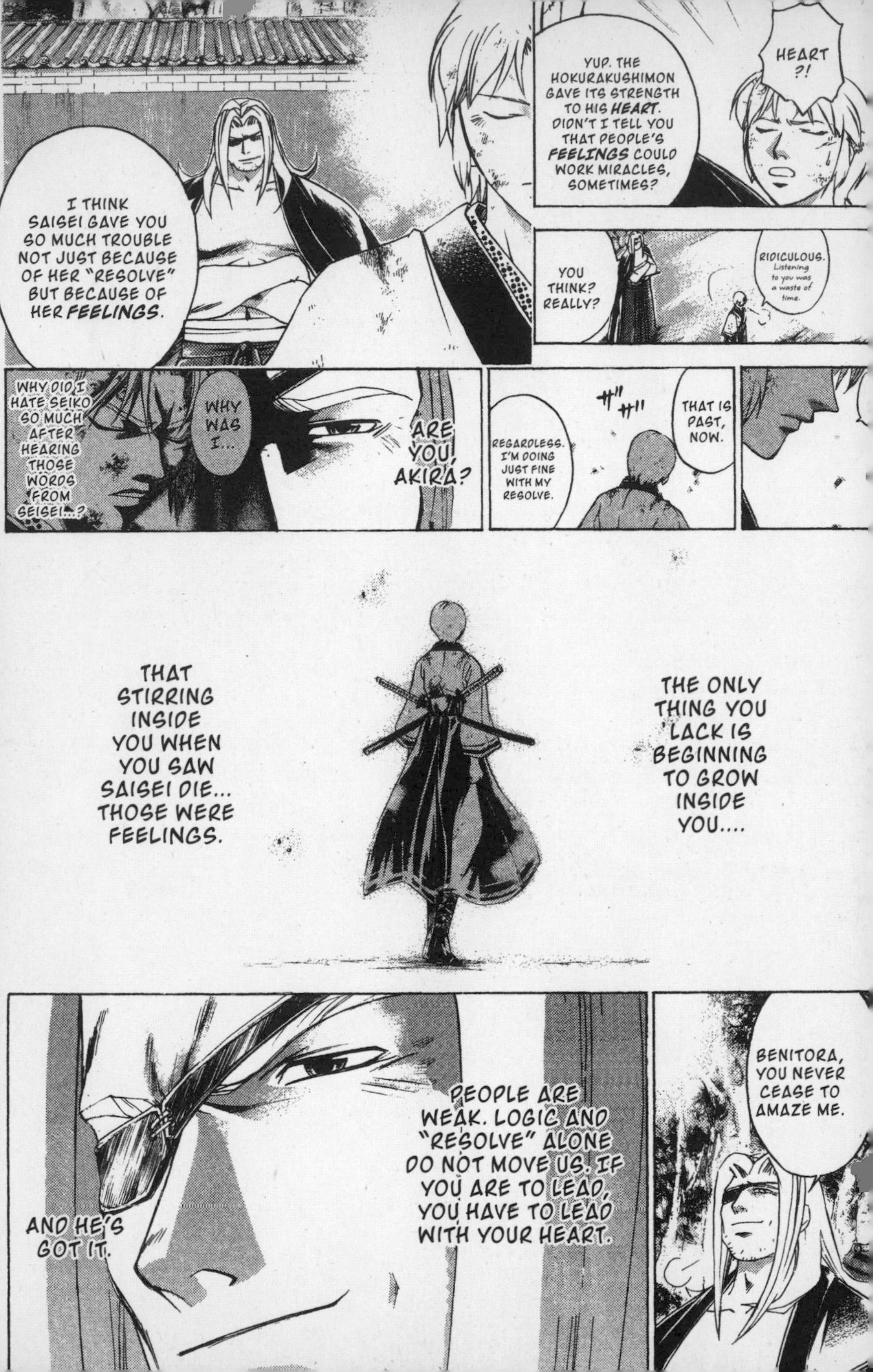
HEART ?!
YUP. THE HOKURAKUSHIMON GAVE ITS STRENGTH TO HIS HEART. DIDN'T I TELL YOU THAT PEOPLE'S FEELINGS COULD WORK MIRACLES, SOMETIMES?
RIDICULOUS. Listening to you was a waste of time.
YOU THINK? REALLY?
I THINK SAISEI GAVE YOU SO MUCH TROUBLE NOT JUST BECAUSE OF HER "RESOLVE" BUT BECAUSE OF HER FEELINGS.
THAT IS PAST, NOW.
REGARDLESS. I'M DOING JUST FINE WITH MY RESOLVE.
ARE YOU, AKIRA?
WHY WAS I...
WHY DID I HATE SEIKO SO MUCH AFTER HEARING THOSE WORDS FROM SEISEI...?
THE ONLY THING YOU LACK IS BEGINNING TO GROW INSIDE YOU....
THAT STIRRING INSIDE YOU WHEN YOU SAW SAISEI DIE... THOSE WERE FEELINGS.
BENITORA, YOU NEVER CEASE TO AMAZE ME.
PEOPLE ARE WEAK. LOGIC AND "RESOLVE" ALONE DO NOT MOVE US. IF YOU ARE TO LEAD, YOU HAVE TO LEAD WITH YOUR HEART.
AND HE'S GOT IT.

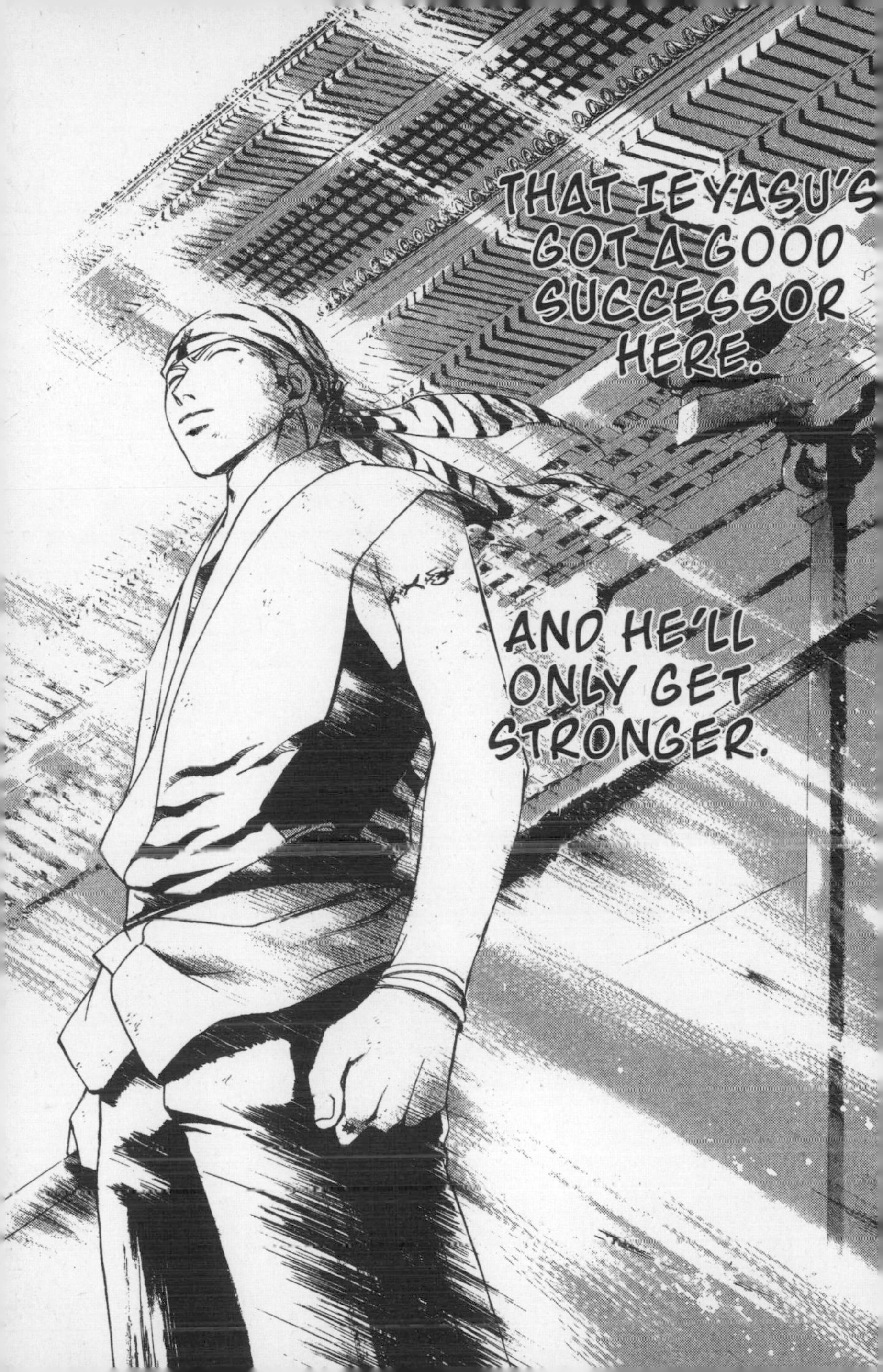
THAT IEYASU'S GOT A GOOD SUCCESSOR HERE.
AND HE'LL ONLY GET STRONGER.

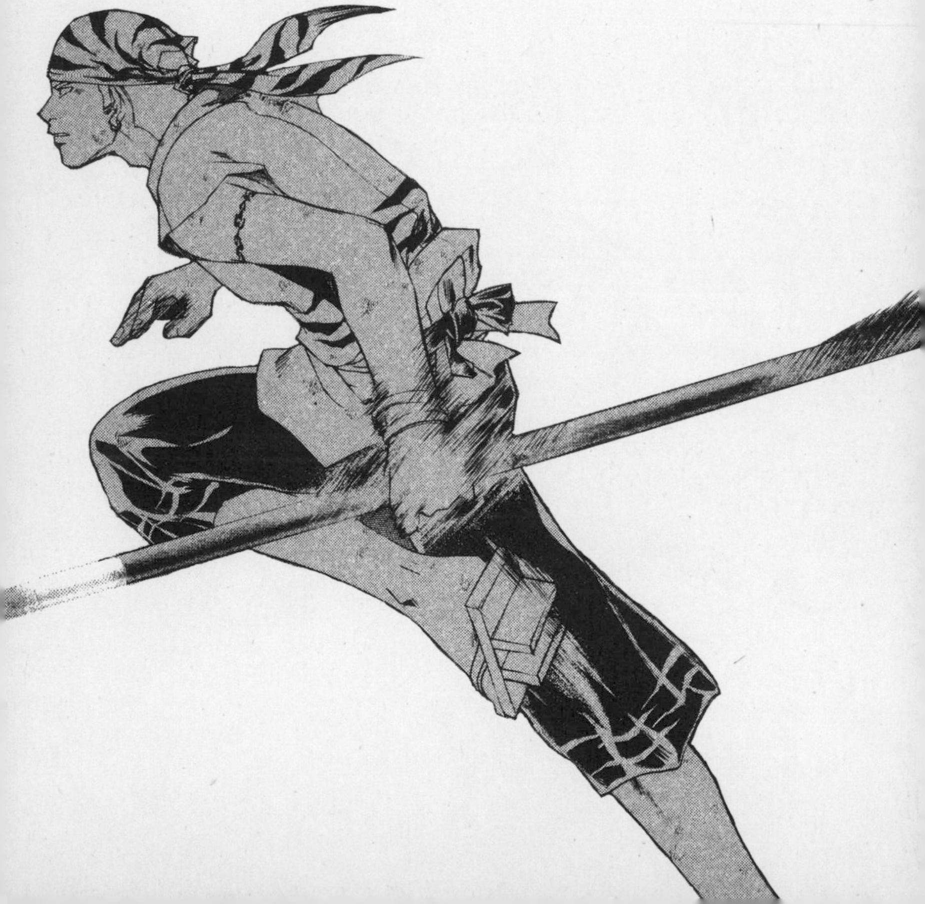

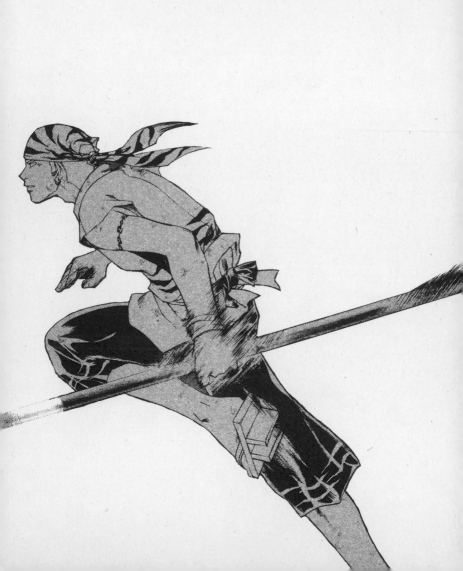

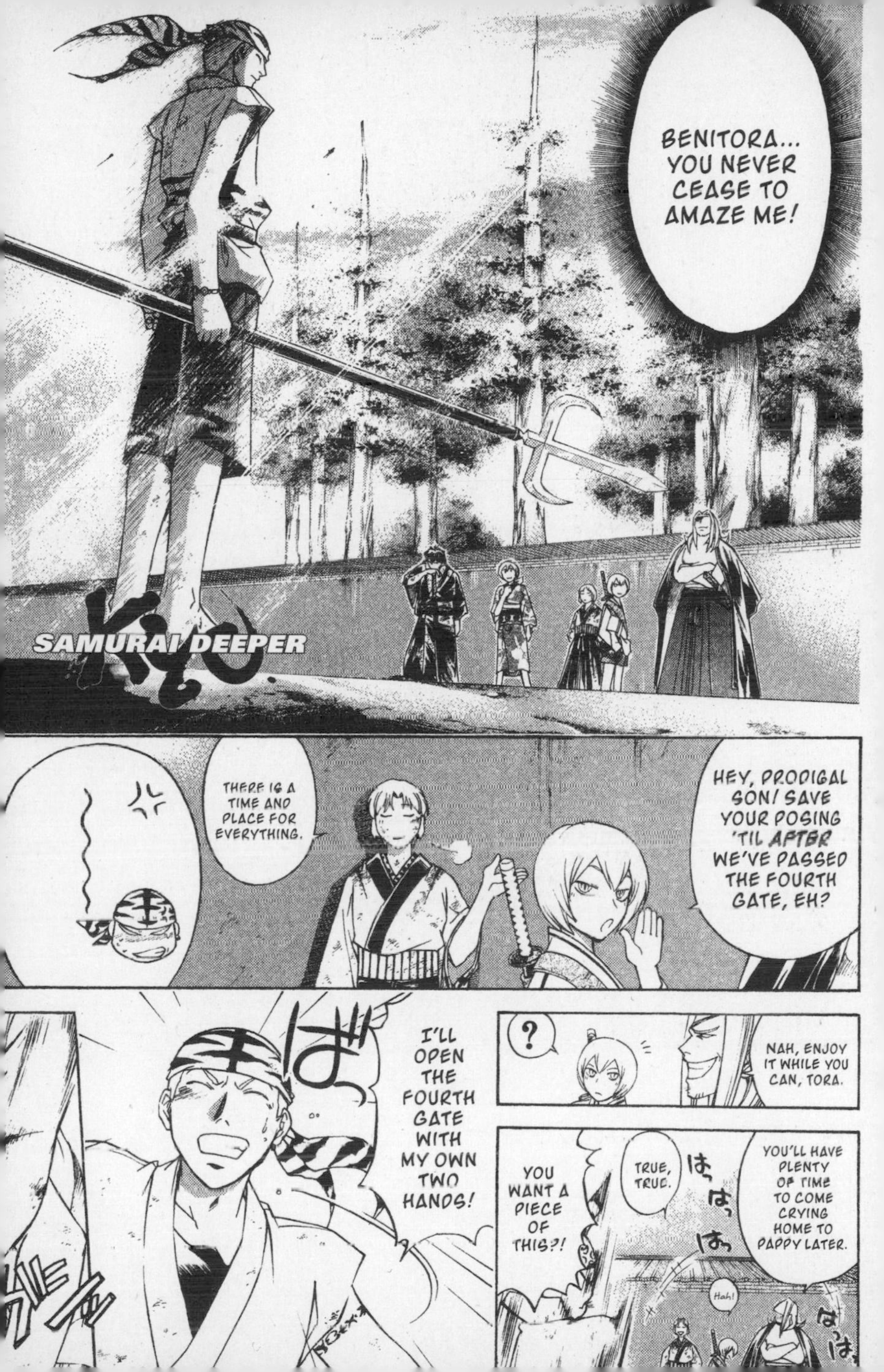
BENITORA... YOU NEVER CEASE TO AMAZE ME!
SAMURAI DEEPER KYO
HEY, PRODIGAL SON! SAVE YOUR POSING 'TIL AFTER WE'VE PASSED THE FOURTH GATE, EH?
THERE IS A TIME AND PLACE FOR EVERYTHING.
?
NAH, ENJOY IT WHILE YOU CAN, TORA.
YOU'LL HAVE PLENTY OF TIME TO COME CRYING HOME TO PAPPY LATER.
はっ はっ はっ
TRUE, TRUE.
YOU WANT A PIECE OF THIS?!
Hah!
I'LL OPEN THE FOURTH GATE WITH MY OWN TWO HANDS!

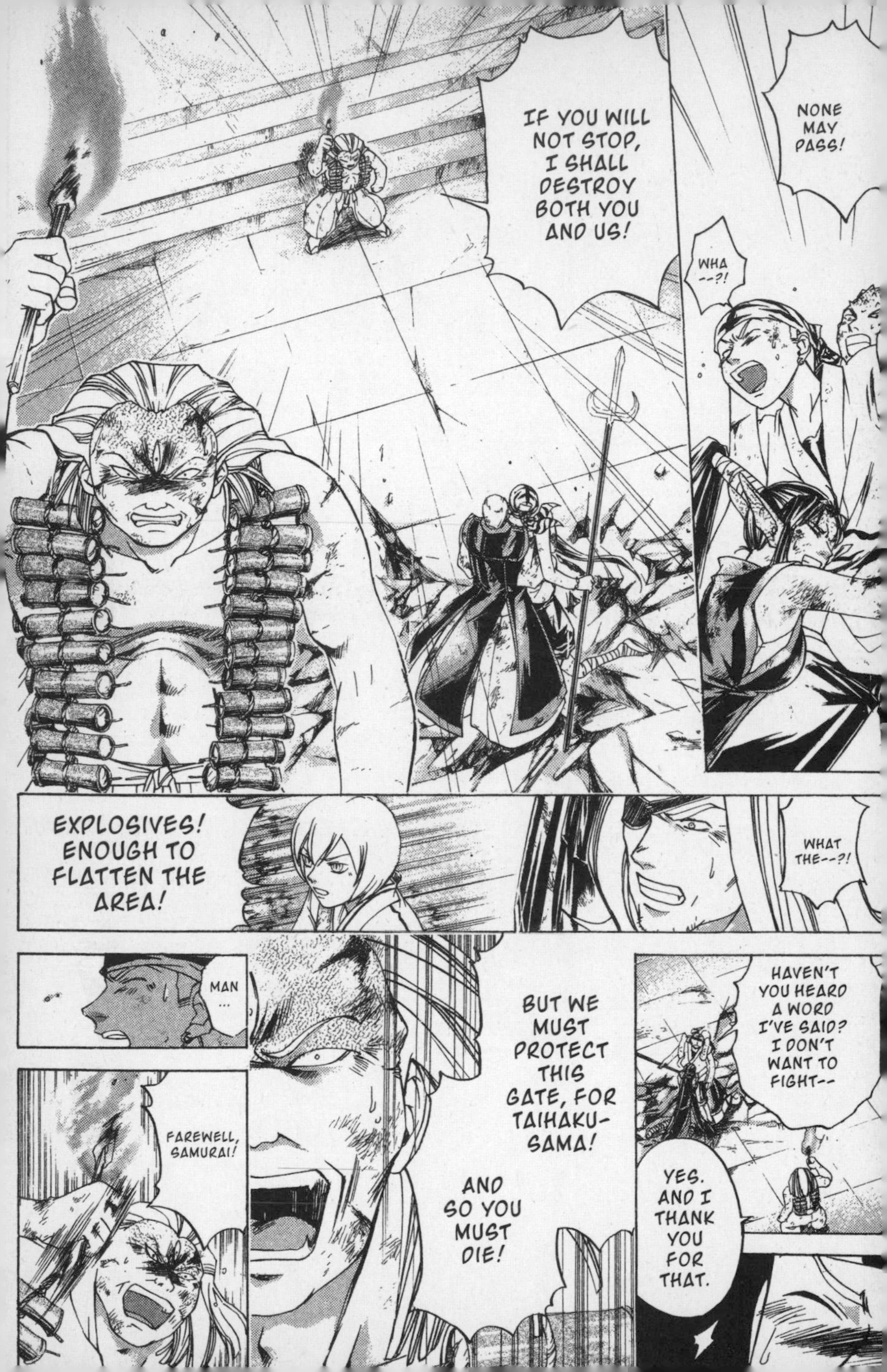
NONE MAY PASS!
WHA--?!
IF YOU WILL NOT STOP, I SHALL DESTROY BOTH YOU AND US!
WHAT THE--?!
EXPLOSIVES! ENOUGH TO FLATTEN THE AREA!
HAVEN'T YOU HEARD A WORD I'VE SAID? I DON'T WANT TO FIGHT--
YES. AND I THANK YOU FOR THAT.
BUT WE MUST PROTECT THIS GATE, FOR TAIHAKU-SAMA!
AND SO YOU MUST DIE!
MAN ...
FAREWELL, SAMURAI!

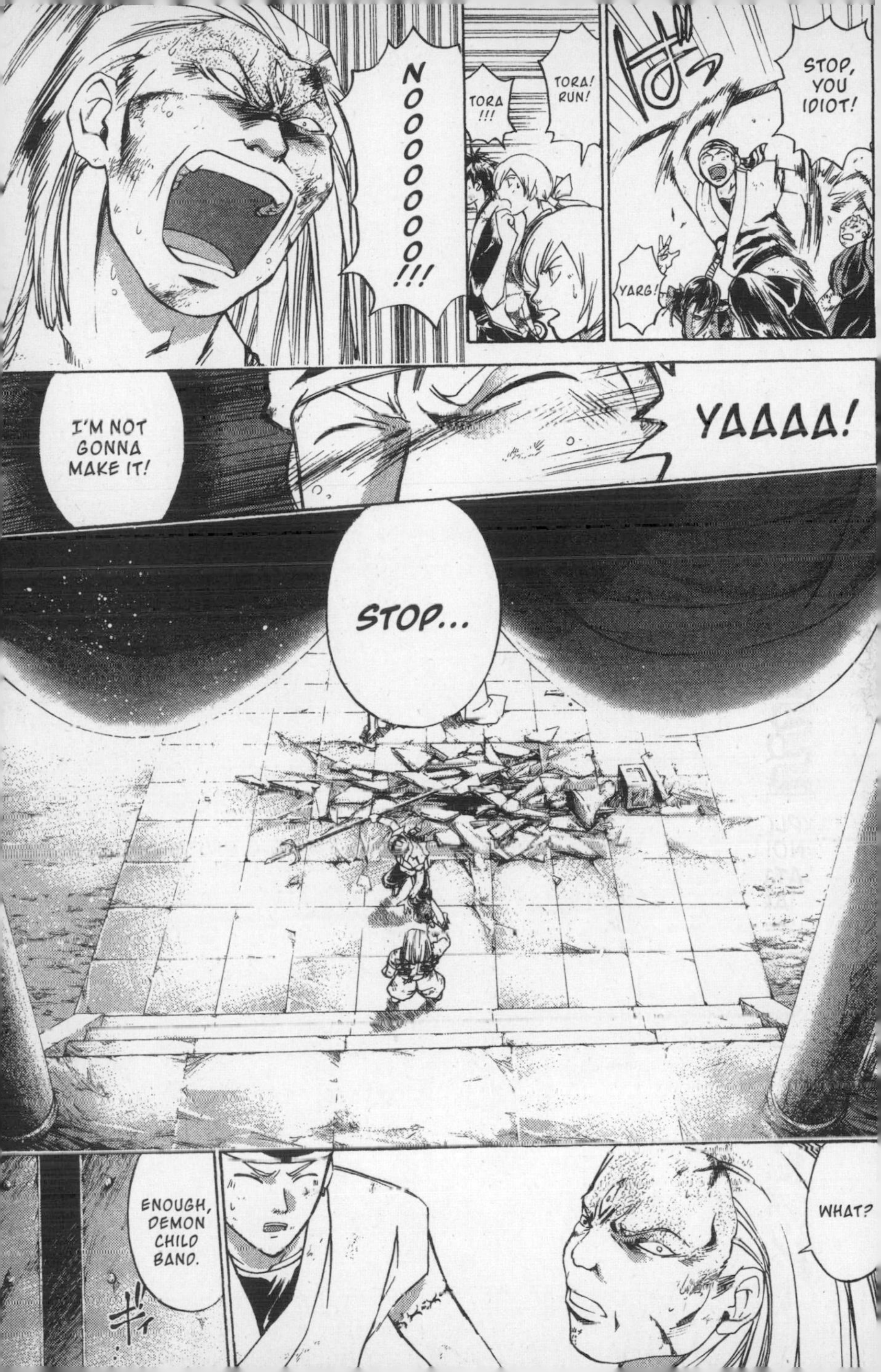
STOP, YOU IDIOT!
YARG!
TORA! RUN!
TORA!!!
NOOOOOOOOOO!!!
YAAAA!
I'M NOT GONNA MAKE IT!
STOP...
ENOUGH, DEMON CHILD BAND.
WHAT?

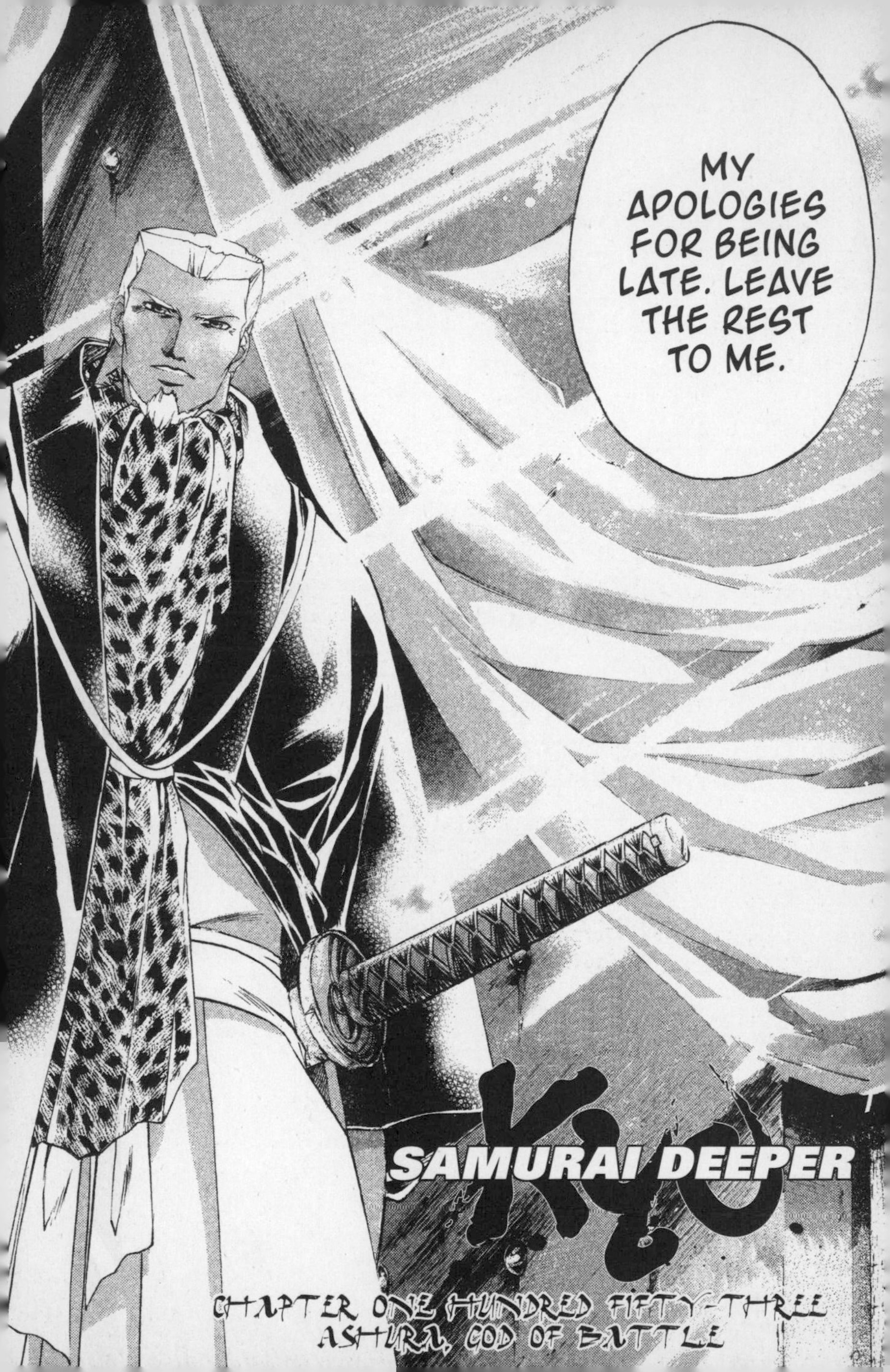
MY APOLOGIES FOR BEING LATE. LEAVE THE REST TO ME.
SAMURAI DEEPER KYO
CHAPTER ONE HUNDRED FIFTY-THREE
ASHURA, GOD OF BATTLE

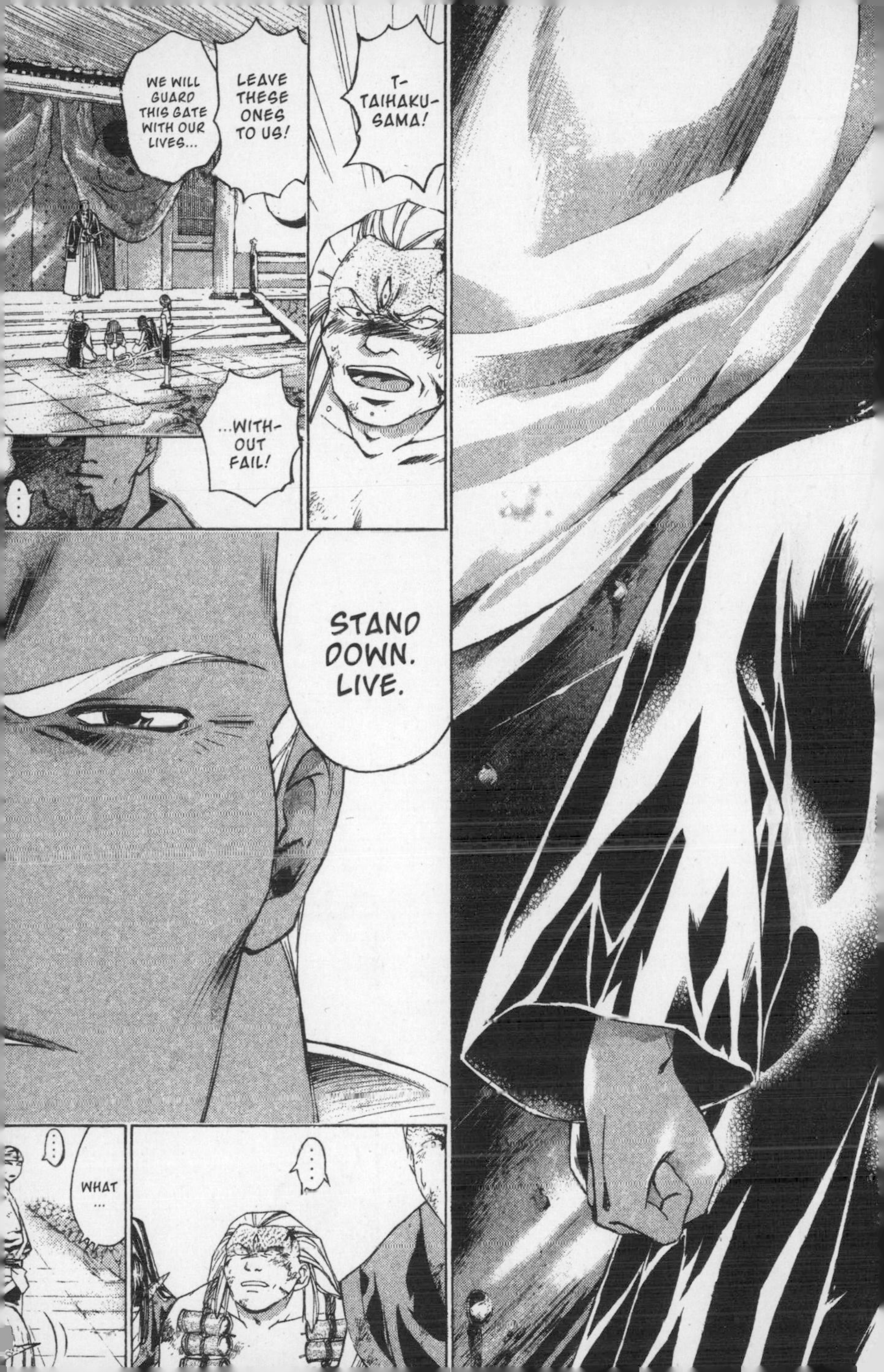
T-TAIHAKU-SAMA!
LEAVE THESE ONES TO US!
WE WILL GUARD THIS GATE WITH OUR LIVES...
...WITH-OUT FAIL!
...
STAND DOWN. LIVE.
...
...
WHAT ...

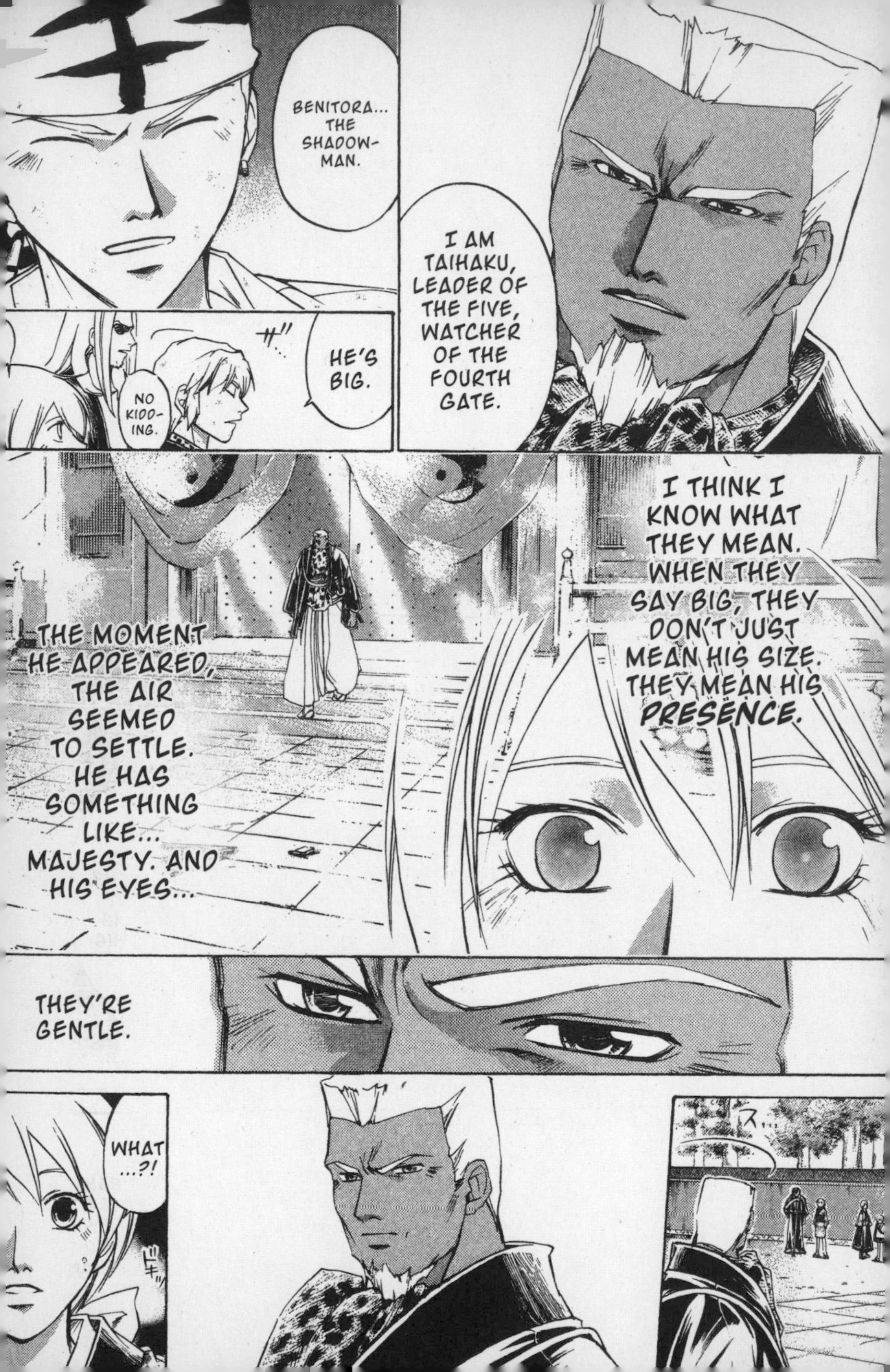
I AM TAIHAKU, LEADER OF THE FIVE, WATCHER OF THE FOURTH GATE.
BENITORA... THE SHADOW-MAN.
HE'S BIG.
NO KIDDING.
I THINK I KNOW WHAT THEY MEAN. WHEN THEY SAY BIG, THEY DON'T JUST MEAN HIS SIZE. THEY MEAN HIS PRESENCE.
THE MOMENT HE APPEARED, THE AIR SEEMED TO SETTLE. HE HAS SOMETHING LIKE... MAJESTY. AND HIS EYES...
THEY'RE GENTLE.
WHAT ...?!

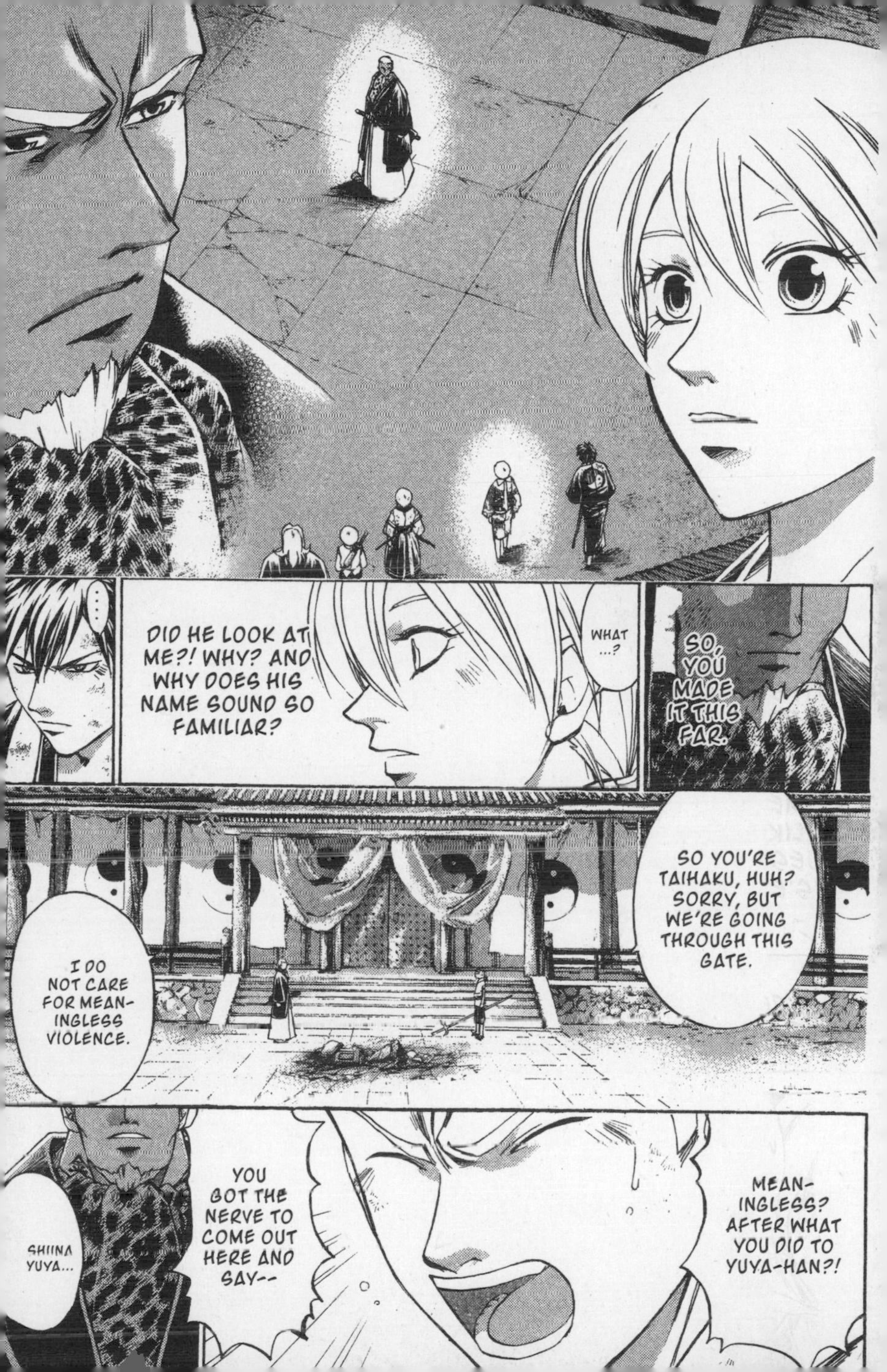
SO, YOU MADE IT THIS FAR.
WHAT ...?
DID HE LOOK AT ME?! WHY? AND WHY DOES HIS NAME SOUND SO FAMILIAR?
....
SO YOU'RE TAIHAKU, HUH? SORRY, BUT WE'RE GOING THROUGH THIS GATE.
I DO NOT CARE FOR MEAN-INGLESS VIOLENCE.
MEAN-INGLESS? AFTER WHAT YOU DID TO YUYA-HAN?!
YOU GOT THE NERVE TO COME OUT HERE AND SAY--
SHIINA YUYA...

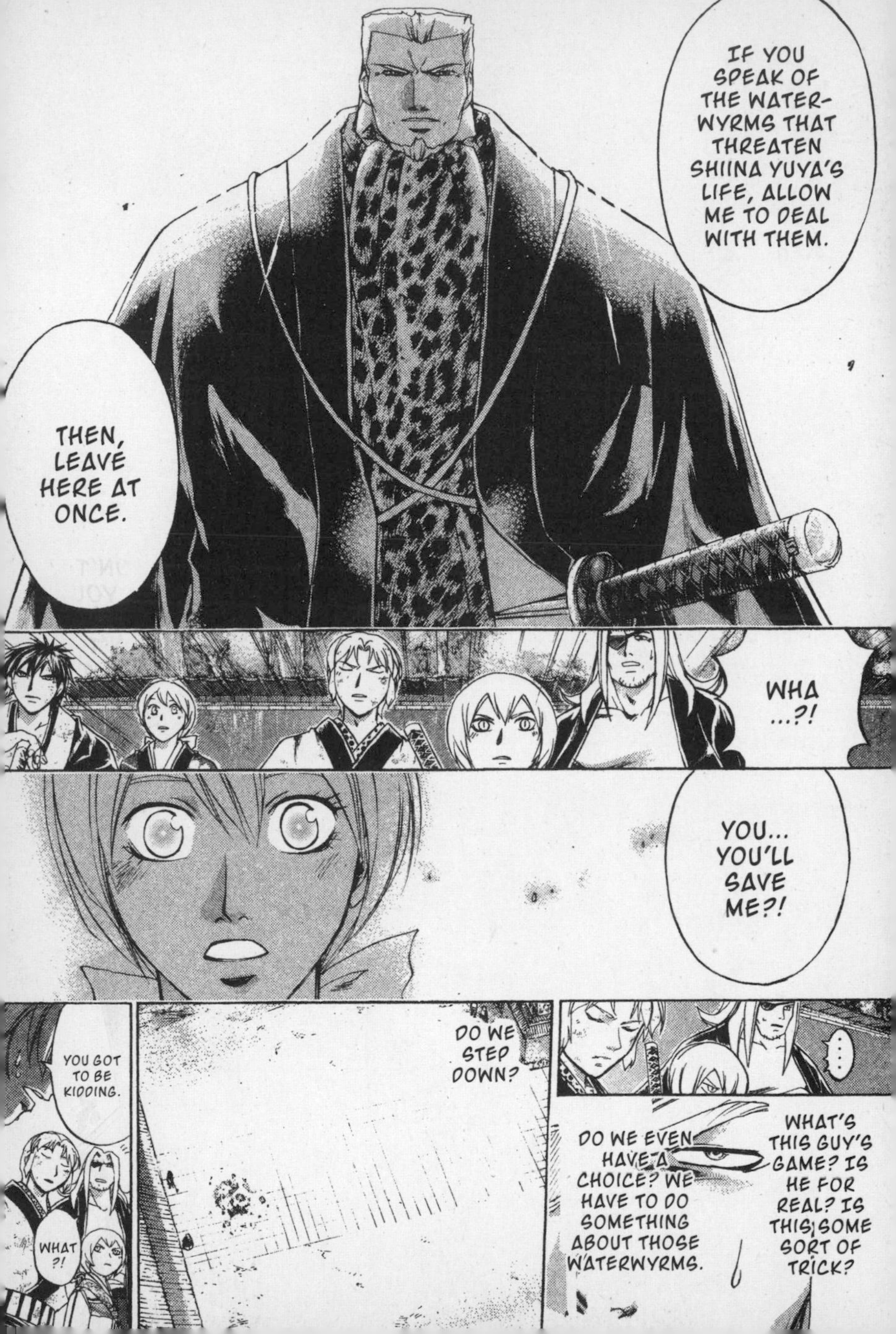
IF YOU SPEAK OF THE WATER-WYRMS THAT THREATEN SHIINA YUYA'S LIFE, ALLOW ME TO DEAL WITH THEM.
THEN, LEAVE HERE AT ONCE.
WHA ...?!
YOU... YOU'LL SAVE ME?!
...
WHAT'S THIS GUY'S GAME? IS HE FOR REAL? IS THIS SOME SORT OF TRICK?
DO WE EVEN HAVE A CHOICE? WE HAVE TO DO SOMETHING ABOUT THOSE WATERWYRMS.
DO WE STEP DOWN?
YOU GOT TO BE KIDDING.
WHAT ?!

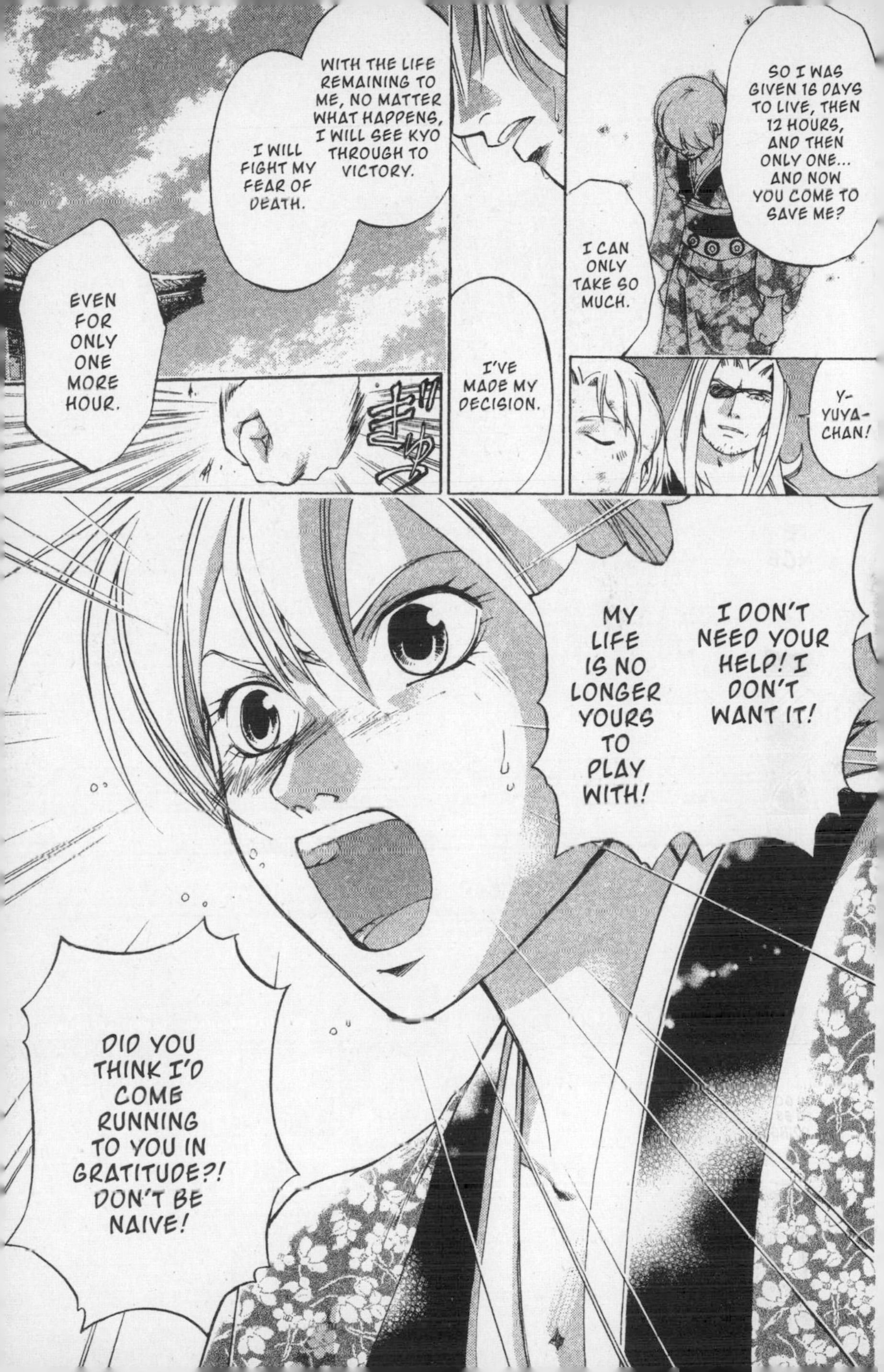
SO I WAS GIVEN 16 DAYS TO LIVE, THEN 12 HOURS, AND THEN ONLY ONE... AND NOW YOU COME TO SAVE ME?
I CAN ONLY TAKE SO MUCH.
Y-YUYA-CHAN!
I'VE MADE MY DECISION.
WITH THE LIFE REMAINING TO ME, NO MATTER WHAT HAPPENS, I WILL SEE KYO THROUGH TO VICTORY.
I WILL FIGHT MY FEAR OF DEATH.
EVEN FOR ONLY ONE MORE HOUR.
I DON'T NEED YOUR HELP! I DON'T WANT IT!
MY LIFE IS NO LONGER YOURS TO PLAY WITH!
DID YOU THINK I'D COME RUNNING TO YOU IN GRATITUDE?! DON'T BE NAIVE!

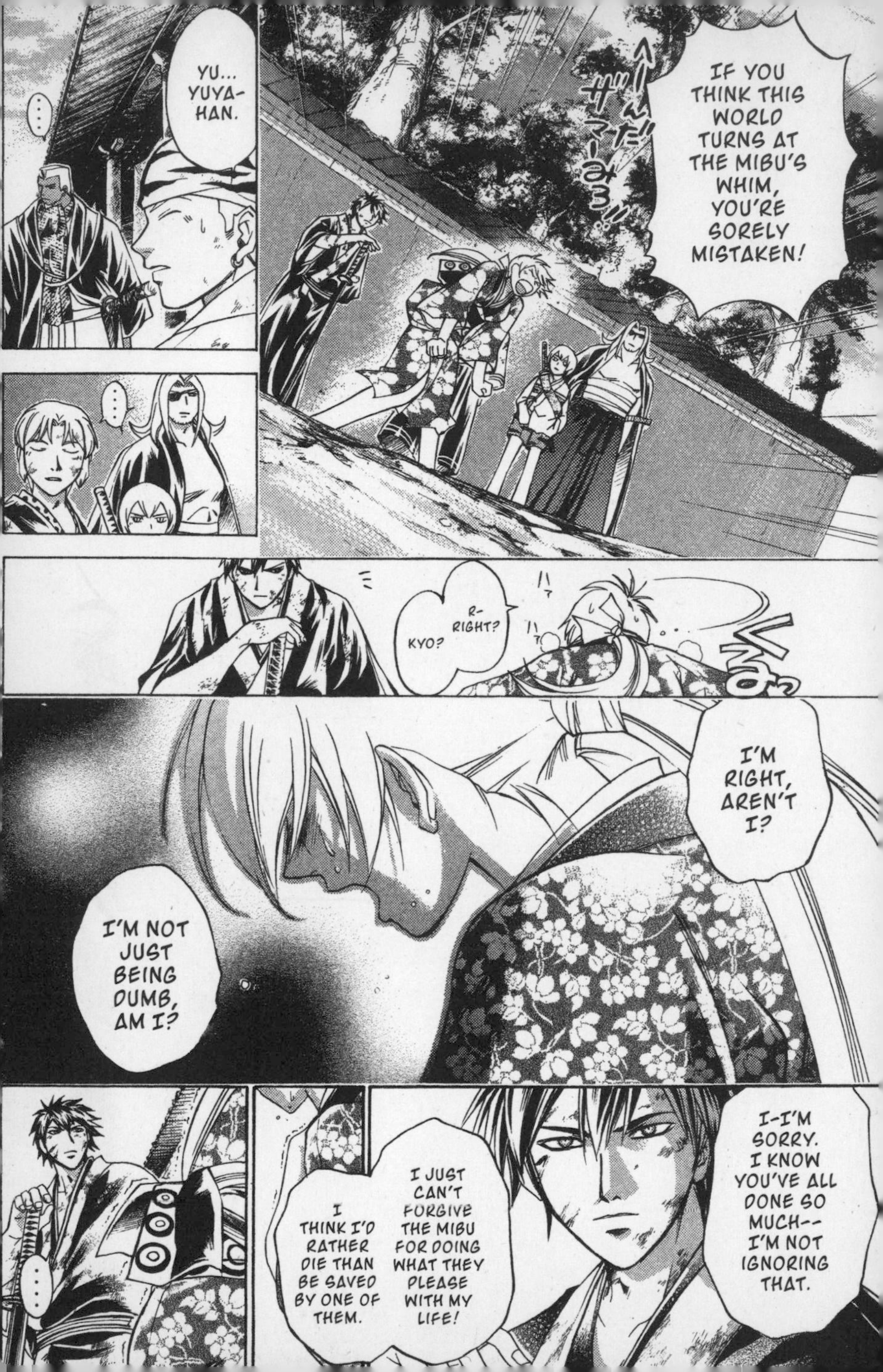
IF YOU THINK THIS WORLD TURNS AT THE MIBU'S WHIM, YOU'RE SORELY MISTAKEN!
YU... YUYA-HAN.
...
...
R- RIGHT?
KYO?
I'M RIGHT, AREN'T I?
I'M NOT JUST BEING DUMB, AM I?
I-I'M SORRY. I KNOW YOU'VE ALL DONE SO MUCH-- I'M NOT IGNORING THAT.
I JUST CAN'T FORGIVE THE MIBU FOR DOING WHAT THEY PLEASE WITH MY LIFE!
I THINK I'D RATHER DIE THAN BE SAVED BY ONE OF THEM.
...

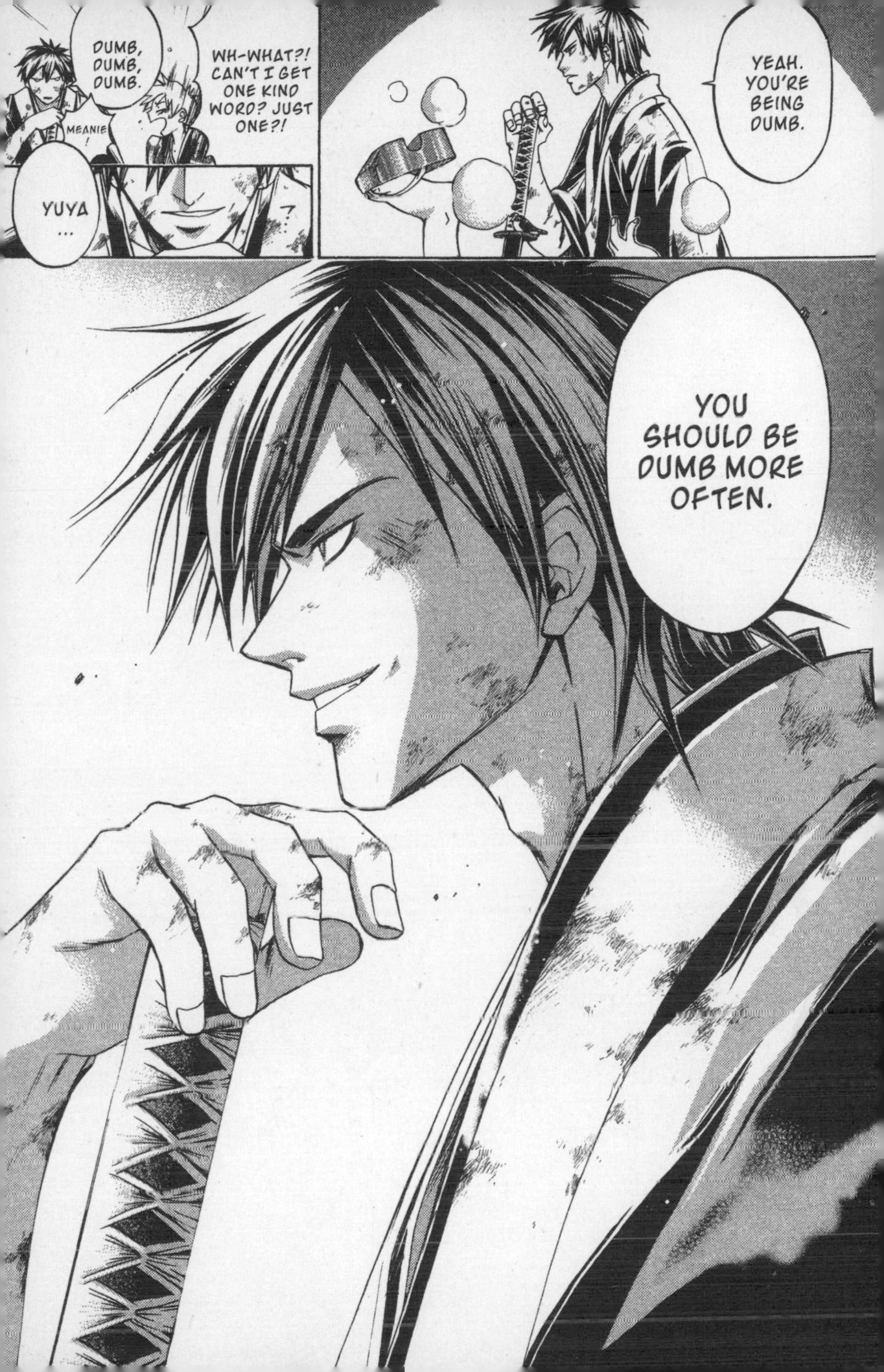
YEAH. YOU'RE BEING DUMB.
DUMB, DUMB, DUMB.
WH-WHAT?! CAN'T I GET ONE KIND WORD? JUST ONE?!
MEANIE!
YUYA ...
YOU SHOULD BE DUMB MORE OFTEN.

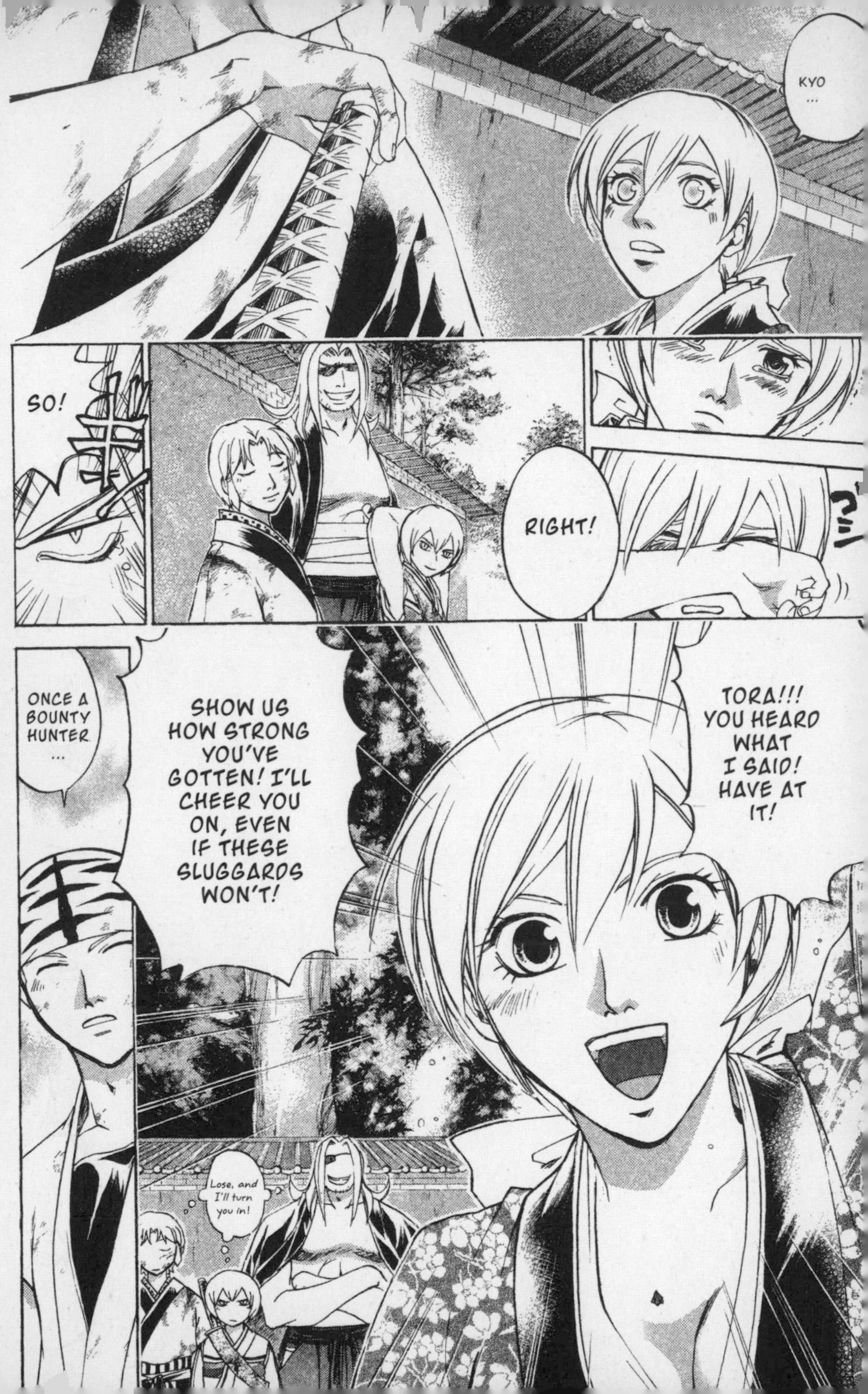
KYO ...
RIGHT!
SO!
TORA!!! YOU HEARD WHAT I SAID! HAVE AT IT!
SHOW US HOW STRONG YOU'VE GOTTEN! I'LL CHEER YOU ON, EVEN IF THESE SLUGGARDS WON'T!
ONCE A BOUNTY HUNTER ...
Lose, and I'll turn you in!

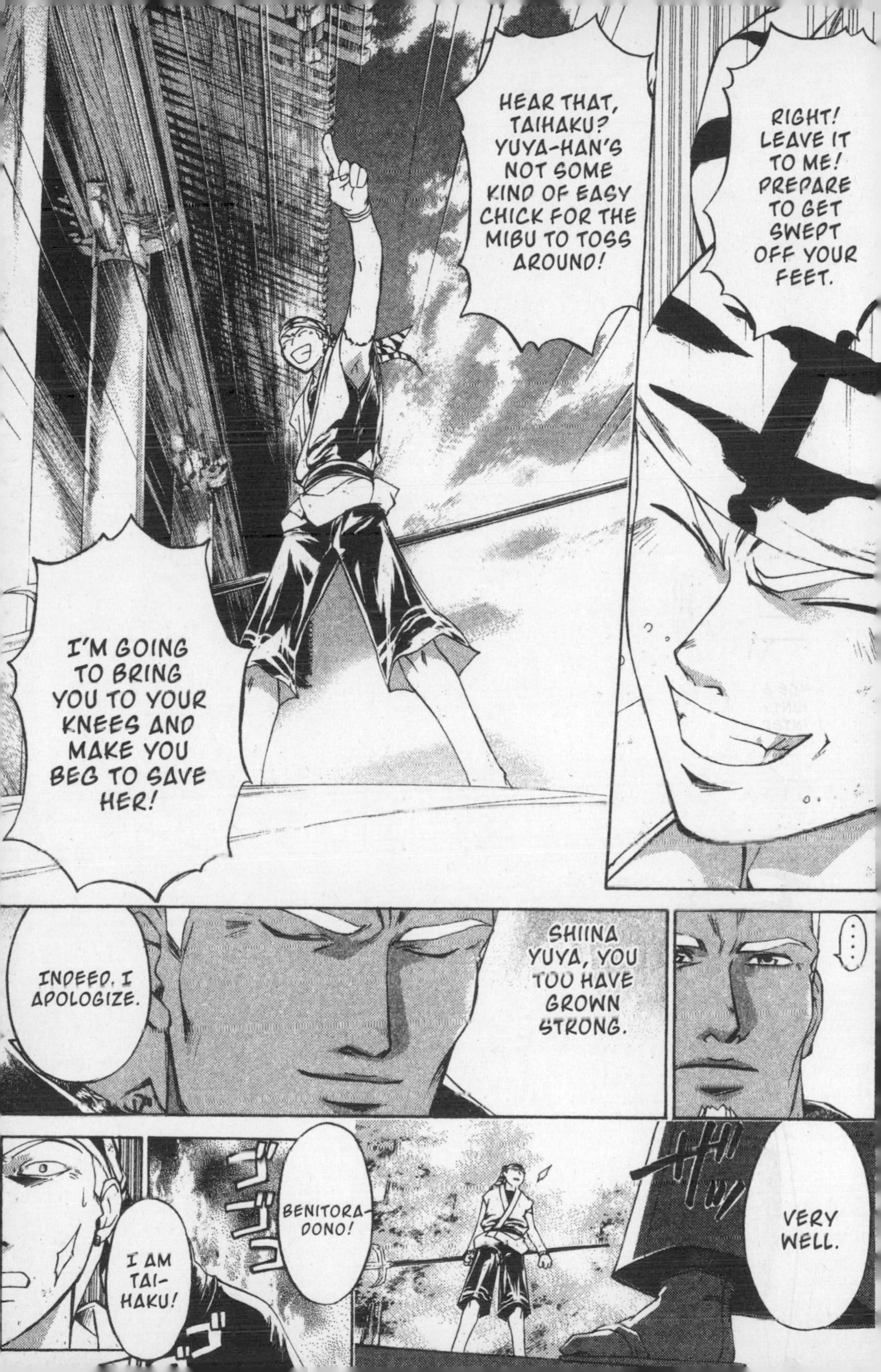
RIGHT! LEAVE IT TO ME! PREPARE TO GET SWEPT OFF YOUR FEET.
HEAR THAT, TAIHAKU? YUYA-HAN'S NOT SOME KIND OF EASY CHICK FOR THE MIBU TO TOSS AROUND!
I'M GOING TO BRING YOU TO YOUR KNEES AND MAKE YOU BEG TO SAVE HER!
...
SHIINA YUYA, YOU TOO HAVE GROWN STRONG.
INDEED. I APOLOGIZE.
VERY WELL.
BENITORA-DONO!
I AM TAI-HAKU!

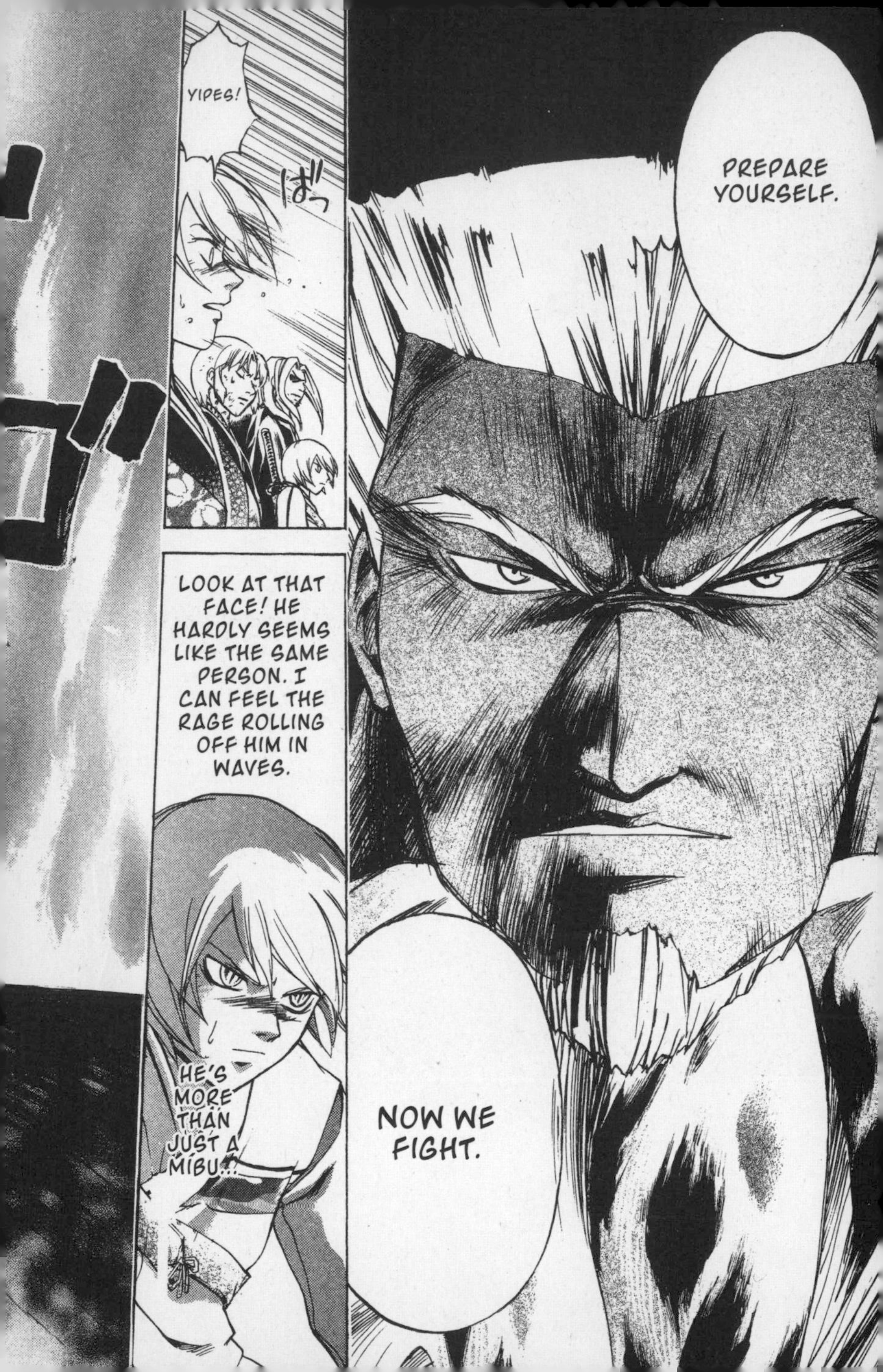
PREPARE YOURSELF.
NOW WE FIGHT.
YIPES!
LOOK AT THAT FACE! HE HARDLY SEEMS LIKE THE SAME PERSON. I CAN FEEL THE RAGE ROLLING OFF HIM IN WAVES.
HE'S MORE THAN JUST A MIBU...!

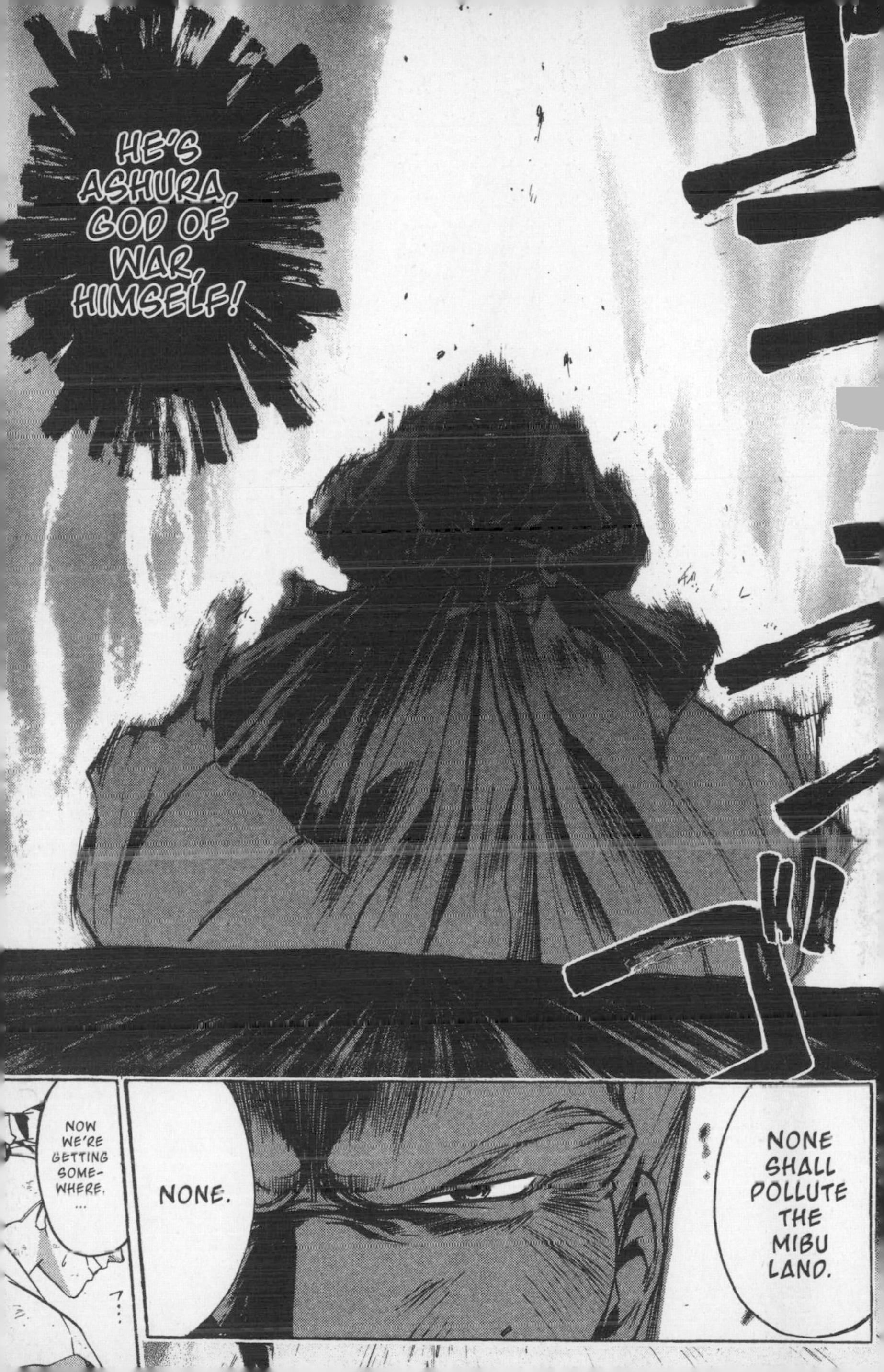
HE'S ASHURA, GOD OF WAR, HIMSELF!
NONE SHALL POLLUTE THE MIBU LAND.
NONE.
NOW WE'RE GETTING SOME-WHERE. ...

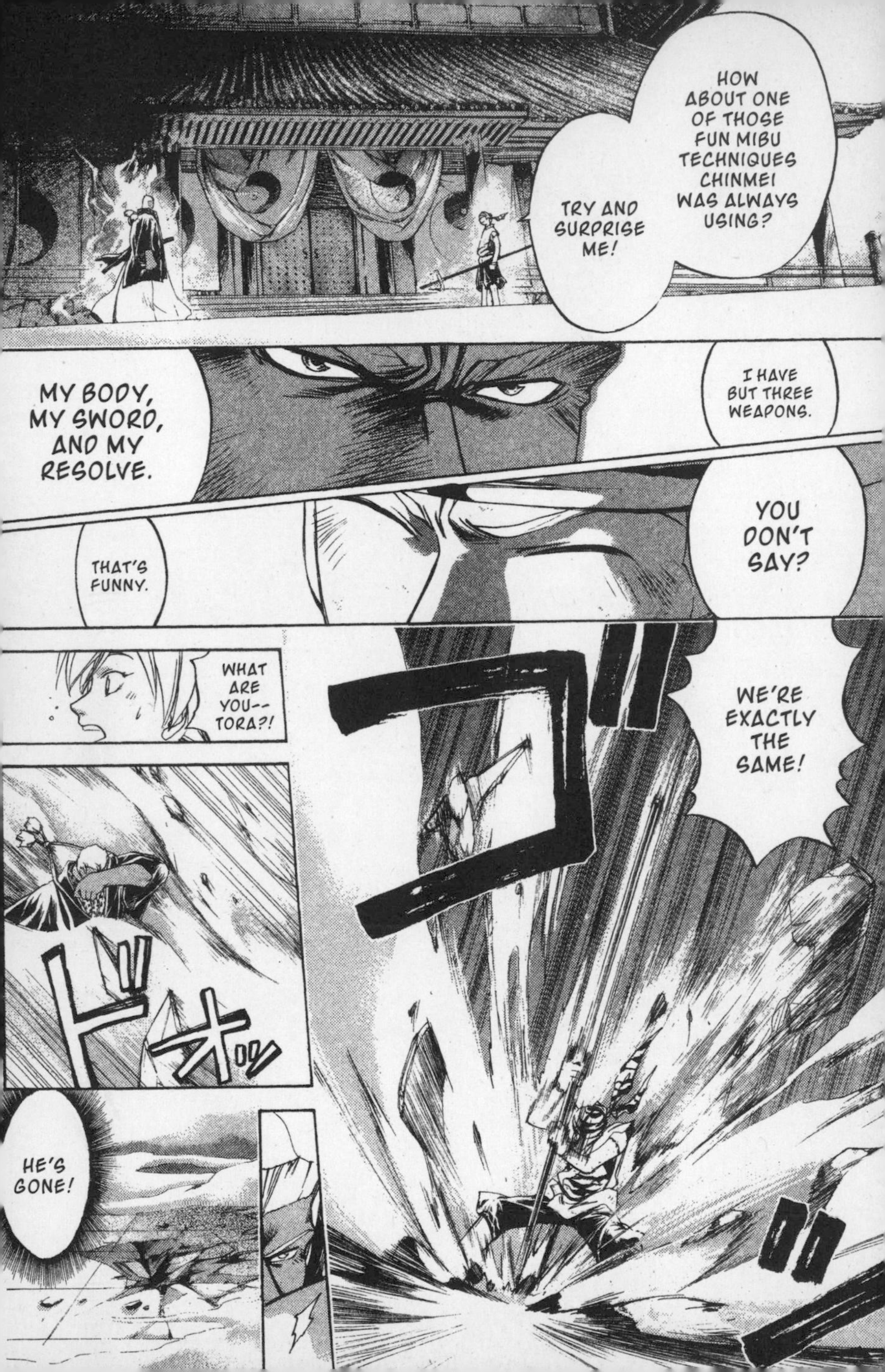
HOW ABOUT ONE OF THOSE FUN MIBU TECHNIQUES CHINMEI WAS ALWAYS USING?
TRY AND SURPRISE ME!
I HAVE BUT THREE WEAPONS.
MY BODY, MY SWORD, AND MY RESOLVE.
YOU DON'T SAY?
THAT'S FUNNY.
ゴ
WE'RE EXACTLY THE SAME!
WHAT ARE YOU-- TORA?!
ドオッ
HE'S GONE!

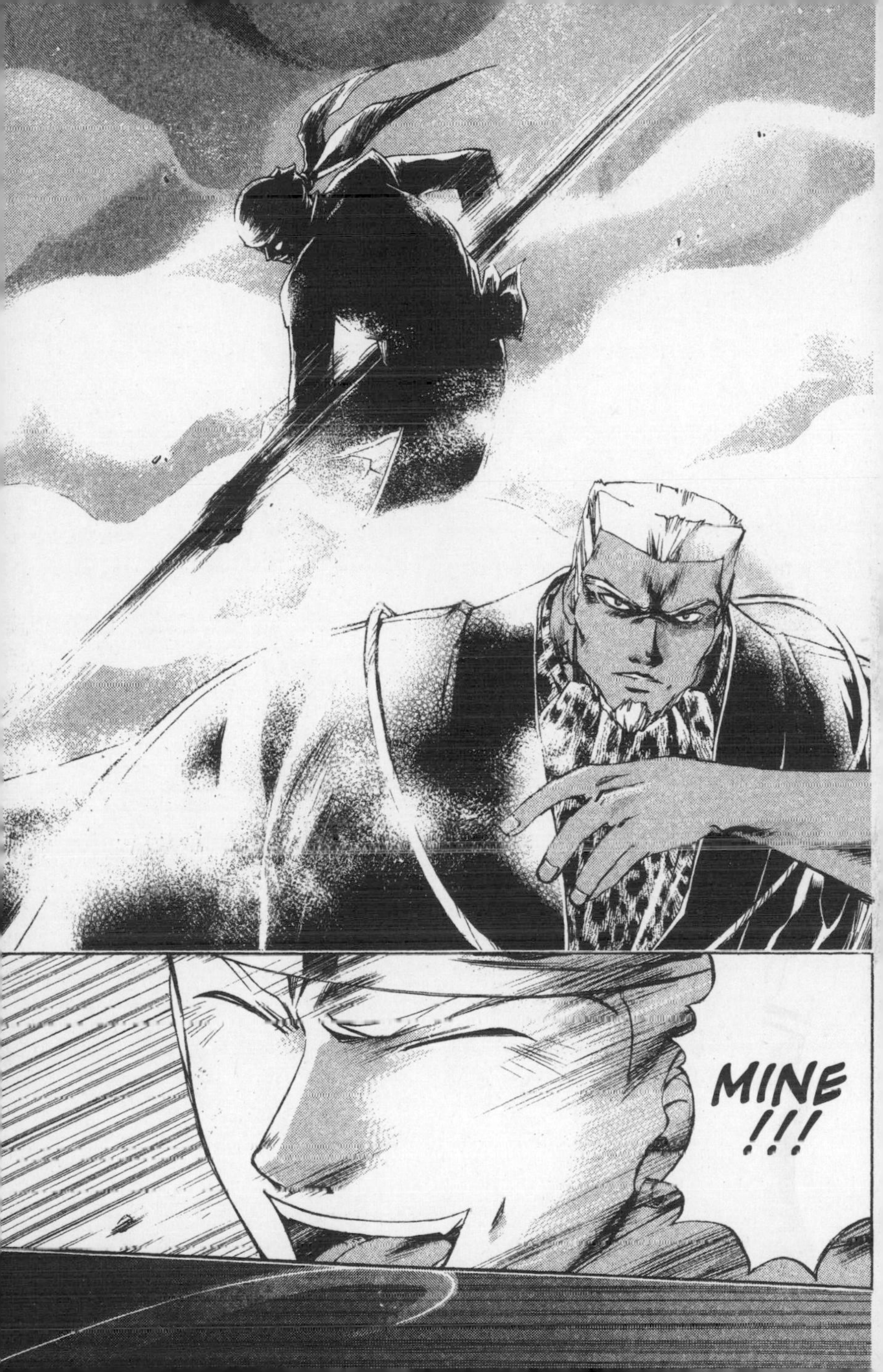
MINE
!!!

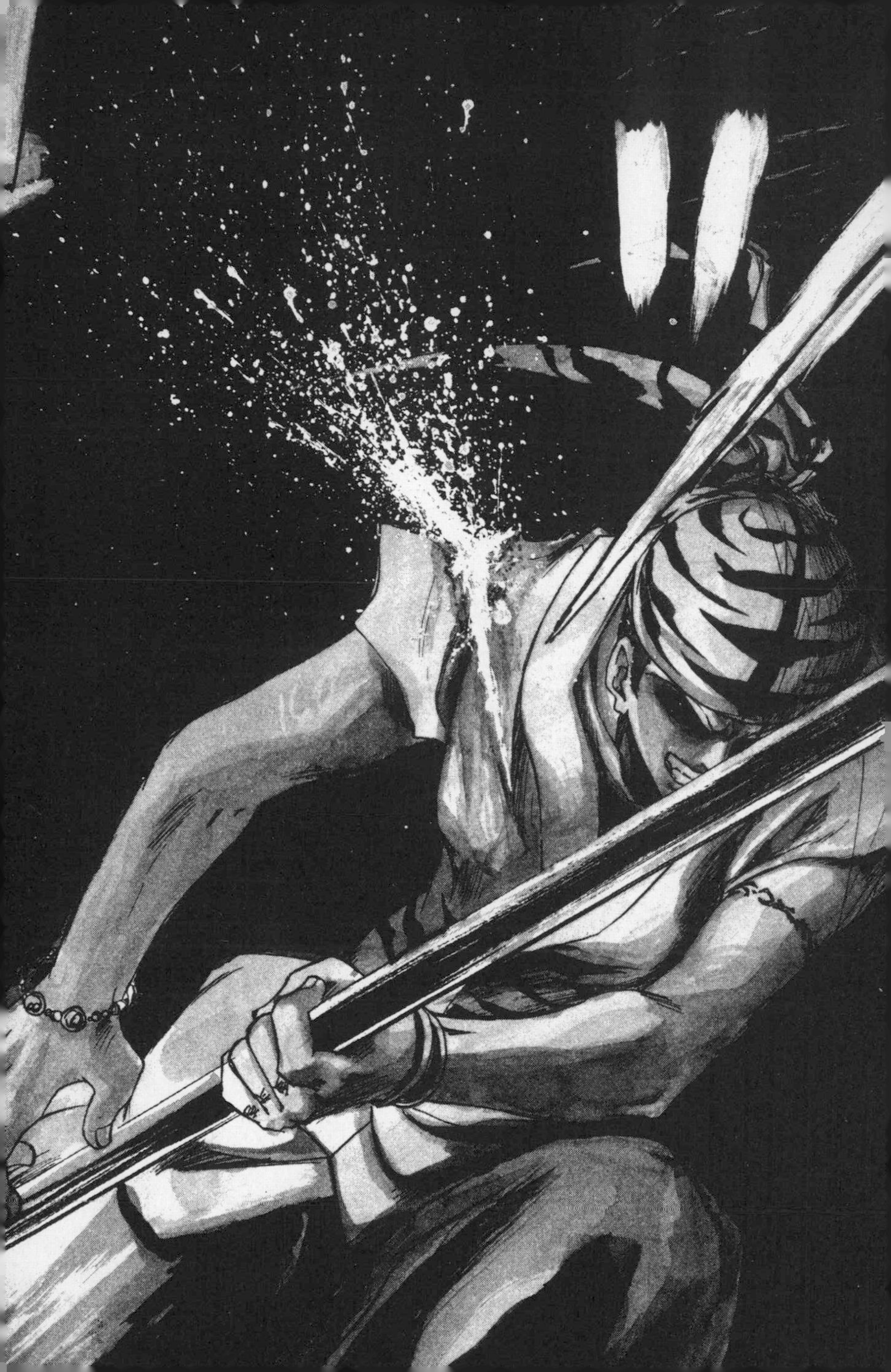

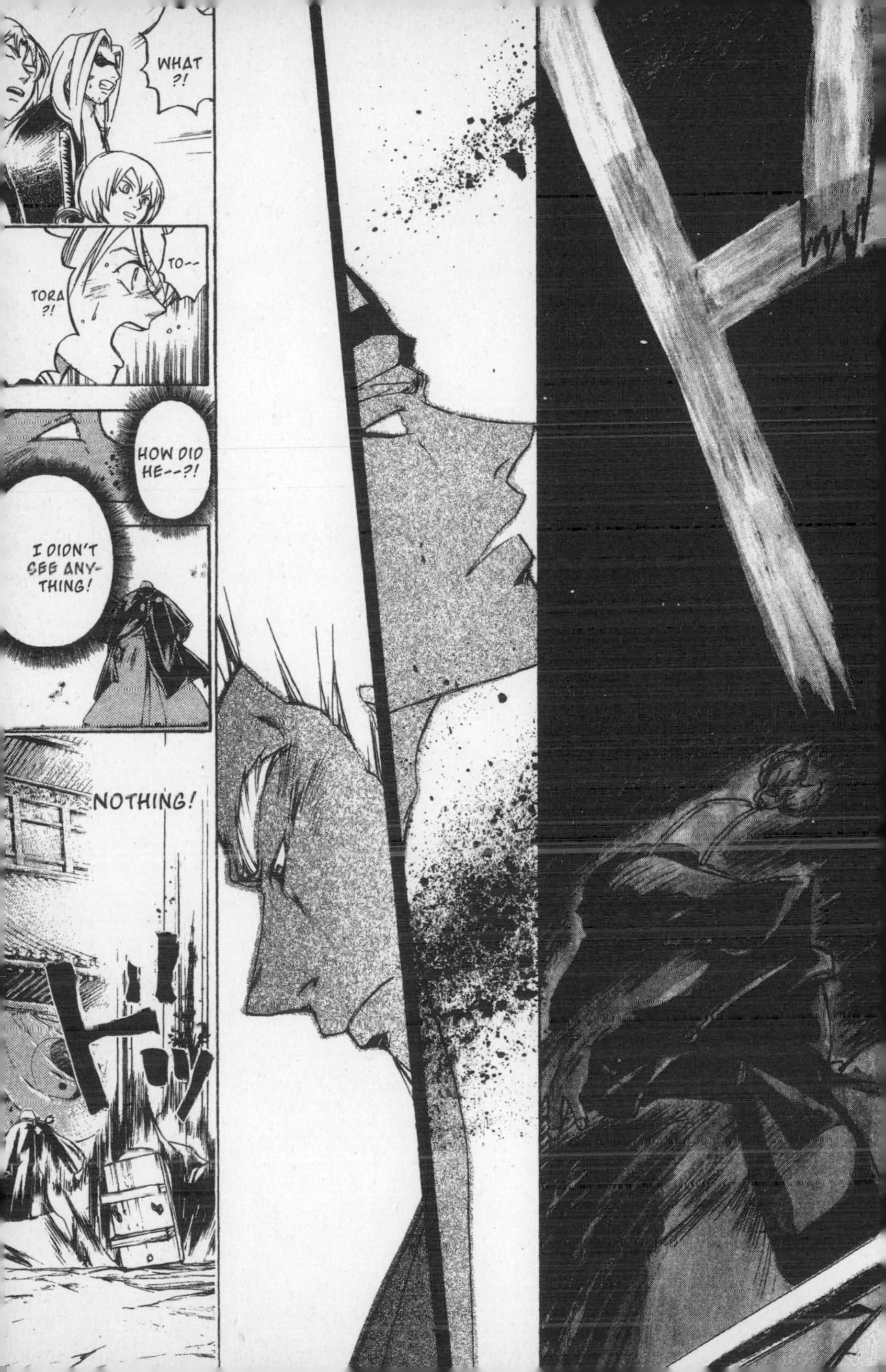
WHAT ?!
TO--
TORA ?!
HOW DID HE--?!
I DIDN'T SEE ANY-THING!
NOTHING!

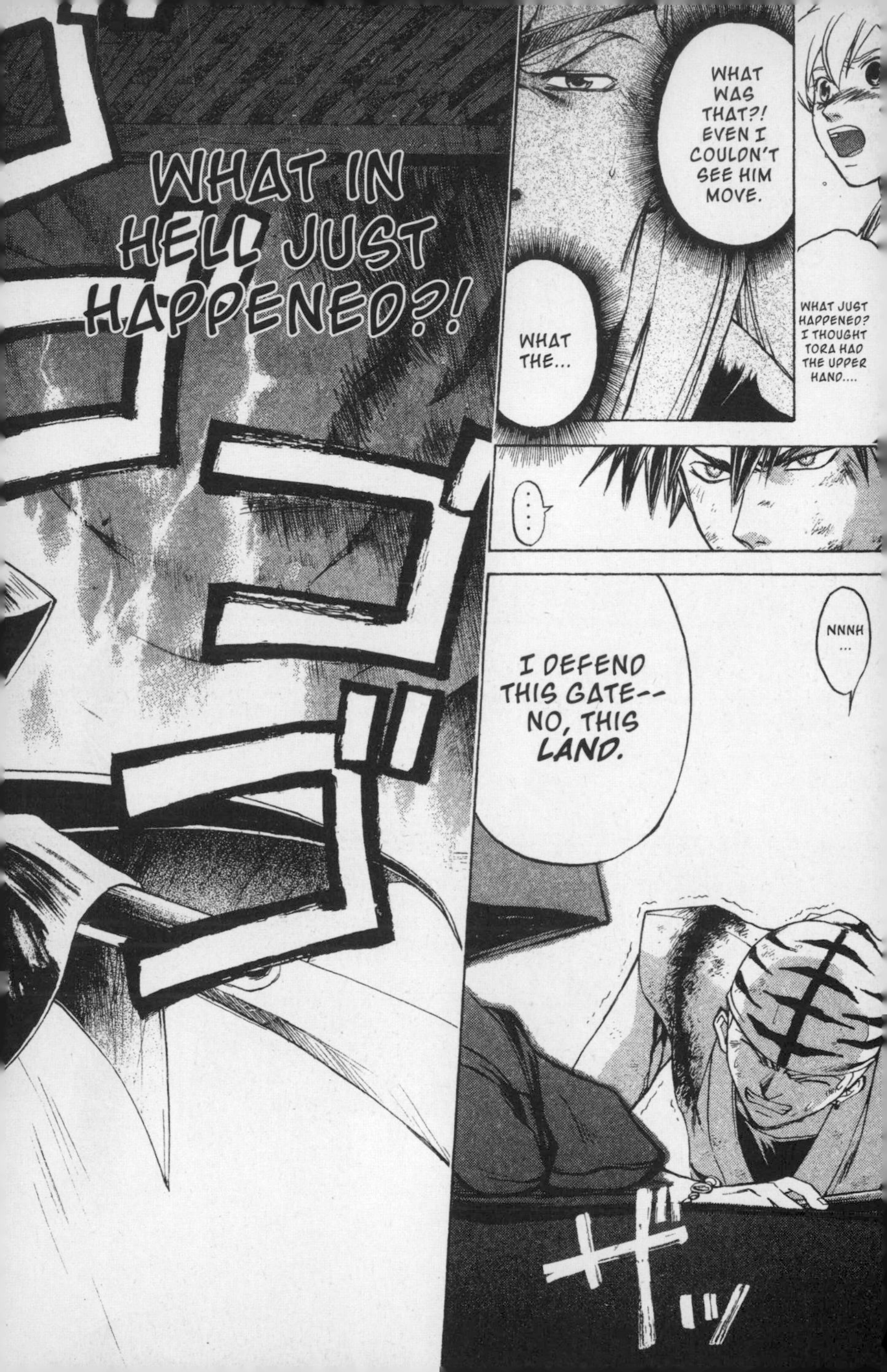

WHAT WAS THAT?! EVEN I COULDN'T SEE HIM MOVE.
WHAT JUST HAPPENED? I THOUGHT TORA HAD THE UPPER HAND....
WHAT THE...
...
NNNH...
I DEFEND THIS GATE--NO, THIS LAND.
WHAT IN HELL JUST HAPPENED?!

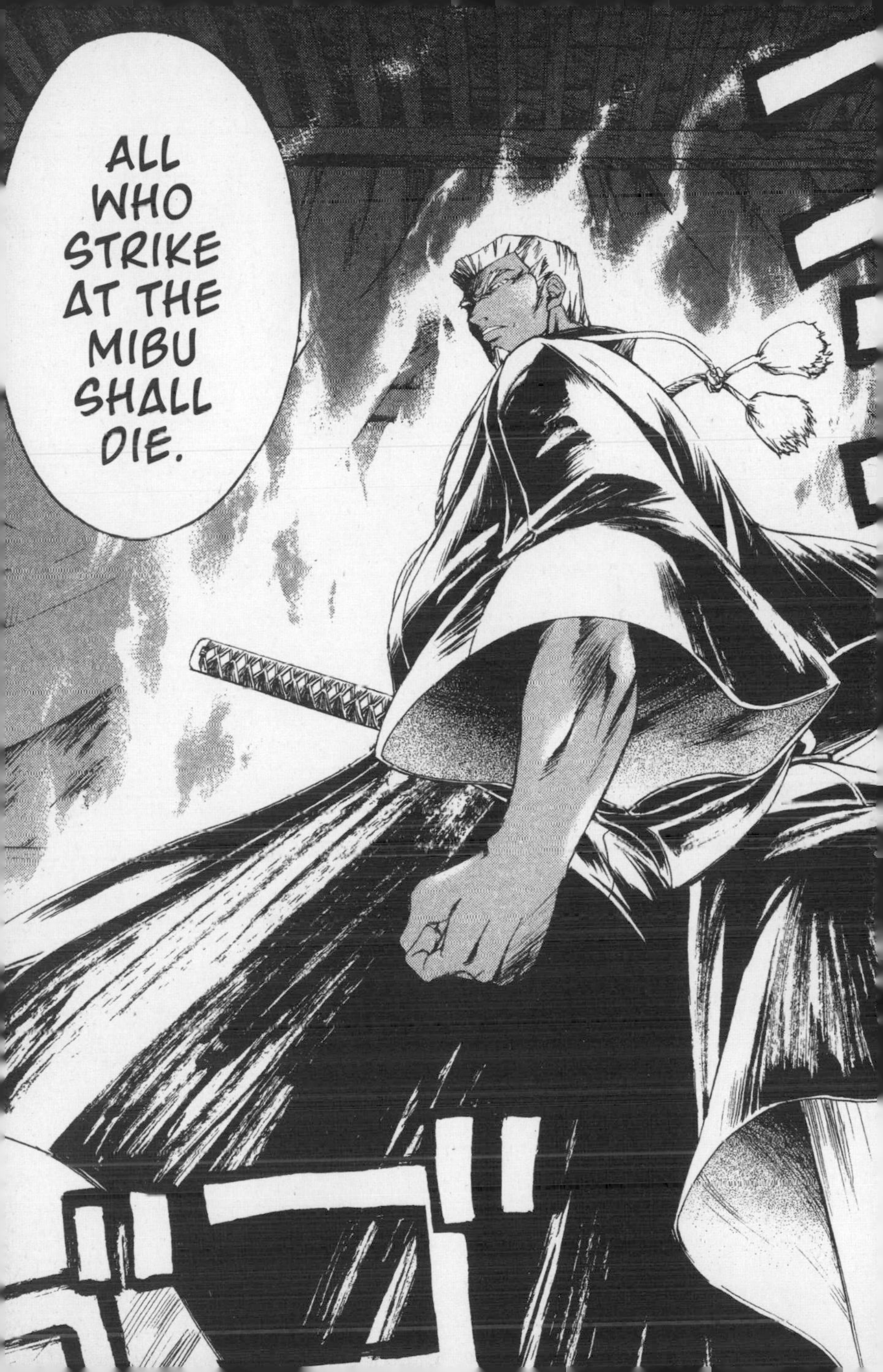
ALL WHO STRIKE AT THE MIBU SHALL DIE.

■THE STAFF ■

Some older people for a change. Note: these aren't the "SDK characters, X years later" or anything like that.

Hazuki Asami
(The Chief)
Soma Akatsuki
(The Sub-Chief)
**The Gentleman
Pumpkin Risa**
(Through Chapter 161
in the next volume...)
Seishi Kamimura
Takaya Nagao
(In the order they joined)

● Risa is moving on! Thanks for all your hard work, Risa!
We look forward to hearing about your many exploits!

■ MANY THANKS ■

To the staff: Thanks for all your hard work on SDK, as always!
Seeing all of you work so hard makes me want to strive all the more.
Keep at it! And thanks also go to Mr. H and Mr. S. Take care of yourselves;
you work too hard! Great job for all of 2002! To Mr. Y, in charge of the
books, and to our designers: Sorry to cause you so much trouble all the
time. Oh, and Mr. Y, thanks for all the pudding! To Mr. K.: Thanks for all
your work on the calendar! Your careful attention to detail was a
lifesaver! And finally, thanks to all the other designers and writers
whom I couldn't mention here. You make it all possible!

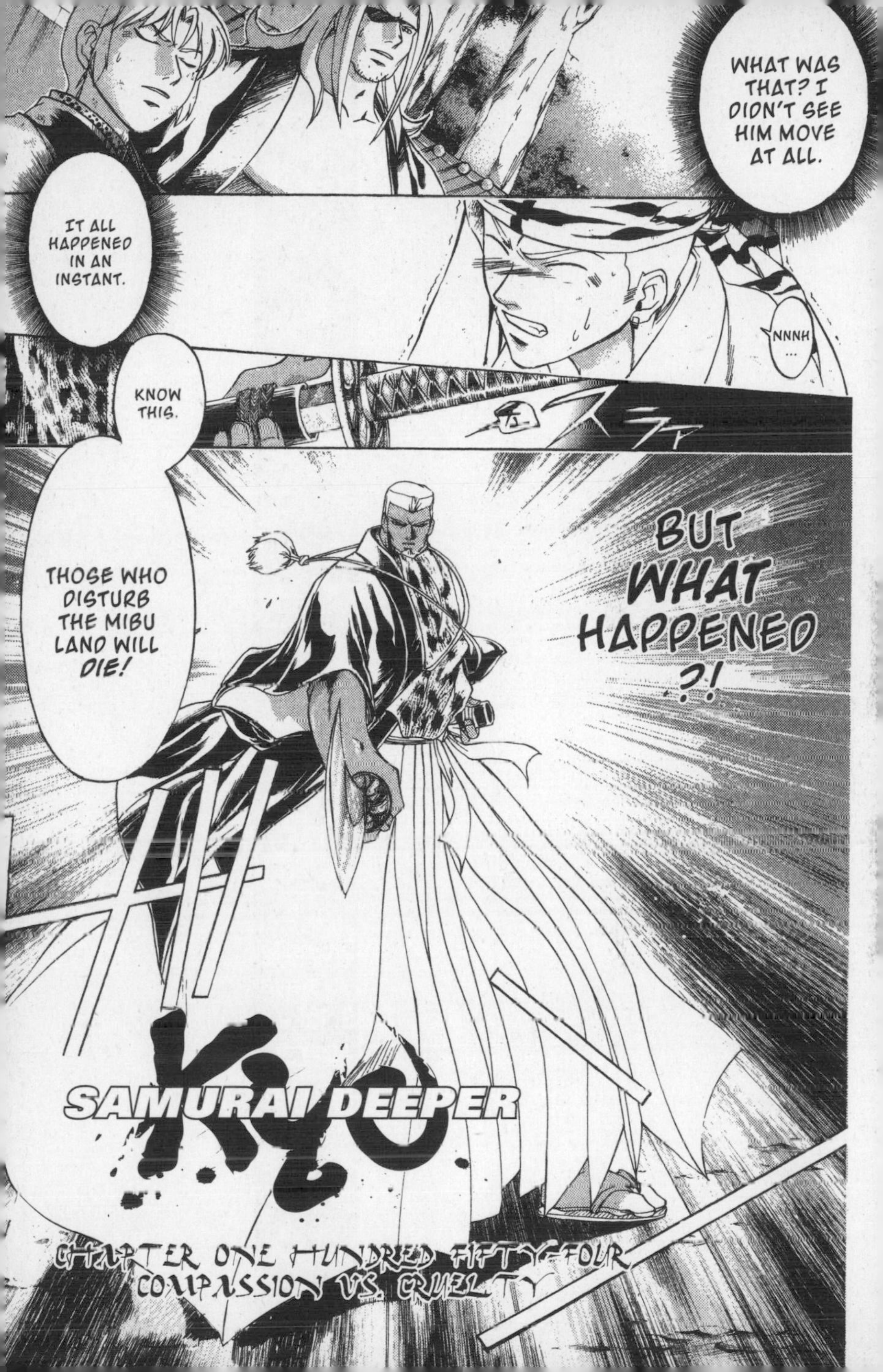
WHAT WAS THAT? I DIDN'T SEE HIM MOVE AT ALL.
NNNH...
IT ALL HAPPENED IN AN INSTANT.
KNOW THIS.
BUT WHAT HAPPENED ?!
THOSE WHO DISTURB THE MIBU LAND WILL DIE!
SAMURAI DEEPER KYO
CHAPTER ONE HUNDRED FIFTY-FOUR
COMPASSION VS. CRUELTY

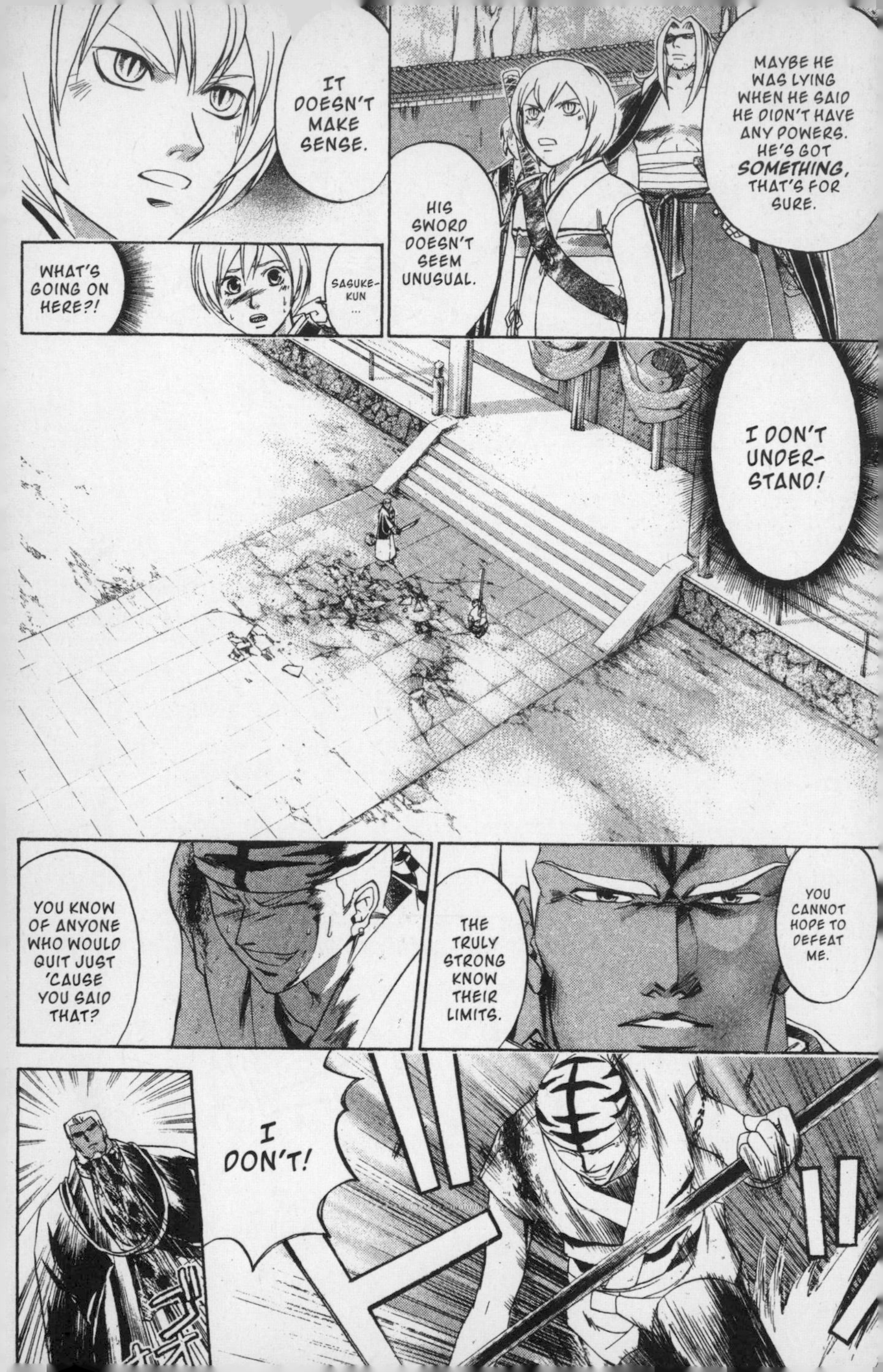
MAYBE HE WAS LYING WHEN HE SAID HE DIDN'T HAVE ANY POWERS. HE'S GOT **SOMETHING**, THAT'S FOR SURE.
HIS SWORD DOESN'T SEEM UNUSUAL.
IT DOESN'T MAKE SENSE.
SASUKE-KUN ...
WHAT'S GOING ON HERE?!
I DON'T UNDER-STAND!
YOU CANNOT HOPE TO DEFEAT ME.
THE TRULY STRONG KNOW THEIR LIMITS.
YOU KNOW OF ANYONE WHO WOULD QUIT JUST 'CAUSE YOU SAID THAT?
I DON'T!

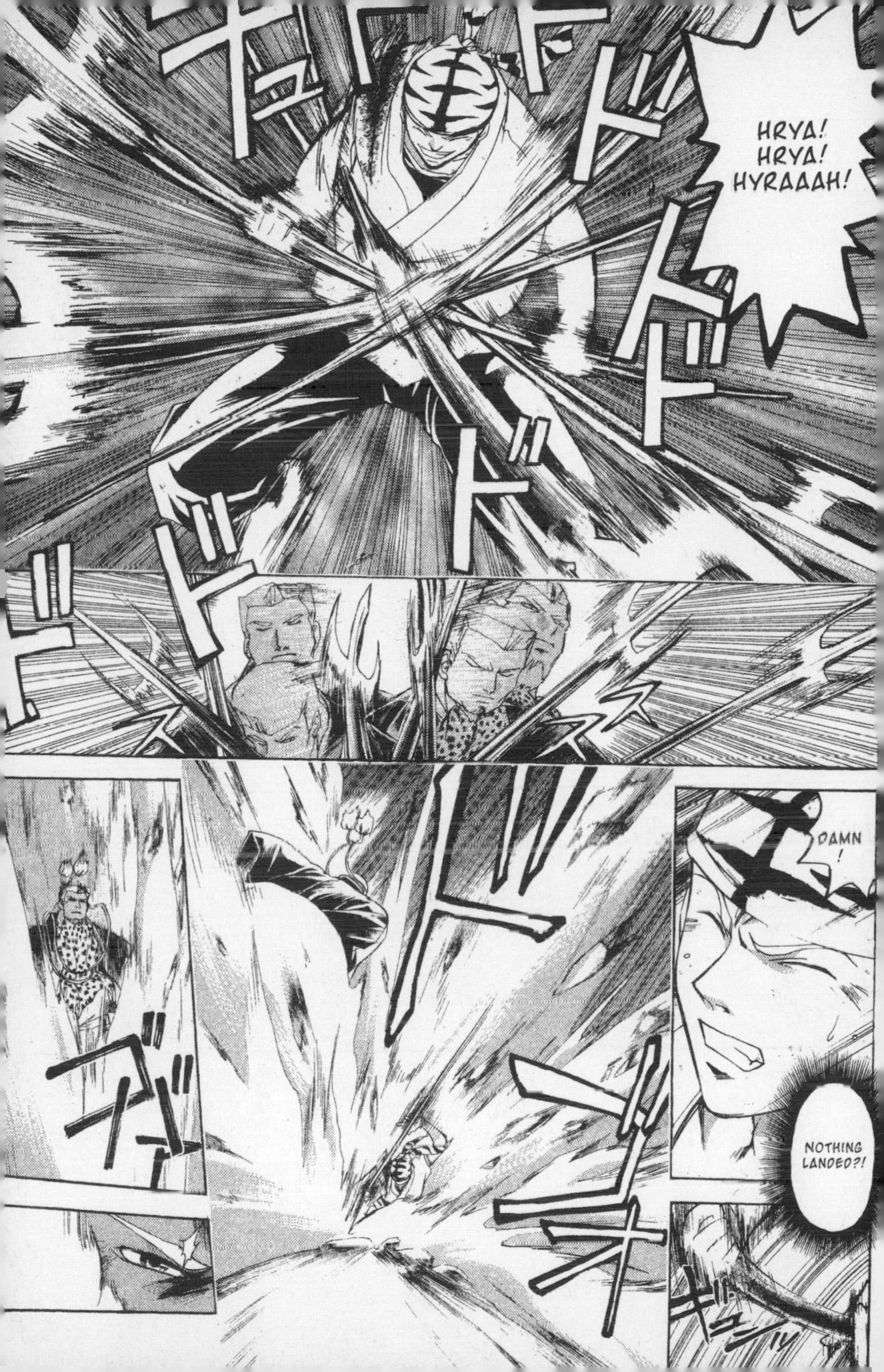
HRYA! HRYA! HYRAAAH!
DAMN!
NOTHING LANDED?!

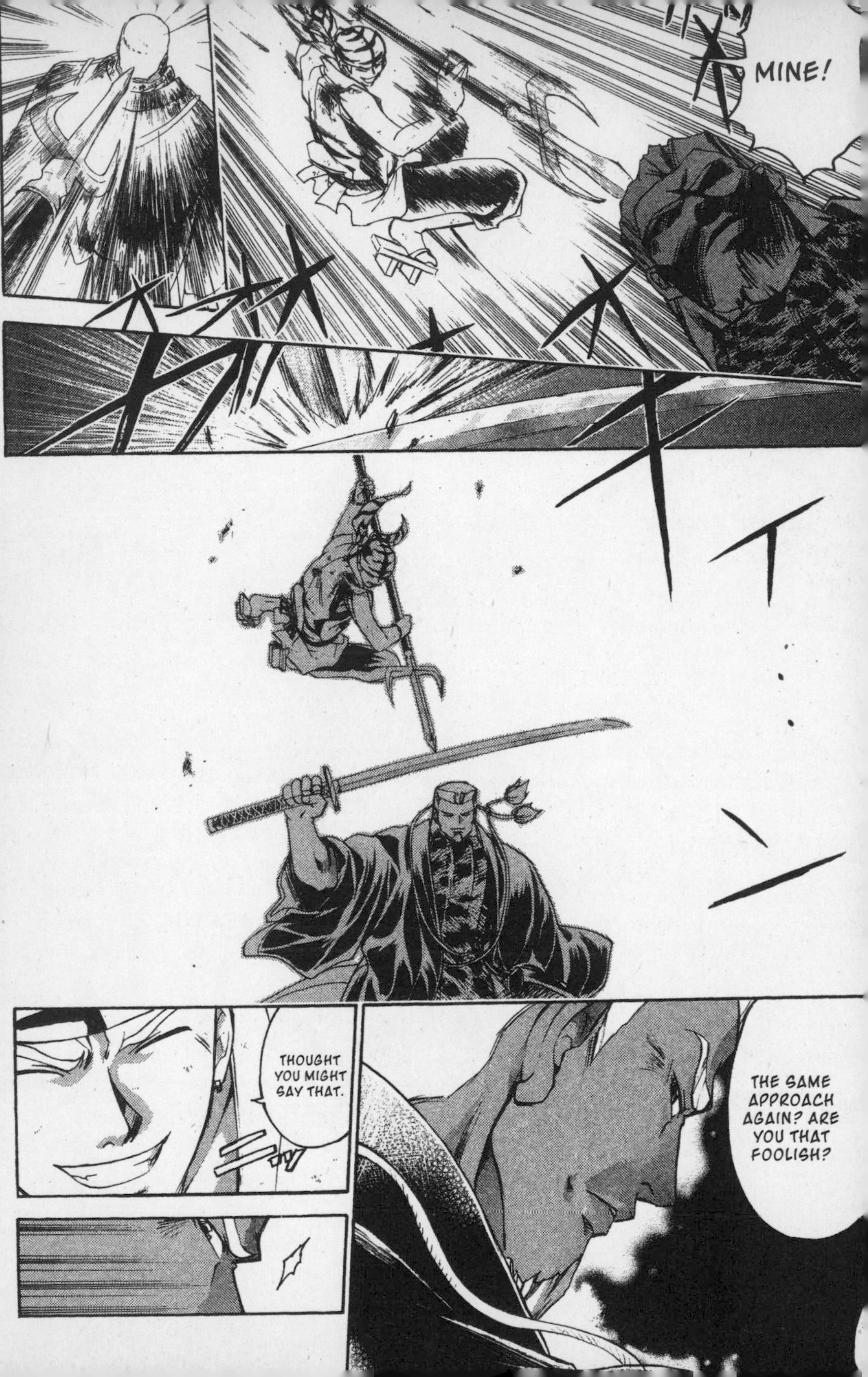
MINE!
THE SAME APPROACH AGAIN? ARE YOU THAT FOOLISH?
THOUGHT YOU MIGHT SAY THAT.

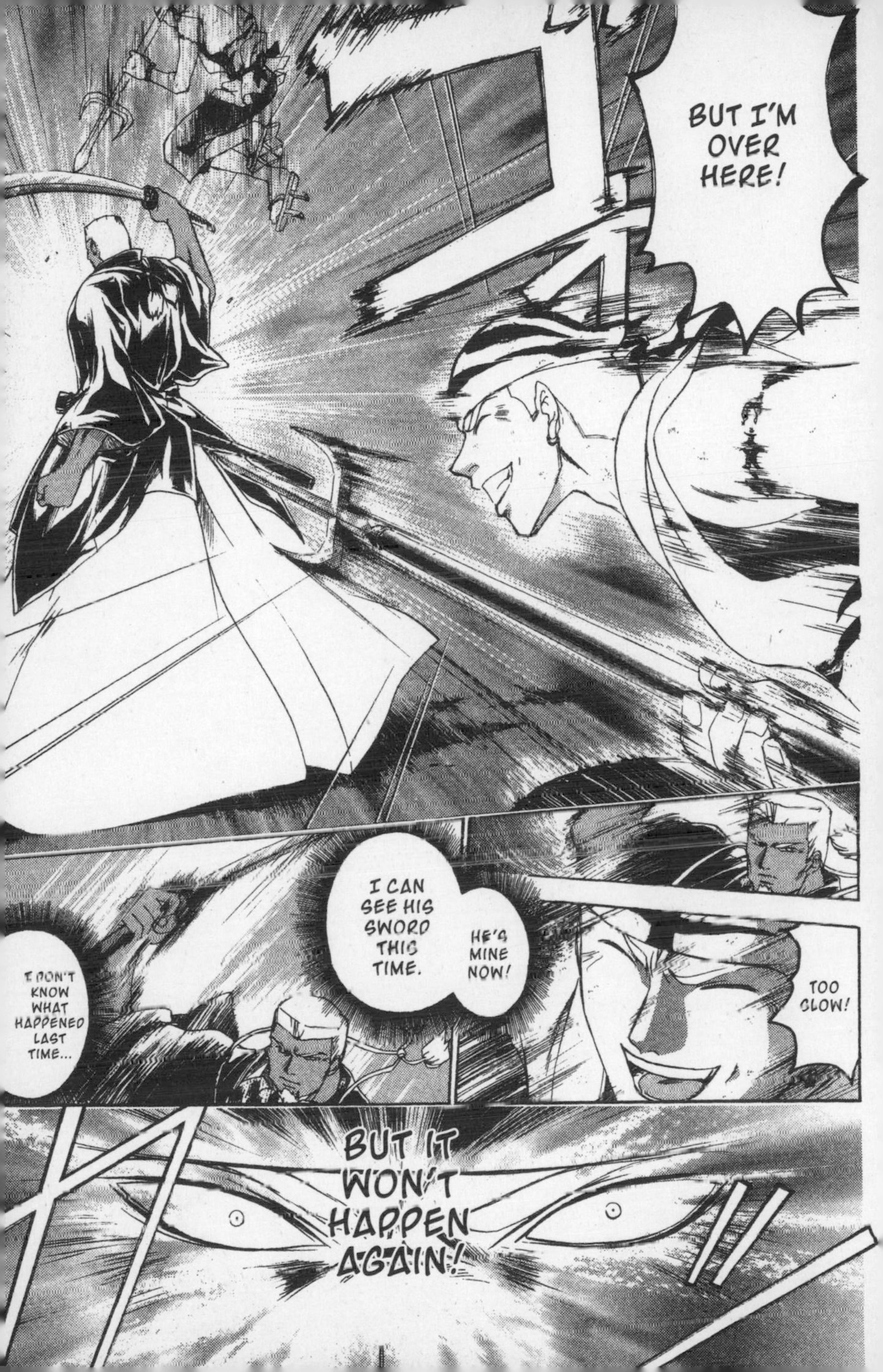

BUT I'M OVER HERE!
TOO SLOW!
I CAN SEE HIS SWORD THIS TIME.
HE'S MINE NOW!
I DON'T KNOW WHAT HAPPENED LAST TIME...
BUT IT WON'T HAPPEN AGAIN!

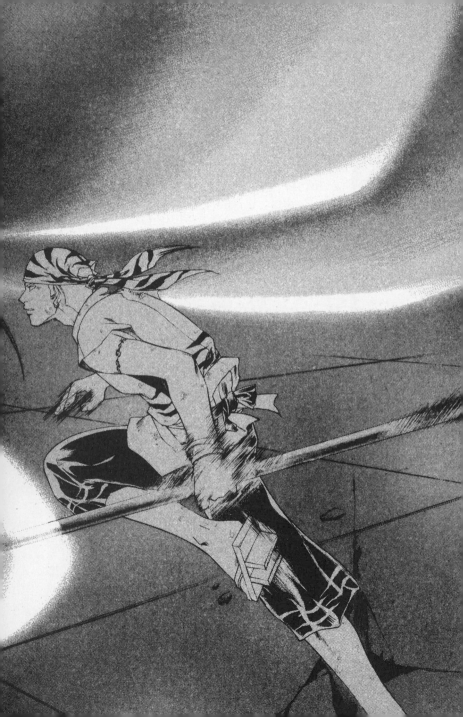

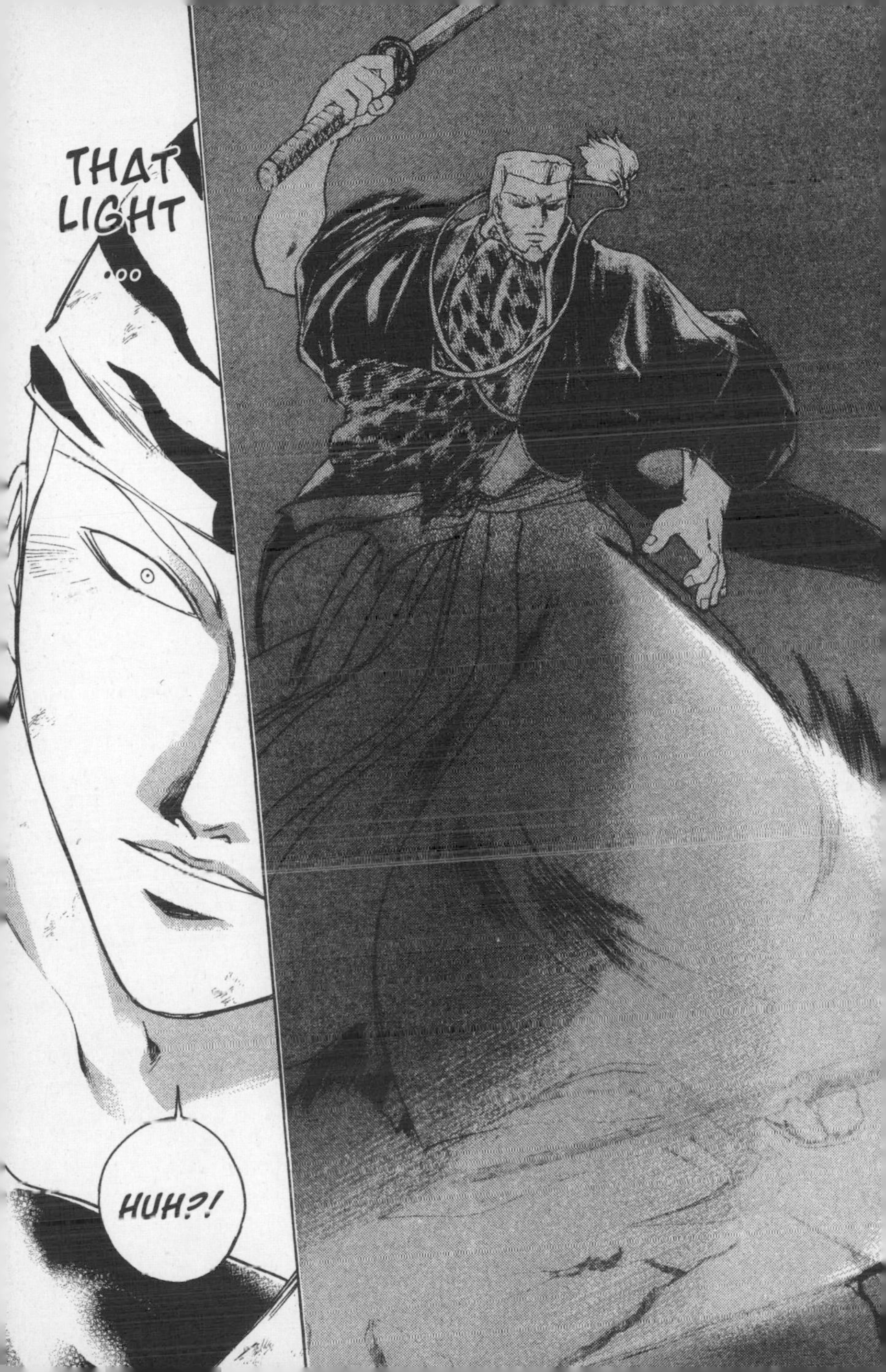
THAT LIGHT ...
HUH?!

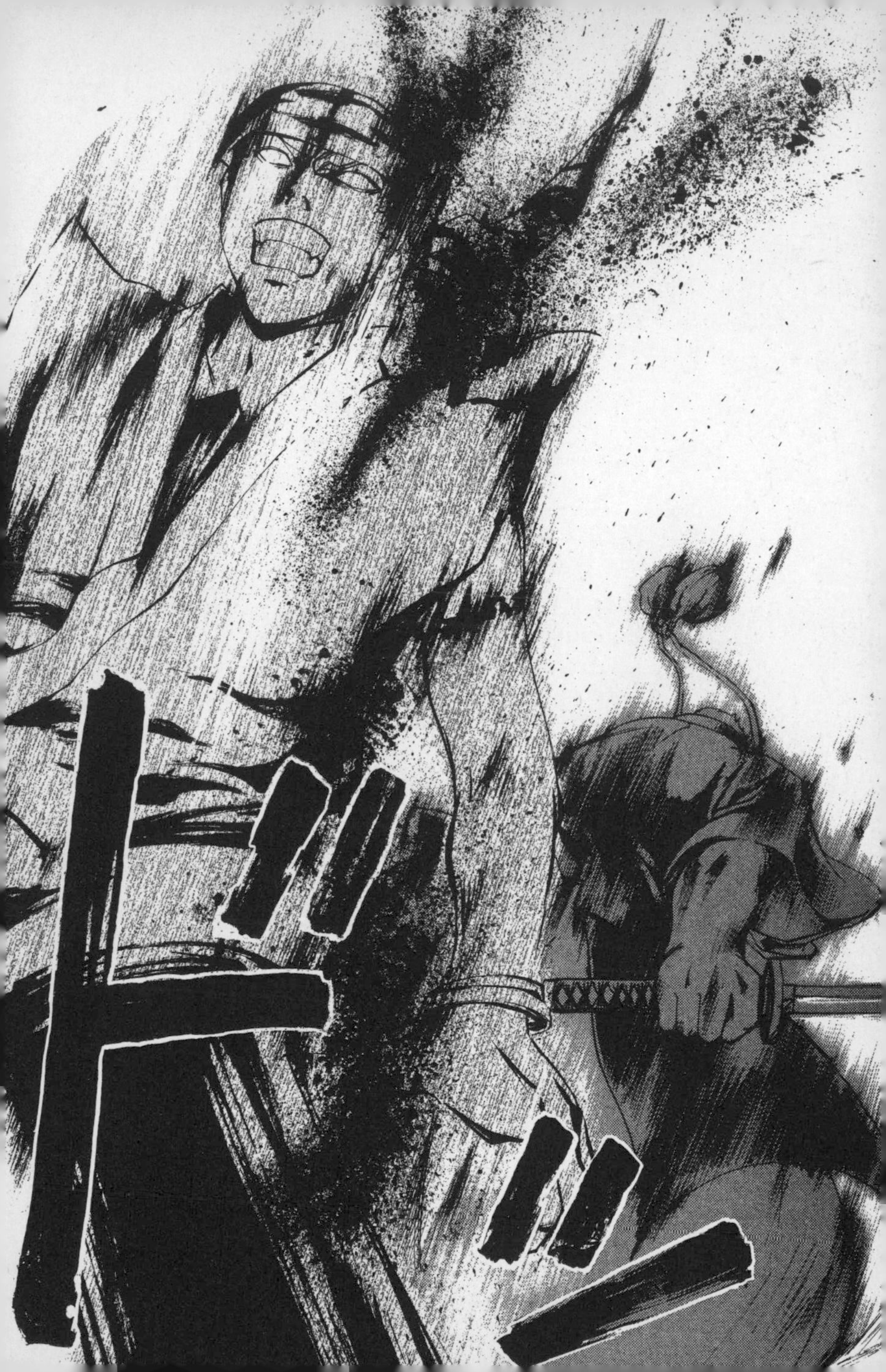
ドッ

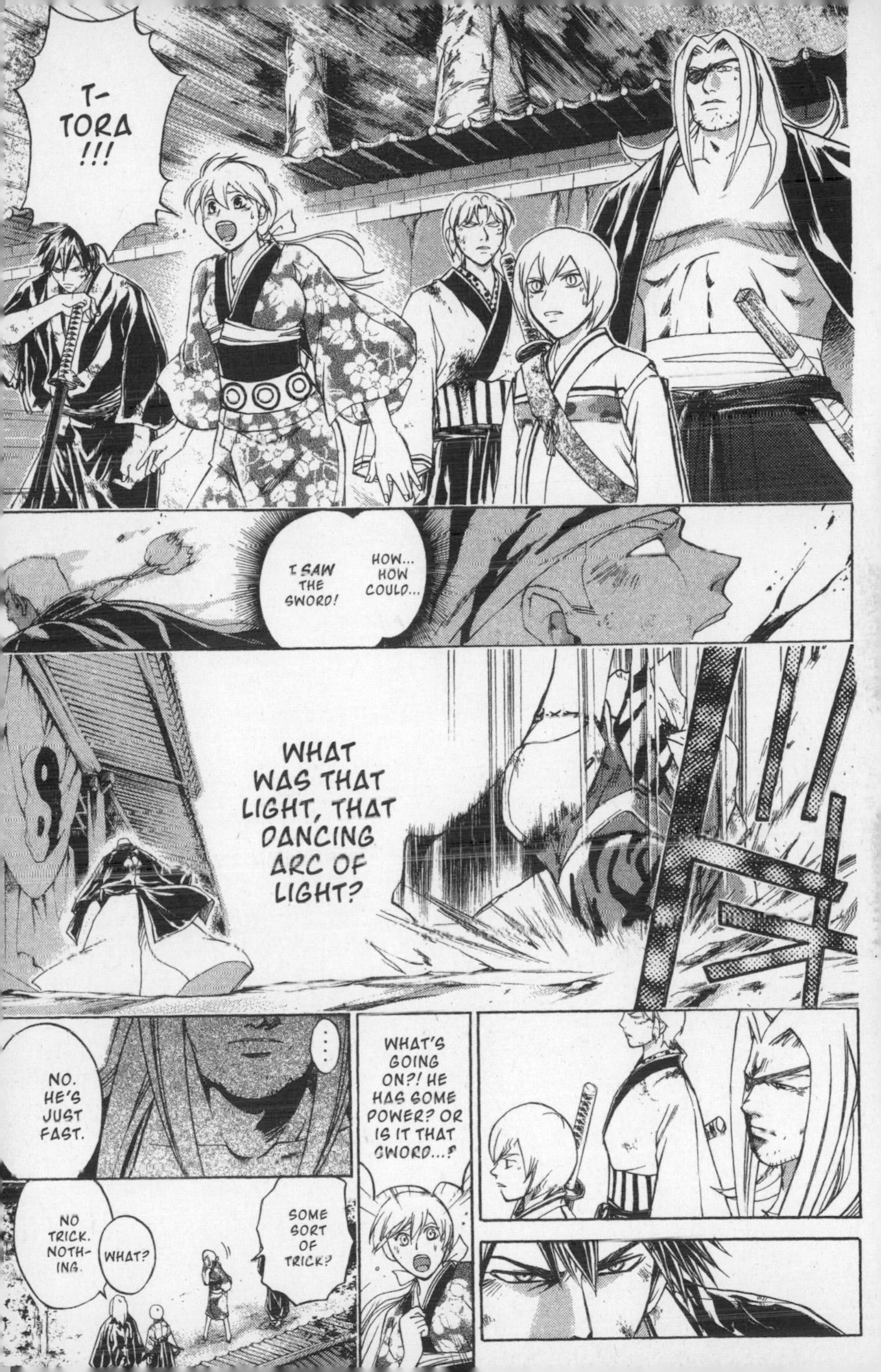
T-TORA!!!
HOW... HOW COULD...
I SAW THE SWORD!
WHAT WAS THAT LIGHT, THAT DANCING ARC OF LIGHT?
WHAT'S GOING ON?! HE HAS SOME POWER? OR IS IT THAT SWORD...?
...
NO. HE'S JUST FAST.
SOME SORT OF TRICK?
WHAT?
NO TRICK. NOTHING.

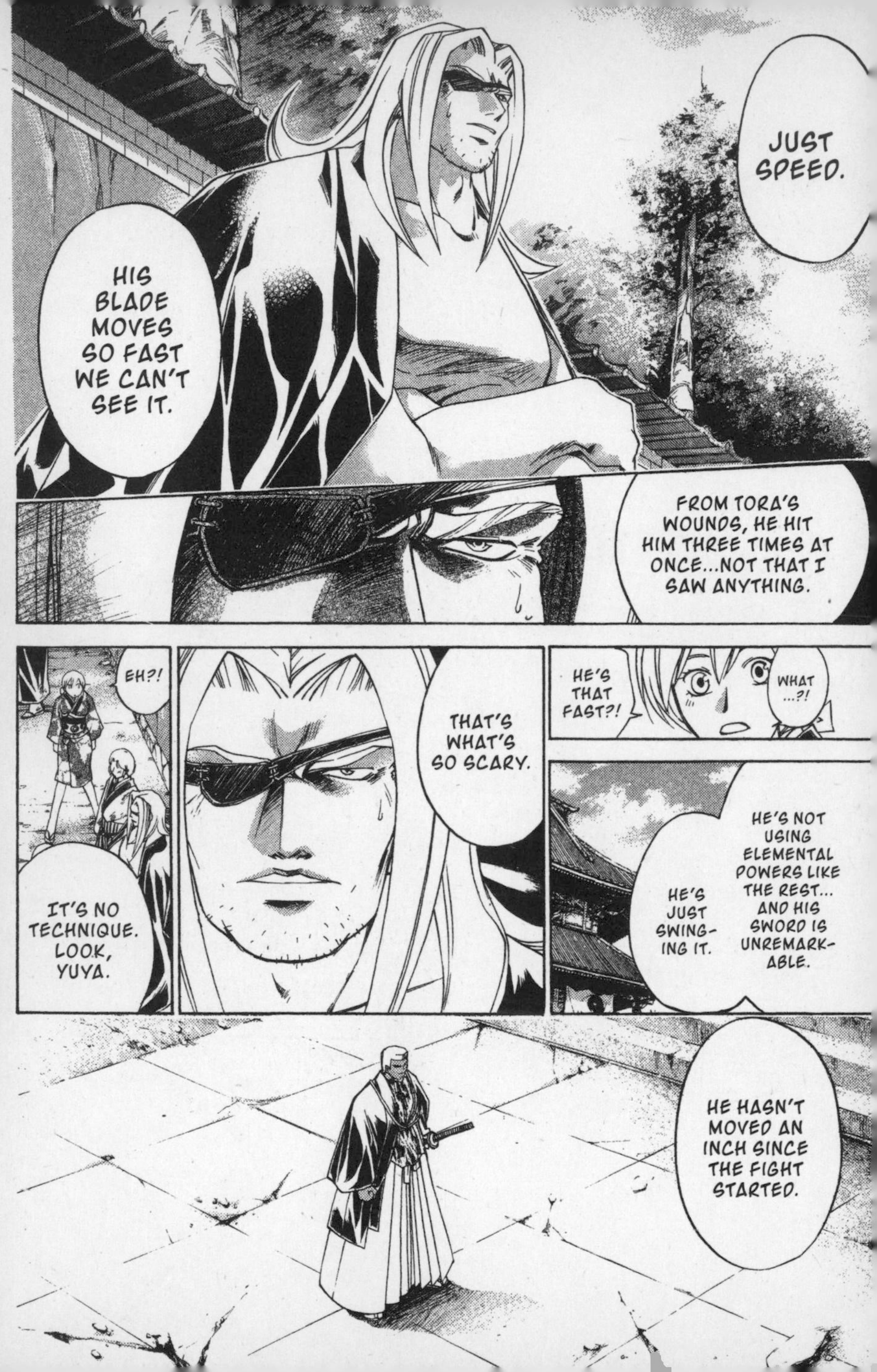
JUST SPEED.
HIS BLADE MOVES SO FAST WE CAN'T SEE IT.
FROM TORA'S WOUNDS, HE HIT HIM THREE TIMES AT ONCE...NOT THAT I SAW ANYTHING.
WHAT ...?!
HE'S THAT FAST?!
HE'S NOT USING ELEMENTAL POWERS LIKE THE REST... AND HIS SWORD IS UNREMARK-ABLE.
HE'S JUST SWING-ING IT.
THAT'S WHAT'S SO SCARY.
EH?!
IT'S NO TECHNIQUE. LOOK, YUYA.
HE HASN'T MOVED AN INCH SINCE THE FIGHT STARTED.

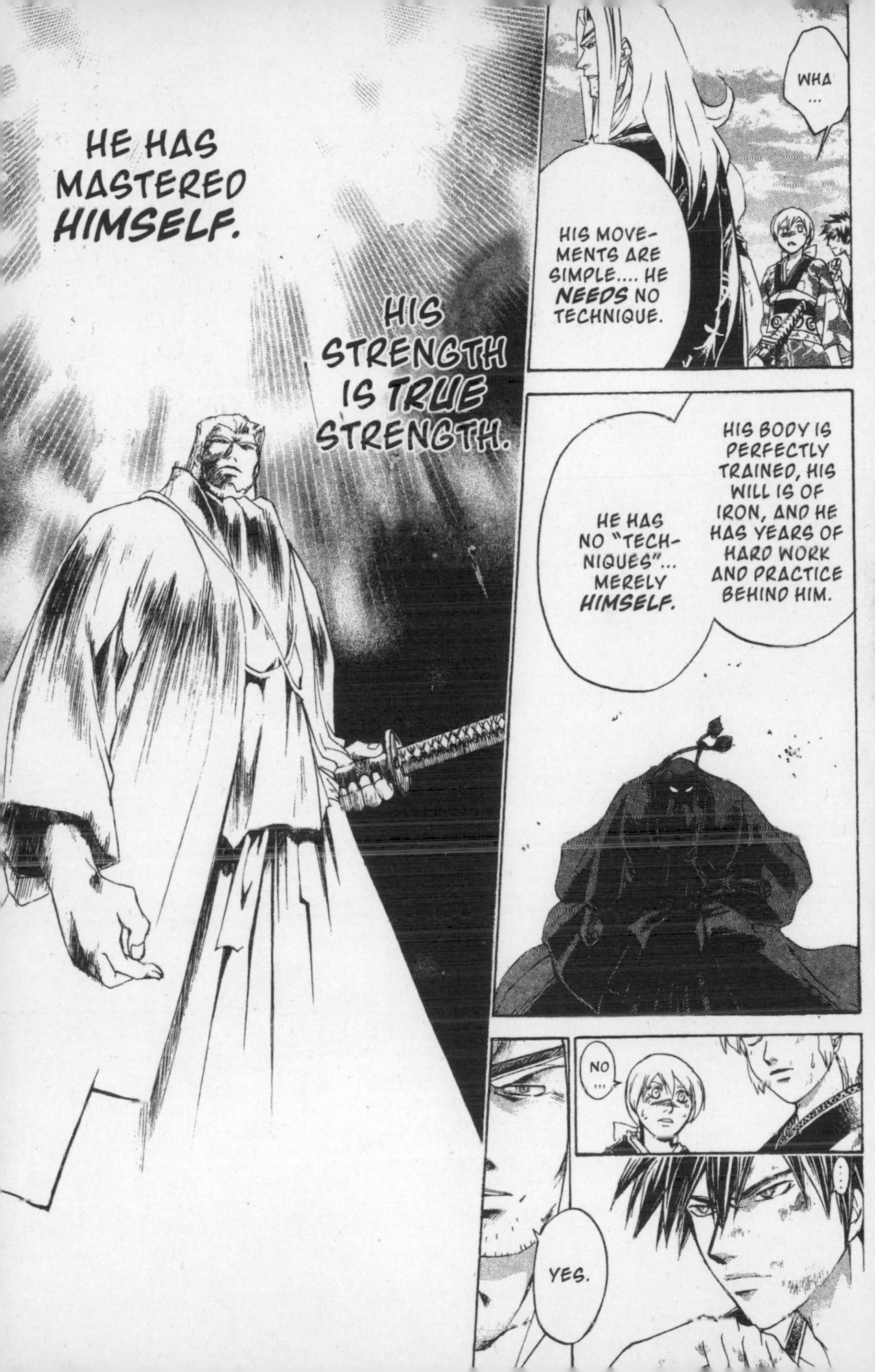
WHA ...
HIS MOVEMENTS ARE SIMPLE.... HE NEEDS NO TECHNIQUE.
HIS BODY IS PERFECTLY TRAINED, HIS WILL IS OF IRON, AND HE HAS YEARS OF HARD WORK AND PRACTICE BEHIND HIM.
HE HAS NO "TECHNIQUES"... MERELY HIMSELF.
NO ...
...
YES.
HE HAS MASTERED HIMSELF.
HIS STRENGTH IS TRUE STRENGTH.

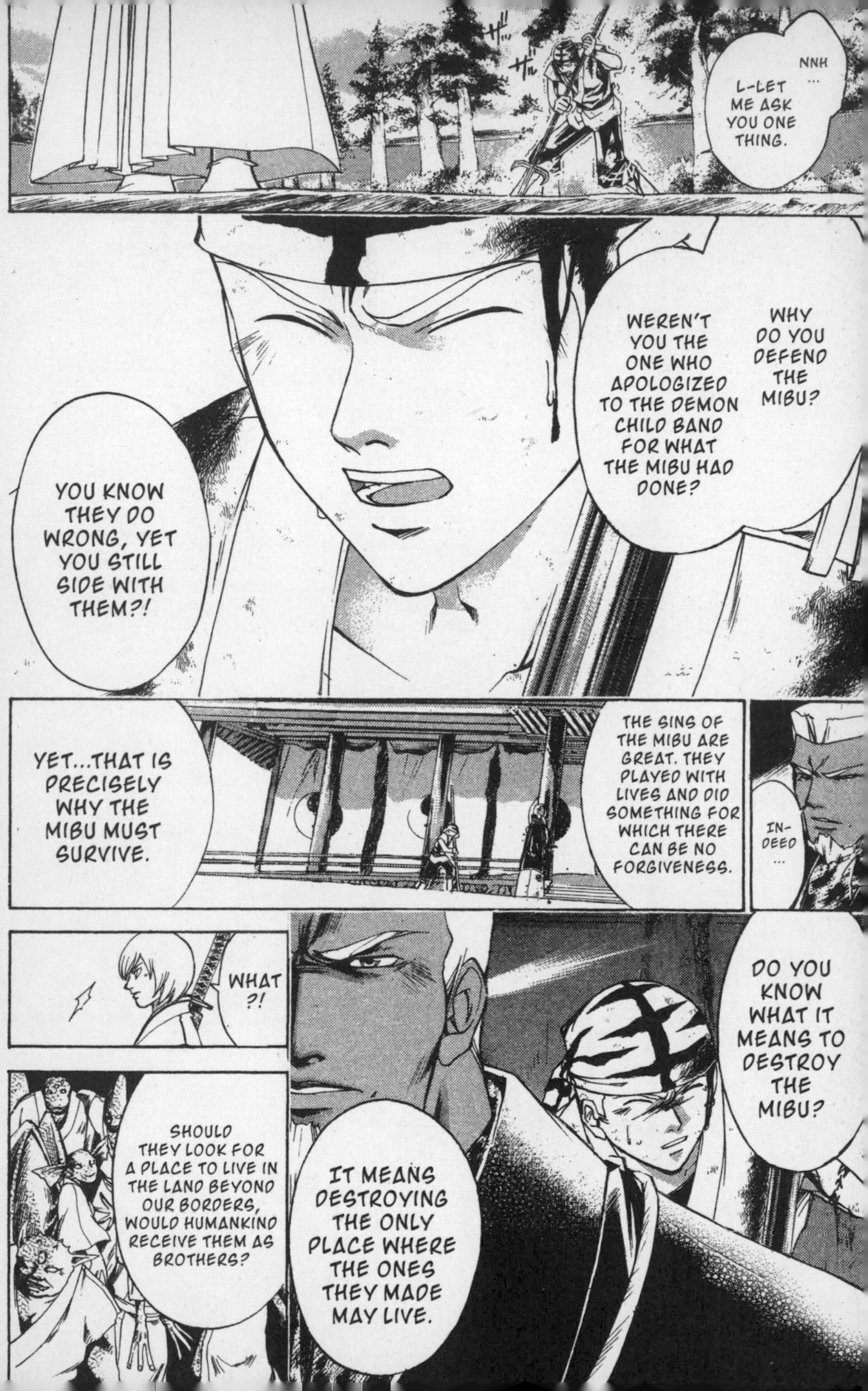
NNH ... L-LET ME ASK YOU ONE THING.
WHY DO YOU DEFEND THE MIBU?
WEREN'T YOU THE ONE WHO APOLOGIZED TO THE DEMON CHILD BAND FOR WHAT THE MIBU HAD DONE?
YOU KNOW THEY DO WRONG, YET YOU STILL SIDE WITH THEM?!
IN-DEED ...
THE SINS OF THE MIBU ARE GREAT. THEY PLAYED WITH LIVES AND DID SOMETHING FOR WHICH THERE CAN BE NO FORGIVENESS.
YET...THAT IS PRECISELY WHY THE MIBU MUST SURVIVE.
DO YOU KNOW WHAT IT MEANS TO DESTROY THE MIBU?
IT MEANS DESTROYING THE ONLY PLACE WHERE THE ONES THEY MADE MAY LIVE.
WHAT ?!
SHOULD THEY LOOK FOR A PLACE TO LIVE IN THE LAND BEYOND OUR BORDERS, WOULD HUMANKIND RECEIVE THEM AS BROTHERS?

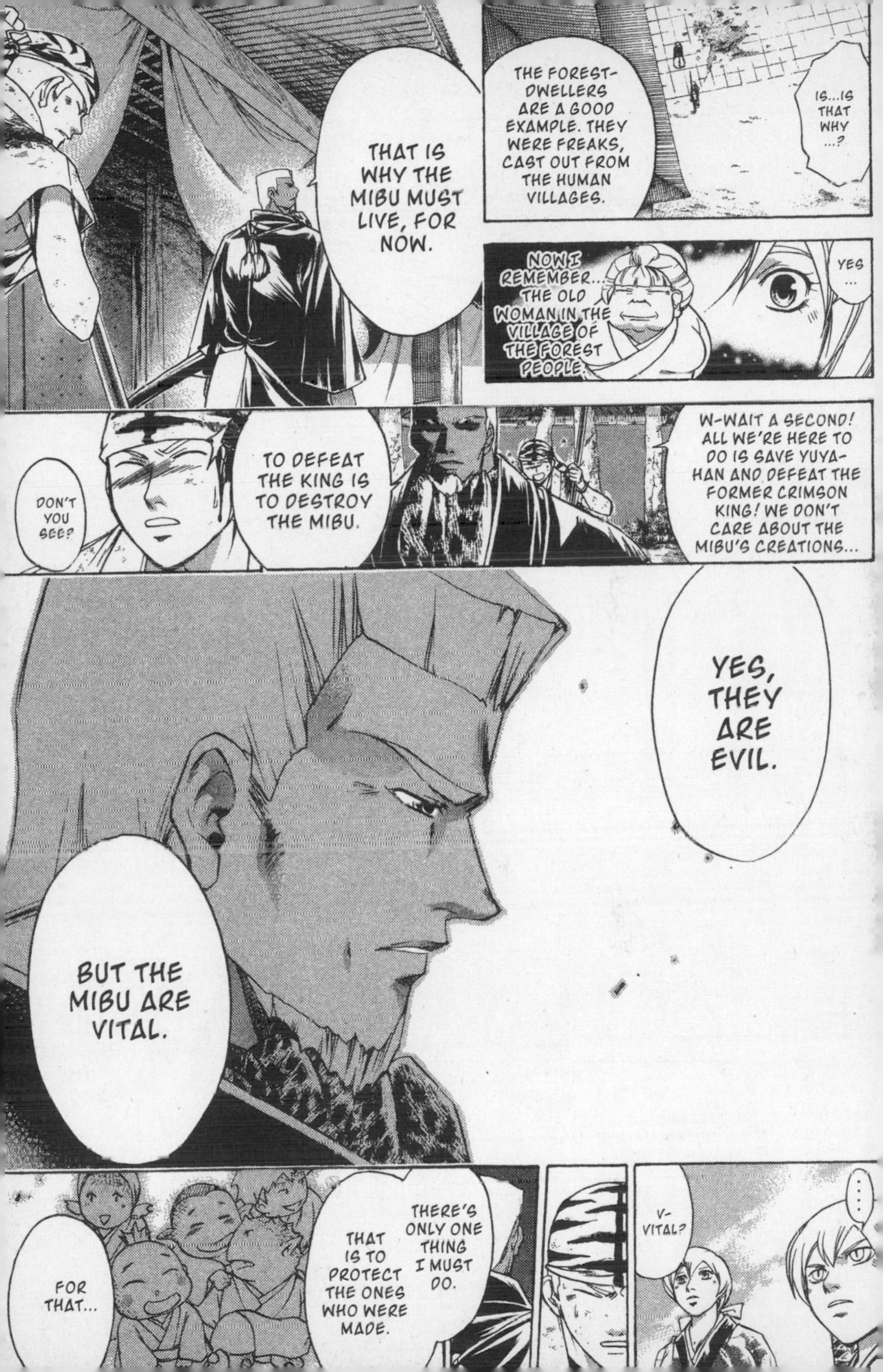
IS...IS THAT WHY ...?
THE FOREST-DWELLERS ARE A GOOD EXAMPLE. THEY WERE FREAKS, CAST OUT FROM THE HUMAN VILLAGES.
YES ...
NOW I REMEMBER... THE OLD WOMAN IN THE VILLAGE OF THE FOREST PEOPLE.
THAT IS WHY THE MIBU MUST LIVE, FOR NOW.
W-WAIT A SECOND! ALL WE'RE HERE TO DO IS SAVE YUYA-HAN AND DEFEAT THE FORMER CRIMSON KING! WE DON'T CARE ABOUT THE MIBU'S CREATIONS...
TO DEFEAT THE KING IS TO DESTROY THE MIBU.
DON'T YOU SEE?
YES, THEY ARE EVIL.
BUT THE MIBU ARE VITAL.
....
V-VITAL?
THERE'S ONLY ONE THING I MUST DO.
THAT IS TO PROTECT THE ONES WHO WERE MADE.
FOR THAT...

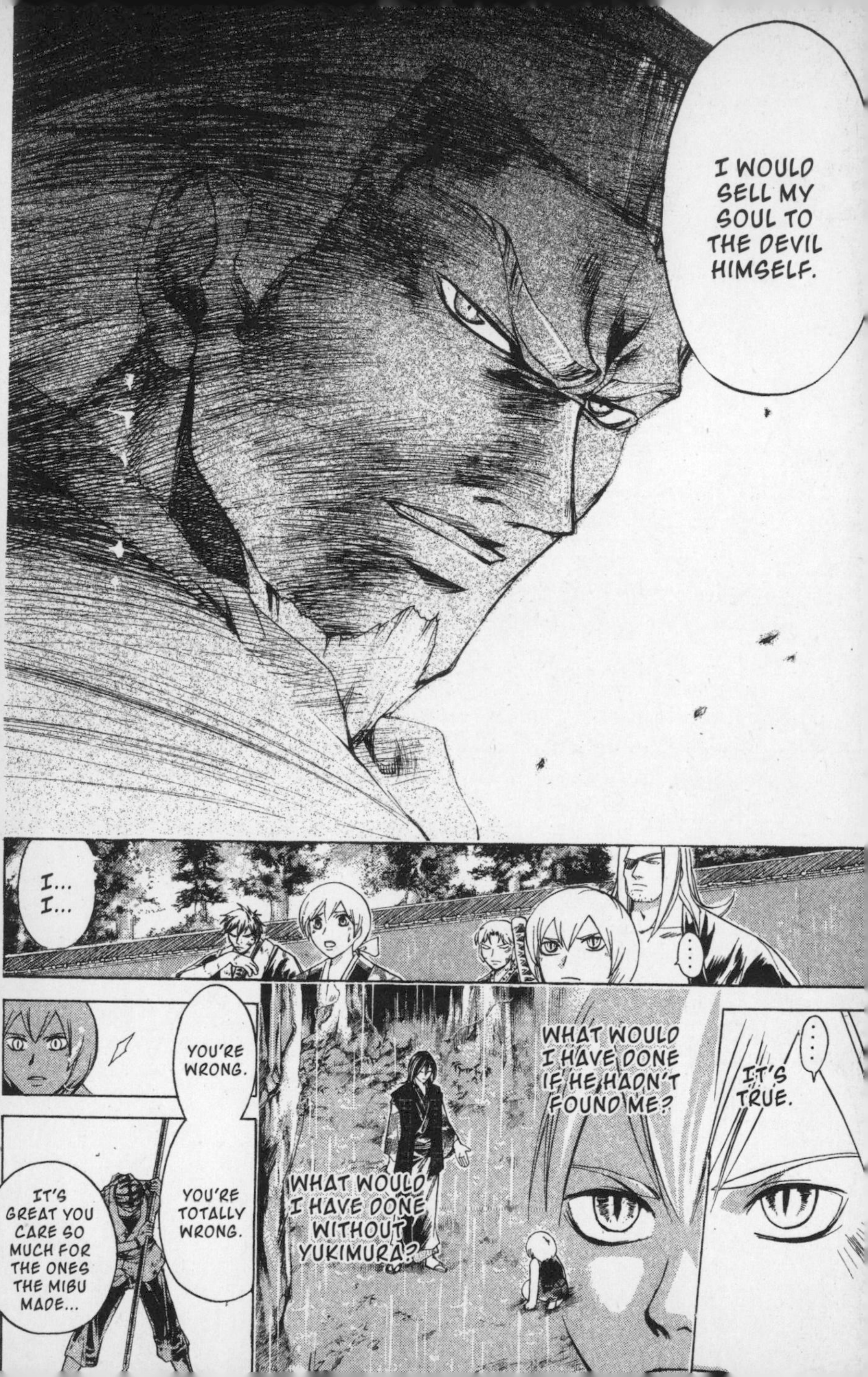
I WOULD SELL MY SOUL TO THE DEVIL HIMSELF.
...
I... I...
...
IT'S TRUE.
WHAT WOULD I HAVE DONE IF HE HADN'T FOUND ME?
WHAT WOULD I HAVE DONE WITHOUT YUKIMURA?
YOU'RE WRONG.
YOU'RE TOTALLY WRONG.
IT'S GREAT YOU CARE SO MUCH FOR THE ONES THE MIBU MADE...

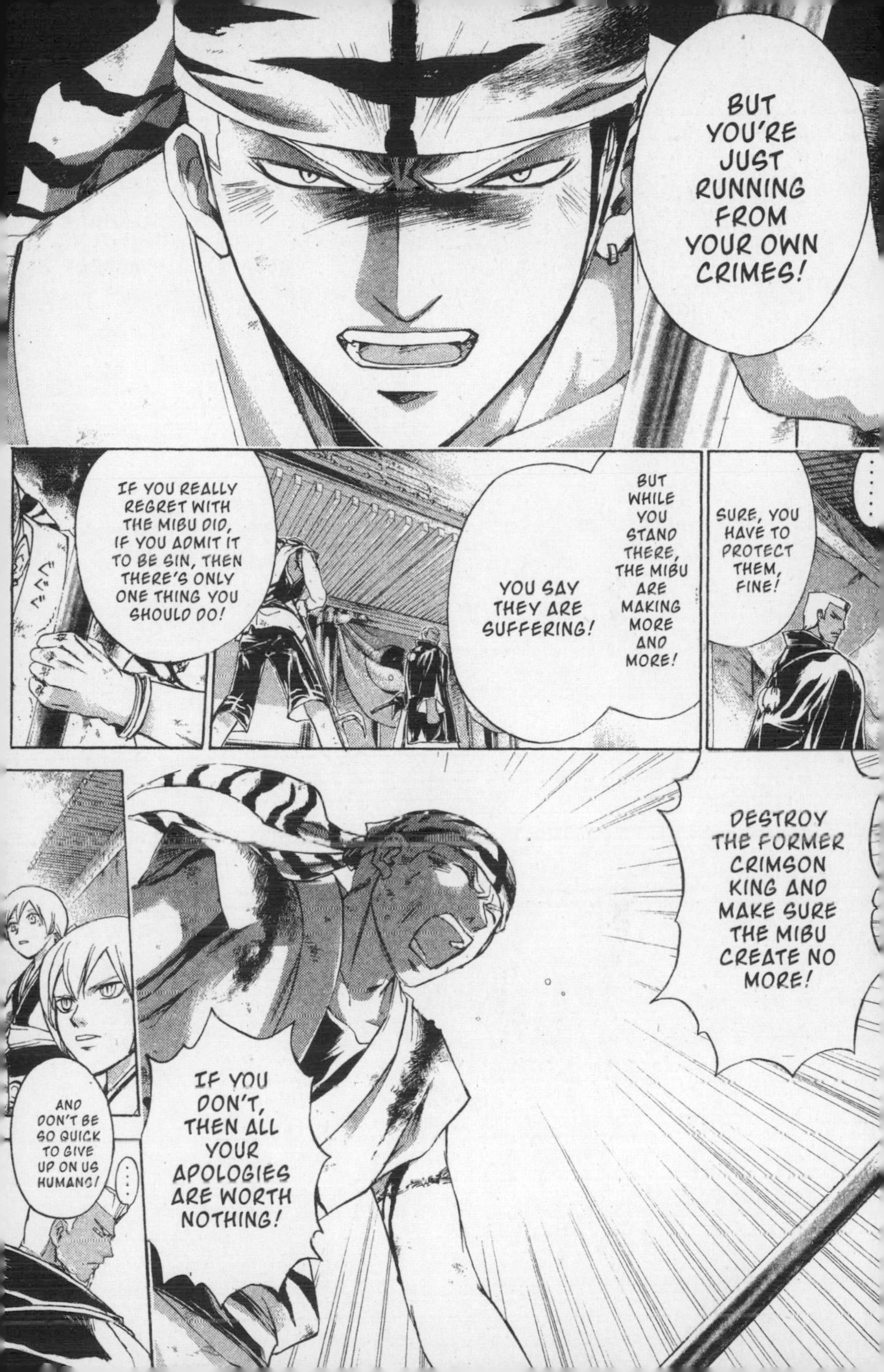
BUT YOU'RE JUST RUNNING FROM YOUR OWN CRIMES!
...
SURE, YOU HAVE TO PROTECT THEM, FINE!
YOU SAY THEY ARE SUFFERING!
BUT WHILE YOU STAND THERE, THE MIBU ARE MAKING MORE AND MORE!
IF YOU REALLY REGRET WITH THE MIBU DID, IF YOU ADMIT IT TO BE SIN, THEN THERE'S ONLY ONE THING YOU SHOULD DO!
DESTROY THE FORMER CRIMSON KING AND MAKE SURE THE MIBU CREATE NO MORE!
IF YOU DON'T, THEN ALL YOUR APOLOGIES ARE WORTH NOTHING!
...
AND DON'T BE SO QUICK TO GIVE UP ON US HUMANS!

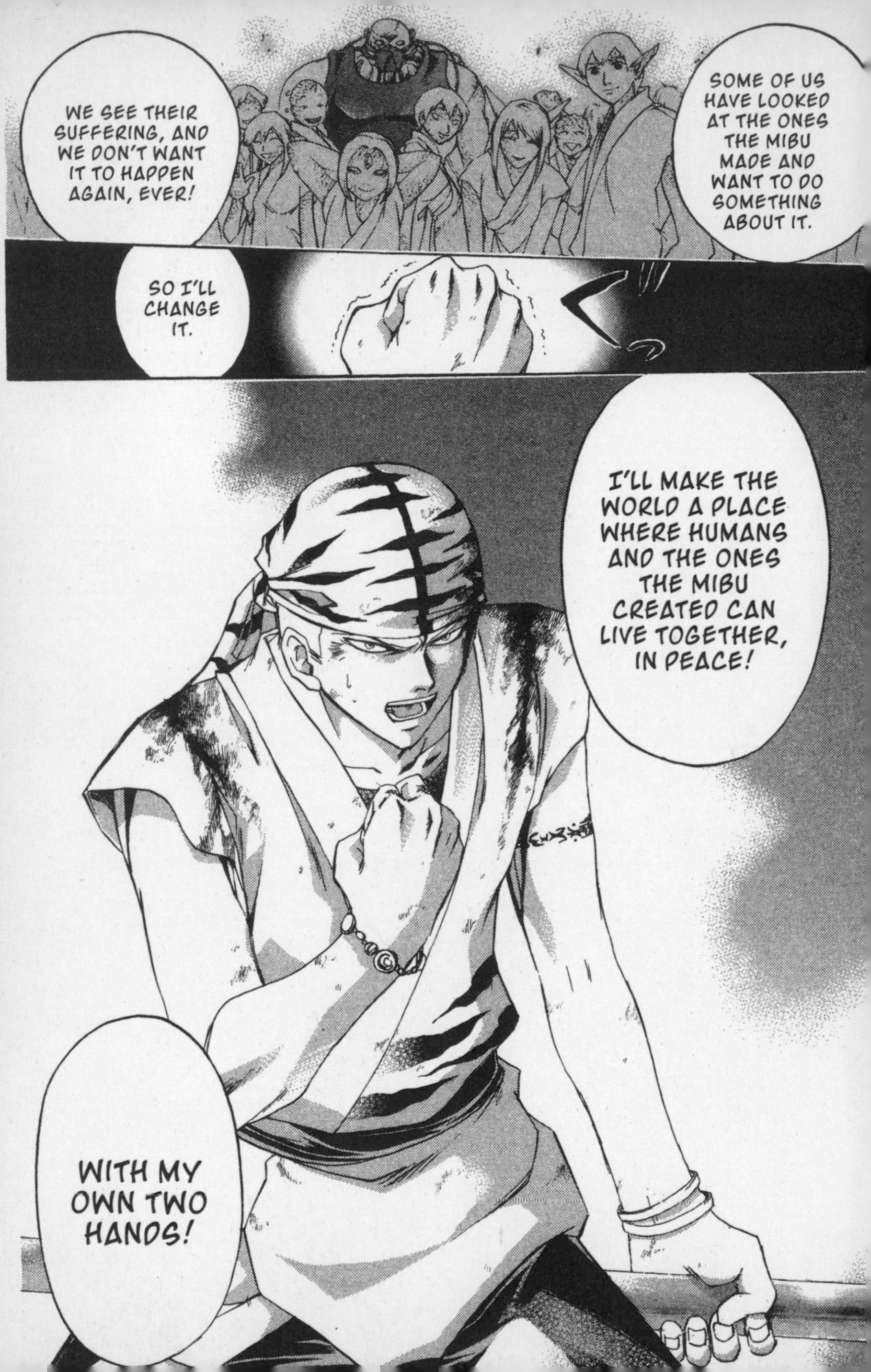
SOME OF US HAVE LOOKED AT THE ONES THE MIBU MADE AND WANT TO DO SOMETHING ABOUT IT.
WE SEE THEIR SUFFERING, AND WE DON'T WANT IT TO HAPPEN AGAIN, EVER!
SO I'LL CHANGE IT.
I'LL MAKE THE WORLD A PLACE WHERE HUMANS AND THE ONES THE MIBU CREATED CAN LIVE TOGETHER, IN PEACE!
WITH MY OWN TWO HANDS!

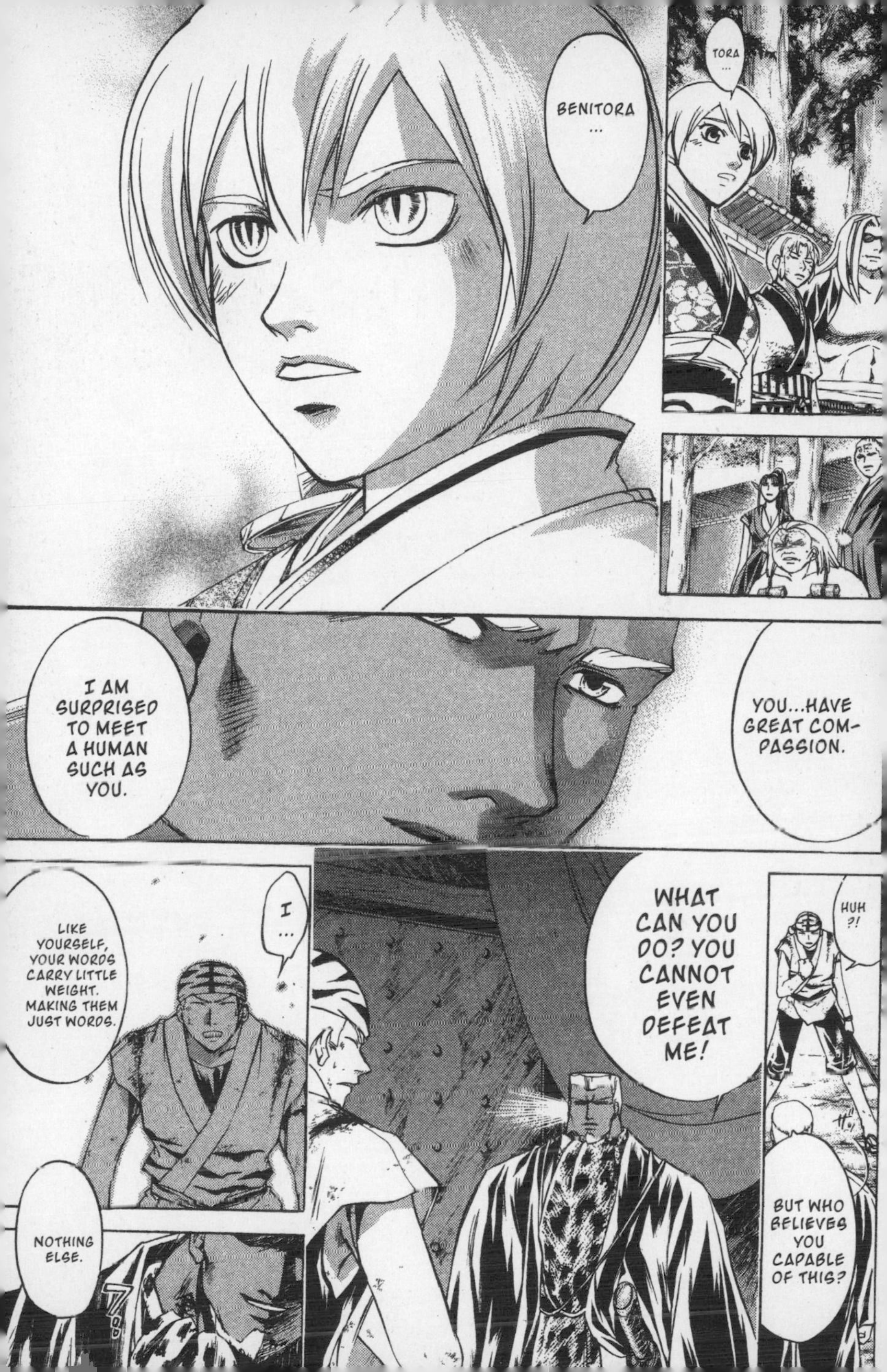
TORA ...
BENITORA ...
YOU...HAVE GREAT COMPASSION.
I AM SURPRISED TO MEET A HUMAN SUCH AS YOU.
HUH?!
BUT WHO BELIEVES YOU CAPABLE OF THIS?
WHAT CAN YOU DO? YOU CANNOT EVEN DEFEAT ME!
I ...
LIKE YOURSELF, YOUR WORDS CARRY LITTLE WEIGHT. MAKING THEM JUST WORDS.
NOTHING ELSE.

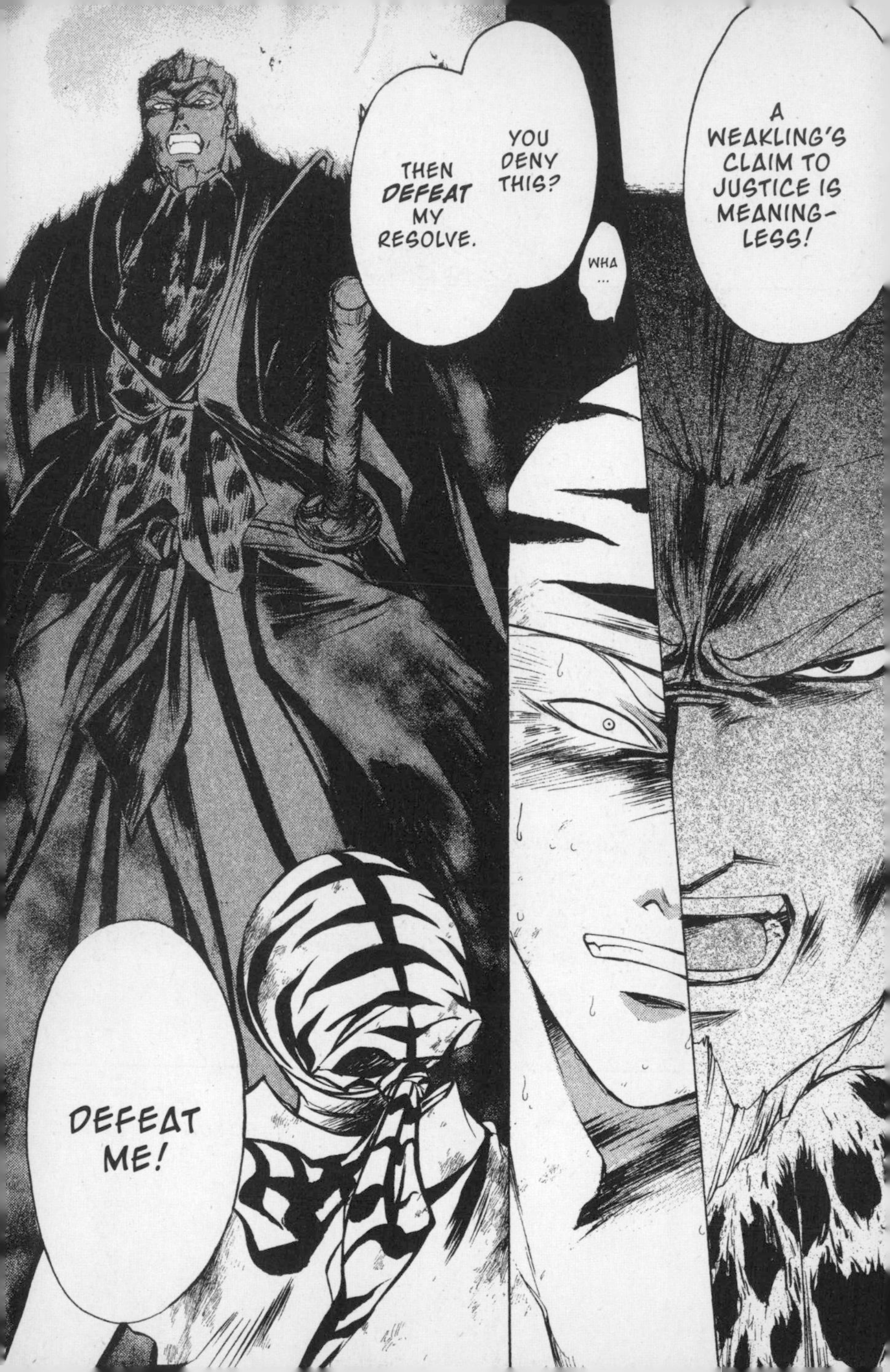
A WEAKLING'S CLAIM TO JUSTICE IS MEANING-LESS!
WHA ...
YOU DENY THIS?
THEN *DEFEAT* MY RESOLVE.
DEFEAT ME!

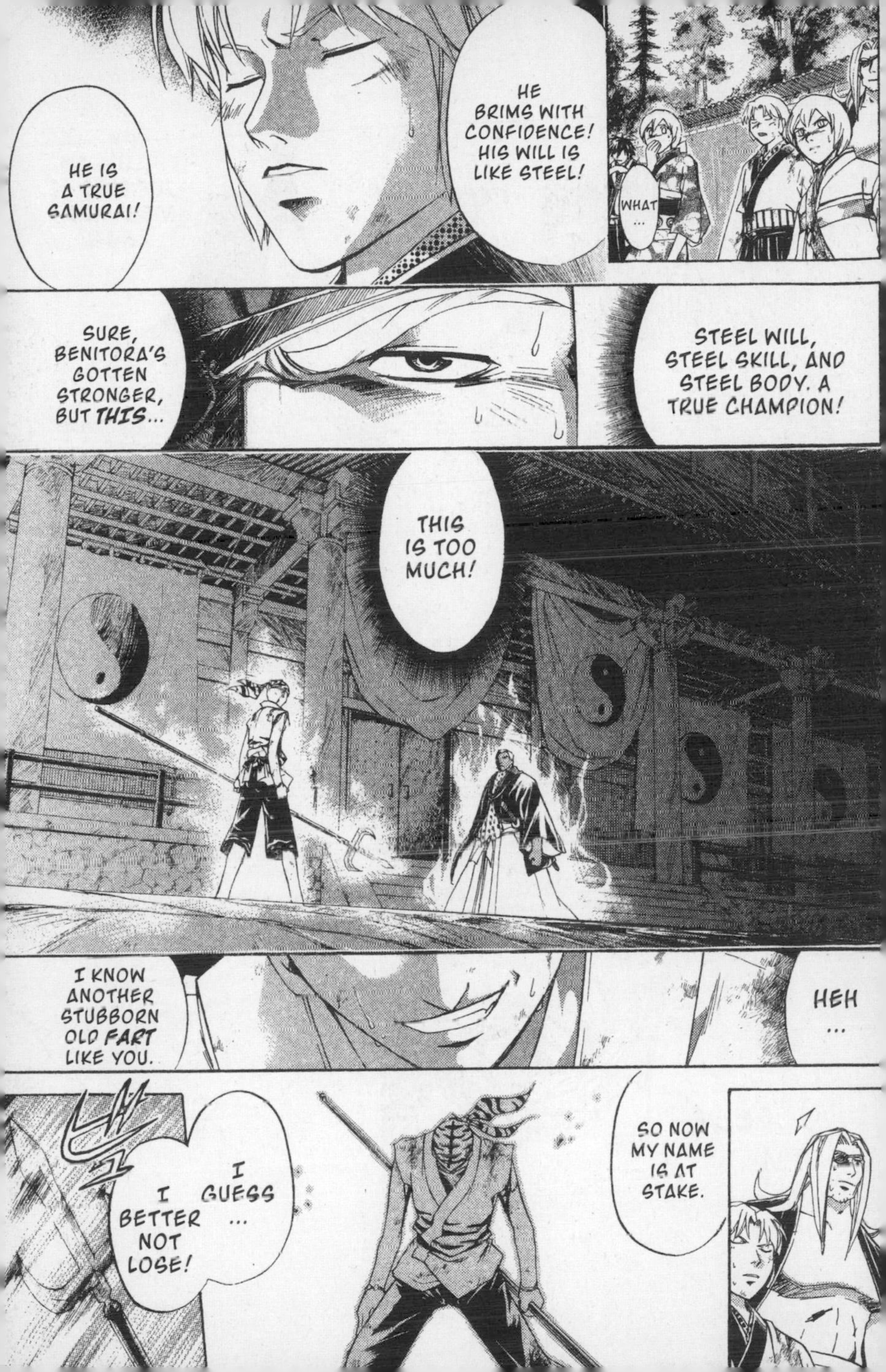
WHAT ...
HE BRIMS WITH CONFIDENCE! HIS WILL IS LIKE STEEL!
HE IS A TRUE SAMURAI!
STEEL WILL, STEEL SKILL, AND STEEL BODY. A TRUE CHAMPION!
SURE, BENITORA'S GOTTEN STRONGER, BUT THIS...
THIS IS TOO MUCH!
HEH ...
I KNOW ANOTHER STUBBORN OLD FART LIKE YOU.
SO NOW MY NAME IS AT STAKE.
I GUESS ... I BETTER NOT LOSE!

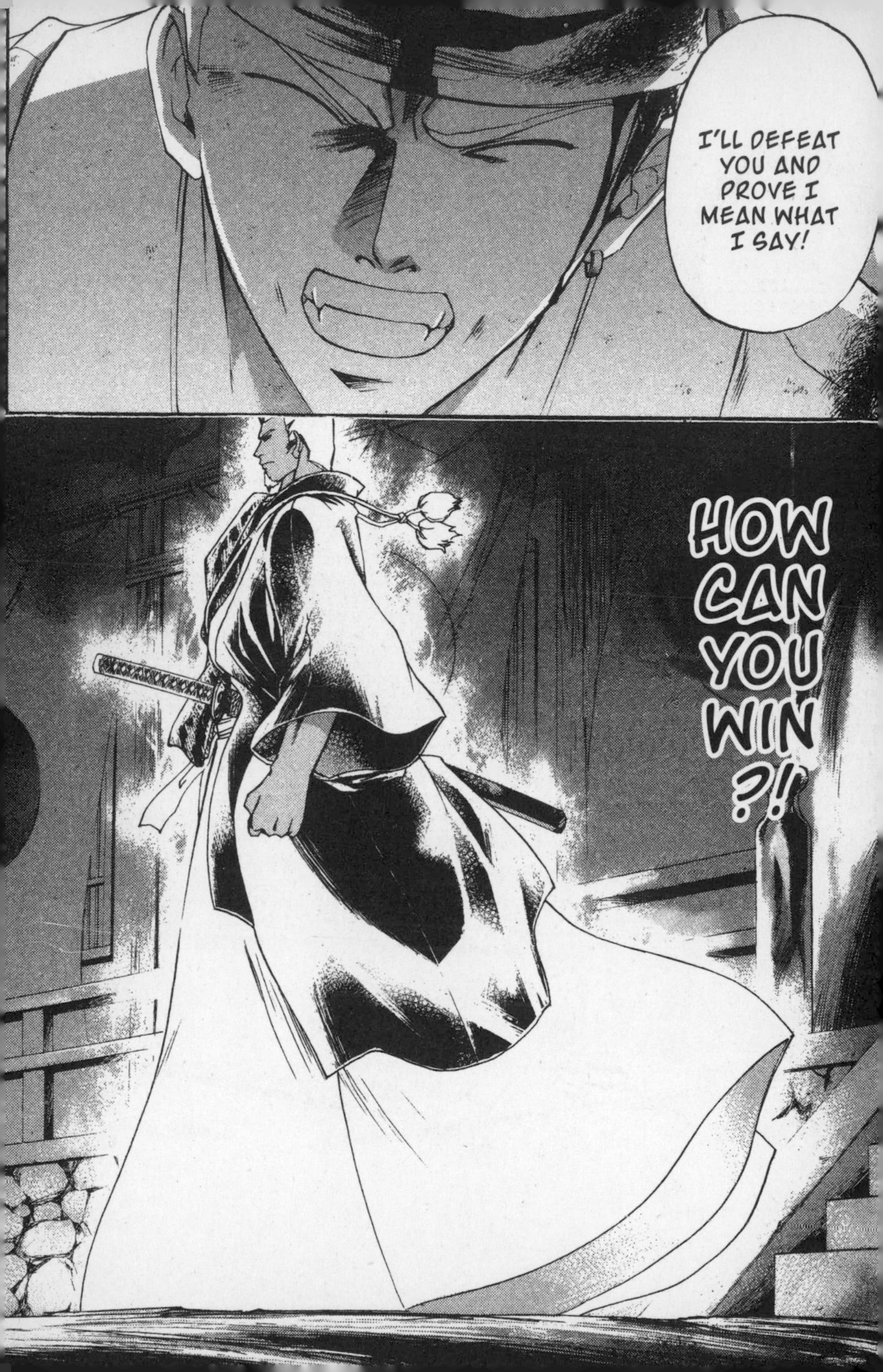
I'LL DEFEAT YOU AND PROVE I MEAN WHAT I SAY!
HOW CAN YOU WIN ?!

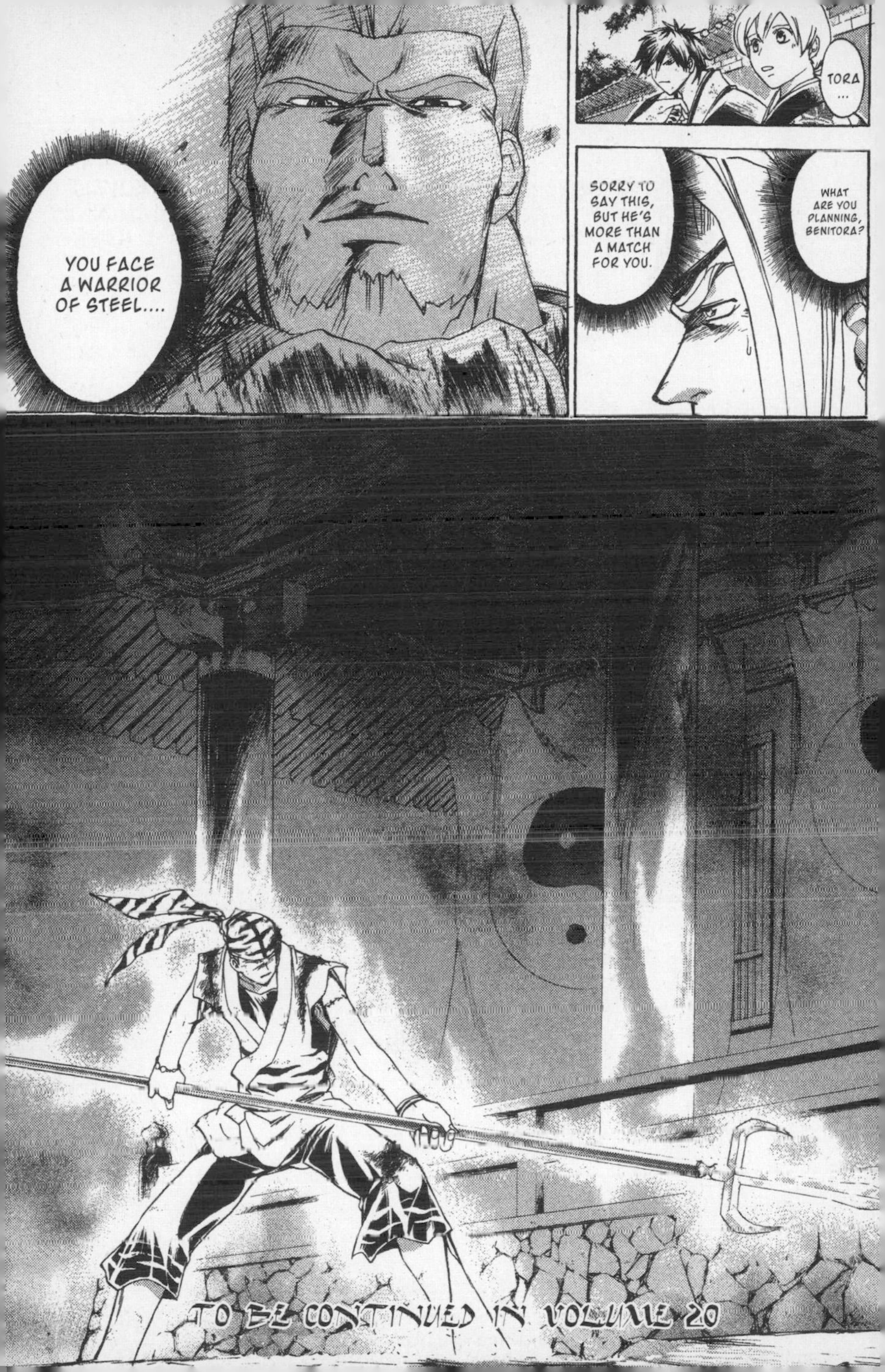
TORA ...
WHAT ARE YOU PLANNING, BENITORA?
SORRY TO SAY THIS, BUT HE'S MORE THAN A MATCH FOR YOU.
YOU FACE A WARRIOR OF STEEL....
TO BE CONTINUED IN VOLUME 20

SAMURAI DEEPER KYO NEXT!

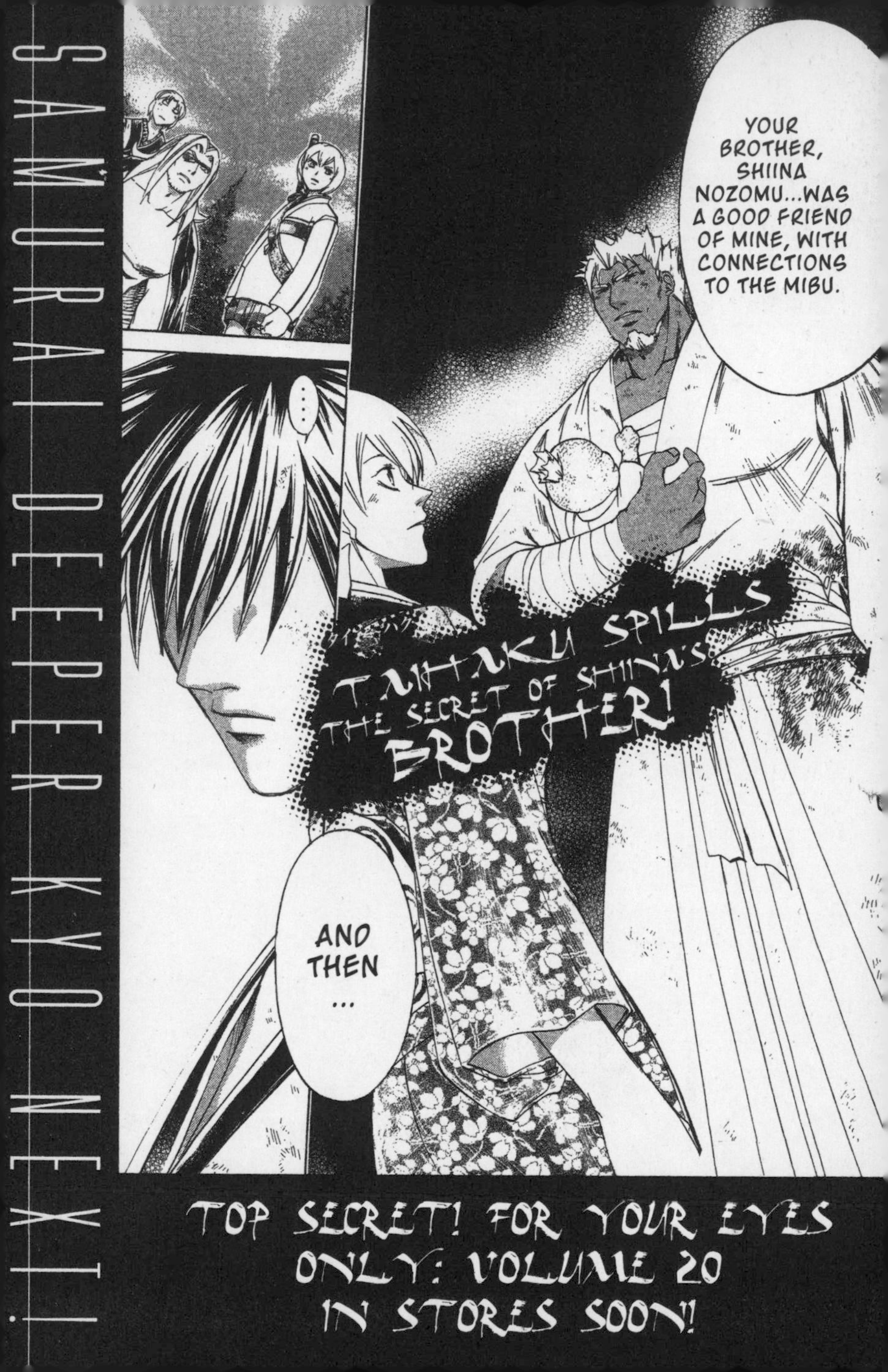
YOUR BROTHER, SHIINA NOZOMU...WAS A GOOD FRIEND OF MINE, WITH CONNECTIONS TO THE MIBU.
...
TAIHAKU SPILLS THE SECRET OF SHIINA'S BROTHER!
AND THEN ...

TOP SECRET! FOR YOUR EYES ONLY: VOLUME 20 IN STORES SOON!

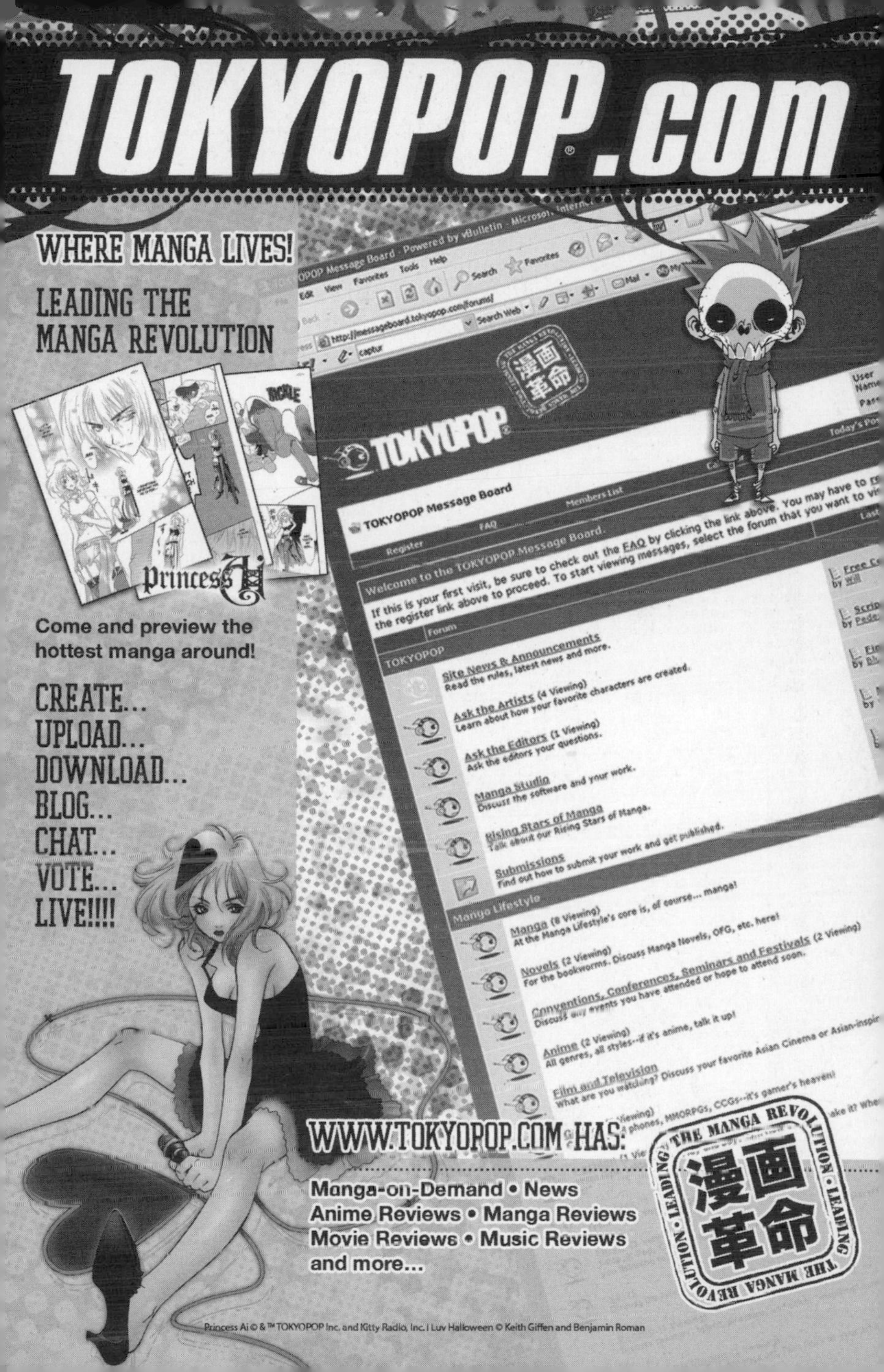
TOKYOPOP®.com
WHERE MANGA LIVES!
LEADING THE MANGA REVOLUTION
Princess Ai
Come and preview the hottest manga around!
CREATE...
UPLOAD...
DOWNLOAD...
BLOG...
CHAT...
VOTE...
LIVE!!!!
TOKYOPOP Message Board
WWW.TOKYOPOP.COM HAS:
Manga-on-Demand • News
Anime Reviews • Manga Reviews
Movie Reviews • Music Reviews
and more...
LEADING · THE MANGA REVOLUTION
漫画革命
Princess Ai © & ™ TOKYOPOP Inc. and Kitty Radio, Inc. I Luv Halloween © Keith Giffen and Benjamin Roman

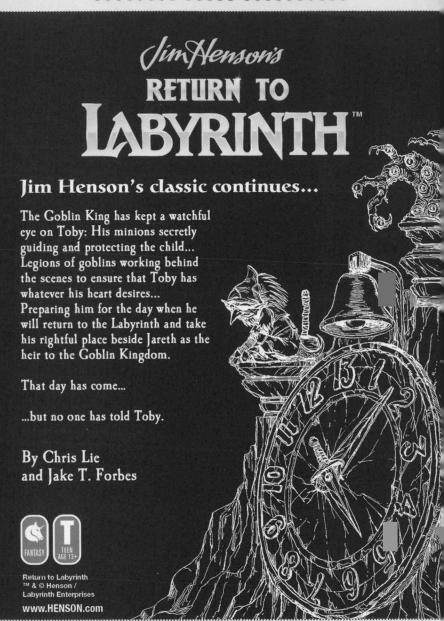

STOP!

This is the back of the book.
You wouldn't want to spoil a great ending!

This book is printed "manga-style," in the authentic Japanese right-to-left format. Since none of the artwork has been flipped or altered, readers get to experience the story just as the creator intended. You've been asking for it, so TOKYOPOP® delivered: authentic, hot-off-the-press, and far more fun!

DIRECTIONS

If this is your first time reading manga-style, here's a quick guide to help you understand how it works.

It's easy... just start in the top right panel and follow the numbers. Have fun, and look for more 100% authentic manga from TOKYOPOP®!